John A. W. Haas

Annotations on the Gospel acording to St. Mark

Volume 3

John A. W. Haas

Annotations on the Gospel acording to St. Mark
Volume 3

ISBN/EAN: 9783337285463

Printed in Europe, USA, Canada, Australia, Japan

Cover: Foto ©Lupo / pixelio.de

More available books at **www.hansebooks.com**

John S. D. Hess

THE LUTHERAN COMMENTARY

A PLAIN EXPOSITION OF THE

Holy Scriptures of the New Testament

BY

SCHOLARS OF THE LUTHERAN CHURCH IN AMERICA

EDITED BY

HENRY EYSTER JACOBS

VOL. III.

New York
The Christian Literature Co.
MDCCCXCV

ANNOTATIONS

ON THE

Gospel According to St. Mark

BY

JOHN A. W. HAAS, B.D.

New York
The Christian Literature Co.
MDCCCXCV

PREFACE.

THE aim and scope of this volume is in part somewhat more scientific and technical than announced in the general plan. It was thought advisable to offer more to scholars, since the practical import of the gospels will be sufficiently treated in the other volumes. Nevertheless the practical need was not overlooked. The matter intended especially for pastors and students has therefore been largely placed in footnotes; and the general text is such in most parts, that it can be readily and easily understood by all readers.

The latest results of exegesis, as far as available, have always been examined even though they were not everywhere adopted. In Biblical Archæology, Geography, Philology, and History, and in the exposition of some few passages, as well as in the maintenance of the historical point of view there has been a real advance. But the modern prevalent method is at fault in this, that constantly looking for the traces of an imaginary original source, it so interprets the individual gospel as to bring it into discord if not disagreement with the others. There is an atomism which disrupts the organism of the gospels. What would be censurable according to the general principles of interpretation, that are used not in the Scriptures alone, is found again and again. Excellent as modern exegesis is in the exact linguistic fixation of the individual word and the true valuation of the peculiarity of the language and expression of the several authors, its great error is the treatment of the Harmony of the gospels. This is generally rejected lightly and summarily. Therefore the conception of unity possessed by Augustine is in essence truer than that of Weiss.

Although the Harmony cannot be established by one principle or through one method, an error of our early Lutheran Harmonists, and must be carefully guarded, nevertheless it is not so useless nor fanciful as modern exegesis largely presupposes by its silence or assumes in its confident tone. The abandonment is due not so much to an actual disproval as to the critical and philosophical position of many exegetes.

The idea of the connection of the Old with the New Testament, and the use of some words of the Old Testament in a messianic sense, directly rather than typically, are not altogether along the line of thought, so generally received, because with all its historicity, it is destructive of the divine factor. The Old Testament is the constant foundation of the truth of the New Testament; and the right understanding of the development of the kingdom of God demands a consideration of its beginning and progress in the times of the Old Testament. But the Old Testament ought not to be regarded as the source whence the Apostles derived the material for their stories of the miraculous. It is no starting-point for the formation of myths. This treatment, arising from an *a priori* rejection of the supernatural, not only undervalues the originality, uniqueness and more than human power of Jesus, but also honors the historical preparation more than the actual appearance of Salvation. It is wrong even on its own historical principles, for it must partly assume a cause of the accounts of the miraculous more striking than its effect, and partly describe an effect for which the cause does not answer.

In the expression of the central thoughts and the practical deductions of many verses, the words of the Church Fathers and of the Reformers together with some later Christian thinkers, notably Starke and Stier, have been frequently employed, not only for their individual value, excellence and suggestiveness; but also to stimulate the study of the whole range of exegetical material and to indicate the deep consensus of biblical exegesis of all times in the Christian Church. The differences in minor points will only serve to make this more apparent.

The text commented upon has not been uniformly abbreviated, but printed in full in italics enclosed between heavy-faced type. This was due to a misunderstanding, which it was too late to correct. The desire to be brief and concise has made this volume somewhat shorter, but, it is hoped, none the less useful and acceptable. An Appendix has been added on the question of the time of the Last Supper, in which nothing new will be found; but the existing material has been thoroughly examined and given fully in all its bearings. This was believed to be not without value for all readers.

Acknowledgment must be made of the ready access which has been granted me to the Library of the Union Theological Seminary, through the kindness of its Librarian, Mr. Gillett.

May the Head of the Church bless this humble endeavor to the stimulation of research among pastors and students, to renewed interest and love in the divine oracles by the people, and to the edification of all believers!

THE AUTHOR.

NEW YORK, *October*, 1895.

INTRODUCTION.[1]

1. *Author.* The second evangelist,[2] John Mark, bears in his name the indication of the divine grace,[3] which sent the Spirit as prime author, and of the peculiar human individuality,[4] which, though borne by the Spirit, shows itself. This name also points to the historical and linguistic Hebrew foundation of the Christian religion, and to the Roman power, which it so soon conquered. And that the gospel might more readily be brought to the Roman Christians, John Mark (Acts 12 : 25; 15 : 37),

---

[1] In addition to the commentaries, cited in the exposition of Mark, the following works have been used or consulted: The N. T. Introductions of Credner, Guerike, Bleek (Mangold, 4th ed.), Köstlin, Holtzmann, Weiss, Reuss (Hist. of Sacred Script. of N. T., Engl. Transl. of 5th ed., Boston, 1884), Grau (Entwickelungsgesch. des N. T., Schrifttums), Nösgen (Introd. to Gesch. der N. T. Offenb.), L. Schulze in Zöckler's Handbuch, etc., Westcott, Davidson, E. A. Abbott in Encyl. Brit., Ebrard's (Wissenschaftl. Kritik der ev. Gesch. 3d ed.) Schaff's Ch. Hist., vol. I.; Güder on Mark and Steitz on Papias in Herzog-Plitt Real-Encyl.; McClintock & Strong & Smith's Bible Dict.; E. Hatch on Mark in Encyl. Brit.; Weiffenbach, Die Papias-fragmente; Zahn, Das Evangel des Petrus; Zahn, Gesch. des N. T., Kanons, I. and II.; Resch, Agrapha in Gebhardt & Harnack, Texte u. Untersuchungen; Farrar, Early Days of Christianity; Fischer, Beginnings of Christianity.

[2] It was conjectured by Spanheim that Mark also wrote the epistle to the Hebrews, by Holtzmann that he composed the epistle of Jude, and by Hitzig that he was the author of the Apocalypse.

[3] John, the Hebrew name, means, Jehovah is gracious, and is equivalent to the German Gotthold.

[4] This is expressed in Mark, a common Latin name meaning "Mallet." Cf. Morison, p. xv.

abandoned his original Jewish name John (Acts 13 : 5, 13), and used Mark alone,[1] in the same spirit of evangelical freedom and wisdom that prompted a Saul to become a Paul. Mark was the son[2] of a certain Mary of Jerusalem, who offered her house as the meeting-place and refuge of the Christians (Acts 12 : 12), and the nephew of the Levite Barnabas (Acts 4 : 36; Col. 4 : 10).[3] On that memorable night, when eagerness led Mark to follow Christ's captors (ch. 14 : 51), and he fled so suddenly, his heart may have been deeply impressed, which made it possible for Peter, who enjoyed the solace of the home of Mark after the delivery from prison (Acts 12 : 12), to convert him (1 Peter 5 : 13).[4] He was soon taken on a missionary tour by Barnabas and Paul, but discouraged in the difficulty of the work returned to Jerusalem (Acts 13 : 13). For this reason Paul in his firmness refused to take him again, although Barnabas

---

[1] After Acts 15 : 39 John never occurs. From the change of names Grotius, Calov, Schleiermacher, Kienlen, Krenkel, Cave and Patrizi argue, that there were two Marks, one Petrine, the other Pauline. The former is claimed as author of this gospel, and the latter as the Mark mentioned in Acts, the companion of Paul. But this distinction is rejected by most scholars.

[2] The name of the father, who was probably the "goodman" of C. 14 : 14, is not known, although a late Coptic tradition calls him Aristobulus.

[3] This relation to Barnabas would make Mark of priestly descent; and there is a tradition (Philosophumena of Hippolytus, VII. 30) that Mark had cut off his thumb to avoid priestly service. Tregelles, Westcott, Morison, suppose, however, that the epithet "stump-fingered" (κολοβοδάκτυλος) refers to poltroonery, because Mark deserted on the first missionary tour, and that this moral idea was in time physically misconstrued. But Zahn (II., p. 20) emphasizing the early occurrence of this tradition, accepts it literally.

[4] There seems no cogent reason to interpret "son" in a natural sense, with Credner, Tholuck and Schanz. On the children of Peter, see McGifford's note on Eus. H. E. (Nicene and Post-Nicene Fathers, 2d series, Christ. Lit. Co., vol. I. 162).

with the kindly feeling of an uncle wished to condone the former fault. A contention and rupture took place (Acts 15 : 39), which was later healed; for Paul mentions Mark as a fellow-worker in the kingdom of God and as a comfort in his imprisonment (Col. 4 : 10; Phil. 24); and asks Timothy (2 Tim. 4 : 11) to bring Mark to Rome, because he was "useful in ministering." This attachment to Paul did not loosen the bonds of affection toward Peter, whom Mark assisted at "Babylon," possibly Rome (1 Peter 5 : 13). According to later tradition [1] Mark labored in Egypt and was the first bishop of Alexandria, where he died.[2] From thence the Venetians, as told in late legends, brought the body to Venice in A. D. 827. They have portrayed this at the entrance of San Marco. The character of Mark is similar to that of his spiritual father in the defects of hastiness and instability, and also in the virtues of vigor and energy.

And upon Peter Mark also depended in his gospel, as the universal testimony of the early church asserts. Papias (first part of 2d century), the scholar of John the Presbyter,[3] relates how John told him that "Mark had been an interpreter of Peter," which most probably means, that through his gospel he interpreted Peter to

---

[1] Eus. H. E. II. 16; Epiph. Hær. LI., 6; Jerome, de vir. ill. 8.

[2] From Eus. II. 24, it follows that Mark died 62 A. D., a date which Jerome adopts. But the earlier and trustworthier tradition of Irenæus, that Mark wrote his gospel after the death of Peter contradicts this. All the accounts of Mark outside the N. T. are doubtful.

[3] Eus. II. E. III. 39, criticises Irenæus (Adv. Hær. V. 33. 4), who calls Papias "a hearer of John," and cites the very words of Papias, in which "John" and "the presbyter John" are mentioned. Unless Eus. was deceived or forged, John the presbyter must be held to be another person than the apostle, as is done by most scholars (Schaff, Ch. Hist. II. 697, McGifford, Eus. p. 170), except Riggenbach, Zahn and Salmon, for whose arguments see Dict. of Christ. Biography, III., p. 398.

those who had not heard him.[1] Justin Martyr (A. D. 100–120) calls the gospel of Mark, the Memoirs of Peter.[2] "Mark, the disciple and interpreter of Peter, did also hand down to us in writing what had been preached by Peter," says Irenæus[3] (A. D. 177–200). And Clement of Alexandria[4] (A. D. 191–202) asserts that upon entreaty of the people Mark wrote out the preaching of Peter. In this he is corroborated by his contemporary, Tertullian (A. D. 190–220), who states[5] that the gospel of Mark "may be ascribed to Peter, whose interpreter Mark was." The great Origen[6] traces Mark's work to Peter's suggestion. Epiphanius[7] (died 402) informs his readers, that Mark "having become an attendant of the holy Peter in Rome, had committed to him the task of setting forth the gospel." And the credulous and inexact Jerome[8] (A. D. 346–420) holds the gospel to have been composed, "Peter relating, and he (Mark) writing." This last form has made the freer relation reported in the earliest testimony

---

[1] This is the position of Zahn (I., 879), who proves that the idea of secretary or dragoman is unhistorical, and therefore the wider sense of "interpreter," which is supported by many classical references, must be accepted. "Interpreter" has been rendered secretary by Hug, Fritzsche, Thiersch, Meyer, Holtzmann, Klostermann, Grau, Weiss, Keil, Schanz; and "translating interpreter" by Kuinoel, Schleiermacher, Bleek, Schenkel, Renan, Weiffenbach (cf. Papias-fragm., p. 37, sq.) That Mark translated the gospel into Latin has been held by Baronius in the interest of the Vulgate. An old Latin copy was supposed to have been found in Venice, but this was a part of the Vulgate (Credner, p. 120).

[2] Justin (Dial. 106) cannot mean Memoirs of Christ, as is evident from the context; nor does he refer to the apocryphal gospel of Peter (Harnack, McGifford), because the general character of the "apomnemoneumata" (Zahn, I., p. 475) is contrary to this notion, and the word "Boanerges," occurring only in Mark 3 : 17, immediately follows.

[3] Adv. Hær. III. 1, 1 ; Eus. H. E. V. 8.
[4] Eus. VI. 14.   [5] C. Marc. IV. 5.
[6] Com. on Matt.   [7] Adv. Hær. XLII.
[8] Letters CXX. to Hedib. XI.

a mere mechanical dictation, and is not supported by internal evidences. For, while there is an intimate correspondence between the sermons of Peter in the Acts and his epistles both in expression and words,[1] no such agreement consists between the gospel of Mark and the writings of Peter. But in its entirety it unfolds the very features of Christ indicated in Acts 2 : 22 and 3 : 16. Its vivid, exact and minute representation[2] can only be the work of an eye-witness, who is Peter as shown in the account of the selection of the first disciples (1 : 16), the visit at Peter's house (1 : 29), the search of Peter for Jesus (1 : 35 sq), the approach of the friends of Jesus (3 : 21), the very words spoken to the daughter of Jairus (5 : 41), the invitation of Jesus to his disciples to rest (6 : 31), the proposal of Peter at the transfiguration with the addition "he wist not what to answer," the omission of Christ's honoring promise to Peter (8 : 28 with Matt. 16 : 17), the suffering at Gethsemane (14 : 32 sq.), and the cock crowing twice (14 : 30, 68, 72).

2. *Sources of the Gospel.* The preaching of Peter is not the only source of Mark; for John, the Presbyter, according to Papias, said that Mark "thus wrote *some* things as he remembered them."[3] But upon what other information Mark relied, and what was its nature, this is a question involving the whole relation and origin of the first three gospels. And in this synoptic problem, so difficult, so much discussed and so little solved, the merest outline can be given, pointing in the direction of what seem to be the most probable facts.

[1] Cf. e. g. 1 Peter 2 : 7 with Acts 4 : 11; 1 Peter 2 : 24 with Acts 5 : 30; 1 Peter 4 : 5 with Acts 10 : 42.
[2] See, e. g., 2 : 23; 3 : 5, 34; 4 : 38; 6 : 3, 39; 7 : 24, 31; 8 : 22; 9 : 21–24.
[3] For this interpretation see Zahn. I., p. 575, who agrees with Klostermann, Meyer, Weiss, as against Weiffenbach (Papias-fragm., p. 63 sq.), who emphasizes "thus." "*As* he remembered *thus* he wrote."

Augustine[1] regarded Mark as the "footman and epitomizer" of Matthew. This theory, but not with as strong a depreciation of Mark, was again taken up by Grotius and adopted by many modern scholars.[2] But a close comparison of Matthew and Mark, although revealing that "one half of Mark is found in Matthew" (Schaff),[3] will nevertheless demonstrate the marked peculiarity of the second gospel, which even in the parts most like Matthew adds many original vivid touches. In the sections from ch. 6 : 45 to 8 : 21, which are parallel to Matt. 14 : 22–16 : 12, there are many additions and original details, as, e. g., "Bethsaida" (6 : 45), "he would have passed them by" (6 : 48), "they were amazed in themselves" (6 : 51), the whole of ver. 52, and 7 : 2, 4, 5, 8, 12, the fullness of 7 : 19 (cf. Matt. 15 : 16 sq.), the sins mentioned 7 : 22, and the independent order of those in ver. 21 (cf. Matt. 15 : 19), "Syrophenician" (7 : 26), the explicitness of 7 : 30 compared with Matt. 15 : 28, the beginning of 8 : 1, "some of them are come from afar" (8 : 3), "having eyes, see ye not? and having ears, hear ye not?" (8 : 18). Even in the chapters 13–15, which are emphasized by those who advocate a partial reliance of Mark on Matthew, Mark's arrangement of ch. 13 as well as ver. 32 and the characteristic conclusion indicate independence; in ch. 14, ver. 3, 5, 15, 31, and in ch. 15, ver. 8, 21, 41, contain information not in Matthew. It is also impossible to accept the use of Matthew by Mark without including Luke, for Mark 1 : 21–28, 35–39 :

[1] De Cons. I., II. 4.

[2] Among those who hold either a total or at least partial dependence of Mark on Matthew are Mill, Bengel, Wetstein, Griesbach, Owen, Hug, Hilgenfeld, Bleek, Ebrard, Greswell, Keil, Klostermann, L. Schulze, and Nösgen.

[3] For an excellent resume of the harmony and variation by numerical estimate of the first three gospels according to their sections, verses and words, see Schaff. Ch. Hist. I., p. 594 sq.

12 : 41-44 are found only in Luke.[1] A combination would therefore be necessary, which would be a veritable patchwork. In a part where the third gospel were followed (Mark 4 : 35—6 : 44) Matt. 13 : 54-58; 14 : 3-12 would be suddenly introduced, and Luke 5 : 39, wanting in Matt., omitted. In the section including Mark 9 : 38 sq., Luke 9 : 49, 50, would be introduced, although the order of Matthew had been previously and subsequently adhered to. Such a method is a modern creation, the conception of imaginative critics.[2] It finds no support in Mark, for such passages where apparently words of Matthew and Luke were artfully combined (as, e. g., 1 : 34, 42; 3 : 4, 5), lose their argumentative power from the fact that there are many other verses, where there is no dependence and the same redundancy, which is a peculiarity of Mark (cf. 1 : 32 with 16 : 2; 2 : 11 with 2 : 9; 5 : 41; 4 : 39 with 6 : 51). In addition there are the sections 4 : 26-29; 7 : 31-37; 8 : 22-26, not in Matthew nor Luke; 45 expressions nowhere else in the N. T.;[3] the frequent mention of the retirement of Jesus (1 : 29, 35, 45; 3 : 7; 6 : 6, etc.); the independent order in the apostolic catalogue (3 : 14 sq.); the designation of Christ as carpenter (6 : 3), the name of the blind beggar at Jericho (10 : 46), and many other similar details, which demonstrate the originality and independence of Mark.

Another supposition is, that an original document, the

---

[1] Clement of Alex. (Eus. H. E. VI. 14) seems to indicate the dependence of Mark on the other synoptic gospels, by giving Mark the third place. This is the position of Griesbach, Fritzsche, Theile, De Wette, Keim, Bleek, Delitzsch. Salmon looks to Luke alone. But "only one third of Mark is in Luke." (Schaff.)

[2] Cf. the construction of C. Baur, as epitomized by Morison, p. XLI.

[3] For the list, see Schaff, Comp. to the N. T., p. 51.

so-called "Urmarkus,"[1] forms the basis of the present gospel of Mark. The historical justification of this view is attempted from the words of John, the Presbyter, as told by Papias, viz., "Mark, having become the interpreter of Peter, wrote down accurately, though not indeed in order, whatsoever he remembered of the things said or done by Christ. For he neither heard the Lord nor followed Him, but afterward, as I said, he followed Peter, who adapted his teaching to the needs of his hearers, but with no intention of giving a connected account of the Lord's oracles, so that Mark committed no error while he thus wrote some things as he remembered them. For he was careful of one thing, not to omit any of the things, which he had heard, and not to state any of them falsely." The accuracy of Mark is asserted, while the order of the things said or done by Christ, i. e., the chronological order,[2] is denied. This, it is claimed, is inconsistent with the gospel that we possess, which has a chronological order. But the sequence of time is not the principle of the arrangement of Mark. The first miracle, which he reports (1 : 40-44), belongs in point of time after 3 : 19.[3] The imprisonment of John (6 : 17 sq.) occurred much earlier, and the manner in which Mark reports it shows that temporal succession was not the motive of his gospel. The section 3 : 20-30 ought to follow 1 : 39. The plucking of the ears of corn by the disciples (2 : 23 sq.) took place most probably after 6 : 56. There is no insurmountable difficulty in applying the

---

[1] This is advocated by Koppe, Lachmann, Weisse, Wilke, Schenkel, Holtzmann, Weizsäcker, Jahn, Meyer, Handmann, Resch, and others.

[2] Such is essentially the exegesis of the "Papias-Fragment" by Zahn (I p. 876), to be preferred to Weiffenbach (p. 44 sq.), who claims the absence of all order from the "Urmarkus" and slights the force of "accurately."

[3] Cf. Luthardt, Tabelle zur ev. Synopse.

words of John, the Presbyter, to Mark; and therefore no reason can be given why an unknown and non-existent document, which the ingenuity of the critics has very boldly, subjectively and arbitrarily reconstructed in many varying and contradictory forms, should be assumed as the basis of the present Mark. Still less reason is there for claiming a partial dependence on the so-called "Logia" (oracles) of Matthew.[1] This theory of sources is a modern fiction. Luke, who knows of many that have taken in hand to draw up a narrative (1 : 1), passes a criticism on these writers; for the word "taken in hand" (ἐπεχείρησαν) in its N. T. usage (Acts 9 : 29; 19 : 13) refers to an undertaking that is a failure. Over against these unnamed writers,[2] that are inexact, Luke has promised an accurate account, based upon what eye-witnesses have "delivered" in oral tradition.[3]

Our gospels are founded on oral tradition.[4] This was the manner of communicating the gospel-story, whether "publicly and from house to house" (Acts 20 : 20), or in private catechetical form (Acts 10 : 37 sq.).[5] The expressions which are used for instruction in the gospel are such as "word," "testimony," "preaching," "speaking," "tradition," "word of message," "message;"[6] and its

---

[1] The words of Papias about Matthew (Eus. H. E. III. 39) have not convinced me of their inapplicability to the present Matthew, in so far as they speak of "Logia," which does not refer to words alone (Weiffenbach, p. 77 sq.), but also to deeds (Zahn, I., p. 892).

[2] The criticism of Luke does not apply to Mark (Joh. Weiss), but to the many partial accounts with their germs of legends. Origen was the first to see this import of the words of Luke (see Zahn, II., p. 625).

[3] Cf. Nösgen, N. T. Offenb. I., p. 34, 52.

[4] This is held by Herder, Gieseler, Credner, Lange, Ebrard, Thiersch, Norton, Alford, Westcott, Godet, Keil.

[5] Westcott, p. 181.

[6] See, e. g., Acts 8 : 4, 5; 9 : 20; 14 : 7; 19 : 13; Rom. 1 : 15; 1 Cor. 1 : 19, 21; 2 Cor. 1 : 19; 10 : 16; 11 : 4; Gal. 1 : 8, 16, 23;

reception is characterized as "hearing,"[1] while "reading" is mostly used of the O. T.[2] The influence of the custom of Palestine was in favor of tradition. The sayings of the elders and the various interpretations of the law were thus preserved. "Commit nothing to 'writing'" was the accepted principle. The memory was schooled to retain not merely facts, but long series of words in the exactest manner. Thus also the gospel-story and the words of Christ would be repeated again and again, and soon obtain a stereotyped form, which was rigidly held. Certain groups of stories would come to be told together, which will often explain connections where chronology is not the determining factor. The early Christian literature shows quite a number[3] of "Agrapha," unwritten sayings of the Lord (cf. John 21 : 25), which are only possible on the supposition of oral tradition. This, too, can explain the high estimate of tradition among even the earliest Church-fathers, before its deformation began. Polycarp (Ad. Phil. VII.) mentions "the word which has been handed down." And Irenæus, notwithstanding his rejection of suspicious traditions, still admits true oral accounts of the wonders and words of the Lord in addition to the four gospels, which are most important to him.[4] With such oral sources the dependence of Mark on the preaching of Peter fully accords.

3. *Characteristic features.* The language and style of

---

4 : 13; Eph. 6 : 19; 1 Thess. 2 : 2, 13; 2 Thess. 2 : 15; 3, 6; Tit. 1 : 3; Heb. 4 : 2.

[1] See, e. g., Acts 17 : 20; Rom. 2 : 13; Eph. 1 : 13; 1 Thess. 2 : 13; 1 Tim. 1 : 13; 2 : 2; James 1 : 22, 23, 25.

[2] See, e. g., Matt. 12 : 3, 5; 21 : 16, 42; 24 : 15; Mark 2 : 25; 12 : 10, 26; 13 : 14; Luke 4 : 16; 6 : 3; 10 : 26; Acts 8 : 28, 30, 32; 13 : 27; 15 : 21.

[3] Resch has undoubtedly overstated their number and significance, often using various readings for distinct Logia.

[4] Zahn, I., p. 168.

Mark are peculiar and characteristic. There is no classical elegance and flow, but the harmony of the Greek language is disturbed by the roughness of the Hebrew. The argumentative " for "[1] is very rare, while the Hebraistic "and" occurs constantly. Provincialism is combined with a limited and repetitious vocabulary. Yet with all this homeliness force and power are united, which appear in the frequent redundancy,[2] the crowding together of participles,[3] the strong negatives,[4] the contrast of opposites,[5] the cognate accusative,[6] as well as in such individual expressions as "rent" (1 : 10), "driveth forth" (1 : 12), "tearing him and crying" (1 : 26), "foameth and grindeth" (9 : 18), and "wailing greatly" (5 : 38). In addition activity and life are everywhere apparent. The word "straightway" occurs 42 times, and "began" is often found.[7] The imperfect[8] and the historical present[9] constantly recur. The events are presented with picturesque vividness. The very words spoken in Aramaic[10] are reported, and the direct speech[11] is preferred to the indirect. The exact time[12] and place[13] are noted. Pictorial participles, such as "looking up," "looking on,"

---

[1] Cf. e.g. 7 : 28; 10 : 45.
[2] 2 : 21; 3 : 7; 4 : 14, 30; 5 : 42; 6 : 25; 7 : 8; 8 : 34, etc.
[3] 5 : 15, 25; 6 : 22, 54; 10 : 17; 12 : 28; 14 : 66, 67.
[4] 1 : 44; 2 : 2; 3 : 20; 7 : 12; 9 : 8; 11 : 14, etc.
[5] 2 : 27; 3 : 26, 29; 4 : 17, 33; 5 : 26, etc.
[6] 1 : 16; 2 : 4; 3 : 28; 4 : 41; 7 : 7; 10 : 38.
[7] e. g. 1 : 45; 2 : 23; 4 : 1; 5 : 17; 6 : 2; 8 : 11, etc.
[8] 1 : 13, 22, 30; 2 : 2, 13, 16; 3 : 2, 1; 5 : 24; 6 : 3, 13, 20; 10 : 13, etc.
[9] From the ninth chapter onward it is found more frequently than "straightway" in the whole gospel, e. g., 9 : 19, 35; 10 : 1, 16, 46, 55; 11 : 2, 4, 15, 21, 33; 12 : 13, 14, 16, 18, 41, 43, etc.
[10] 3 : 17; 5 : 41; 7 : 34; 14 : 36; 15 : 34.
[11] 4 : 39; 5 : 8, 9, 12; 6 : 9, 23, 31; 7 : 5; 8 : 16; 9 : 11, 25; 14 : 58, etc.
[12] 1 : 35; 2 : 1; 4 : 35; 6 : 2; 11 : 1, 11, 19; 15 : 25; 16 : 2.
[13] 2 : 13; 5 : 20; 7 : 31; 12 : 41; 13 : 3; 14 : 68; 15 : 39; 16 : 5.

"looking around," "groaning," are employed as also the affectionate diminutives.[1] Simplicity and naturalness, living power and striking force, freshness and fragrance are the prominent features.

The great commotion of the people and their thronging[2] around Jesus, whom they seek even when he would retire, are graphically represented; while the enmity[3] of the leaders of the Jews, particularly of the Jerusalemites, and the non-receptivity of the people and even of the disciples[4] are not forgotten. But the central figure, real and living, is Jesus, shown in his true humanity, needing sleep and repose (4:38; 6:31), subject to hunger (11:12), moved by wonder (6:6), pity (6:34), grief (7:34; 8:12), and anger (3:5; 8:33; 10:14); and yet as the mighty lion[5] of Judah, with power over sickness (1:23; 3:1; 6:56) and victorious strength over demons, the servants of Satan, who dread him. (cf. e. g. 1:23, 26; 3:11; 5:15; 7:26, 29, 30, etc.). Miracles are ever wrought by him, who is "the Son of God."[6] The gospel of Mark is the gospel of miracles, which are however not overvalued (cf. 8:11 sq.). It is in itself an evidence

---

[1] 5:23, 39, 41; 7:27; 14:47.
[2] 1:22, 27; 2:12; 3:10, 32; 4:1, 41; 5:21; 6:2 etc.
[3] See, e. g., 2:6; 3:6; 7:1 sq.; 8:11 sq.; 9:14 sq.; 12:1 sq., etc.
[4] 4:11, 40; 5:17, 40; 6:6, 52; 7:18; 8:17, 32, etc.
[5] It is this representation of Christ's power which makes the lion the appropriate symbol of Mark. It was not always his symbol, for Irenæus (Adv. Haer. III., 11, 8), seeing in the first verse the coming down of the prophetical spirit from on high, and speaking of "the winged aspect of the gospel," ascribes the eagle to Mark. Later, however, the lion is applied to Mark, for, says Victorinus (Com. on Apoc.) in him "is heard the voice of the lion roaring in the desert." Through Jerome this symbol gained general acceptance, though Augustine (De Cons. I. 6) assigns the man to Mark. All of the symbolic attributes rest on the vision of Ezekiel (1:15 sq.; 10:1; 11:22). See Schaff, Ch. Hist. I., p. 585.
[6] For the frequent occurrence of this name see 1:1.

against those, who, while accepting its primacy, deny the supernatural and attempt to reduce to a lifeless skeleton the vigorous creation of heavenly power.

4. *Integrity of the gospel.* There is only one section of Mark, about whose genuineness there is a reasonable doubt, ch. 16 : ver. 9–20: but this has been much discussed.[1] It is wanting in the oldest manuscripts, the Sinaitic and Vatican of the fourth century, and all the more exact manuscripts known to Jerome and Eusebius, who states that the gospel ended " they were afraid " (16 : 8). In the Regius manuscript L of the seventh century, several MSS. of the Ethiopic version, and the best Coptic MSS., there is a shorter ending,[2] which has been substituted for the longer in the Codex Bobiensis (k) of the Old Latin Version. This outward testimony of the MSS. is apparently corroborated by the difference of the style and language of this section from the rest of Mark. There is no "straightway," nor any other frequent characteristic expression of Mark. The words "disbelieved" (ἠπίστησαν, ver. 11), "walked" (πορευομένοις ver. 12), "manifested" (ἐφανερώθη ver. 14), "seen" (θεασαμένοις ver. 14), "speak with new tongues" (ver. 17),

---

[1] It is rejected by Credner, Griesbach, Lachmann, Wieseler, Tischendorff, v. Hofmann, Tregelles, Alford, Westcott & Hort, Reuss, Klostermann, Keim, Holtzmann, Meyer, Weiss, Zahn, etc., and defended by Simon, Mill, Bengel, Hug, Schleiermacher, De Wette, Strauss, Köstlin, Bleek, Ohlshausen, Hilgenfeld, Lange, Ebrard, Keil, Schanz, Nösgen, Scrivener, Burgon, Morison, Cook, etc.

[2] This ending is: "All things announced to them about Peter they told briefly. After these things Jesus himself was manifest; from the east to the west he sent out through them the holy and incorruptible preaching of the eternal salvation." The form and vocabulary of this conclusion show its late date and spuriousness. See Zahn, II., p. 920 sq.; Westcott & Hort, II. Append., p. 30, 38, 44 sq.

"drink any deadly thing" (ver. 18), "first day of the week" (ver. 9) (πρώτῃ σαββάτου)[1] are found nowhere else in Mark. The promise of ver. 7 is not told as fulfilled, and in the account of the appearances there is an apparent climax not natural to Mark.

But this testimony is outbalanced by opposite witnesses. The disputed section, which is full of apostolic elements and admitted by Zahn to have been known in certain circles far earlier than the middle of the second century, is found in most of the MSS., beginning with the Alexandrine[2] of the fifth century, and in most ancient versions, the Itala (k excepted), the Vulgate, the Peshito, the Curetonian Syriac, the Coptic, Gothic, the Ethiopic, in the Greek and Syrian lectionaries. Irenæus, much earlier than Eusebius, knows it and quotes a part of the 19th verse (Adv. Haer. III., 10, 6), and Tatian includes it in his "Diatessaron," the first harmony of the gospel (in the second half of the second century). The ending of ver. 8 is also a very improbable one. And the difference in language is partially explained in the case of "speak with new tongues," "drink anything deadly," "disbelieved" and "manifested," which are rare in the N. T. (Luke 24 : 11, 41 ; John 21 : 1), from the nature of the matter related. What appears unsolved is largely outweighed by correspondences with the other parts of Mark "The whole creation" (ver. 15) reminds of 13 : 19 "the beginning of creation ;" (κτίσεως) "lay hands on the sick" (ver. 18) of "the sick" 6 : 13 (ἀρρώστια); "Signs" (ver. 17 σημεῖα) point to 13 : 22, and "word" (ver. 20 τὸν λόγον) to 2 : 2 ; 4 : 14, etc. And the "hardness" of the disciples' hearts (ver. 14) is a peculiar feature of Mark

---

[1] In the enumeration of these peculiarities almost all scholars have drawn on Credner, p. 106.

[2] The others are C, D, X, Γ, Δ, Σ etc.

found previously 6 : 52 and 8 : 17. There is then no overwhelming argument against this part of Mark, which may possibly have been added later, because Mark was suddenly interrupted in a Neronian persecution.[1]

5. *Purpose and Plan.* The opening of the gospel shows its purpose to be the relating of the beginning[2] of the glad tidings of the Messiah-king.[3] His wonderful work as still carried on through his disciples (16 : 20) is to be unfolded in its inception. The gospel as a power is to be traced to its beginning and source. Its preparatory announcement was made by John, who called for the repentance necessary to enter the kingdom to come, and preached the "mightier one" (1 : 2-8), who then appeared, and, endowed by the Spirit, began to call the first disciples and to proclaim the kingdom with mighty word and wonderful deeds in every part of Galilee (1 : 9-45). This soon aroused the enmity of the leaders of the people, who accuse Jesus of blasphemy, unholy walk, disregard of sacred traditions, permissive and active breaking of the sabbath; but he, showing his healing power, his call to sinners, the joyous newness of his kingdom, the fight of necessity and his lordship over the sabbath, triumphs, though a dangerous hate is aroused. (2 : 1-3 : 6). The knowledge what it would bring and the changeableness of the multitude move the Lord to select the Apostles as companions of his life that they might be assistants in his work (3 : 7-19). They are to be tried, for Christ is assailed by friends, enemies and his own kin (3 : 20-35); and to learn their peculiar privilege in having unfolded the mysteries of the kingdom

---

[1] See Keil, Com., p. 145 sq.; Morison, p. 463 sq.; Schaff, I., p. 643 sq. Zahn, II., p. 911.

[2] Grau renders this "Urevangelium," wrongly inverting the order.

[3] See 1 : 1.

hidden to the people (4 : 1-34). And by the wonderful testimony of Jesus of his power over nature (4 : 33-41), over Satan (5 : 1-19), sickness and death (5 : 20-43), which can be apprehended by faith, they are to be led to believe in him, who is not to be refused because of his humble earthly home (6 : 1-6). Taught thus the twelve are sent on a trial missionary journey (6 : 7-13). The first part of Mark ends here, and the introduction to the second is the death of John the Baptist, which announces the end of him, whose herald John was. But as Herod thinks John has arisen, there is a prophecy of Christ's final victory (6 : 14-29). He now desires to lead the disciples through the miracle of the feeding and the stilling of the storm to the clearer consciousness how salvation is conditioned by the dignity of his own person (6 : 30-52). But not yet are they able to see this, although in companionship with Jesus they are freed from the externalism of Judaism and instructed in the true law of purity (7 : 1-23). The borders of Israel are crossed and Jesus, who with difficulty gains real followers among the Jews, though many crowd about him, shows how freely he gives salvation even to the Gentiles, if only the right confession of faith be made (7 : 24-37). Then the disciples aroused by a second miracle of feeding, and warned against the contaminating influence of Pharisaism, are, like blind men gradually receiving sight, brought to see and confess the Christ, as distinct from all heralds (8 : 1-29). But this confession is not yet for the people, for it is not even fully understood by the disciples, who cannot think of a suffering Messiah and self-denial as the way to glory (8 : 30—9 : 31). Therefore but a select few can see the revelation of the essential divine glorious Sonship of Christ, into the fruition of which he enters by way of suffering, that a new time may come when his visible presence is not needed, but his present power is received by the prayer of faith (9 : 2-29). This in the congregation, founded on the crucified and risen Son of man, would bring the new law of greatness, the tolerant, non-offending and self-preserving love (9 : 30-50). And the new life was to show itself in the home, in the sanctity of the marriage-bond, the proper estimate of children and possessions (10 : 1-31). Then begins the way to suffering, which, to be inflicted by Jews and Gentiles and so little understood even by the select disciples, is the deed of ministering love that ransoms, and even now heals (10 : 32-52). For a short moment the Messiahship is recognized even at Jerusalem, but the Jews are unfruitful and cursed, and their leaders again surround Christ with wicked designs, which he overcomes though prophesying his near end, in contemplation of which the prophecy of the last things is given (10 : 32—13 : 37). The last sufferings begin and are borne to their bitter end, and the rescuing love of the God-man, though met by human self-confident weakness, avaricious betrayal, fierce hatred, vacillating injustice, cruel abuse and mockery, saves those that are to be saved (14 : 1—15 : 47). Then arisen and ascended the Lord and King of salvation sends out his servants working through them in the word and confirming them by signs (16 : 1-20).[1]

6. *Place and time of composition.* This gospel was, as reported by Clement of Alexandria, most probably written at Rome and for Roman readers. Storr alone conjectured that it was composed at Antioch. But it contains Latin terms,[2] mentions Roman measures and coins (12 : 15, 42), and watches (13 : 35); and describes a house in Roman style (4 : 21). It speaks of a Roman pikeman

---

[1] In this plan I have largely followed Klostermann, but with some changes.
[2] e. g. ʼεσχάτως ἔχειν (5 : 23), τὸ ἱκανὸν ποιεῖν (15 : 15).

(6 : 27), centurion (15 : 39), the Prætorium (15 : 16), and adds a remark interesting to the friends of Rufus at Rome, (15 : 21 cf. with Rom. 16 : 13).

Its composition could not have taken place after the destruction of Jerusalem (A. D. 70), because that catastrophe is regarded as future in chap. 13. Nor could it have been given to the church sooner than the death of Peter (between 64-69 A. D.), for Irenæus (Adv. Haer. III., 1, 1) relates that it was written after the death [1] of Peter and Paul. And if Clement Alex. (Eus. VI., 14, 5 sq.) says that Mark wrote while Peter was alive, who when he "became cognizant of this he neither laid an interdict on the undertaking nor urged its fulfilment," this does not contradict Irenæus, for the beginning of the undertaking, not its completion and giving to the Church, is spoken of. The probable date of Mark would therefore be about 68 or 69 A.D.

[1] μετὰ δὲ τὴν τούτων ἔξοδον can only mean death not departure. (cf. 2 Pet. 1 : 15). See Zahn, note in I., p. 887.

CHAPTER I.

1. The beginning of the gospel of Jesus Christ, the Son of God.

Ver. 1. The beginning of the gospel of Jesus Christ is not to be restricted to the prophecy[1] concerning John the Baptist (ver. 2) nor to his preparatory labor (ver. 4 sq.), but it includes the appearance and all the consequent work of Jesus while in the flesh. It is a characteristic title of the whole gospel according to Mark, who depicts the historical beginning of Christ's mighty works, which are to continue (chap. 16:17 sq.). To announce these is the purpose of the **gospel** which is the preaching of the glad tidings of salvation, and not a written record.[2] (1:15; 13:10; 14:9; Matt. 24:14; Luke 4:18 sq.) It is not the preaching by Christ, which would simply be gospel (1:15, Luke 20:1), or gospel of God (1:14) if the divine authorship were to be designated (1:14; 1 Thess. 2:2, 8; 1 Peter 4:17), but it is the gospel, whose content[3] (cf. 8:35; 10:29) is **Jesus Christ.** This name

---

[1] Thus Origen ag. Celsus, II. 4.

[2] This usage of the word gospel prevailed down to the second century. (Zahn, Geschichte des N. T. Canons, I., 842, 869, note.) An evidence of this is also found in the superscriptions of the gospels. In Mark this superscription was εὐαγγέλιον K. M. except in ℵ. B & F, which have only κατὰ Μάρκον (accdg. to Mark). Late cursives read τὸ κατὰ M. ἅγιον εὐαγγ. (the holy gospel accdg. to Mark), and seem to point to a time, when the gospels were already gathered into one volume. Keil. p. 16: Weiss. p. 11). On the meaning of the superscriptions, cf. Zahn, I., 164 sq.

[3] Winer N. T. Grammar (7th ed.) p. 186; Cremer, Bibl. theol. Wörterbuch der N. T. Gräcität (7th ed.) p. 31.

of the Lord occurs in this combination in the gospels only here and Matt. 1 : 1, 18; John 1 : 17. By its use Mark confesses Jesus to be the Christ (Matt. 16 : 16; John 20 : 31). **Jesus** is the personal name of the Lord, but as it expresses His saviourhood (Matt. 1 : 21) it receives an official signification in Acts 19 : 14 (the Jesus, τοὺς Ἰησοῦν).[1] **Christ** (Messiah) is used primarily as the official title of honor for the anointed of God; prophet (Isai. 61 : 1), high-priest (Lev. 4 : 3), king (1 Sam. 2 : 10; 12 : 3; 16 : 6, etc.; 2 Sam. 1 : 14; 19 : 21, etc.; Ps. 2 : 2; 18 : 50; 20 : 6; 89 : 38, etc.). But it is also applied personally to Jesus (9 : 41; Rom. 5 : 8; 6 : 4; 8 : 10; 1 Peter 1 : 11, 19, etc.). Mark shows pre-eminently the kingship of the Christ, who is **the son of God**[2] (1 : 11; 3 : 11; 5 : 7; 9 : 7; 13 : 32; 14 : 61). This title received in its messianic use in the O. T. (2 Sam. 7 : 12-14; Ps. 2 : 7) a dignity, which made it more than human; and in the expectation of the synagogue the son of God was infinitely superior to all other servants of God.[3] In the N. T. the son of God as Messiah, is always the eternal, supermundane son.[4] The central idea of the divine Sonship of Christ is that of likeness of image and identity of essence.[5]

[1] Possibly Jesus may originally have had this force in the combination Christ Jesus (Rom. 3 : 24), although in most cases there is no trace of it (Rom. 8 : 2; 15 : 1; 1 Cor. 4 : 15; Eph. 1 : 1; Phil. 3 : 3, etc.), Cremer, p. 947.

[2] This name is wanting in ℵ and therefore rejected by Tischendorf, Wesct. & Hort. Iren. (ag. Her. III. 11, 8), and frequently Origen omit it. But it is found in all the other uncials and cursives, as well as in Iren. III., 10, 15; 16, 3; and occurs so often in Mark and is so characteristic, that it is doubtless original. The article the (τοῦ) is not supported by ℵ, B, D, L, and is probably spurious.

[3] Edersheim, Life and Times of Jesus the Messiah (5th ed.) I., 173, sq.

[4] Cremer, p. 920.

[5] Nösgen, Gesch. der N. T. Offenb. I., 153, defines all sonship as likeness of image and essence. In Christ likeness of essence is replaced by identity. (John 10 : 30; cf. Matt. 11: 27; Lk. 10 : 22.)

(Hebr. 1 : 1, sq.) How glorious is the title of the gospel of Mark; in itself a message of gladness of the divine Redeemer-King!

> 2–8. Even as it is written in Isaiah the prophet,
> Behold, I send my messenger before thy face,
> Who shall prepare thy way;
> The voice of one crying in the wilderness,
> Make ye ready the way of the Lord,
> Make his paths straight;
> John came, who baptized in the wilderness and preached the baptism of repentance unto remission of sins. And there went out unto him all the country of Judæa, and all they of Jerusalem; and they were baptized of him in the river Jordan, confessing their sins. And John was clothed with camel's hair, and *had* a leathern girdle about his loins, and did eat locusts and wild honey. And he preached, saying, There cometh after me he that is mightier than I, the latchet of whose shoes I am not worthy to stoop down and unloose. I baptized you with water; but he shall baptize you with the Holy Ghost.

Ver. 2. As ... written. As, referring to an implied "thus" at the beginning of the 4th verse, introduces the only quotation from the O. T. used by Mark himself in his gospel. His appeal to the O. T. prophecy, establishes the truth of prophecy by its fulfilment, shows the providential preparation for the gospel, and exalts the written record of the O. T. as the sure Word of God. In this emphasis of the written Word Mark but follows Christ's example. (7 : 6; 9 : 12; 11 : 17; 14 : 21, 27; Matt. 4 : 4; 7 : 10.) The written word is cited as in **Isaiah ... prophet**,[1] but the first part (ver. 2) is a quotation from Mal. 3 : 1, and only the latter half (ver. 3) is found in Isaiah (40 : 3). These two prophets are cited under the name of one, not because of a lapse of memory,[2] nor

---

[1] This reading is sustained by ℵ B, D, L, Δ., the Itala, Peshito, and the principal fathers. The Rev. version "in the prophets" was an amendation to escape a difficulty.

[2] Thus with a polemical purpose Porphyry, and among modern commentators from a critical bias, Griesbach, Bleek, Meyer, Weiss.

because Isaiah was "more full and better known," (BENGEL,) nor because Mark wishes to quote briefly, (KEIL), but to show the inward relationship of the prophets and to exhibit the organic nature of prophecy. The prophet whose book stood at the head is named, and a prophecy from him, who occupies the last place, is introduced, to include the whole range of prophecy from Isaiah to Malachi, as it comes to be fulfilled.—KLOSTERMANN. Isaiah has the melody, and Malachi adds the harmony. (Cf. similar cases Matt. 21:5; Rom. 9:27.) The whole passage, which agrees closely with the Hebrew original, is different in substituting "thy" for "my" before "face" and "way." This accords with the time of fulfilment, in which the Father speaks to the Son. Here the difference of persons is noted, while in Malachi the identity of essence is brought out. This prophet announces in God's name: **Behold . . . messenger.** As a remarkable immediate act the Lord of Hosts (Mal. 2:16) makes known the sending forth of His own peculiar messenger to the Christ, as taking place before his **face**, which is here a descriptive pleonasm for "before," and expresses temporal precedence. It is to be the work of the messenger to **prepare thy way.** The roads in the East are mostly wretchedly constructed and not at all kept.[1] When, therefore, a king or noted personage comes a special quartermaster must build a road.[2] And the construction

---

[1] Thomson (The Land and the Book, I. 65,) called the road par excellence between Beirut and Sidon "a villainous path."

[2] But even such preparations or repair of former roads often leaves them in bad condition. Thus Dr. Trumbull (Studies in Oriental Social Life, p. 217) relates: At Hebron as our party entered the Holy Land from the desert below, we were told that the Crown Prince of Austria was just before us, and that the word had gone out from the Turkish authorities to prepare his way in advance. At this our dragoman was delighted, as he was sure we should find the roads in excellent condition all the way northward.

of such a highway is a sign of royal greatness. But how much greater is He for whom a spiritual way was to be prepared, as was proclaimed by the, Ver. 3, **voice . . . wilderness.** This voice is suddenly heard, calling with great earnestness; and it is "a voice" because the message is to be everything, the messenger nothing. He is merely the crier in the **wilderness,** which symbolized the condition of Israel. Living in the land of promise they had made it a spiritual wilderness of individual and social religious desolation and corruption. In such a state the crier, because of the immediate coming of the Lord, should call: "**Make . . . Lord.**" The people should prepare themselves by removing the hills of pride and self-righteousness, and filling up the hollows of sin in their hearts by sincere repentance. Thus a way would be made not for men to come to God, but for God to come to men. It is the **Lord's way,** on which His kingship is to appear. It was made by His command and to serve His purpose in His gracious approach to men,[1] who were to **make . . . straight**, by laying aside all crookedness, hypocrisy, and deceit (Luke 3 : 7). Thus there would be a real plain (Is. 40 : 4). In accordance with this prophecy, Ver. 4, **John came.** Corresponding to the expectancy created by the prophecy John is introduced in the midst of his labor, as he **who baptized.** Baptizing is mentioned before preaching, not as in Matt. 28 : 19 for its initiatory character; but Mark loving to dwell upon activity, points out the most characteristic work of John (11 : 30), which

---

Again and again he said gratefully: "This road has been prepared for a prince. I wish there was always a prince before us." He evidently thought that the road was better than usual; but we did not see how it could ever have been worse.

[1] Cf. Trumbull, Primitive Idea of "The Way" (Studies in Oriental Social Life, p. 219 sq.)

was performed **in the wilderness.** This was the wilderness of Judæa, which beginning at Jerusalem extends southeast to the Dead Sea and is about fifteen miles broad. It is a "frightful desert"—ROBINSON, "the hottest chasm in the world"—HUMBOLD, "a dreary waste of rocky valleys; in some parts stern and terrible—the rocks cleft and shattered by earthquakes and convulsions into rifts and gorges."—GEIKIE. In this desert John **preached**[1] **... sins.** This baptism, preached and administered, had its O. T. prediction in Ez. 36 : 25; Zech. 13 : 1. It went beyond the symbolical purifications of the O. T. in its condition of repentance, which it not only illustrated, but required of those seeking baptism, and sealed in baptism. This **repentance,** is not merely a change of mind, affecting the whole personality, and the adoption of entirely new motives, but it is fundamentally a change of attitude toward God in the inwardness of man's nature by thorough conversion. (Matt. 3 : 11; Luke 3 : 3; Acts 13 : 24; Rom. 2 : 4; 2 Cor. 7 : 10; 2 Tim. 2 : 25). Such repentance receives in baptism **remission of sins.** It was a baptism into remission, i. e. God's free forgiveness (Luke 1 : 77; 3 : 3, Acts 2 : 38). Forgiveness was not only symbolized, nor regarded as a distant purpose, but it was really imparted by baptism as means to the repentant heart. But this baptism did not give the new life of the Christian "baptism of regeneration," for it did not bestow the Spirit. (Acts 19 : 2, sq.; John 7 : 39; Acts 2 : 38; Tit. 3 : 5.) (See Excursus 1, p. 29.) John's work was so novel, that, Ver. 5, **there ... Jerusalem.** "John came not to men, but they had to go to him"—KLOSTERMANN, and **all,** i. e. the great mass of the people, came not only from the province of Judæa, but from the capital, to

---

[1] Preaching (κηρύσσων) does not possess its usual N. T. signification of heralding the gospel, because otherwise determined by it object.

satisfy their curiosity. But many were won and **baptized
... Jordan**, which designates the location, and not the
mode of baptism. To this they were admitted, after
confessing their sins. The confession (ἐξομολογούμενοι) was
an outspoken admission of transgressions (Acts 19 : 18 ;
James 5 : 16 ; 1 John 1 : 9.).[1] Such an open confession
before men, and especially before those called of God, is
salutory because of its humiliation and the consolation
received.[2] Ver. 6. **And ... hair.** He wore a rough
coat made of thick cloth woven from the coarse woolly
tufts on the hump of the camel.[3] And the coat was girt
up with *a leathern girdle*, a plain strap of untanned
leather used by the poor, instead of the costly silk or
linen girdle (Jer. 13 : 1 ; Ezekiel 16 : 10), which was often
ornamented with gold or silver (Rev. 1 : 13 ; 15 : 6), and
possessed by the wealthy. This austere garb fitted to the
plain fare of John, **locusts ... honey.** The former allowed by the law as food (Lev. 11 : 21, 22) were eaten
raw. To-day they are sold in the bazaars cooked, fried
or scalded. **Wild honey** is found largely in the clefts and
fissures of the limestone rocks, but also in trees, and at
times even in the skulls of dead animals.[4] This food
shows the ascetic life of John, which was a living sermon
reproving worldliness and calling to repentance. To the
announcement of this (Matt. 3 : 4-12 ; Luke 3 : 7-18),
described by Mark only in its striking action and not in
its leading words, John adds the heralding of Christ and his
relation towards Him, for, Ver. 7, **he ... I.** Although

---

[1] The synoptical gospels do not contain the deeper conception of sin as a quality and condition, even in Matt. 12 : 31 sin (ἁμαρτία) means an act, cf Mark. 3 : 28.

[2] Cf. Luther's Sermon v. d. Beicht u. d. Sacrament (Erl. Ed. 11, p. 166 sq.). Tischred. Erl. Ed. 59 : 78. Sermon v. Sacr. d. Leibs u. Bluts Christi (Erl. Ed. 29 : 352.) [3] Geikie, N. T. Hours, I., p., 308.

[4] Thomson, II., p. 362. Geikie, I., p. 336.

not yet knowing as after Christ's baptism the majesty of His person and therefore the secret of His might, John still sees in Christ one of greater power in His preaching and baptism, as well as in person. Of Him he says **the latchet . . . undo.** Mark reports the confession of John which most strikingly exhibits his deep humility; for he deems himself not only unworthy to "bear Christ's sandals" (Matt. 3 : 11), but even to stoop and unloose their thongs, a most menial service. The dignity of the "mightier" is so much greater than that of his greatest herald (Luke 7 : 28), that the lowest service is too great an honor. "Humility is the best adornment of a teacher (1 Peter 5 : 3)"—STARKE. In such humility John says: Ver. 8, **I . . . water.** The baptism, looked upon as completed, is designated merely according to its outward element. Its efficacy (ver. 4) is not mentioned, because less than that of Christ, who would baptize **with . . . Ghost.** This baptism, as is evident by the addition "fire" (Matt. 3 : 11; Luke 3 : 16), refers primarily to the first outpouring of the Spirit (Acts 2 : 2 sq.), but it also includes the ordinate coming of the Spirit in Christian baptism (John 3 : 5).

9–11. And it came to pass in those days, that Jesus came from Nazareth of Galilee, and was baptized of John in the Jordan. And straightway coming up out of the water, he saw the heavens rent asunder, and the Spirit as a dove descending upon him: and a voice came out of the heavens, Thou art my beloved Son, in thee I am well pleased.

Ver. 9. **And . . . days,** i. e. in the days of John's baptizing and preaching, that **Jesus . . . Galilee,** His place of abode,[1] which is beautifully situated on the lower slope of rounded hills, that enclose a sequestered hollow, and at a distance of about 14 miles from the sea of Galilee.

---

[1] For an excellent description of Nazareth, see Ninck, Auf biblischen Pfaden, p. 176 sq.

And ... John. The baptism of Jesus was not the dedication to His work, but the entrance upon it, by fulfilling righteousness (Matt. 3 : 15), in taking upon Himself a baptism not needed,[1] for the purpose of His identification with sinful men and the fulfilling for them righteousness, which they could not of themselves attain.[2]

Ver. 10. **Straightway**[3] **... asunder.** From the Jordan where Christ had stood to be baptized, not necessarily by immersion,[4] He came out, and as Mark forcibly reports the heavens were rent asunder,[5] for He was here, through whom heavenly blessings and messengers could descend and men ascend (John 1 : 51). Upon Him came the **Spirit ... descending.** The dove was a fitting embodiment for the Spirit, because of its purity (Song of Songs 6 : 9) and therefore its use in purifications (Lev. 14 : 22), as well as its gentle, peaceful simplicity (Ps. 74 : 19; Matt. 10 : 16). But it is the dove in its descent, which the Spirit employs, to symbolize the brooding warmth[6] in the inception of redemption even as in creation (Gen. 1 : 2). The dove of Noah has found its antitype, for

---

[1] In the gospel of the Hebrews, Christ is said to have been invited by his mother and brothers to come to the baptism of John, and to have answered: "What have I sinned, that I should go and be baptized of him? Unless, perchance, this very thing I have said is ignorance." The latter part shows the heretical influence of the Nazarenes, as they begin to cast a doubt upon Christ's sinlessness. Cf. Resch. Agrapha, p. 345 against Handmann, Hebräerevangelium, p. 67 sq.

[2] Nösgen, p. 189; also in his Com. Matt. 3 : 11; Luther, sermon in House postil for Epiphany. Erl. Ed. I. p. 142.

[3] This word so characteristic of Mark is rendered uniformly in the Rev. version. In the Auth. version it is translated in seven different ways, as straightway, immediately, forthwith, as soon as, by and by, shortly, anon. Cf. Schaff's Companion to Greek and Engl. version, p. 359.

[4] Cf. Weidner, On Mark, p. 52.

[5] Matt. and Luke have simply "opened."

[6] Cf. Creuzer, Symbolik, as quoted by v. Hofmann, Weissag. u. Erfüll. II., p. 73.

"therefore the dove also appears, not bearing an olive branch, but pointing out to us our Deliverer from all evils, and suggesting the gracious hopes."—CHRYSOSTOM. To accomplish this deliverance Jesus is anointed to His messianic work by the Spirit (Isai. 61 : 1), and " now He begins rightly to be Christ."—LUTHER. And He is further attested, for, Ver. 11, **a voice . . . heavens.** The voice of the Father[1] confirms the extraordinary witness of the Spirit, and " we behold and see as it were in a divine spectacle exhibited to us the notice of our God in Trinity."—AUGUSTINE. This voice[2] is directed to John and Christ, although Mark reports only its import for Christ. To Him the Father said : **" Thou . . . Son."** The Son is beloved, not merely as the obedient or chosen one (Luke 9 : 35 ; Rom. 11 : 28), but as *the only Son* (Jerem. 6 : 26 ; Am. 8 : 10).[3] " He is the Beloved (Eph. 1 : 6), through whom as the Son of His love (Col. 1 : 13) the love of the Father is given to the whole human race (John 3 : 16 ; 17 : 26)."—STARKE. And in this Son the Father is *well pleased*, not merely because of their eternal relation, but because of the Son's obedience in the work of redemption (Isai. 42 : 1, 2 ; John 4 : 34 ; Rom. 5 : 19).

12, 13. And straightway the spirit driveth him forth into the wilderness.

[1] The heretical gospel of the Hebrews, reports a threefold voice, and has the Spirit calling Christ his Son. And yet Handmann would have us believe that these inventions are the basis of the simple gospel story. Sancta Simplicitas !

[2] This voice could not have been inserted in the gospel as a Jewish notion, as found in the Rabbinic " Bath-Qol," because the Bath-Qol came after the Spirit ceased, is rarely an echo of the divine voice, and the occasions on which it is used are often " shocking to common and moral sense." Edersheim I., p. 285.

[3] Cf. the Septuag. Zech. 12 : 10; Judg. 11 : 34; Ps. 22 : 20, where μονογενής is used. Nösgen on Matt. 3 : 16; Cremer, p. 18.

And he was in the wilderness forty days tempted of Satan; and he was with the wild beasts; and the angels ministered unto him.

Ver. 12. **The ... forth**. The Spirit becomes a mighty force impelling the only-begotten Son above the measure of other sons of God (Rom. 8 : 14); and the Son willingly goes **into the wilderness**, which is, according to the traditional supposition, the wild region near Jericho round about Mount Quarantania.[1]

Ver. 13. In this He remained **forty days**, like Moses and Elijah, and the people of Israel. During this time He was **tempted of Satan** again and again, by temptations not mentioned by Matthew, and prior to the last three (Matt. 4 : 1). The possibility of temptation is given in Christ's human nature. Its necessity was that of His work both for Himself, and for us as the second Adam. It was no dream, phantasy or mental occurrence, but a real outward event. Christ was really tempted, but was sinless (Hebr. 4 : 15); He could feel (sentire) the temptation, but could not assent (consentire). "With a peccable human nature He was impeccable; not because He obeyed, but being impeccable He so obeyed, because His human was inseparably connected with His divine nature."—EDERSHEIM.[2]

And ... beasts. This describes the utter lonely and forsaken state of Christ, in which He was without all human comfort. But **angels ... him**. They who desired to look into the deep mysteries of redemption (1 Peter 1 : 12) were sent to cheer and sustain their Lord bodily and spiritually, and to be witnesses of His victory. "Temptation preceded, that victory might follow. The

---

[1] Thomson, II., p. 450.
[2] Cf. Ullmann's Sinlessness of Jesus (Engl. Trans.) p. 264; Frank, Chri. Wahr. II., p. 174; Nösgen I., p. 196; Nebe, Ev. Perikopen II., p. 86 sq.

angels ministered that the dignity of the victor might be attested."—JEROME.

14, 15. Now after that John was delivered up, Jesus came into Galilee, preaching the gospel of God, and saying, The time is fulfilled, and the kingdom of God is at hand: repent ye, and believe in the gospel.

Ver. 14. **After . . . up** into the hands of Herod Antipas (6 : 17 sq.), **Jesus . . . Galilee**, and began His ministry there. His preaching was **the . . . fulfilled**. The fulness of time (Gal. 4 : 4 ; Eph. 1 : 10), the proper time divinely appointed and wrought out in the history of Israel had come. This Christ, the fulfiller, but not John, could announce ; and therefore when Christ preaches (ver. 13), "**The . . . hand**," He takes up the proclamation of John (Matt. 3 : 3), pronounces nearness of the kingdom as presence. The kingdom is at hand in the King. The **kingdom of God**, although made known by O. T. prophecies (Isai. 2 : 11 ; Jer. 23 : 5 ; Ezek. 34 : 23 ; Micah 4) and typified in God's royal rule over Israel to Israel's blessing and salvation (Exod. 15 : 19 ; Deut. 7 : 6 sq. ; 33 : 5), is in its fulness a N. T. conception, for that order of things in which God's rule, i. e., the assertion of His will, appears for the realization of His plan of salvation.—CREMER. Its foundations are the treasures (Matt. 13 : 44 sq.) and free gifts of salvation (Matt. 22 : 1 sq. ; Luke 14 : 16 sq.) ; its life-principle is the divine Word (Matt. 13 : 19 sq. ; Mark 4 : 13 sq.) ; its character in this life mixed, owing to the Enemy (Matt. 13 : 24 ; Matt. 13 : 47) ; its nature inward and spiritual (Luke 17 : 20 ; John 3 : 5 ; Rom. 14 : 17), but not hidden, for it comes into view (Matt. 11 : 12 ; 12 : 28 ; 13 : 11, 19). Its development ever continuing (Matt. 13 : 31 ; Mark 4 : 30 sq. ; Matt. 13 : 33) it is present (Matt. 4 : 17 ; 10 : 7 ; Mark 12 : 34 ; Luke 11 : 8 sq.). But it is also future, and its consummation comes at the end of this present world (Matt. 6 : 10; 25 : 34; Mark; 14 : 25; Acts 14 : 22; 1 Cor. 6 : 9, etc.).[1] The condition of entrance into this kingdom Christ announces with the words: Ver. 15, "**repent . . . gospel.**" The preaching of repentance by John is confirmed by the use of the same term: and faith, which John had directed to the person of Jesus (1 : 7; John 1 : 15, 19 sq., 29 sq.), is by Jesus Himself at first centred upon His message. From this Christ in proper time leads to His person. The faith required is the trust, which is concentrated and fixed upon its object.[2] The double demand of Jesus includes the whole saving truth, for " as in the first member Christ convicts of sin, in the latter He consoles us and shows the remission of sins."—Apology of Augs. Conf.

16–20. And passing along by the sea of Galilee, he saw Simon and Andrew the brother of Simon casting a net in the sea : for they were fishers. And Jesus said unto them, Come ye after me, and I will make ye to become fishers of men. And straightway they left the nets, and followed him. And going on a little further, he saw James the *son* of Zebedee, and John his brother, who also were in the boat mending the nets. And straightway he called them: and they left their father Zebedee in the boat with the hired servants, and went after him.

Ver. 16. **Passing . . . Galilee,** in an incidental walk,

[1] Cremer, p. 194; Nebe, I., p. 163; Schmid, Bibl. Theol des N. T. (5th ed.) p. 115; Frank, Chrl. Wahrheit, II. 375; Nösgen, I. 280 sq. 342, 345; and especially Jul. Köstlin, Religion u. Reich Gottes, in which the idea of Ritsch'l, that the kingdom of God is merely an ethical community, is thoroughly refuted by a comparison of N. T. teaching. Cf: also Schnedermann, " Jesu Verkündigung und Lehre vom Reich Gottes," especially II., 37 sq., 77 sq.

[2] Believe ($\pi\iota\sigma\tau\epsilon\acute{\iota}\epsilon\iota\nu$) is used with $\dot{\epsilon}\nu$ (in, permanence) only here in the gospels, and Eph. 1 : 13; Gal. 3 : 26; with $\dot{\epsilon}\pi\acute{\iota}$ and the accus. Matt 27 : 42 expressing direction and rest upon ; and with $\epsilon\dot{\iota}\varsigma$ showing direction towards and into Mark 9 : 42; Matt. 18 : 6. See Keil; Winer, N. T. Gram., p. 213; Cremer, p. 766; Thayer, Lexicon, p. 184, 511.

which had its deep purpose, Christ came to the shores of the **Sea of Galilee**, also called Gennesaret (Luke 5 : 1) and Tiberias (John 6 : 1) in the N. T. It is a pear-shaped lake about 13 miles long and from 4 to 6 miles broad, and broadest at the north end. Its depth is about 160 feet, and its level 600 feet below the sea. Its water, which is somewhat salty, is filled with many species of fish. The shores, in Christ's day, very fertile and populous, recede at the plain of Gennesaret, Tiberias, and at the outflow of the Jordan; but mostly they are steep limestone and basalt hills.[1] At the shores of this sea Jesus saw **Simon**, the son of Jonas, who is thus named until 3 : 16, and thereafter always Peter, except when rebuked by the Lord in the Garden of Gethesemane (14 : 37). By nature impulsive and fiery, in temperament sanguine, Simon was enthusiastic, bold, straightforward, but at times fearful.[2] With Simon Jesus found **Andrew**, Simon's brother, who had originally called Simon to discipleship (John 1 : 41), before the present call of Christ to apostleship. Of the character of Andrew we have but two glimpses (John 6 : 8; 12 : 22); he seems to have had some of the forwardness of his brother, but less energy and faith.[3] These two brothers were *casting a net*, which

---

[1] Smith's Bible Dict.; Tristram, Land of Israel, p. 426 sq.; Thomson, I., 541.

[2] Beyond the testimony of the Acts and the Epistles of Peter, nothing is known of his later labors. The tradition of his martyrdom (John 21 : 19), is first mentioned by Clement of Rome (Ad. Cor. 5.), who does not however name the place. But this must have been Rome. (Ign. Ad. Rom. 4.) That Peter was bishop in Rome rests only upon late and uncertain tradition. (First found in Jerome, de vir. ill. 1.) Cf. Notes on Eusebius H. E. by Dr. McGifford, Nicene and Post Nicene Fathers, 2d Series, Vol. I., pp. 115, 129, 132.

[3] The traditions about Andrew, his labor in Scythia and his crucifixion, are very contradictory. The traditions concerning the later labors of the various apostles are supposed by Lipsius to be connected originally with that

was neither the drag-net (Matt. 13 : 47, 48), nor the bag-net (Luke 5 : 4 sq.), but the casting-net, "which, when skillfully cast from over the shoulder by one standing on the shore or in a boat, spreads out into a circle, as it falls upon the water, and then sinking swiftly by the weight of the leads attached to it, encloses whatever is below it" (Trench, N. T. Synonyms).[1] As the brothers were thus at work, the call of Christ came. Ver. 17. **Come ... me** (cf. 2 Kings. 6 : 19), which asked them to forsake their present calling, and in following after Jesus to be prepared for their higher calling, upon which they were to enter later. They were to be **Fishers of men** (Jer. 16 : 16), and to catch human souls with the gospel-net (Matt. 13 : 47). "It is God's manner to invite every one to Himself, with a voice most comprehensible to each one" (CHEMNITZ), and therefore fishers are called to gospel-work under the name of their human work, which would indicate to them at once the difficulties of their new calling (Luke 5 : 5), as well as the need of divine blessing (Luke 5 : 6). The men of "low degree" are chosen to the noblest work (1 Cor. 1 : 26 sq.). Ver. 18. **And ... him.** As sudden as their call had been, they were prompt in self-denying obedience. "Their heart was then such, that if they had much, yea the whole world, they would have left all. It is not to be wondered at that they arose so quickly and followed Christ without a prophecy and promise, but only that they should be fishers of men; but what does Christ's word not effect, when it comes into the heart? It is a living,

---

of their separation at Jerusalem. But "the efforts to derive from varying traditions any trustworthy particulars as to the apostles themselves is almost wholly vain." (McGifford on Eusebius, p. 132.)

[1] On the various modes of fishing, see Thomson, II., p. 79 sq.; Geikie, I., p. 220.

active, fiery word, it does not return without profit and blessing."—LUTHER. After this, Ver. 19, Christ going a little further saw **James . . . Zebedee,** one of the three favored apostles, who was the proto-martyr among them, being beheaded by Herod Agrippa, A. D. 44 (Acts 12 : 2).[1] The epithet " the Elder " was added to distinguish him from James the Little (Mark 15 : 40), James, the son of Alphæus (Mark 3 : 18) and James, the brother of the Lord, surnamed "the Just" (Gal. 1 : 19). With James was **John his brother,** the evangelist. A second pair of brothers follow Christ. " Blessed are such brothers, whose natural bond of brotherhood grace sanctifies and confirms." [2]—BESSER. These brothers were **in . . . nets,** preparing to begin their work, when called. Some, as James and John, are called in the preparation for their earthly labor, others, as Simon and Andrew, when already in the midst of work. Upon the invitation of Christ, James and John, Ver. 20, **left . . . servants.** The fact that Zebedee had hired servants, shows that his business must have been more extensive than that of Simon and Andrew, and may indicate that James and John were men of some means, thus helping to explain John 19 : 26, 27. They could with less sacrifice than the sons of

---

[1] On the way to martydom. Clement relates in Hyptop., Bk. VII. (Eus. H. E. II. 9), according to a tradition not improbable, " that the one who led James to the judgment seat, was moved, and confessed that he was himself a Christian. They were both therefore led away together; and on the way he begged James to forgive him. And he, after considering a little said, " Peace be with thee " and kissed him. And thus they were both beheaded at the same time." Epiphanius, who probably confuses this James with the brother of the Lord, says that he was unmarried and a Nazarite. Equally untrue are the Latin legends of James' labors in Spain and his burial in Compostella. McGifford, Eus., p. 111.

[2] Besser reminds of the similar cases of Moses and Aaron, Basil and Gregory of Nyssa.

Jonas leave their work; but in leaving their father they left more (Matt. 10 : 37).

21-28. *And they go into Capernaum; and straightway on the sabbath day he entered into the synagogue and taught. And they were astonished at his teaching: for he taught them as having authority, and not as the scribes. And straightway there was in their synagogue a man with an unclean spirit; and he cried out, saying, What have we to do with thee, thou Jesus of Nazareth? art thou come to destroy us? I know thee who thou art, the Holy One of God. And Jesus rebuked him, saying, Hold thy peace, and come out of him. And the unclean spirit, tearing him and crying with a loud voice, came out of him. And they were all amazed, insomuch that they questioned among themselves, saying, What is this? a new teaching! with authority he commandeth even the unclean spirits, and they obey him. And the report of him went out straightway everywhere into all the region of Galilee round about.*

This healing, although occurring after Christ's remarkable sermon in Nazareth (Luke 4 : 31) is characteristically selected by Mark to introduce Christ in His power.

Ver. 21. **And they go.** The "and" used almost always by Mark to introduce a new scene, does not imply temporal connection unless indicated, but serves to bring on the various pictures in quick succession. Thus Christ is shown with His newly-called apostles entering into **Capernaum**, Christ's own city (Matt. 9 : 1), as the place of His abode, and scene of some of His most remarkable works. Its exact site is one of the unsettled questions of Palestinian topography, for it has been so brought down into the dust (Matt. 11 : 23). The Scriptural data, that it was on the lake of Galilee (Matt. 4 : 13), a place of custom (Mark 2 : 14), near Bethsaida and Chorazin (Matt. 11 : 21), are not sufficient to determine the dispute. Most scholars favor Tell Hum,[1] two miles southwest of the en-

---

[1] The supporters of Tell Hum are Dr. Wilson, Major Wilson, Thomson, Stanley, Dixon, Ritter, Baedeker, Delitzsch, Plumptre, Schaff, Edersheim, Farrar. Porter, Kiepert, Sepp, Geikie, after the lead of Robinson select

trance of the Jordan into the sea of Galilee. In Capernaum Christ and His disciples on the *sabbath day*, which they kept as Israelites obedient to the law, entered into the *synagogue*. If Tell Hum be the site of Capernaum we have a slab of the lintel, which was over the entrance to the synagogue, built by the centurion (Luke 7 : 5), and on it is pictured a pot of manna (John 6 : 31 sq.). The synagogue was probably built of marble, a rectangular hall with pillared portico. Within at the south end, opposite the gallery reserved for the women at the north, was the holy ark containing the rolls of the law and the prophets, before which sat the rulers and elders. In the centre was the platform (Bima) from which Christ *taught* after the prayers were said and the selection from the Pentateuch (Perashah, pericope) was read. Such teaching was in accordance with the general privilege of an Israelite.[1] Ver. 22. **And . . . authority.** Christ's preaching rested upon His mighty "I say unto you," upon the authority of His person, which like glorious heavenly sunshine broke forth through His meekness and lowliness. Sweet and gentle as were His words, they were mighty withal, thrusting home at the conscience, uncovering sin in its deepest recesses and unfolding the greatness of the Father's love and mercy. It is not to be wondered at, that men were astonished at such teaching, the like of which they had never heard, for Christ taught *not as the scribes*, who in their office as copyists of the law had allowed exactness to become quibbling about

---

Khân Minyeh, about 3 miles south of Tell Hum and near the shore. Tristram (Land of Israel, p. 442) supposed 'Ain Mudwarah to be the correct site, but afterward abandoned it. See Smith's and Schaff's Bible Dict., Thomson, I., p. 542 sq., Edersheim, I., 365 sq., Ritter, Jordan, p. 335 sq., Wilson, Lands of the Bible, II., 139 sq.

[1] Vitringa de Synag. Vet. III., 1 : 7 ; On the whole structure of a synagogue, Edersheim, I., p. 433; Farrar, Life of Christ (rev. ed.), p. 157.

the letter, and had degraded their instruction into discussions about subtle niceties and distinctions. They ever sought for minute differences, and relied for every statement upon some authoritative rabbinical interpretation. Thus their teaching was dead formalism, without life and power.[1] Ver. 23. **And ... spirit.** Even the synagogue is not free of the unclean, for there is present a man possessed with a demon, who is called an unclean spirit[2] because of his unholy, wicked, Satanic nature. (On demoniacal possession see EXCURSUS II. p. 31.) The demon, Ver. 24 *cried out*, using the voice of the man possessed, and **saying**[3] ... **thee.** What is there to us and thee; why dost thou interfere? "Thou hast thy kingdom, leave us ours."—CHEMNITZ. The demon speaks for the other demons, who "make common cause with each other."—BENGEL. The "very presence of Christ was felt to be an interference."—MORRISON. Him the demon at once addresses as *Jesus of Nazareth*,[4] not by diabolical artifice, nor to despise Him (John 1 : 46). It is simply Christ's human name, by which He was ordinarily known. Continuing, the demon says: **art ... us?** It is better with Luther to make this an affirmation, thou comest to destroy us. There is no

---

[1] Edersheim, I., p. 94 sq. Farrar, p. 189. For a clear exposition of the difference between Christ's teaching and that of one of the noblest scribes, Hillel, see Delitzsch's monograph : "Jesus u. Hillel."

[2] Mark uses unclean spirit almost as often (1 : 23, 26, 27 ; 3 : 11, 30 ; 5 : 2, 8, 13; 6 : 7; 7 : 25) as demon (1 : 32, 34, 39; 3 : 15, 22; 5 : 15, 18; 6 : 13; 7 : 26; 29, 30; 16 : 9, 17. Matt. employs it only 10 : 1; 12 : 43; and Luke less than demon (4 : 36; 6 : 18; 8 : 29; 9 : 42; 11 : 24).

[3] The interjection (ἔα) "let us alone," found in the Auth. version is wanting in ℵ B, D, Itala, Peshito, etc., and was probably interpolated from Luke. 4 : 34.

[4] Mark makes use of the adjective "Nazarene" (Ναζαρηνός) in 10 : 47 ; 14 : 67 ; 16 : 6, which occurs elsewhere in the gospels only Luke 4 : 34. Matt. and John always use Ναζωραῖος.

doubt with the demon, that Christ has come to give him and his fellow-demons over to judgment and destruction (1 John 3 : 8); for he confesses tremblingly (James 2 : 19) **I . . . art**, and adds to the human name the divine,[1] the *Holy One of God.* Christ is *the Holy One* (Luke 4 : 34; Ps. 16 : 10; Acts 3 : 14) above the holy prophets (Luke 1 : 70), priests (Ps. 106 : 16), apostles (Eph. 3 : 5), saints (Acts 9 : 13; Rom. 1 : 7), not as the one especially and above measure (John 3 : 34) anointed as Messiah by the Holy Spirit and sent into the world as sanctified (John 10 : 36), but as the absolutely sinless Son of God (Acts 4 : 27, 30).[2] The holiness of Christ is the greatest dread of the unclean spirit, because it augurs the certainty of the defeat of sin and the power of Satan. This Satanic spirit Christ (ver. 25) *rebuked*, for " He would not that the truth should proceed from an unclean mouth,"—ATHANASIUS, by which Satan sought to impress men that Christ was in league with him (Luke 11 : 15). Therefore Christ said, Ver. 25: " **Hold . . . him.**" Christ muzzles the demon like a beast (1 Cor. 9 : 9; 1 Tim. 5 : 18), and by His word of power ejects him. Ver. 26. **And . . . him**, throwing about the man in convulsions into the midst of the people (Luke 4 : 35), and **crying . . . voice**, making a terrible outcry, came out of him. Ver. 27. **And . . . amazed** (9 : 15; 10 : 24; 14 : 33; 16 : 5). The astonishment, which had arisen during Christ's teaching (ver. 22), now rose to such a height, that those present begin in feverish excitement to discuss with each other: " **What**[3] **. . . him !**" (Isai. 34 : 16).

---

[1] Cf. *Iren.* ag. Her. IV. 6, 6. *Tertull.* ag. Praxeas, 26. *Augustine* On Baptism ag. Donatists, chap. 10; On John, Tract VII., 6.

[2] Cf. Keil on this passage as against Meyer & Weiss.

[2] The reading, " A new teaching with authority," supported by ‫א‬ B, L, 33, etc, but unknown to the fathers, is to be preferred (v. 22).

Ver. 28. And the report of Christ went everywhere **into ... about**, i. e. into all the province of Galilee out from and about Capernaum.

29–31. And straightway, when they were come out of the synagogue, they came into the house of Simon and Andrew, with James and John. Now Simon's wife's mother lay sick of a fever; and straightway they tell him of her: and he came and took her by the hand, and raised her up; and the fever left her, and she ministered unto them.

Ver. 29. **When**[1] **... synagogue.** The succeeding event is connected temporally with the previous account. Christ and His disciples **come ... Andrew.** Andrew, who is not mentioned in this connection by Matthew, originally lived with Simon who was probably the head of the household, at Bethsaida (John 1:44); but afterward they removed to Capernaum. At their home they may have found no festal meal, as was customary, on this sabbath, for, Ver. 30, **Simon's**[2] **... fever.** This "burning fever," which is still prevalent in the Galilean lake region, was in all probability caused by the miasmic vapors, arising from the marshy plains.[3] Ver. 31. **And straightway,** when Jesus entered the house, the people of the

---

[1] The reading "they" is found in א, L, A, C, while "he" occurs in B, D, Σ.

[2] The N. T. tells us nothing further of Simon's wife, than that she accompanied her husband on his missionary travels (1. Cor. 9:5). But an old tradition, which there is no reason to doubt, reported by Clement Alex. (Strom. VII. 11) and quoted by Eus. H. E. III. 30, relates this account of her martyrdom: "They say, accordingly, that when the blessed Peter saw his own wife led out to die, he rejoiced because of her summons and her return home, and called to her very encouragingly, and comfortingly, addressing her by name, and saying 'Oh, thou remember the Lord.' Such was the marriage of the blessed, and their perfect disposition toward those dearest to them." Canon Cook, who has used this account in his Com. on Mark, calls it exceedingly beautiful and free from the monastic taint found in later writers.

[3] Thomson, I. 547.

household run up and **tell him**, as the physician, from whom they expect help. And *He*, before whose presence all evil flees, **took ... hand** (5 : 41), and by His simple touch from which there went out power (5 : 30) gave her strength, and **raised her up** to health, for the *fever* [1] *left her* immediately. **And ... them.** Christ came to minister, and not to be ministered unto, but yet He receives the loving service of those whom He helped. To serve Him is the best use of health regained. This use Simon's wife's mother made, in performing the first deaconess-work for Christ and His disciples.

32-34. And at even, when the sun did set, they brought unto him all that were sick, and them that were possessed with devils. And all the city was gathered together at the door. And he healed many that were sick with divers diseases, and cast out many devils; and he suffered not the devils to speak, because they knew him.

Ver. 32. **At even,** which Mark defines more accurately: **when ... set,** and therefore the sabbath ended, *they brought unto* Christ, who was still at Simon's house, the sick and the demoniacs. Ver. 33. **And ... city,** i. e. the body of the people, was at the door. Ver. 34. Christ healed **divers diseases,** for He was Lord over all sicknesses, which are distinguished from demoniacal possession, that was *sui generis*. The demons cast out were not suffered to speak (ver. 25) for they knew Him.[2]

---

[1] Edersheim (I. 486) shows very aptly how altogether different in "sublime simplicity" the healing of Christ was from the magical methods of the Jews, by referring to the remedy, which the Talmud prescribes for the same disease, "of which the principal part is to tie a knife wholly of iron by a braid of hair to a thornbush, and to repeat on successive days Ex. III. 2, 3, then verse 4, and finally verse 5, after which the bush is to be cut down, while a certain magical formula is pronounced."

[2] The addition "to be Christ" rests upon the authority of B, C, G, L, M, but it was probably inserted from Luke 4 : 41.

35-39. And in the morning, a great while before day, he rose up and went out, and departed into a desert place, and there prayed. And Simon and they that were with him followed after him; and they found him, and say unto him, All are seeking thee. And he saith unto them, Let us go elsewhere into the next town, that I may preach there also; for to this end came I forth. And he went into their synagogues throughout all Galilee, preaching and casting out devils.

Ver. 35. **In the morning** (Matt. 20 : 1), is more closely defined as **a . . . day**, when it was yet very nightly (ἔννυχα) and dark, long before dawn,[1] Christ **rose up** (Ps. 57 : 8) and **went out** of the house unto a **desert place**, an uninhabited barren region, that, undisturbed, He might gain strength for new work and new victory. More than once such retirement took place: and Mark, who portrays most strikingly the constant activity of Christ, mentions more frequently than any other evangelist these times of withdrawal (1 : 45; 3 : 7 sq.; 6 : 6, 31, 32; 7 : 24; 8 : 27; 9 : 2; 11 : 11; 11 : 19). At this time Christ **prayed** (6 : 47; Ps. 63 : 1), and "made the desert place a temple of God by His prayers."—LANGE. His injunction (Matt. 6 : 6) He confirms by His own life, which was one of prayer (Matt. 26 : 36; Luke 5 : 16; 9 : 29; 22 : 32; John 17 : 1 sq.). Ver. 36. And in the morning **Simon and they . . . him**, i. e. Andrew, James, John, together with the multitude (Luke 4 : 42) *followed after* Christ; they sought, hunted, pursued with great earnestness, until they, Ver. 37, *found Him*. Blessed are those that seek Christ, for they shall find him (Matt. 7 : 7). As they find Jesus they say : "**All . . . thee**." It was the desire of most to find Christ, not for their souls, as the preacher of the Word, but for their bodies as the Healer of their diseases. Therefore, Ver. 38, **he . . . them**, His

---

[1] Wyclif renders this very quaintly: "in the morenynge ful erly."

disciples, **let ... elsewhere.**[1] The divine blessing is not to be restricted to one city, but to be spread first into the *next towns,* or village, cities (κωμοπόλεις), of which Galilee was very full. Josephus (Jew. Wars, III., 3, 2; Life 45), exaggerating somewhat, mentions 204 cities and villages, of which the least was said to contain 15,000 inhabitants. The population in the thickly sown cities and villages, was so dense owing to the richness of the soil.[2] In these places Jesus wished to preach, for He says: **to this ... forth,** not from Simon's house or Capernaum, but from the Father, who sent me into the world (Luke 4 : 43; John 8 : 42; John 13 : 3; 16 : 27). Christ's first work was to preach the gospel, and His deeds were to call attention to and confirm the Word. The miracles of Christ were to be but attestations of His truth. Ver. 39. **And ... preaching.** The order of the Greek original is the better, "he went preaching into their synagogues," because it emphasizes the preaching. This took place at the appointed houses of worship (Matt. 4 : 23), except where the multitudes came to Christ in the open. Notwithstanding the enmity shown Christ in some of the synagogues, He became no separatist. (Hebr. 10 : 25). His preaching in the synagogues He confirmed by **casting ... devils** everywhere. "Where Christ's kingdom is to be planted, the devil's kingdom must be destroyed "(2 Cor. 6 : 14, 15).—STARKE.

40-45. And there cometh to him a leper, beseeching him, and kneeling down to him, and saying unto him, If thou wilt, thou canst make me clean. And being moved with compassion, he stretched forth his hand, and touched him, and saith unto him, I will; be thou made clean. And straightway the leprosy departed from him, and he was made clean. And he strictly charged

---

[1] This word has been replaced by Tischendorff on the authority of א, B, C, L, 33.

[2] Delitzsch, Jüdisches Handwerkerleben zur Zeit Jesu, p. 11.

him, and straightway sent him out, and saith unto him, See Thou say nothing to any man: but go thy way, shew thyself to the priest, and offer for thy cleansing the things which Moses commanded, for a testimony unto them. But he went out, and began to publish it much, and to spread abroad the matter insomuch that Jesus could no more openly enter into a city, but was without in desert places: and they came to him from every quarter.

This event is placed by Matthew after the Sermon on the Mount. Mark and Luke give no chronological setting, although the latter in the arrangement of his gospel puts it before the Sermon on the Mount, and describes it as having taken place in "one of the cities." (Luke 5 : 12). Ver. 40. **And . . . leper,** who was probably affected with that variety of leprosy, which is called the white (lepra mosaica). It begins with small scabby postules, having minute spots in the centre, which are somewhat depressed (Lev. 13 : 34). The hairs near the scabs become white (Lev. 13 : 3, 20, 25). The postules, as they spread (Lev. 13 : 8) generate inflammation (Lev. 13 : 10, 14). The skin becomes white and dry, the eyelids cramped while the eyes lose their brightness. All the senses lose their power, and the extremities rot away. In its development the disease becomes exceedingly loathsome.[1] It was regarded as a special plague of God (2 Kings 5 : 27), excluding for sanitary[2] and ceremonial reasons from all men (Lev. 13 : 43; Num. 5 : 1, 2; 12 : 10, 14). It is a striking picture of sin, in its small beginning, its constant development, its uncleanness and hideousness, its incurableness by men, its heredity and contagiousness, and in its terri-

---

[1] Winer, Reallexicon; Smith, Bible Dict.; Trench, Miracles, p. 165 sq. Robinson, Bibl. Researches, I. 359; Thomson II. 516; Geikie, p. 186; Nebe, I.; p. 428.

[2] Trench rejects the contagiousness of leprosy, arguing from the case of Naaman. But Naaman's was probably a different variety. There can be no doubt from the testimony of Scripture and the Ancients, that white leprosy was contagious.

ble end... The leper came to Christ, breaking through the crowds and not heeding the legal restrictions. **Beseeching... down**[1] to Him, the afflicted man renders not only profound reverence toward a superior or "a man of God," but he adores the Christ, **saying... clean.** In great faith the leper ascribes to Christ the power and never doubts about it, although he is not certain if it be Christ's will to heal him. This uncertainty is no questioning of Christ's love; nor does it arise from the consciousness of special guilt; but it is rather the submissive humility of faith, which knows, that everything good is willed by Christ, but not all that is desired may be good. If this desire be for heavenly, spiritual blessings there can be no doubt, "for God's will is evident, that He will have His glory and our salvation unhindered. But it is not meant thus in temporal things. One can be poor, sick, miserable, and despised, and yet be saved.—Who therefore prays for rescue and help, shall truly believe that God can and will help; but he should place his will in God's will."—LUTHER. Thus the leper prays with true wisdom, for "who believes rightly, prays rightly."—LUTHER. Upon this prayer the Lord, Ver. 41, **being... hand.** The deepest compassion is stirred up in the Lord for the wretched sufferer, and "are not the pitying heart, the healing hand and the mighty word of Jesus foundations upon which one can be supported and rely?"—Tüb. Bible, STARKE. The hand of Jesus **touched** the leper, for Jesus is not afraid of impurity. Him the absolutely pure nothing can defile (Tit. 1:15). His touch is healing. "Jesus touched the leper to cleanse him in a twofold sense, freeing him not only as the multitude heard, from the visible leprosy by visible contact, but also from that

---

[1] "Kneeling down to him" is properly retained, although wanting in B, D, G, F.

other leprosy, by His truly divine touch."—ORIGEN. After the touch Christ said **I . . . clean**. This is the "prompt echo to the mature faith of the leper," coming from Him who is God (2 Kings 5 : 7), and whose will is deed. The humble "if thou wilt" combined with the mighty "thou canst" moves Christ's deep love to His powerful word: **Be thou clean.** What Christ commands, is accomplished at once (Ps. 33 : 9). The leper does not become clean as he goes, but, Ver. 42, **Straightway . . . departed.** It was an immediate and thorough cure. Christ heals where other healers fail. Ver. 43. **And . . . out.** Literally, "speaking to him sternly he drove him forth." This sternness, as the following injunction shows, was necessary because the healed man was in danger of "talking too much of the grace of God, to his own and others' harm." —GERLACH. Therefore Christ said, Ver. 44, **See . . . man,** for thy and My sake. Christ wishes to avoid being sought after as a mere worker of miracles (Mark 8 : 30; Matt. 16 : 20; 17 : 9; Luke 9 : 21), not only because of the wrong notion men would gain of Him, but also from His humility. "Why, O sweet Lord, dost Thou now say this: tell it to no one? On account of my humility, He says, on account of my sweetness, that you might be taught, when you have done anything good, not to glory, not to seek praise, nor wish to be uselessly placed before men."—ORIGEN. The man made whole is told: **Go . . . priest.**[1] By this order Christ demonstrates that He has not come to destroy the law. He subjects Himself to its provisions, and gives honor to whom it is due (Matt. 23 : 2, 3). To us He gives an "example of love, because He, who had power, does not wish to withhold from the priests, what was given and

---

[1] Cyprian employs these words to prove the right of priestly authority. Letters, LIV. 4; LXIV. 2.

granted them by God, in order that we should permit every one to remain in his rights, and take from no one, what is due."—LUTHER. Further the man restored to health is told: **Offer ... commanded.** These offerings (Lev. 14: 1 sq.) were at first two sparrows, of which one was killed over a vessel with spring water, while the other was dipped into this water and blood, together with a small bunch of hyssop, a piece of cedar wood and some crimson wool, which had been put under the tip of the tail and the tops of the wings. The hand of the restored leper was then sprinkled seven times and the bird let loose. On the eighth day a second burnt-and-sin-offering was brought (Lev. 14 : 9, 10, 11).[1] It is significant that Christ ascribes this ceremonial law not to some late scribe, but to Moses himself (cf. also 7 : 10; 10 : 3; 12 : 19, 26). The sacrifice before the priests was to be a testimony unto them; for they were to receive knowledge of Christ's power, that they might decide about Him. Thus although preaching in Galilee Jesus sent His testimony to Jerusalem, so that "the priests might be rendered without excuse, if they did not receive Christ's as the servant of God."—CALVIN. Ver. 45. But the **Leper ... abroad.** Disobedient to Christ's injunction the leper everywhere proclaimed the account of what Jesus had done, and He **could ... city**, for He was besieged on every side by masses, seeking Him for their outward ailments or to satisfy their curiosity. Then He remained without in *desert places*, but the people came to these **from ... quarter**, i. e. every part of Palestine (Matt. 4 : 25), and Christ could not keep concealed.

---

[1] See McClintock & Strong, Cyclopædia, sub. Leprosy.

EXCURSUS I.

THE BAPTISM OF JOHN. The baptism of John, standing between the Old and New Testament, occupies as to its effect and fruitage an intermediate position. It contained more than the shadow (Col. 2 : 17) of legal purifications and circumcision, because it was "a baptism of repentance into remission of sins." Its condition was repentance, for it was administered only to those who had heard the preaching of repentance (Matt. 3 : 2) and had confessed their sins (Matt. 3 : 6). In it repentance was also confirmed (Matt. 3 : 11), for it was truly "a seal of repentance." (Tertullian). It communicated as a means the forgiveness of sins (cf. Mark 1 : 4, with Acts 2 : 38). But it was less than Christian baptism, for it was a baptism of water (Mark 1 : 8) and not of the Spirit. It did not regenerate. Thus John's baptism agrees with his whole position. He was less than the least in the kingdom of God (Matt. 11 : 11) because he was not within. His preaching had much legal earnestness and severity (Matt. 3 : 5 sq.; Luke 3 : 7 sq.) and in his temptation about the Messiahship of Jesus (Matt. 11 : 3 sq.) the sterner aspect of the Christ and His day had influenced John (cf. Isai. 40 : 5; Mal. 3 : 2; 4 : 6). But withal John was the greatest of those born of women (Matt. 11 : 11); he was nearer to Christ than any other prophet, and as the friend of the bridegroom rejoiced in the bridegroom's voice (John 3 : 29). He saw the light of which he bore witness (John 1 : 8) and applied Isaiah's prophecy (Isai. 53 : 7) to Jesus, whose greatness and eternity he clearly proclaimed (John 1 : 29). Knowing this place of John the Fathers did not regard his baptism as equal to Christian baptism. Tertullian says: "That baptism was *divine* indeed (yet in respect of *command, not in respect of efficacy* too, in that we read that John was *sent by the Lord* to perform this duty) but *human* in its nature: for it conveyed nothing celestial, but it fore-ministered to things celestial; being, to wit, appointed over repentance, which is in man's power.—But if repentance is a thing human, its baptism must necessarily be of the same nature; else *if it had been celestial, it would have given both the Holy Spirit and the remission of sins.*" (On Baptism, X.). And this Tertullian, who in guarding John's baptism from over valuation deprives it of all efficacy, maintains, because "he who prepares does not himself perfect, but procures for another to perfect." Origen likewise in his Com. on John holds, that "the baptism of regeneration came not by John, but only with Jesus through his disciples." Augustine also (Enchir. 49) is of the opinion, that "those who were baptized in the baptism of John, by whom Christ was himself baptized, were *not regenerated;* but they were prepared through the ministry of His forerunner, who cried, Prepare ye the way of the Lord, for Him in whom only they could be regenerated. For His baptism is not with *water only, as was that of John.*" But John's baptism is more than this to Augustine, who (Ag. Donat. V. 11) says: "To none of the prophets, to no one at all in Holy Scripture, do we read that it was granted to baptize in the *water of repentance for the remission of sins*, as it was granted to John." Chrysostom was not as near the truth, when he affirmed (Hom. X. on Matt.), that John's baptism "had not remission, but this gift pertained unto the baptism, that was given afterward.—John verily preached a baptism of *repentance (he saith not of remission)*." But Cyril (Cat. Lect. XX) has correctly summed up in a consistent manner what Augustine had not fully declared, when, treating of Christian baptism, he stated: "Let no one then suppose that baptism is merely the grace of remission of sins, or further, that of adoption; as John's was a baptism, *conferring only remission of sins.*"

Luther holds, that John's baptism did not purify, for John said: "I purify *with water, not as though you are purified by it,* but through Him, who comes after me, who will purify with the Holy Spirit." (Erl. Ed. 47 : 91). With the prophets John points to Christ, saying: "I will take you as witnesses, that I am *not of the opinion, that my baptism saves;* but therefore I baptize, that you should accept Christ." (Erl. Ed. 47 : 106). But Luther has other utterances, which attribute to John's baptism the value of a real purification almost equal to that of Christ. "They have believed that John with *his baptism purified. For he hangs you with his baptism upon Christ,*" (Erl. Ed. 47 : 44), which is "as well instituted and confirmed by God as afterward the baptism of Christ." (Erl. Ed. 19 : 471.) "The baptism of John *is not far from the baptism of Christ.*—Therefore there *is no other difference, but that they who received John's baptism believed in the future Christ,* but we believe on Him, who has come." (Erl. Ed. 19 : 487). In this latter position, which ascribes even more than remission of sins to John's baptism, Luther was the leader of the Lutheran dogmaticians of the 16th century, who, from Chemnitz on, held, that the difference between John's and Christian baptism was that of the "word, concerning Christ coming and Christ exhibited," and that although the manner of publication was different, yet "as to its *substance it is the same* and has the *same effect* on believers." This view became prevalent in a polemical interest against the canon of the council of Trent on baptism, which declared : "If anyone say that the baptism of John has the same power as that of Christ, let him be anathema." Nevertheless other interpretations were not absolutely rejected, for Chemnitz, in his treatment of the various opinions on Acts. 19, which he has reviewed, states: "there is not sufficient cause, why he who embraces one opinion, should immediately by anathema condemn those who think differently." (Cf. *Chemnitz,* Exam. Conc. Trid. Loc. II. Sec. 1. *Gerhard,* Loci. XXI. Chap. IV. § 43 sq. *Aeg. Hunnius,* Artic. de Sacr. vet. and nov. test.) Calvin also (Com. Matt. 3 : 11) would not have the baptism of John to be distinguished from that of Christ. Among the modern Lutheran theologians Philippi (Kirchl. Glaubenslehre V. 2 : 195) adheres to the position of Chemnitz and Gerhard, giving a higher value to John's baptism than Hengstenberg (Christ. III. 1 : 663), who attributes repentance and faith in a weaker degree to John's baptism. Thomasius (Christi Person u. Werk, III. 2 : 10 sq.) holds, that forgiveness of sins on condition of repentance is imparted, an opinion which v. Hofmann defends (Schriftbew, II. 2 : 159.) Nösgen (N. T. Offenb. I. 139) attributes to this baptism a preparatory character for the remission of sins, in as far as it "generates the negative side of repentance, the godly sorrow and the desire for the full salvation." Höfling (Sacr. der Taufe, § 17 Anm. 27), Luthardt (Comp. § 71 : 1), Frank (Chrl. Wahr. II. 264) see in it only a symbol. (Cf. also v. Zezschwitz, Katech, I. 224; Nebe, Ev. Perik. I. 226 sq.)

EXCURSUS II.

DEMONIACAL POSSESSION. The casting out of demons by Christ is frequently and vividly pictured by Mark. He makes it his special object to show Christ's victory over these Satanic powers in emphasizing a feature of Christ's work reported by all synoptists, but rarely by St. John (John 7 : 20; 8 : 48, 49, 52; 10 : 20, 21), who "does not relate the prevailing over Satan by power, but his moral vanquishment: he (John) portrays not the struggle carried on in the periphery, but that which takes place in the centre." (Steinmeyer). Now the synoptists are not inserting individualistic conceptions into Christ's miracles, when they represent him as casting out demons, because not only in their descriptions but in Christ's own words the demons are accepted as real powers. And if we impugn the veracity of the evangelists in these reports of Christ's words, their trustworthiness as witnesses of other statements becomes doubtful. If the synoptists were deceived in these miracles, all miracles and consequently the whole N. T. record becomes uncertain. It cannot then but be accepted, that Christ treated the demonized as reported. And in such treatment we cannot attribute to Christ unconscious acceptance of the superstitions of his day (cf. Jewish Demonology, Edersheim, Life and Times of Jesus the Messiah, Vol. II., Appen. XIII., p. 755 sq.,) because His manner of healing was totally different from that of the exorcists, who performed temporary cures (Matt. 12 : 27; Mark 9 : 38) by magic formulas ascribed to Solomon, by incantations, fumigations, etc., (Jos., Jew. Wars, VII. 6, 3; Antiq. VIII. 2, 5). Christ cured by the simple power of His divine word. In Him there can be no superstitious ignorance, for this would be inconsistent with the whole gospel-picture of Jesus, who was the truth, and exhibited knowledge far superior to His own and all times. Nor can it be held with Bleek, (Synopt. Erklär. der ersten drei Evan. I. 219) that Christ accommodated Himself to popular notions, and entered upon the idiosyncracy of those affected, not only because such a supposition rests upon the misconception that the insane are cured by acquiescing in their ideas, but also because it is not in accordance with the truthfulness of Jesus, who gave his disciples power to cast out demons (Matt. 10 : 1, 8; Mark 16 : 17,) spoke to them about the proper preparation for this work (Matt. 17 : 21; Mark 9 : 29), and in every way regarded demoniacal possession as a fact and reality. (Luke 10 : 17 sq.) The demons were real spirits (Matt. 8 : 16; Mark 9 : 20), unclean (Matt. 10 : 1; Mark 1 : 23, 26, 27, etc.), wicked (Luke 7 : 21), satanic (Luke 10 : 18), not the souls of departed criminals (Jos. Jew. Wars, VII. 6, 3), nor the giants born of "the sons of God" and the "daughters of men" (Gen. 6 : 2). (Justin, Apol. II. 5; Tatian, ag. the Greeks. c. 16; Tertull. Apol. 22; Commodianus, Christ. Discipl. 3; Lactanius, Div. Inst. II. 15), but fallen angels (Augustine, City of God, XIX. 9). As spirits they enter into the spiritual nature of man, occupying his psychical powers, which is evident from the synonymous use of "to have a demon" and "to be mad" (John. 10 : 20), and the general classical use of "demonized" and "insane." In this insanity the demons are at times clairvoyant, recognizing Christ as the Son of God (Matt. 8 : 29; Mark 1 : 24; 3 : 11; Luke 4 : 34), and Paul and his companions as the servants of God (Acts 16 : 17), and they know what doom awaits them (Matt. 8 : 29; Mark 1 : 24, 5 : 7; Luke 4 : 34, 8 : 28). Into the very self-consciousness they intrude themselves and at intervals unseat the ego (Mark 5 : 9). From their central location within "holding the spirit in a state of siege" (Delitzsch), they are sheltered in the capacities of the soul, but not in the nervous system (Ebrard), nor on the border between the soul and the nervous organism (Delitzsch). From their citadel they act upon the nervous system, which is so intimately connected with the soul, by bringing on mania (Matt. 8 : 28; Mark 5 : 3; Luke 8 : 28; 9 : 39), epilepsy (Mark 9 : 18; Matt. 17 : 15), lunacy (Matt. 17 : 15). They take possession of speech (Matt. 8 : 29, 31; Mark 1 : 26; Luke 4 : 34; Acts 16 : 17), and sometimes cause dumbness (Matt. 9 : 32; 12 : 22; Luke 11 : 14), blindness (Matt. 12 : 22), and as "spirits of infirmity" bring on the permanent loss of motory power (Luke 13 : 11). This possession (obsessio corporalis) is to be distinguished from the moral possession (obsessio spiritualis) (John 13 : 2, 27), which is the result of special sin and takes place with the freest volition of the one possessed. But in no case of casting out a demon does Christ forgive sins, or is it anywhere intimated that because of sin in general or for special sins (Luther, Erl. Ed. 11 : 132; 58 : 127), or heathenish impurities these possessions came about. They are reported not only as taking place in Galilee, although most frequent there, but also in

Judæa (Matt. 10:1, 8; Mark 6:13; Luke 10:17; Acts 10:38). Only the New Testament reports such possession, for the case of King Saul (Jos. Antiq. VI. 8, 2) is to be diagnosed as moral possession. It was but natural that in the fulness of time when the Son of God appeared to destroy the works of Satan, that Satan would make every endeavor to hinder Christ's work, and in an extraordinary manner bring men under his yoke. In the deliverance from Satanic power, and by relegating the demons to the place of death, where they cannot exercise their abusive power (Matt. 8:29; Luke 8:31), Christ proved himself to be "the man of God, who could redeem life from the power of the enemy of all life, and lock up this enemy in his own domain, that of death" (v. Hofmann). This serves to explain why demoniacal possession became rare after Christ's departure, in evidence of which the testimony of the Fathers may be cited, who, while adding many superstitious elements to demonology and ascribing to the demons great influence over spirit and body, mention comparatively few cases of real exorcism and show the complete cessation later. (Justin Martyr, Apol. II. 6; c. Tryph. c. 30; Tertull. Apol. c. 23; Ad Scap. IV.; Origen adv. Celsus I., 6; Minucius Felix, Octav. c. 27; Theophilus ad Autol. II. 8; Lactantius, Div. Inst. II. 16; IV. 27; V. 22; Cyprian, Epistles, LXXIV. 10; Eusebius, Praep. Ev. III. 6; the pseudo Clementine Recogn. and Homilies, the Apocrypha; Martyrdom of Matt. the Apostle, Acts of the Holy Apostle and Evangel. John. Cf. Ffoulkes, in Smith and Wace Dict. of Christian Biography, I., p. 810b sq.; Zahn, Gesch. des N. T. Kanon I. 14, Note 2). Luther, whose "knowledge was literally world-wide," while attributing all disorders of nature, all diseases, all accidents, in short almost every evil to demons and Satan, and who is quite bound up in the superstitions of his day in this particular (Köstlin, Luther's Theol. II. 312 sq.), mentions few clear cases of bodily possession (cf. e. g. Erl. Ed. 1 : 279), which he distinguishes from "obsessio spiritualis" (Erl. Ed. 18:66; 59:315). The former, according to him, shows itself in insanity (Erl. Ed. 60 : 10). But the rarity of demoniacs after Christ's day does not prove that demoniacal possession has entirely ceased (Mark 16:17). This it would be difficult to maintain, especially since the experience of Johann Christoph Blumhardt (see Meusel, Kirchl. Lexicon, I. 482). (On the whole subject, Nebe, Ev. Perik. II. 131 sq., Ebrard in Herzog and Plitt Realencycl. III. 440; Edersheim, I. 479 sq., 607; Delitzsch Bibl. Psychology (Engl. Transl.) 345 sq.. Keil's Handbuch der bibl. Archäologie, 567; Twesten, Dogmatik. II. 1, 374; Nösgen, N. T. Offenb. I. 248 sq. Trench Miracles, on Demoniacs in the country of the Gadarenes, p. 117 sq. Demon Possession and Allied Themes, by J. L. Nevins, D. D., espec. Chap. XIV., p. 243 sq. For a modern negative view, Hand-Commentar zum N. T., Vol I., by Holtzmann, p. 73.

CHAPTER II.

1-12. And when he entered again into Capernaum after some days, it was noised that he was in the house. And many were gathered together, insomuch that there was no longer room *for them*, no, not even about the door: and he spake the word unto them. And they come bringing unto him a man sick of the palsy, borne of four. And when they could not come nigh unto him for the crowd, they uncovered the roof where he was: and when they had broken it up, they let down the bed whereon the sick of the palsy lay. And Jesus seeing their faith saith unto the sick of the palsy, Son, thy sins are forgiven. But there were certain of the scribes sitting there, and reasoning in their hearts, Why doth this man thus speak? he blasphemeth: who can forgive sins but one, *even* God? And straightway Jesus, perceiving in his spirit that they so reasoned within themselves, saith unto them, Why reason ye these things in your hearts? Whether is easier to say to the sick of the palsy, Thy sins are forgiven; or to say, Arise, and take up thy bed, and walk? But that ye may know that the Son of man hath power on earth to forgive sins (he saith to the sick of the palsy), I say unto thee, Arise, take up thy bed, and go unto thy house. And he arose, and straightway took up the bed, and went forth before them all; insomuch that they were all amazed, and glorified God, saying, We never saw it on this fashion.

Christ's popularity soon arouses the envy of the Jewish leaders, who are inwardly angered at Him. Accusation and attack follow, which, though answered in gentleness by Christ, grow into enmity. The development of this Mark depicts down to chap. 3 : 6 in a series of vivid pictures.

Ver. 1. **And** . . . **Capernaum,** His own city, which as the place of His first great success (1 : 32 sq.), was now to become the city, where enmity first met Him; **after** . . . **days,** lit. through days, i. e., after a number of days intervened, **it . . . noised,** lit. it was heard, everywhere because reported throughout the city, that *he was in the house*.[1] He had gone into the house and was there [2] at the home, which He occupied when at Capernaum, probably the house of Peter. Blessed the house, where Jesus is at home (Luke 19 : 9). Ver. 2. **Many . . . together,** in such multitude, **so . . . door.** If the house was that of Peter, it could not have been a low, flat house like these occupied by the poor,[3] in the front room of which Jesus was staying; but one containing a courtyard and similar to the dwellings of the middle class. The whole courtyard was thronged to the place beyond the door in the street. And Jesus **spake . . . word,** discoursing on the kingdom (1 : 15), proclaiming the Word of God (1 Pet. 1 : 23; 3 : 1; 1 Thess. 2 : 13), not in the upper chamber,[4] but in the covered gallery, which surrounded the courtyard. "Perhaps He was standing within the entrance of the guest-chamber, while the scribes were sitting within that apartment or beside Him in the gallery."—EDERSHEIM. As Christ was speaking there, Ver. 3, *they came*, i. e. four men **bringing . . . palsy,** by which name various kinds of muscular and nervous diseases, that deprive of sensation or motion, are designated. But most cases described in the N. T. (Matt. 4 : 24; 12 : 10 sq.; Luke 6 : 6; John 5 : 5 sq.), seem to have been apoplexy, paralysis of the whole system. In a severe form the limbs remain incurably rigid, and death occurs shortly (Matt. 8 : 6).[5] The paralytic, now brought to the true physician, was **borne . . . four,** each one carrying one

---

[1] The better reading is εἰσ οἶκόν accdg. to A, C, T, Δ, Π., etc.
[2] Cf. Winer, p. 415.
[3] Thomson, II., p. 6, sq. Robinson, Morison, Keil, Holtzmann, Cook.
[4] Lightfoot, Meyer, Weiss, Lange, Trench.
[5] Farrar, N. T. Hours, p. 185. Schaff, Bible Dict. sub. Palsy.

corner of the pallet. Ver. 4. **And**[1] **... crowd**. The impossibility of approach would not have been so great had the people filled only a room of a small one-story hut, rather than a courtyard, the passage to which was completely blocked up. But ministering love, although meeting with obstacles, is inventive, and with eagle-eye detects a way to accomplish its desire; for **they ... was**. If Christ stood upon the gallery, the difficulty of digging through a roof, paved with stones and having hard beaten earth and rubble underneath, as well as the danger to those below from the falling débris is avoided. The gallery easily reached from above by an outside approach to the roof could readily have its covering of tiles, which rested upon light frame-work, unroofed; and in a short time an opening would be dug out.[2] When *they had broken up* the roof as described, they **let ... lay**. The narrow couch, similar to a camp-bed, upon which only one person could lie, was lowered not "merely by stooping down and holding the corners of the couch," —THOMSON, but by means of cords. Thus love, born of faith, triumphed. "Where there is love in the heart we bear, we drag our neighbor until he is brought to Christ."—MÜLLER. Greater service cannot be performed for the sick, than to bring them to Christ with the strong arms of loving prayer. Ver. 5. **And ... faith**, which "refers not merely to those who brought

---

[1] The reading "to bring him unto him," is supported by B. L. 33.

[2] This view adopted by Faber, Jahn, Kitto, Wordsworth, Webster, Wilkinson and Edersheim solves all difficulties most satisfactorily. Even if we suppose with Robinson, that the covering of the roof was only earth, it could still not be dug out without at least inconveniencing those below. This objection is also fatal to the idea that it was an upper chamber. The size of the family in Simon's house (1:29 sq.) and his social position demand the kind of dwelling that has been presupposed in the above explanation.

the man,[1] but also to the man who was brought."—CHRYSOSTOM, because spiritual gifts are only given to personal faith. God may give bodily health or any outward blessing on account of the faith of others, but remission of sins cannot be obtained without our own faith.[2] In suffering himself to be brought and let down through the roof the paralytic exhibited the courage of faith; and his bearers showed that "through all things faith will penetrate."—BENGEL. In view of this faith, **Jesus**[3] . . . **forgiven.**[4] The palsied man is

---

[1] The faith is conceived as that of the carriers only by Cyprian, Ambrose, Jerome, Luther, and Stier.

[2] The question as to whether the faith of others has any direct effect upon spiritual life, has an important bearing upon infant baptism. In this connection it has been often treated by Luther, who in a sermon on Maunday Thursday, 1518, still held to the prevalent doctrine, that children were brought in the faith of the Church, which the Lord would regard, as the faith of the child was wanting, (Erl. Ed. 16:29). But in the Com. on Gal. (1519) faith was attributed to the child, because of the divine word spoken. (Op. Lat. 31:258). From this position Luther never again receded, but he combined it with the former; and thus in 1520 he maintained, that the congregation bringing the child in faith must be included, for by the prayer of the Church offering and believing the child is changed and renewed. (Babyl. Capt. Op. Lat. 36:71). This power of the faith of the Church, Luther also affirmed against the errorists of Zwickau; and he has summed up and adjusted his view most consistently in the sermons of the Church-postil for the third Sunday after Epiphany and the nineteenth Sunday after Trinity (Erl. Ed. 11:65; 14:202 sq.), when he says: "this we call the power of the faith of others; not, that any one can be saved by the same, but that through it, as through its intercession and help, one may obtain of God a faith of one's own to be saved by it." The bearers of the paralytic "in their faith asked Christ on behalf of the paralytic for faith of his own. Thus the faith of others helps, that I may receive faith of my own. Thus I baptize the child not in my faith or that of Christendom, but my faith and that of Christendom brings the child, for the purpose that God may give it a faith of its own." Cf. also Erl. Ed. 14:372; 59:25.

[3] *Thy* σοῦ instead *thee* σοὶ is found in B, D, G, L.

[4] The form ἀφίωνται found in A, C, D, L, and others, is Doric, perf. pass.

cheered by the address of the Lord, who calls him **Son**, in order to encourage and sustain him (Matt. 9 : 22; Mark 10 : 24). Christ exhibits His loving condescension, in which He assures the sufferer, **Thy . . . forgiven**. The forgiveness is an accomplished fact, now declared. The sins were forgiven before God, the moment faith began, but the paralytic is to possess the blessed consciousness of this divine grace, which Christ seals by His word. Thus Christ " first loosed the bonds of the real and true palsy," which " was that of the soul by sins." —CHRYSOSTOM. Although the paralytic was not sick because of special transgressions (John 5 : 14), he had learnt in his suffering the deep inward connection of sin and sickness, and had applied it practically and personally. He had searched his conscience and found much wrong; and the moment when his darkness of sin was placed in the radiant light of Christ's holiness he felt his sinfulness the more, and was unable to utter his petition for help. But Christ gave the true help first, because it was most desired, and because the soul is greater than the body (Matt. 16 : 26) and its health salutary to bodily well-being (James 5 : 14, 15). Now the paralytic was blessed (Ps. 32 : 1 sq.), for " with the forgiveness received the punishment has in reality been taken away, the remaining suffering is no longer punishment to the reconciled."—STIER. (Rom. 8 : 1, 18). Christ's word was not a savor of life to all, for, Ver. 6, **there . . . there**. These punctilious copyists of the law, students and observers of tradition, had come to find something against Christ, and after His word began **reasoning . . . hearts**, for they were afraid as yet to make charges, but inwardly they condemned Christ, saying, Ver. 7, **Why . . . speak?**

But a similar form ἀνέωνται is Ionic. Cf. Kühner's Ausführl. Griech. Gram., § 285, 4; Winer, p. 80.

In a contemptuous manner they call Christ "this man," and accuse Him: **He blasphemeth.** Blasphemy, speaking evil of (1 Cor. 4:13; Tit. 3:2), is supposed by the scribes to have been committed and directed against God, because Christ attributed to Himself a prerogative of God;[1] (Matt. 26:65; John 10:36) for **Who ... God?** In ascribing to God alone this power the scribes were correct (Isai. 43:25), for against Him mainly are all sins directed (Ps. 51:4). And that Christ exercised this right as God is clear, because He forgave not in God's name as a prophet (2 Sam. 12:13), nor as a priest after a sacrifice. Even these functions did not belong to Christ in the opinion of the scribes, much less the power to announce forgiveness in His own authority. But that this inward accusation of Christ rested upon a misapplication of truth is at once proved, for, Ver. 8, **straightway ... hearts?** Jesus saw their thoughts, and thus demonstrated His divinity, for before God alone the meditation of our hearts are as apparent as visible deeds (1 Sam. 16:7; 1 Chron. 28:9; 2 Chron. 6:30; Jer. 17:10, etc.). Since Jesus knows what is in man, without being told (John 2:25), His *spirit* is more than human. By His own spirit, and not by the leading of the Holy Spirit, He perceived, for His self-conscious inwardness is divine intuitiveness. The scribes, who from previous deeds should have known Christ, were thinking evil in their hearts (Matt. 9:4), and therefore "did not see God present."—AUGUSTINE. "Exposing to the Pharisees what they silently thought in the inmost recesses of their hearts, He showed Himself more than man; and by the same power, divine indeed, by which He saw the secrets of hearts, He could also remit sins."—GERHARD.

---

[1] Blasphemy against God also takes place, when improper attributes are given God, or proper ones denied (Bengel).

The accusers already convicted, are to be thoroughly routed, and Christ says: Ver. 9, **Whether ... walk?** Undoubtedly the scribes had reasoned, it is easy for Jesus to assume divine power by forgiving sins, for this power cannot be seen and tested; it would be much more difficult to heal by a word, and thus to authenticate His authority. But in reality it is different, and Christ may well ask which is easier to say. Either is equally hard; both presuppose the same divine might. He who has the power of the one must possess the power of the other. The one is conditioned by the other; forgiving of sins must show its effects in removing the results of sin, although not immediately, and outward healing can be no real blessing without a whole soul. To the eyes that truly see, the effects of forgiveness of sins are no more hidden, than the results of the word of bodily healing. But the former Christ will demonstrate by the latter, Ver. 10, **that**[1] **... sins.** Jesus calls Himself **The Son of man.** This was no name of Messianic import among the Jews,[2] for it sounded strange to them (John 12:34). In it Christ takes up an O. T. term, which designates man according to his lowliness, weakness and suffering (Ps. 8:4; Job 25:4, 6; Ezek. 2:1; Dan. 8:17), and declares Himself fully man with the same humble condition and suffering. But the definite article **the,** of this title, which in the gospels is used only by Jesus,[3] gives him an unique position, not as the second Adam, but as the one whose work it was to bear man's lowliness, although not as "misunderstood Messiah."—CREMER. With this name

---

[1] This order of words, which places "on earth" emphatically before "forgive sins" is attested by ℵ, C, D, L, M.

[2] Against Schnedermann, Verkünd. u. Lehre vom Reich G., II. 206.

[3] "The Son of man" occurs about seventy-five times in the gospels; and Acts 7:56, Rev. 1:13; 14:14.

not only Christ's poverty (Matt. 8 : 20 ; Luke 9 : 58), bodily need (Matt. 11 : 19; Luke 7 : 34), suffering and death (Mark 8 : 31 ; 9 : 31 ; 14 : 21 ; Luke 9 : 22 ; Matt. 17 : 12, 22; 26 : 2, etc.) are combined, but also glorious divine attributes, as forgiving sins (Matt. 9 : 6 ; Luke 5 : 24), lordship over God's day (Matt. 12 : 8 ; Luke 6 : 5), resurrection (Mark 9 : 9; Matt. 17 : 9), and glorious coming to judge the world (Mark 8 : 38 ; 13 : 26 ; Matt. 10 : 23 : 16 : 27 ; 19 : 28, etc.). Thus human lowliness has been exalted by union with the divine nature in Christ, and the prophecy of glory attached to " a son of man " (Dan. 7 : 13), has been brought into agreement with the prevalent O. T. conception by its fulfilment in Jesus. Son of man reaches with its apex into the divine. Christ is therefore "*the* Son of man because He is the Son of God."—VON HOFFMAN.[1] He has power *on earth* to forgive sins. Because the son of God has become man, the power of forgiveness has been brought to earth ; and the objection of the scribes why one standing before them in human form should forgive sins, is answered. This authority upon earth was not temporary, for as the word of the Son of man remained upon earth so also this power inherent in the word, which has been relegated to Christ's servants (Luke 10 : 16 ; Matt. 16 : 19 ; 18 : 18 ; John 20 : 22). If any minister uses Christ's word and says : " Thy sins are forgiven, then believe it as surely as if God Himself had said it."—LUTHER. " Through such power, that we men forgive or bind among ourselves, God's honor is not taken, nor are we made gods, as the unskilled people speak of it. For we have nothing more than the office.

---

[1] See Nösgen I., p. 157 sq.; Schmid, Bibl. Theol. des N. T. (5th ed.), p. 113 sq.; Cremer. p. 909 sq.; von Hofmann, Weisag. u. Erfüll. II., p .19 sq.; Franz Sieber, Anhang in Schnedermann, II. 257 sq. Cf. also the subtle argument of Tertull. ag. Marcion, IV., 4.

If you believe the word you have it; if you do not believe you have nothing."—LUTHER. Because of such faith Christ not only forgave the sins of the paralytic, but also said, Ver. 11, **Arise ... house.** The reality of forgiveness is now proved to the objectors, for they witness in the immediate effect of bodily health through Christ's word, the evidence of the same immediate blessing to the soul. This is likewise accomplished without appealing to the Father. Ver. 12. And the paralytic **arose ... all.** The man arose at once, and bore his pallet, "the sign of his sickness being now the sign of his cure."—TRENCH. It was quickly rolled up,[1] and a way being made the man passed out. **All ... fashion.** The people were not only amazed, but filled with fear (Matt. 9 : 8) in the presence of such divine might. But fear soon gave way to joy, in which they expressed their exultant praise to God for this marvellous power never before seen by men. "The inestimable blessing of forgiveness is well worth all praise and gratitude" (Ps. 103 : 3). —STARKE.

13-17. And he went forth again by the sea side; and all the multitude resorted unto him, and he taught them. And as he passed by, he saw Levi the *son* of Alphæus sitting at the place of toll, and he saith unto him, Follow me. And he arose and followed him. And it came to pass, that he was sitting at meat in his house, and many publicans and sinners sat down with Jesus and his disciples: for there were many, and they followed him. And the scribes of the Pharisees, when they saw that he was eating with the sinners and publicans, said unto his disciples, He eateth and drinketh with publicans and sinners. And when Jesus heard it, he saith unto them, They that are whole have no need of a physician, but they that are sick: I came not to call the righteous, but sinners.

Ver. 13. Jesus **went ... again** from Capernaum to **the sea side,** soon after the healing of the paralytic

---

[1] Possibly it was a simple, light mattress, such as is still the only bed of many in the East.

to avoid the people (1 : 45). But **all ... them**, availing himself of their avidity to see miracles by preaching the word. Ver. 14. After this passing on he **saw ... Alphæus**, whose name became Matthew[1] (Matt. 9 : 9), the "manly"[2] (cf. Matt. 16 : 18). His father was not the Alphæus whose son was James the Less (3 : 18), otherwise Matthew and James would be named together in the apostolic catalogues, like Andrew and Peter, James and John. Of the work of Matthew beside his writing of the gospel,[3] we possess but uncertain information.[4] His character, as indicated by his name and position in the list of the apostles beside Thomas[5] according to the principle of contrast, seems to have been one of decision and firmness.[6] By Christ Levi was called, while **sitting ...**

---

[1] Orig. ag. Cels. I. 62, says Levi (Lebes) "was not of the number of the apostles," although in his introduction to Romans he identifies Levi with Matthew. Heracleon, the Valentinian (Clem. Alex. Strom. IV. 9), distinguishes Matthew and Levi, as also Grotius, Ewald, Michaelis, Sieffert, Nicholson; but the synoptists permit no distinction. (Cf. Mt. 9 : 9 sq.; Lk. 5 : 27 sq.).

[2] The best derivation of "Matthew" is from the rare singular Mettm (manly) (Grimm), although Noeldeke argues for Āmătăy (faithful man). Holtzmann, p. 84.

[3] That Matthew did not write the gospel, which bears his name either in the Hebrew original (Papias, Euseb. III. 39; Iren. ag. Her. III. 1 : 1; Eus. III. 24), or in the Greek redaction is one of the unproved assumptions of modern critics.

[4] Such various countries as Ethiopia (Socr. H. E. 1 : 19), Persia, Macedonia, are claimed as the fields of Matthew's labor; but neither Origen (Eus. III. 1), nor Eusebius himself (III. 24), know of any such tradition, which even the credulous Jerome did not accept (De vir. ill. 3).

[5] Some suppose that Thomas was a twin-brother of Matthew, because of the epithet "Didymus" (twin).

[6] The ascetic character ascribed to Matthew by Clem. Alex. (Instr. II. 1), who says: "the apostle Matthew partook of seeds, nuts and vegetables without meat" is unwarranted. The story of Matthew's martyrdom unknown in early tradition (Clem. Alex. Strom. IV. 9) is due to the inventions of the apocryphal "Acts and Martyrdom of Matthew." Much of the

toll. Sitting is the general attitude in Syria when at work. The carpenters work sitting on the ground. The merchants in their bazaars sit cross-legged upon their booths. Thus Levi was probably sitting upon his toll-booth, ready to collect customs upon the various goods that were conveyed along the great road between Tyre and Jerusalem. He was not a general tax-collector (gabbai), but an inferior official (mohkes).[1] Upon Christ's call, Ver. 15, **he . . . him,** "breaking himself at once away from all worldly things, by his complete obedience he bare witness, that He who called him had chosen a good time." —CHRYSOSTOM. And "although the people, who have to do with money, are hard to convert (Acts 8 : 20 ; Matt. 19 : 21), Jesus exhibits His power, and can accomplish it with a single word."—QUESNEL, STARKE. After his conversion Levi made a great feast of rejoicing **in his**[2] **house** (Luke 5 : 29), and with Jesus there were reclining at the table **many . . . sinners.** The joining of **publicans** with **sinners,** people of ill-repute (Luke 7 : 39) known and shunned as great sinners, shows in what estimation they were held. They were called a criminal race, traitors of their country, because they served the hated Gentile rulers. Their testimony was to be rejected, their alms were not to be received. Even though they forsook their calling, the defilement of it was believed to adhere to them always. With such men Jesus and **his disciples,** who are here first mentioned as accompanying him, sat down.

wrong tradition attached to Matthew has arisen from a confusion of Matthew and Matthias.

[1] These officials were most hated. "The very word Mohkes seems in its root-meaning associated with the idea of oppression and injustice. He was literally, as really, an oppressor." (Edersheim).

[2] This is the correct interpretation of Mark, although Jesus has just before been designated "he." The word "Jesus" following corroborates this view.

And there *were many* of the disciples (Weiss, Nösgen), and their number was no doubt increased from among the publicans. That Jesus met with them offended, Ver. 16, **the . . . Pharisees**,[1] the learned scholars of the Pharisaic party. The **Pharisees** arose out of the earlier " Chasidim " (pious ones) at the time of Jonathan, successor of Judas Maccabbee, between 160 and 143 B. C. (Jos. Ant. XIII. 5 : 9) and were the Puritan tendency within Judaism. Two vows were taken by them, to be very exact in rendering all religious dues and to observe most strictly the Levitical laws of purity. They were conservative in belief, but slaves of tradition. These Pharisees after the previous defeat of the scribes (ver. 6), not venturing to approach Jesus Himself, come to the disciples, as they leave the feast, and say :[2] **He**[3] **. . . sinners!** This is an utterance of great contempt for one, who claiming to be a teacher (rabbi) would thus lower himself and eat with the dregs of the population, and by his association with them sanction their wickedness. Enmity puts on the guise of godliness (Matt. 7 : 15 ; 2 Tim. 3 : 5). But, Ver. 17, when **Jesus heard** the accusation aimed at Him, He said : **They . . . sick.** Christ answers with a " truism on the physical side of things."—MORISON. The very nature of His work as physician of the soul, and the actual condition of men (sick in sin), necessitate His going to them. He goes not to become as they are, but to make them as He is. But He can help only those who know their condition. " Would that you were aware of your

---

[1] These words, supported by ℵ, B, D, L, 33, are to be preferred to "the scribes and Pharisees."

[2] ὅτι is simply equal to a quotation mark, and has no interrogative import (against Tischendorf), Winer, p. 457.

[3] "And drinketh," found in A, C, L, Δ, E, is wanting in ℵ, B, D, but it was probably omitted on account of Matt. 9 : 11 (Meyer).

sickness, that ye might seek a physician."—AUGUSTINE. As physician, Christ says: **I . . . sinners.** The righteous are those that are whole, the sinners the sick. Although it is not stated whether there are such righteous men or not (Weiss, Holtzmann), yet the fact of Christ's mission to all makes it impossible. Christ knows no men, whom he could call righteous.[1] Therefore the Pharisees are righteous in their own imagination. For them as they are Christ has not come, because they will not see that they are sinners. They "grudged sick men a physician, and being more sick than those, they slew the physician." —AUGUSTINE. "Christ calls to repentance, and not to a profligate life; **would** you enjoy him, prepare yourself for repentance" (Joel 2 : 2, 13).—OSIANDER, STARKE.

18-22. And John's disciples and the Pharisees were fasting: and they come and say unto him, Why do John's disciples and the disciples of the Pharisees fast, but thy disciples fast not? And Jesus said unto them, Can the sons of the bride-chamber fast, while the bridegroom is with them? as long as they have the bridegroom with them, they cannot fast. But the days will come, when the bridegroom shall be taken away from them, and then will they fast in that day. No man seweth a piece of undressed cloth on an old garment: else that which should fill it up taketh from it, the new from the old, and a worse rent is made. And no man putteth new wine into old wine-skins: else the wine will burst the skins, and the wine perisheth, and the skins: but they put new wine into fresh wine-skins.

Ver. 18. **John's disciples**, who had not attached themselves to Jesus (John 1 : 35 sq.), possibly from a wrong spirit of jealousy for John the Baptist, still adhered to John's asceticism (Matt. 11 : 18). They and the Pharisees, who used them in their innocence to carry out hostile plans against Jesus, **were fasting.** The meal at Levi's house had taken place on one of the traditional weekly fast-days (Monday or Thursday), which were sincerely kept by John's disciples, but which the Pharisees used to

---

[1] δικαίους without the article confirms this interpretation.

obtain, as they supposed, the merit of forgiveness of sins, not because they mourned for sin (Is. 58 : 5), but because they underwent an external minute ritual of self-mortification. **And they**, representatives of John's disciples and of the Pharisees **came** to question Jesus why His disciples transgressed the accepted religious observance. Ver. 19. **Jesus . . . them ?** *The sons of the bride-chamber* is a common[1] oriental expression for the attendants of the bridegroom, who accompany him on the way to the bride and the bridal chamber,[2] and in their gladness shout for joy. Such groomsmen are the disciples of Christ, who is the **bridegroom**, because in Him are fulfilled all the prophecies of God's intimate union with His people (Ps. 45 ; Song of Songs ; Isai. 54 : 1, 5, 6 ; Hos. 2 : 19, 20). This union (2 Cor. 11 : 2 ; Eph. 5 : 24 sq. ; Rev. 19 : 7 sq.) must be a joyous one without fasting.[3] Wherever Christ is, there is joy. " Jesus, who before has called Himself physician, now calls Himself bridegroom, by these names He reveals certain unspeakable mysteries."—CHRYSOSTOM. As long as He is with the deciples **they . . . fast**, for the " truth of outward fasting is inward mourning."—STIER. Ver. 20. **But . . . them**, or rather shall have been torn away ($\alpha\pi\alpha\rho\theta\tilde{\eta}$)[4] by violent death. So early, while triumphant, does Christ announce His death by more than human foresight. **When He is taken, then . . . day.** Beginning with the one sad day they shall fast, for " the day of

---

[1] Trumbull, p. 242.

[2] For an excellent account of weddings and wedding-customs in the East, see Trumbull, p. 7 sq.

[3] The Messianic expectation of the Jews confirms this. Maimonides says : " All fasting will cease in the days of the Messiah, and there shall be no other days than good days, and days of joy, as is written, Zech. 8 : 19."

[4] Morison sees in this word a "fine mystical meaning," and believes it covertly to refer " to what began with the crucifixion and ended with the ascension."

the bridegroom's removal is one, the days when he is removed and absent are many."—BENGEL. They shall **fast,** for their souls are bowed down, and they bear the fast-day divinely ordered, but not self-imposed. This fasting will be more than mere external abstention from food, a deep inward mourning. For outward fasting there is no law in the new dispensation; and although the apostles and early Christians fasted (Acts 13 : 2 ; 14 : 23 ; 1. Cor. 7: 5, etc.), it was their voluntary deed and no yoke laid upon them (Col. 2 : 16 ; Gal. 4 : 9 ; 1 Tim. 4 : 1 sq.)[1] To illustrate the incongruity of the old with the new, Christ says : Ver. 21. **No man . . . made.** A patch of new, unfulled cloth will by shrinking, when exposed to moisture, tear the old garment; therefore no one will patch the old with the new. The Lord employs this parable not to justify the disciples of John in their adherence to fasting (Beyschlag, Weiss); but to prepare for the force of the following illustration (ver. 22) He argues first from the point of view of the old, and to those that adhere to it He brings home the impossibility of adopting a single feature of the new without endangering what is still useful of the old. " The completeness ($\pi\lambda\eta\rho\omega\mu\alpha$) takes away from the garment, the new completeness from the old garment."—LIGHTFOOT. An entire change is necessary. The new cannot be a patch upon the old. As the old cannot adopt a new custom, the new cannot use old forms. Ver. 22. **No man . . . wine-skins.** The *wine-skins* are the skins of goats, which, after being steeped in

---

[1] This is the position of the Lutheran church, which sees in fasting "a good external discipline" for subduing the body (1 Cor. 9 : 27), but makes it neither legal nor meritorious. The assertion that "fasting avails for the extinguishing and prevention of guilt" (Aquinas) is utterly rejected. Cf. Augs. Conf. Art. XXVI.; XXVIII.; Apol. VIII. Smald. Art. III.; Small Catech. IV.; Form of Conc. X.

tannin with the hairs on and exposed to the sun, are carefully sewed up and pitched. In them all liquids are carried in the East. Old skins could not bear the distension caused by the fermenting of the new wine. It required new strong skins. Thus the new gospel of Christ, fittingly symbolized in its joyousness by wine (Ps. 104 : 15 ; Isai. 55 : 1, 2), demands new forms in which religious life expresses itself, because of the power of life (ferment) and the spirit of freedom (wine) inherent in the gospel. "The new spirit was to be embodied in wholly renovated forms; the new freedom was to be untrammelled by obsolete and long meaningless limitations; the spiritual doctrine was to be sundered forever from the elaborate externalism of cancelled ordinances."—FARRAR. Every syncretism is therefore dangerous and a failure.[1]

23-28. And it came to pass, that he was going on the sabbath day through the cornfields; and his disciples began, as they went, to pluck the ears of corn. And the Pharisees said unto him, Behold, why do they on the sabbath day that which is not lawful? And he said unto them, Did ye never read what David did, when he had need, and was an hungered, he, and they that were with him? How he entered into the house of God when Abiathar was high priest, and did eat the shewbread, which it is not lawful to eat save for the priests, and gave also to them that were with him? And he said unto them, The sabbath was made for man, and not man for the sabbath: so that the Son of man is lord even of the sabbath.

Ver. 23. **On the sabbath-day,** near the passover (Luke 6 : 1), Jesus with His disciples *was going* along a road, which passed between ripe *cornfields.* **His**[2] . . . **corn.**[3]

---

[1] Lange suggests the historical examples of Ebionitism and the Interims of the period of the Reformation.

[2] This second part of the sentence is not dependent upon "it came to pass" (ἐγένετο). Winer, p. 578.

[3] The interpretation referred to in the margin of the Rev. Vers., that the disciples made either a new way or followed an old path overgrown by corn (Holtzmann) through or alongside of the field by pulling out the grain (Winer, Meyer, Lange, Schenkel), rests upon the exact classical meaning of ὁδὸν ποιεῖν,

As they passed they took some ears of corn from the fields on either side. Ver. 24. When **the Pharisees**, who probably stood incidentally at the place where Jesus passed with His disciples, saw this, they said to Christ: **Behold**, look what a terrible transgression is taking place; **why** do thy disciples **on the . . . lawful**. It was not unlawful to pluck and eat a few grains (Deut. 23 : 25), but being done on the sabbath it involved according to rabbinic law the double sin of plucking, which was regarded equivalent to reaping, and rubbing in the hands,[1] which was considered to be a species of threshing.[2] This transgression of rabbinic statutes was held to be a greater sin than breaking God's own law. Ver. 25. But Jesus said **Did . . . did**. David, whose need broke the law (Lev. 24 : 9), is referred to not only because he is the great king and the Messiah his son, but because his very case is vindicated by Jewish tradition, on the principle that "danger to life superseded the sabbath-law."[3] In such danger David committed what otherwise was also unlawful; he, Ver. 26, **entered . . . God**, the holy place, and this he did under the sanction of the high-priest. It happened **when**[4]

but overlooks its hellenistic usage, which is rather to be expected in the N. T. According to this ὁδὸν ποιεῖν is to make a journey (Judg. 17 : 8, Sept.). The use of στάχυας (ears) and not blades likewise militates against the marginal translation. Cf. Klostermann, Keil, Weiss, Nösgen.

[1] This was done after plucking, and is still to be seen. Thomson (II. 510) relates: "I have often seen my muleteers, as we passed along the wheat-fields, pluck off ears, rub them in their hands, and eat the grains unroasted, just as the apostles are said to have done."

[2] Even treading upon the grass was thought to be threshing. But the casuistry of the scribes often relaxed this severity. Thus, if a person laid a sheaf of wheat upon a spoon it could be removed, because the spoon might be removed. See Edersheim, II. 56 sq.; Lightfoot, Hor. Hebr. 206; Farrar, 266, 304. 418 sq., 669.

[3] Edersheim, II. 57.

[4] The rendering "in the days," as far as the article "the" is concerned, is

... **high-priest.** The mention of Abiathar instead of Ahimelech (1 Sam. 21 : 1 sq.) is no error of memory (De Wette, Bleek, Meyer, Weiss, Holtzmann, Keil), nor due to the acceptance from tradition of the mistake in 2 Sam. 8 : 17 ; 1 Chron. 18 : 16; 1 Chron. 24 : 6 (Nösgen), in which passages Ahimelech (Ahiah, 1 Sam. 14 : 3), is called the son of Abiathar. That Abiathar was present with his father (1 Sam. 22 : 20) and a party of the act (Wordsworth), would not entitle him to be called high-priest; nor can he legally have been high-priest conjointly with his father (Luther, Edersheim). The solution traditional since Victor of Antioch, which ascribes to father and son both names according to the custom of double names (Judg. 6 : 32 ; 2 Sam. 11 : 21), is still the easiest.[1] In Abiathar's presence, David did eat the **shewbread**, the "loaves of the Face" (Lev. 24 : 5 sq.), which were kept before God, one for each tribe, to remind them that "what pertains to the life of Israel comes from the presence of Jehovah."—BÄHR.[2] These it was **not . . . priests**, who every sabbath partook of the loaves of the past week in the sanctuary. (Lev. 24 : 9). But in his great emergency not only David ate of them, but **gave . . . them**, who were in dire need. Therefore Christ's disciples in their hunger might take the ears of corn. "Love and necessity transcend every commandment."—QUESNEL, STARKE. Ver. 27. **The** . . .

---

supported by A, C, Δ, 33, but outweighed by א, B, L, E, G, H, etc.; and it is not as precise a translation of ἐπὶ as "when."

[1] "Even this explanation is not without its difficulties ; but in all such apparent discrepancies, whether they can be solved or not, it is well to remember Luther's words: "It is absurd to imitate the great boldness, which, when difficulty occurs, immediately cries out, a manifest error has been committed, and dares to amend the books of others without shame." (Op. Lat. 3 : 71.)

[2] Öhler's O. T. Theol. (Am. ed.), p. 256.

man; it was ordained of God for the bodily rest (Exod. 23 : 12) and spiritual advancement (Exod. 20 : 8) of man, and as an anticipation of eternal rest (Hebr. 4 : 9). But **man ... sabbath,**[1] to be the slave of a day. The day has its purpose not in itself; it is only a means for man's highest good. "Since God has done everything for man's sake, man should do everything for God's sake, and have His glory as his aim."—STARKE. If even sinful man is no slave of the sabbath, much less *the Son of man*, for He not only "as God,"—NOVATIAN, but as *the* man, who has glorified human weakness (ver. 10), is, Ver. 28, **lord ... sabbath.** This sacred institution of God is also under the lordship of the Son of man, who does not desire to abrogate it with its blessing (Matt. 5 : 17), but to redeem it from Jewish legalism, and renew it in its universal features, that it may be held in the freedom of the Spirit, who working in the church has prepared the "Lord's day." Thus Christ "prepared anew the sabbath, without a literal commandment as in the Old Testament."[2]—STIER. "Believers are with Christ and through Christ lords of the sabbath, that they may use it for their own and their neighbor's necessities."—QUESNEL, STARKE.

---

[1] For a similar but less expressive rabbinical saying, see Holtzmann, p. 91; Edersheim, II., p. 58.

[2] This word of Christ is the germ of the apostolic words (Rom. 14 : 4, 5, 17; Col. 2 : 16, 17). With this N. T. doctrine the Lutheran Church agrees, holding to the liberty as well as to the necessity of the Lord's day (Augs. Conf. XXVIII. Large Cat. I. 3). Cf. also Luther's Sermon for 17th Sunday after Trinity, 1544 (Erl. Ed. 20, II. 220). Th. Zahn, Geschichte des Sonntags, 1878.

CHAPTER III.

1–6. And he entered again into the synagogue; and there was a man there which had his hand withered. And they watched him, whether he would heal him on the sabbath day; that they might accuse him. And he saith unto the man that had his hand withered, Stand forth. And he saith unto them, Is it lawful on the sabbath day to do good or to do harm? to save a life, or to kill? But they held their peace. And when he had looked round about on them with anger, being grieved at the hardening of their heart, he saith unto the man, Stretch forth thy hand. And he stretched it forth: and his hand was restored. And the Pharisees went out, and straightway with the Herodians took counsel against him, how they might destroy him.

Ver. 1. Jesus *entered again* on the following sabbath (Luke 6 : 6) *into the*[1] *synagogue* in the town, where the last conflict had taken place (2 : 23); and **there**[2] . . . **withered** (1 Kings 13 : 4). By some disease the right hand of the man had become atrophied.[3] "A withered member of the body is a picture of death."—CANSTEIN, STARKE. Ver. 2. **And they**, certain of the Pharisees (ver. 6), who had probably placed the man in a prominent position to ensnare Jesus, **watched**[4] Him, with close,

---

[1] א, B, omit the article, but it is found in A, C, D, L, etc.

[2] The description of this man by the gospel of the Hebrews as a stone-mason, and his petition: "I am a stone-mason seeking for food by my hands. I pray thee, Jesus, to restore to me my health, that I may not basely beg food," far from being original (Handmann, p. 86), shows its apocryphal character in its prolix form, and in its Ebionitic tinge by strongly motivating Christ's breaking of the sabbath law (Resch. p. 379).

[3] The exact form of Mark 'εξηραμμένην proves, as Bengel suggested, that it was no congenital defect.

[4] Better "kept watching" (παρετήρουν) accdg. to א, D, C, L., etc.

eager observation and hostile purpose (Luke 6 : 7; 14 : 1; Acts 9 : 24; Gal. 4 : 10), **whether . . . him.** His act on this day, at this place, and before so many witnesses [1] would offer a clear case to the spies, who "are very urgent about ceremonies, but do not care about true discipline and honorableness."—OSIANDER, STARKE. Ver. 3. But Jesus **saith . . . forth.** Having him arise and come into the midst of the Pharisees, that they might see him, Christ does His work openly, and exhibits the mighty contrast between the wise directness of the Light, and the invidious scheming of the children of darkness (1 John 2 : 11). "The Light itself has come, it removes the shadows."—AUGUSTINE. This Light says, Ver. 4: **Is . . . kill?** Christ appeals to the conscience of the Pharisees by going back to the fundamental law of the sabbath, whose force their traditional misconstructions could not totally obscure, for they admitted that "the danger of life abolishes the sabbath." [2] Although no immediate danger threatened the man with the withered hand, yet to heal was doing good. But not doing good, when it was required, was doing evil (James 4 : 17); and not saving life now, when it could be done, was this not finally to kill, and a transgression of God's law? (Exod. 20 : 13). The Pharisees must choose between God's law of love and their narrow limitations. It is really a question not about the observance of a day, but about saving or killing, i. e. about good or evil. **But . . . peace.** The Pharisees do not wish to sanction Christ's deed, therefore they do not assent to what their conscience and God's law tells them to be right; and they fear to deny because they would be convicted of

---

[1] Cf. Luther, Ann. on Matt., Walch. St. Louis, Ed. VII., p. 149.

[2] On the minute discussions about healing on the sabbath and the evasions, see Edersheim, II., p. 60.

merciless unholiness. In their silence they give evidence of their hypocrisy. Thus the wicked, who have set themselves against Christ, utterly fail (Ps. 7 : 15 sq.) Ver. 5. **And . . . them,** still waiting for an answer, but only seeing their determined silence, He was filled **with anger,** which was the holy, divine indignation of love, because they shut themselves up against the truth. But with His anger, Christ is **grieved,** and combines deepest compassion with holiest indignation. "Divine zeal must be united with love of compassion and sympathy, that we are zealous against sin, but compassionate against the sinner. The foe of sins is the friend of men" (1 Cor. 5 : 3-5).—MAJUS, STARKE. Christ, the best friend of His enemies, is sad, because of **the hardening . . . hearts,** by which they are rendering themselves obdurate to the impressions of truth (2 Cor. 4 : 4), and subject to God's judgment.[1] Therefore Christ turns from them to the man and says: **Stretch . . . hand.** Without touching the man, and therefore not even transgressing the sabbath-law, Christ heals by the direct power of His word (John 4 : 49 sq.). And the man in faith stretched forth his hand, which **was restored.** In this restoration Jesus acted "after the example, the gentleness, the mercy and the prediction of the Creator."—TERTULLIAN. "How quickly can Christ change a great misfortune with a word or sign" (Matt. 8 : 26).—STARKE. But neither word nor sign convinces the Pharisees, for, Ver. 6, they **went out** with deeper hatred of Christ, whose compassion for them had been in vain, and **straightway** repaired to the

---

[1] Cf. the hardening of Pharaoh, in which the relation of divine judgment to individual choice is shown. Ten passages refer to Pharaoh's decision, and ten to God's action ; and, except in Ex. 4 : 21 ; 7 : 3, where the announcement of divine judgment is made to Moses, hardening is always first traced to the will of Pharaoh.

Herodians, who were probably a political party favorable to Herodian rule, not because it saved from absolute dependence on Rome, but rather because it represented the mighty, victorious Roman rule.[1] With these unpatriotic, time-serving men of the world, the Pharisees **took counsel** against Christ, **how . . . him.** The pious Puritans invoke the aid of the civil power to do away with the hated Jesus. "If the enemies of God can no longer answer from the Bible, they fight with the iron bible; then Herod and Pilate become friends."—CANSTEIN, STARKE.

7-12. And Jesus with his disciples withdrew to the sea: and a great multitude from Galilee followed: and from Judæa, and from Jerusalem, and from Idumæa, and beyond Jordan, and about Tyre and Sidon, a great multitude, hearing what great things he did, came unto him. And he spake to his disciples, that a little boat should wait on him because of the crowd, lest they should throng him: for he had healed many; insomuch that as many as had plagues pressed upon him that they might touch him. And the unclean spirits, whensoever they beheld him, fell down before him, and cried, saying, Thou art the Son of God. And he charged them much that they should not make him known.

Ver. 7. From the unknown inland town of Galilee, **Jesus . . . withdrew** to find rest at the sea, but a great multitude followed not only *from* Galilee, but also **from Judæa,** and, Ver. 8, **Jerusalem;** and from **Idumæa,** the province called by Josephus Amaleketis (Ant. II. 1, 2) including the south of Palestine and extending southeast; the country of the Edomites, which had been conquered and subjected to Jewish law by John Hyrcanus; the original home of the Herodian family. People also came from **beyond Jordan,** out of Peræa, which Josephus describes (Wars III. 3, 3) as bounded on the west by the Jordan, on the east by Philadelphia, on the north by Pella, and on the south by the castle of Machærus. As the crowds

[1] Cf. Nebe, III. 419.

were approaching from the west and the extreme southeast, a contingent arrived from about **Tyre** and **Sidon**, the northwestern confines, all desirous to see the great things of which they heard. "The report of Christ does not save, but it must direct and lead to Christ" (Rom. 10 : 13-17).—STARKE. So many came to Christ, that He desired, Ver. 9, **that . . . him**, which His disciples were to hold in constant readiness; for, Ver. 10, **as . . . plagues**, i. e. diseases (5 : 29, 34; Luke 7 : 21), in which the consciousness was present "that they were strokes (μάστιγας) or blows inflicted by God,"—TRENCH, **pressed upon Him**, actually fell upon Him (ἐπιπίπτειν, Luke 15 : 20; Acts 10 : 44, etc.) in their eagerness to *touch Him*, believing this to be necessary. "Divine Love makes no distinction, but does good even to those who come impetuously and at an unsuitable time" (Luke 11 : 8).— QUESNEL, STARKE. Before this strong Love the demons, Ver. 11, **fell down** (5 : 33) in terror and acknowledged the **Son of God** (1 : 1), who, Ver. 12, **charged** them sharply **not . . . known** (1 : 25).

13-19. *And he goeth up into the mountain, and calleth unto him whom he himself would; and they went unto him. And he appointed twelve, that they might be with him, and that he might send them forth to preach, and to have authority to cast out devils: and Simon he surnamed Peter; and James the son of Zebedee, and John the brother of James; and them he surnamed Boanerges, which is, Sons of thunder: and Andrew, and Philip, and Bartholomew, and Matthew, and Thomas, and James the son of Alphæus, and Thaddæus, and Simon the Canánæan, and Judas Iscariot, which also betrayed him.*

Ver. 13. From the seashore Christ goeth up into **the mountain**, probably a well-known height near Capernaum,[1] and **calleth . . . would**, according to His author-

---

[1] The traditional site is Tell Hattin, the Mount of Beatitudes. See Robinson, Bibl. Researches in Palestine, III., p. 240.

ity as God's apostle (Hebr. 3 : 1), choosing His sub-apostles (John 17 : 18). This "He willed, from the will of the Father."—BENGEL. His calling was mediate and yet immediate, but altogether without human interference. Ver. 14. **And . . . twelve,**[1] to correspond to the twelve tribes of Israel, to whom they were at first sent (Matt. 10 : 6). They were to **be with him**, as His constant and special attendants, without the exclusion however of the other disciples (Luke 10 : 1), that they might learn of Him. "Who would be thorough in the work of the Lord, must first be with Christ to be instructed, sanctified and prepared by Him."—Tübingen Bible, STARKE. After the twelve had been well-schooled Christ would **send . . . devils**. The work of Christ, whose important and first part was preaching (1 : 39), was to be thus spread and perpetuated. This clearly defines the activity of the apostles, whom the two words "send" and "authority" describe as authorized messengers.[2] Their names were, Ver. 16, **Simon** (1 : 16) **surnamed Peter** (Matt. 16 : 18); Ver. 17, and **James** (1 : 19) and **John** (1 : 19), **them . . . Boanerges**,[3] **. . . thunder**,

---

[1] The addition "whom he named apostles (א, B, C, Δ) does not occur in A. D. L., etc., and is probably inserted from Luke 6 : 13. The word "apostle" used frequently by Luke (6 : 13; 9 : 10; 11 : 49; 17 : 5; 22 : 14; 24 : 10), is found only in Mark 6 : 30 and Matt. 10 : 2.

[2] For proof see Cremer, p. 863; Nösgen I., p. 310; Holtzmann, p. 97. The supposition, that the apostolate was derived from the Hebrew Shāluāch, is historically untenable, and would include the notion, that the apostles were congregational delegates, while their "mission is a descending delegation in relation to Christ's mission by the Father." (Nösgen.)

[3] This is the Aramaic form of B'nē-R'gōsh. While it may be impossible that Sheva has become oa (Weiss) in the Aramaic (Nösgen, Com. 209), yet the indication that B'ne was sometimes pronounced Bone (Edersheim I. 514) can form the link between the Hebrew and the Greek transliteration of the Aramaic. R'gōsh need not be amended R'gōz (Kautzsch), for it receives in Aramaic the meaning, noise, rushing, raging. The substitution of Jerome

not because of their mighty preaching (Greg., Naz., Luther), nor because of the occurrence, Luke 9 : 54, but rather for their fiery, zealous temperament, of which that event and Mark 9 : 38 is an evidence. The truth of this name, which is no reproach, is likewise seen in 1 John 2 : 22; 3 : 8; 2 John 7 sq., and in the seven letters of the Apocalypse.[1] Ver. 18. Christ further appoints **Andrew** (1 : 16), and **Philip** of Bethsaida, who seems to have been of a realistic turn of mind (John 14:8), but cautious and timid (John 12 : 21);[2] and **Bartholomew**, Nathaniel of Cana,[3] the former name being his patronymic (son of Tolmai), who was of quick judgment, but guileless in spirit, and earnestly prayerful (John 1 : 47 sq.);[4] and **Matthew** (2 : 14), and **Thomas**, inclined to despondency (John 11 : 16) and doubt (John 14 : 5; 20 : 25);[5] and **James**, the son of

followed by Luther (Bnehargem) is a translation into Hebrew. Cf. Delitzsch's Hebrew N. T.; Morison, p. 76; Thayer, p. 103.

[1] The tradition of John's leaving the bath-house, in which Cerinthus was (Iren. ag. Her. III. 3, 4; Eus. H. E. III. 28; IV. 14), and his search for the young convert, who had become a robber (Clem. Alex. Quis Dives salv. XLII.) confirm the fitness of Christ's appellation, which should correct the prevalent impression, that the meditative apostle of love had no active zealousness.

[2] The tradition of Philip's labor and death together with his daughters at Hierapolis (Eus. III. 31; V. 24), probably rests upon a confusion with Philip, the Evangelist, an error which Polycrates and Clement Alex. had introduced. (McGifford's Eus. p. 162.)

[3] Augustine (On John, I. 17), whom Chrysostom and Gregory the Great followed, claims that Nathaniel was no apostle.

[4] Bartholomew preached in India (Eus. V. 10; Jerome, De vir. ill. 36), a tradition, which seems more probable than Lipsius' suggestion of Sindia. (McGifford, Eus. p. 225.) The later traditions of Bartholomew's martyrdom are unreliable.

[5] The identification of Thomas with Judas (Thaddæus) (Eus. I. 13; Acts of Thomas, where he is called Judas Thomas) probably arose from a mistaken tradition of Edessa; and cannot be used to correct the list of the gospels. The jugglery of Resch (Agr. 424), by which James, the son of Alphæus, and Judas are made twins, whose common name was Thomas

Alphæus, who is not to be identified with James, the
Little, the son of Clopas and Mary, and made a cousin
of Christ[1] and **Thaddæus** (the son of the bosom), also
called Lebbæus (full-hearted) (Matt. 10 : 3), and Jude of
James (Luke 6 : 16; Acts 1 : 13); and **Simon the Cananæan**,[2] or zealot, from an unknown Canaan (not Cana;
Luther), who belonged originally to the anti-Roman,
fanatical, revolutionary party of the zealots, founded by
Judas, the Gaulonite (Acts 5 : 37) (Jos., Wars, IV., 3 sq.).
Ver. 19. And finally **Judas Iscariot** (the man of the city
of Kerioth (Josh. 15 : 25), the only apostle from Judæa,
the Jew *par excellence*, who **betrayed Christ**. With this
description Judas is always characterized to his own
eternal shame and the constant warning of all disciples.
In his betrayal he is a type of the Jewish people. For
the motives of his act see 14 : 10. In this catalogue of
the apostles Mark agrees with all (Matt. 10 : 2 sq.; Luke
6 : 14; Acts 1 : 13) in placing Peter first, Philip fifth;
and Bartholomew and Judas Iscariot in the sixth and
last place respectively (except Acts 1 : 13). The principle of prominence rather than relationship seems to
underlie the classification of Mark.

(Didymus, twin), completely violates the gospel record. Parthia was said to
be the field of the labor of Thomas, as well as of Thaddæus and Simon, the
Cananæan.

[1] This is the opinion of most scholars at present, and seems to accord
best with the parallelism of John 19 : 25, while avoiding the possible but not
probable identity of Clopas with Alphaeus. (Cf. John 19 : 25; Mark 15 : 40,
41; Luke 24 : 10.) (Schaff, Ch. Hist. I., p. 272; McGifford, Eus., p. 99;
Geikie, N. T. Hours, p. 269.)

[2] καναναιος (B, D, C, L), as against the amended καναυιτης of א, which
seems to bring out more clearly Kānānō (zealot) (Weiss, Das Markusev. u.
seine syn. Parall., p. 121), although καναναιος is also equivalent to zealot
accdg. to some. (Stellhorn, Wörterbuch zum griech. N. T., p. 73; Thayer,
p. 324; Robinson's Harm. (rev. ed.) p. 217.)

20-30. And he cometh into a house. And the multitude cometh together again, so that they could not so much as eat bread. And when his friends heard it, they went out to lay hold on him: for they said, He is beside himself. And the scribes which came down from Jerusalem said, He hath Beelzebub, and, By the prince of the devils casteth he out the devils. And he called them unto him, and said unto them in parables, How can Satan cast out Satan? And if a kingdom be divided against itself, that kingdom cannot stand. And if a house be divided against itself, that house will not be able to stand. And if Satan hath risen up against himself, and is divided, he cannot stand, but hath an end. But no one can enter into the house of the strong *man*, and spoil his goods, except he first bind the strong *man*; and then he will spoil his house. Verily I say unto you, All their sins shall be forgiven unto the sons of men, and their blasphemies wherewith soever they shall blaspheme: but whosoever shall blaspheme against the Holy Spirit hath never forgiveness, but is guilty of an eternal sin: because they said, He hath an unclean spirit.

Ver. 20. Christ after working in Galilee (1:39) **cometh . . . house,** i. e. "Jesus comes home" (nach Hause, Luther) to Capernaum to Simon's house (2:1): Ver. 20, **and the multitude** (ver. 7, 8) gathers, so *that they*, Jesus and His apostles, **could . . . bread,** because the thronging mass pressed in; much less find leisure to speak of the kingdom. "Preachers should be slaves of souls; and even forget the necessity of life if the harvest is great and a good opportunity is offered" (1 Cor. 9:19 sq.).—QUESNEL, STARKE. Ver. 21. **When his friends,** lit. those from beside Him, not about Him (apostles, Luther); His relatives (1 Mac. 12:52), not His mother and brethren (Meyer, Weiss, Holtzmann),[1] **heard** of His untiring work, **they went out** from their home, possibly Nazareth, **to . . . him,** by force seize Him and restrain Him from wearing Himself out; **for they said** (ἔλεγον), i. e. were of the opinion: **He . . . himself.** These relatives could account in no other way for the extraordinary power and work of Jesus, than by holding Him to be carried beyond Himself by ungoverned ecstasy

[1] Cf. Keil, p. 44.

($\dot{\epsilon}\xi\dot{\epsilon}\sigma\tau\eta$ cf. 2 : 12 ; 2 Cor. 5 : 13), that bordered on insanity. They measure Him by "the cold moderation, which the world loves so well."—BRAUNE, LANGE. But divine work must be done zealously, and can suffer no human relationship to interfere. Ver. 22, While Christ's kinsmen are with Him, **the scribes** arrive, **which . . . Jerusalem**, deputed no doubt by the Sanhedrim to find a cause against the popular teacher not of their schools. They *said*, after the healing of a blind and dumb demoniac (Matt. 12 : 22 sq.), **He hath Beelzebub,**[1] which denotes Satan, not as fly-lord (2 Kings 1 : 2), nor by a witticism of the Jews as filth-lord, but as "lord of the house" (Z'vūl), which is his kingdom (Matt. 12 : 28).—MEYER, VOLKMAR.[2] He, according to the scribes, dwells in Christ, and **by**, lit. in i. e. in the power of **the . . . devils.** By this terrible charge the scribes seek to destroy the effect of Christ's healing of the demoniacs, the reality of which they cannot deny. Three times was this same charge repeated (Matt. 9 : 34; John 8 : 48; 10 : 20). "It is terrible that the world ascribes what is from God to Satan, and thus makes God Satan."—STARKE. Ver. 23. Upon this accusation Christ **called . . . parables,** which in short gnomic form (Matt. 7 : 17; Luke 4 : 23; 6 : 39) were first used by Christ in defence (Mark 2 : 19; Luke 4 : 23), and afterward as detailed descriptions were his constant mode of instructing the people (4 : 34) to reveal and conceal (4 : 11) the truth of the Kingdom in pictures of actual life and real processes of nature. In the use of the parable, which Christ first developed,[3] and which is "His peculiar form of in-

---

[1] The best reading is Beelzebul (Bāăl-Z'vūl).

[2] Klostermann, (p. 77) like Lange interprets "lord of the possessed," deriving Beelzebub from the Syriac Baal Ssebero. Holtzmann (p. 134) appealing to Eph. 2 : 2 regards the air as the dominion of Beelzebub, and follows Jahn. For an excellent résumé see Nebe, II. 159.

[3] Nösgen, I., p. 256.

struction, in which no one else has equalled him,"—
HOLTZMANN. He witnesses to the inward analogy of nature and religion; and adopts a form, which is infinitely above the fictitious fable, as well as the poetic allegory and metaphor, in its reality, truthfulness, instructive and convincing power.[1] The truth, that Christ would now illustrate is, **How . . . Satan?** This would be the greatest inconsistency, for "wolf does not eat wolf, and Satan does not cast out Satan" (Tüb. Bible. STARKE). And, Ver. 24, **If . . . stand.** With this truism and not by a word of Scripture Jesus shows the unreasonableness of the attack of the scribes even according to common sense. "It is necessary that we should mark closely, that Christ says that Satan has a kingdom, a very harmonious kingdom, which keeps well together."—LUTHER. The unity of this kingdom, whose king (Job 18:14; Jude: 8, 9; Rev. 2:10; 9:11) is the god of this world (2 Cor. 4:4), consists in the constant opposition to God's kingdom.[2] In a kingdom there are houses (Judg. 18:14), Ver. 25, **and . . . stand.** This second parable is no meaningless parallel, but referring to the parts of the kingdom (von Hofmann), depicts more minutely the disunion as within the individual groups of families, and suggests the organization of Satan's kingdom into principalities and powers (Rom. 8:38; Eph. 6:12). These powers Christ conquers by casting out their subjects (demons). For if Satan is in Christ, then, Ver. 26, **Satan . . . himself** in all his power to subdue himself in his ministering servants; and **is divided** in his kingdom as king against sub-

---

[1] On the parables, see Trench, Introd. to Parables, p. 7 sq.; Nebe, I. 447 sq.; Nösgen, I. 343 sq.; Holtzmann, p. 88; and in a popular form, Taylor, "The Parables of our Saviour," p. 1 sq.

[2] Are not moral statistics, when properly balanced, also an evidence of a kingdom of evil, with its laws of development?

[3] ἐμερίσθη belongs to the previous clause.

jects, and also in his own house, family, as lord against vassals. If this be so, **he . . . end**; he cannot retain his power over men, and his influence is at an end. But such self-defeat is inconsistent with Satan, and manifestly absurd. From this *reductio ad absurdum* Christ passes to the explanation of his power over demons, saying, Ver. 27, more than this, **no . . . house**. The entrance into Satan's stronghold has been effected by healing the possessed; but these healings could not have been accomplished had the breaking in of Christ not been succeeded by *binding* Satan (Rev. 20 : 2) who had bound men (Luke 13 : 16). Christ came to *spoil* (διαρπάσαι), i.e. thoroughly plunder Satan's stolen goods, human souls; *and then finally he would spoil his house* also by completely overthrowing it. Satan, the *strong* one, in constant, decided, consistent, wicked purpose, and in higher power as a spirit, is to be feared. (1 Pet. 5 : 8; Rev. 12 : 3). But Christ, the mightier (1 : 7) has bound him; and therefore He alone can evict Satan from the heart. But even He is powerless, where men absolutely harden themselves. This the scribes are beginning to do, and to them Jesus therefore says: Ver. 28, **Verily . . . you,** which is an expression of great earnestness, frequently used in the gospels, and always reduplicated in John, to introduce an important word. (Mark 8 : 12; 9 : 1; 10 : 15, etc.) **All . . . men.** Unto the *sons of men*, as weak beings (cf. 2 : 10), inclined to sin (Gen. 8 : 21) forgiveness is promised as an absolute certainty, under "the presupposition of repentance,"—HOLTZMANN, for *all sins*. These words are emphatically prefixed to show that the whole range of sins are included, even the **blasphemies . . . blaspheme**[1]

---

[1] τύπος (א, B, D, E, G) is a favorite word of (Mark 2 : 19; 3 : 8; 5 : 19; 9 : 13, etc.).

(2 : 17). The great sins of open blasphemy against God and Christ, as Son of man (Matt. 12 : 32) will find pardon, for God's grace is far above the sins of men. (Rom. 5 : 20.) But one sin is not forgiven. Ver. 29. **Whosoever ... sin.** This unpardonable sin, whose binding guilt, ἔνοχός (1 Cor. 11 : 27; Jas. 2 : 10) is *eternal* (αἰωνίου),[1] endless in all future, began on the part of the scribes in imputing to Christ an unclean spirit (ver. 30), by which utterance they wilfully and consciously rejected the prevenient illumination of the Spirit, after whose coming their sin would be completed (John 16 : 8 sq.). The sin unto death (1 John 5 : 16), which presupposes the clear inner conviction by the Spirit, is a special, conscious denial and attack of the truth with a distinct blasphemy, and cannot be identified with the wilful relapse of the regenerated, which is an unpardonable condition, that may lead to the act of *the* sin against the Holy Spirit (Heb. 6 : 4; 10 : 26). The unpardonableness is due to the absolute rejection of God's saving presence.[2] If a person

---

[1] Cf Cremer, p. 99.
[2] This sin attributed by the Didache (XII. 7) to false prophets, by Irenæus to the Montanists (III. 11), by Tertullian to Hymenæus and Alexander (De pud. XIII.), by Cyril to Manes (Cat. Lect. VII. 25), is supposed by Origen (De Prin. I. 3, 2), to attest the "exceeding majesty of the Holy Spirit," while Theognostus of Alex. (Frag. Hyp. III. in Athan. De Decret. Nic. Syn. XXV.), correctly ascribes the unpardonableness to "having tasted the heavenly gift" (Heb. 6 : 4), Augustine (Civ. Dei XXI. 24; Ep. CLXXXV. 11, 48; Serm. XXI.), followed by Chrysostom (Hom. on Matt. XLI. 5), holds it to be persistent impenitence (impoenitentia finalis), a view adopted by v. Oettingen, Meyer, Ritschl, Keil, Schaff. Luther (Sünde wid. d. Heil. G. 1529; Erl. Ed. 23 : 70 sq.; 64 : 192), believes it to be "battling against truth recognized" (impugnatio veritatis agnitæ), and despising of the gospel and its work; but he also enumerates five other sins, spiritual pride, stiff-neckedness, despair, envy of the brethren because of grace, final impenitence (Walch, St. Louis Ed. VII. 174). The Luth. Dogmaticians (Schmid, Engl. Transl. p. 276), analyze this sin into the elements, (1) denial of truth, (2) hostile attack, (3) voluntary and atrocious blasphemy; but Heb.

has committed this sin, "he is no longer in Satan's power and deception, but has himself become a voluntary and conscious Satan."—STARKE.

31–35. *And there come his mother and his brethren; and, standing without, they sent unto him, calling him. And a multitude was sitting about him; and they say unto him, Behold, thy mother and thy brethren without seek for thee. And he answereth them, and saith, Who is my mother and my brethren? And looking round on them which sat round about him, he saith, Behold, my mother and my brethren! For whosoever shall do the will of God, the same is my brother, and sister, and mother.*

Ver. 31. And shortly, **his mother**, Mary, desiring as in Cana (John 2 : 3) to show her motherly prerogative, and forgetful of Christ's word in the temple (Luke 2 : 49), arrives with **his brethren** (6 : 3), the sons born to her after her first-born (Luke 2 : 7).[1] These **standing without** the house where Jesus was, **sent . . . him**: his mother, from true anxiety, fearing the enmity of the leaders of Israel, and troubled by the apparent over-exer-

---

6 : 4, is not sufficiently distinguished from Matt. 12 : 31. Harless (Ethics, Engl. Trans. 6. Ed. p. 290), conceives of it as, "obduracy against a preparatory knowledge." Cf. Stier, Reden, Jesu, II. 38 sq.; Cremer, p. 52; Nösgen, Com. p. 75; Martensen's Ethics (3 Ed. German) II. p. 147 sq.; Frank, Chrl. Sittlichkeit, I., p. 277 sq.; Herm. Schmidt in Herz. Realencyl. XV. 41; the monograph of L. Lemme, 1883.

[1] This view, exegetically the best, because adopting the most obvious meaning of ἀδελφός, agreeing with the use of ἀνεψιος, accounting for Matt. 1 : 18, 25 ("*before* they came together;" "knew her not *till* she had a son,") and confirmed by Mary's constant appearance with her sons (Matt. 12 : 46; 13 : 55; John 2 : 12), has been stigmatized with the heretical name "Helvidian," although held by Tertullian. It is the prevalent opinion of modern exegetes, as Stier, Wieseler, Meyer, Weiss, Nebe, Farrar, Schaff, etc. That the brothers were sons of Joseph by a former marriage, is advocated by Clem. Alex., Orig., Eus., Greg. of Nys., Epiph., Cyril, Lightfoot, Plumptre, Morison, etc. The opinion of Jerome and Augustine, that the brothers were cousins, children of Alphæus (Clopas) and Mary, the sister of the mother of Jesus, finds favor with Luther, Calvin, Mill, Ohlshausen, Schnekenburger, Nösgen. Cf. Nebe, I., p. 245 sq.; Schaff, Ch. Hist. I., p. 272 sq.

tion of Jesus; but His brethren from envious unbelief (John 7:5). Ver. 32. And before **the multitude ... him** (2:14) in the courtyard, *they*, who repeated the call, **say**.[1] **... thee.** To some this was a welcome interruption, and others may have "been laying a snare for Jesus, to see whether He would prefer flesh and blood to His spiritual task."—JEROME. Ver. 34, 35. Therefore **looking ... him**, on the good hearers and especially His apostles, **he ... mother.** Those, who fulfilled the *will of God* in believing on Christ (John 6:40) and living holily (Matt. 7:21; 5:48), Christ claims as His true relatives. This made Mary His mother indeed, for "what the Lord magnified in her was, that she did the will of the Father, not that flesh gave birth to flesh."—AUGUSTINE. By real, spiritual affinity every one in whom Christ is born can be a Mary (Stier); and all who are united with Him by heavenly love He is not ashamed to call brethren and sisters (Heb. 2:12). But no one can be His father, but *the Father*, from whom all this spiritual relationship proceeds. And "he who doeth the will of God to the end makes an eternal covenant with God as his father (Deut. 7:9 sq.) with Jesus Christ as his brother, with the angels and all the blessed as his sisters (Matt. 23:8), with the heavenly Jerusalem as his mother (Gal. 4:26)."—QUESNEL, STARKE.

---

[1] The words "thy sisters" have been wrongly inserted by some MSS. They do not occur in ℵ, B, C, G, K, etc.

CHAPTER IV.

1-9. And again he began to teach by the seaside. And there is gathered unto him a very great multitude, so that he entered into a boat, and sat in the sea; and all the multitude were by the sea on the land. And he taught them many things in parables, and said unto them in his teaching, Hearken; Behold, the sower went forth to sow: and it came to pass, as he sowed, some *seed* fell by the wayside, and the birds came and devoured it. And other fell on the rocky *ground*, where it had not much earth; and straightway it sprang up, because it had no deepness of earth: and when the sun was risen, it was scorched; and because it had no root, it withered away. And other fell among the thorns, and the thorns grew up, and choked it, yielded no fruit. And other fell into the good ground, and yielded fruit, growing up and increasing; and brought forth, thirtyfold, and sixtyfold, and a hundredfold. And he said, Who hath ears to hear, let him hear.

Ver. 1. **Again**, after being with the twelve (3:13) and the disciples in a house (3:20), Christ **began ... sea-side**, where **there.**[1] .. **multitude** (3:7), so that He made a *boat* (3:9) His pulpit, and **sat ... sea** (Ps. 77:19; 95:5), discoursing to the masses upon the shore. "Jesus makes the little ship His pulpit; if we do not diligently hear and obey He departs with His little ship and pulpit (Acts 13:46)."—CRAMER, STARKE. Ver. 2. From it He **taught**[2] ... **parables** (3:23), the first of which He began with the word, Ver. 3, **Hearken**, and concluded with the injunction to hear (ver. 9). "Preachers should often encourage their hearers to a diligent and proper hearing of the Word" (2 Tim. 4:2).—MAJUS, STARKE. That the attention to the Word be still more aroused Christ adds: **Be-**

---

[1] The present συνάγεται is the best reading. (א, B, C, L, Δ, etc.)
[2] The expression πολλά occurs 15 times in Mark.

hold, possibly pointing to some sower at work on the distant hills, whom He characterizes as *the sower* from his special vocation. **The ... forth** from his village [1] to the open ground, not to do the preparatory work of clearing the field, but to *sow*.[2] Ver. 4. **As ... way-side** (παρὰ τὴν ὁδόν) which was not the road bounding the field (Weiss, Edersheim), but rather a trodden pathway running through the midst of it,"—STANLEY, which, although it had been ploughed up, was again made by frequent passers seeking a short-cut. And the **birds**, who after the winter were eager to pick up the first seeds of spring, *came*, making the time of sowing their harvest, and *devoured* quickly what was not trodden down. Ver. 5. **Other ... ground,** not upon earth mingled with stones, but upon a thin coating of mould, which covered a large surface of rock.[3] This seed **sprang up,** and was apparently not wasted like the seed that fell upon the wayside; but its early appearance and sudden growth was deceptive. It lasted only for a time, because *it had no deepness of earth:* Ver. 6, **and ... away.** Its roots having soon exhausted the moisture of the scant layer of ground, could not furnish the additional refreshment from the depth to counteract the increasing heat of the sun, which was necessary to ripen the grain. Therefore the sun, the source of life, became to this seed the source of death.[4] Ver. 7. **And ... thorns,** which before the seed-time had probably been burnt, but not dug up with their roots. *And the*

---

[1] Thomson, I., p. 115.

[2] "According to the Jewish authorities there was a twofold sowing, as the seed was either cast by the hand, or by means of cattle. In the latter case, a sack with holes was filled with corn, and laid on the back of the animal, so that as it moved onwards, the seed was thickly scattered." Edersheim, I. p. 586.

[3] This was the view of Origen (De Prin. III. 1 : 14.)

[4] For interesting illustrations from the classics see Nebe II. 41.

thorns grew **up** by their native power more quickly and strongly than the good seed, from which they took the nourishment of the soil and the light of the sun; and they **choked** *it, and it yielded no* **fruit.** The unfruitfulness was in this case due neither to hard nor shallow but to impure ground. Ver. 8. **Others**[1] *fell into the good* **ground.** These seeds fell into ground that was free from the imperfections of the three other kinds of soil. It was neither hardened, shallow nor impure, but soft, deep, pure and rich. These seeds **yielded** *fruit, growing up and* **increasing.**[2] The corn-stalks (Matt. 13: 26; James 5: 18), designated broadly as *fruit*, which in the classics " means generally that which grows in the field,"—MEYER, are called *growing*, in contrast with the seed by the wayside, and *increasing* to distinguish them from the seeds upon the rocky and thorny ground. The seeds in the good ground **brought** *forth thirtyfold, and sixtyfold, and a* **hundredfold.** The yield, in no case small, increased in proportion to the fertility of the soil up to a hundredfold, which is not unheard of in the East (Gen. 26: 12),[3] especially on the fertile shores of Lake Gennesaret.[4] Ver. 9. And finally Christ said, **Who ... hear.** This injunction is used to call attention to what has preceded[5] (ver. 23; Luke 8: 8; 14: 35). It emphazises the responsibility of hearing and the danger of neglecting to hear with the "ear of a diviner kind,"—ORIGEN, the inward perception

---

[1] ἄλλα (א, B, C, L, 33, etc.) is to be preferred to ἄλλο which, conforms to the previous verses.

[2] These participles (ἀναβαίνοντα καὶ αὐξανόμενα) (A, C,) rather than (א, B,) ought to be connected with "fruit" and not "others," (ag. Klostermann, Weiss, Morison, Riddle). Cf. Keil, p. 48.

[3] Thomson, I., p. 117.

[4] Robison, III., p. 285.

[5] This usage invalidates Trumbull's illustration of the royal crier (p. 237), because **he** calls out before his message.

of the heart. But too often "Him, who made the ear, man will not hear."—GOSSNER, LANGE.

10–20. And when he was alone, they that were about him with the twelve asked of him the parables. And he said unto them, Unto you is given the mystery of the kingdom of God: but unto them that are without, all things are done in parables; that seeing they may see, and not perceive; and hearing they may hear, and not understand; lest haply they should turn again, and it should be forgiven them. And he saith unto them, Know ye not this parable? and how shall ye know all the parables? The sower soweth the word. And these are they by the wayside, where the word is sown; and when they have heard, straightway cometh Satan, and taketh away the word which hath been sown in them. And these in like manner are they that are sown upon the rocky *places*, who, when they have heard the word, straightway receive it with joy; and they have no root in themselves, but endure for a while; then, when tribulation or persecution ariseth because of the word, straightway they stumble. And others are they that are sown among the thorns; these are they that have heard the word, and the cares of the world, and the deceitfulness of riches, and the lust of other things entering in, choke the word, and it becometh unfruitful. And those are they that were sown upon the good ground; such as hear the word, and accept it, and bear fruit, thirtyfold, and sixtyfold, and a hundredfold.

Ver. 10. **And . . . alone,** the crowds having gone for a time, **they . . . him,** the wider circle of disciples **with . . . parables.**[7] Their inquiry was turned not only to the reason of parabolic teaching (Matt. 13 : 10), but also to the unfolding of the parables, with a special desire for the proper understanding of the parable of the sower, so important for them, who are later to do the work of sowers. And Christ said, Ver. 11, **Unto . . . God.** The disciples that ask receive the gift of the truth, "as a grace bestowed from above,"—CHRYSOSTOM; because they have open ears, and then approach Him, in whom are all the treasures of wisdom. "The spirit gives it to you, that you not only see and hear but know with your heart and believe."—

[7] The plural is supported by ℵ, B, C, L, Δ, etc.

LUTHER. Their faith shall possess *the mystery of the kingdom of God*, which is the knowledge of the saving truth not revealed before, named thus not because of its obscurity, but for its secrecy [1] (Rom. 16 : 25 ; 1 Cor. 4 : 1 ; Eph. 1 : 9). Its content is comprehensively designated " the kingdom of God " (1 : 15) ; [2] and it is kept from the people. **Unto** *them that are without, all things are done in* **parables.** They receive the instruction that conceals (3 : 23), not because of an unjust discrimination of Jesus, who reserved the truth for an exclusive circle, acting among Jews as a Jew would against Gentiles, or instituting an esoteric doctrine after the manner of heathen religions. But they have excluded themselves by hearing and not inquiring.[3] From this careless obduracy it arose, Ver. 12, **that . . . them.** This judgment of Christ himself (ag. **Jülicher,** Holtzmann) is the confirmation of Is. 6 : 9, which is quoted with the change of the precedence of " seeing " before " hearing " owing the appearance of the Word. It is shown to be the purpose of God to completely fulfil what was then threatened and to harden finally His people, so that in their *seeing they may* physically *see* but not spiritually *perceive*, and outwardly *hear* but not inwardly *understand*. This takes place in the teaching of the parables, which are a savor of death to the non-receptive.[4] Mark sees in actual occurrence

---

[1] Cremer, p. 626. J. H. Foster, The word " Mystery " in the N. T., in The Thinker, Vol. VIII. 5, p. 408.

[2] The genitive is objective and not possessive (Schnedermann).

[3] Schnedermann distinguishing between " Verkündigung " (announcement) and " Lehre " (doctrine) of the kingdom, and seeing in the former the preparatory heralding of the coming kingdom, whose truths the latter was to unfold, holds that the non-acceptance of the invitatory announcement was the cause of the self-exclusion that followed.

[4] Jülicher (Die Gleichnisreden Jesu, 1888, p. 146), although ascribing these severe words only to the disciples, must still admit to the detriment

what Matthew portrays as a result. "Because the ears, which they have, they neither have nor use; therefore as Christ knows, He speaks, that their inability is judged as unwillingness."—STIER.[1] Because of this unwillingness, in which they are afraid that they might be converted and receive forgiveness, God withholds every opportunity, "leaving them in the darkness, which they have chosen for themselves."—IRENÆUS. But the disciples have chosen the light, therefore Christ saith unto them, Ver. 13, **Know . . . parables?**"[2] Recurring to their question (ver. 10) Christ answers with a question, not merely to deepen the consciousness of their ignorance, but to arouse them to inquire about *all the parables*, which they would hear. But *this parable* of the sower must be unfolded first because of its fundamental character, which would enable them to trace the lessons of other parables more readily. "The longer man retains and studies any one divine truth, the more manifest it becomes, and itself brings all others to light."—GERLACH, LANGE. Therefore Christ begins a detailed explanation and says, Ver. 14, **The . . . word.** *The sower*, as in the parable (ver. 3), is introduced first not to lead most briefly to the "word," but to place prominently before the disciples as their example the divine sower in His activity. He as the eternal Word is the author of "*the word*" (2:2), which is to be implanted in the hearts (James 1:21), that by it

---

of his position according to the clear import of this passage: "It is true that the parable has exercised a judgment of hardening. Who did not comprehend the doctrine of the kingdom, of the love of God, of the earnestness of sin even in this form, upon him it (the parable) had executed the judgment of hardening, because he was executing it upon himself."

[1] Reden Jesu II. 80 sq.; Nebe. II., p. 49 sq.; Schnedermann, note p. 150.
[2] Meyer and Weiss are correct in combining these questions. Thus the article "the" is better accounted for, and the apparent censure of the disciples, which is evidently impossible (ver. 11), is avoided.

as the power of God (Rom. 1 : 16) men may be begotten again (1 Pet. 1 : 23). This it accomplishes because it is the Creator's word (Col. 1 : 16), far superior in its life-giving power to the word of the Old Testament, which is but the preparatory snow and rain (Is. 55 : 10.). "The law brings no fruit, as little as human inventions."—LUTHER. Ver. 15. **And these**, pointing forward, **are . . . sown.** This concise statement, picturesquely characterizing the people according to the condition of their hearts, at once brings into prominence the main lesson to be learnt, that the character of the hearers is the condition of the fruitfulness of the word. The wayside people are not such, "that persecute the Word and do not hear, but such that hear and are pupils, that are called Christians and wish to live among the Christian community,"—LUTHER; but **when . . . them.**[1] Upon the heart the word falls, but not into it, because of its obduracy, caused by the constant passing of worldly and sinful thoughts. The word not immediately received is *straightway* taken by *Satan*, who sends out his *birds*,[2] the little and apparently innocent thoughts and cares. "Men are troubled if anything is stolen from them; but the most unhappy theft for their souls is when Satan takes away the word of God."—STARKE. Ver. 16. And in **like manner** of interpretative application it is with those, **that . . . places,** (ver. 5), i. e. in such with whom the seed has fallen upon rocky ground. The inexact form is due to the prominence given the persons, who are identified with the seed sown,[3] (see Matt. 13 : 38). **When . . .**

---

[1] ἐν (א, C, L, Δ) is to be preferred to εἰς (B) as more consistent with the whole description.

[2] Birds are appropriate symbols of Satan (Eph. 2 : 2).

[3] Farrar (p. 229) well says: " It is a part of the divine boldness of Christ's teaching, and the manner in which it transcends in its splendid paradox all

word Satan does not take it, but **straightway** . . . **joy**, not with the deep inward gladness which will sacrifice everything for the gospel (Matt. 13 : 44), but with the quick flash of an aroused superficial feeling, that lacks earnest purpose. But this reception is of no avail, for, Ver. 17, **they . . . themselves.** The word is not deeply rooted in *themselves*, in their conscience (1 Tim. 3 : 9), but in the shallow covering of changeable sensations. Therefore they **endure** only for a while, as long as the hot summer-time of **tribulation**, the pressure of the enemies of the word, or **persecution**, the more violent pursuit into which the pressure has developed, does not arise. But in this heat, as necessary for the growth of the Christian (Acts 14 : 22 ; Rom. 5 : 3 ; 1 Pet. 4 ; 12) as the sun for the seed, *they* **stumble**, and become "scandalized." Persecution entraps them, and "anon they fall."—TYNDALE. "Not the beginning should be inquired after in a Christian, but the end ; to begin is the part of many, to arrive at the end belongs to few."—JEROME. Ver. 18. And **others . . . thorns** (ver. 7) come not to ripeness, although not stumbling in tribulation, because gradually there enter in the, Ver. 19, **cares** *of the* **world**, which divide the hearts of men (Matt. 6 : 25) in their struggles for wealth, in the possession of which they learn the **deceitfulness** *of* **riches ;** for they do not free from care and bestow what they promised, but are a snare (1 Tim. 6 : 9, 10); often leading to the **lusts** *of other* **things** (1 John 2 : 16), the desire after all kinds of worldly engagements, pleasures, and possessions, which are as deceitful as riches and brings cares upon cares. "As the thorns are unfruitful, so these things ; as thorns tear those that handle them, so do these passsions."—CHRYSOSTOM. They *choke*

ordinary modes of explanation, that in His explanation of the parable, the seed when once sown is *identified with* him who receives it."

(ver. 7), the word and **it** *becometh* **unfruitful.** Thus they, who seemed most hopeful and whose sanctification had begun, do not reach maturity, for the roots of the old nature were not removed. Ver. 20. But those **sown . . . ground,** prepared by prevenient grace that was not rejected, *accept* the word firmly and keep it patiently, and **bear . . . hundredfold.** The difference in fruitfulness is due to the variety of God's gifts and to the degree of man's faithful use of them. But all, that are good ground, bring fruit to eternal life, therefore " those who bear more fruit should not despise others and become proud."— MAJUS, STARKE.

21–25. And he said unto them, Is the lamp brought to be put under the bushel, or under the bed, *and* not to be put on the stand? For there is nothing hid, save that it should be manifested; neither was *anything* made secret, but that it should come to light. If any man hath ears to hear, let him hear. And he said unto them, Take heed what ye hear: with what measure ye mete it shall be measured unto you: and more shall be given unto you. For he that hath, to him shall be given: and he that hath not, from him shall be taken away even that which he hath.

Ver. 21. Jesus said to His disciples: **Is .**[1] **. . bushel,** the Roman measure about equivalent to our peck and probably used for the Hebrew household measure, seah; or **under** *the* **bed,** the couch used to recline upon at meals and also employed as a bed; and *not to be put on the stand?*[2] This illustration, which Christ also employed to

[1] "The lamps of Palestine are, to-day, no doubt, just what they were two thousand years ago; small clay toys, holding two or three spoonsful of oil; a hole at one end for the rag which serves for a wick, and a teacup-like handle at the other, to let it be carried about." (Geikie, N. T. Hours, p. 356.)

[2] Canon Cook is scarcely correct in holding this to be a description of the common houses with their single room, containing the flour-bin, lamp-holder and bed. A house of the better class, where Roman customs had obtained, is pictured, as shown by the μόδιον, κλίνην, and the stand not found in ordinary houses.

suggest to His disciples their duty as light-bearers (Matt. 5 : 15), and to enjoin the brightness of the spiritual eye (Luke 11 : 33), is here meant to enforce the duty of communicating the truth of the Light (John 1 : 9; 9 : 5). Ver. 22. **For ... light.** From the preceding parable of the light the general principle is deduced, that truth is to be revealed in due time, and its secrecy to be made public. Therefore it is Christ's purpose to hide truth only temporarily in the parables, and to conceal even from His disciples some doctrines, that they cannot at once understand (John 13 : 7; 16 : 12); but finally the light is to appear (1 Cor. 2 : 7 sq.). "Do not suppose that what I now commit to you in secret, I would have concealed forever; the light is kindled by me in you, that by your ministry it may disperse the darkness of the whole world." —ERASMUS. And again, Ver. 24: **Take** *heed* (1 Cor. 16 : 10; Eph. 5 : 15) *what ye* **hear** (Luke 8 : 18). This warning adds to the previous injunction to hear well (ver. 23) the obligation of the matter heard: for, **with ... you** (Matt. 7 : 2; Luke 6 : 38). According to your standard of attention and earnestness in the reception and use of the word, you shall receive a new measure of truth: **and ... you.** God's gift from His abundant grace will be beyond the exact measure of retribution. "We may do what we will, there is no comparison between what we do for God, and what God does for us."— QUESNEL, STARKE. Ver. 25. It is His law that: **He ... hath** (Matt. 13 : 12; 25 : 29; Luke 8 : 18; 19 : 26). This truth, constantly exemplified in every sphere of life, is applied to show, that faithful hearing and learning of the word, will increase the capacity to receive and digest, and therefore enable God to give more; while neglect will weaken the receptive power, stop growth and bring about decrease. "A faithful diligent soul has a great treasure, its wealth enters into eternity; but an idle soul becomes daily poorer, until finally all is lost."—QUESNEL, STARKE.

26-29. *And he said, So is the kingdom of God, as if a man should cast seed upon the earth; and should sleep and rise night and day, and the seed should spring up and grow, he knoweth not how. The earth beareth fruit of herself; first the blade, then the ear, then the full corn in the ear. But when the fruit is ripe, straightway he putteth forth the sickle, because the harvest is come.*

Ver. 26. And, not long after the first parable, *Christ said:* **So . . . earth.**[1] The man is not the "son of man," but a disciple,[2] sowing the word of the kingdom. Ver. 27. It is as if this man **should . . . day.** The sleep is no carnal security, but the necessary rest succeeded by rising and the work of the day. The *night* proceeds not because it first followed the sowing of the seed,—MORISON, but because human activity can do nothing, while "the fruitful bosom of night,"—STIER, is maturing the seed. Although the *day* intimates work and care, yet all labor is in vain except God give the increase (Ps. 127 : 2; 1 Cor. 3 : 6, 7). But while man cannot make the seed grow, it **springs . . . how.** By its inward power of life the seed sprouts and grows into a stalk with its spike, but man does not understand this mysterious process. "All sprouting, growing, budding in the kingdom of

---

[1] The assumption of Ewald, Strauss, reasserted by Weiss, that this parable is that of the tares changed by Mark, rests with Weiss upon the idea, that Mark cannot have a "Logion" not found in the older source (Com. p. 77; Markusev. u. seine syn. Parall., p. 158). Volkmar, Holtzman find in the parable of the tares an allegory of this parable. Both positions are untenable, if the plain distinct features of the two parables are not obscured by an unfair criticism of pre-supposition. Cf. Keil, p. 57.

[2] This appears inconsistent with v. 29, but Christ cannot be the man as v. 29 proves. The human activity of sowing is to be characterized, and this individual, subordinate feature dare not be pressed, for "omne simile claudicat." Thus Stier, Morison, as against Ohlshausen, Trench, Keil.

nature and grace is open only before God, because it is His work."—STIER. This should exclude all anxious probing into the growth of the spiritual life, and lead to trust in God's powers, for "though the seed of the Word be concealed and choked for a time, Christ enjoins pious teachers to be of good courage, and not to allow their alacrity to be slackened through distrust."—CALVIN. For,[1] Ver. 28, **The . . . herself.** The growth is spontaneous (αὐτομάτη, Acts 12 : 10)[2] owing to the fertility given the earth by God (Gen. 1 : 11), and excludes human influence. Thus in the tilled land of human hearts, the power of divine grace causes the fruitfulness; therefore although we are "God's fellow-workers" (1 Cor. 3 : 9) in the ministry, we must remain humble. But still the growth not caused by man can be seen by him. There appears **first** *the blade, then the ear, then the full corn in the* **ear.** In the first stage there is no difference between the *blade* and ordinary grass.[3] The "young babes in Christ" are "carnal" (1 Cor. 3 : 1). But the "little children" become "young men" when the ear appears, and as it fills up with precious wheat they are "fathers" (1 John 2 : 12, 13). Growth is progressive, and therefore perfection is not to be expected at the beginning, but God will give it increasingly (1 Thess. 5 : 23). Finally, Ver. 29, **when . . . ripe,**[4] when all the work that does not require man's help is accomplished by the soil and weather, and the fruit "delivers itself up," then **straight-**

---

[1] The Rev. version has properly omitted "for" according to A, B, C, etc.

[2] Winer, p. 464; Thayer, p. 85.

[3] χόρτον generally means grass (6 : 39; John 6 : 10; 1 Pet. 1 : 24; etc.).

[4] This free rendering of παραδοῖ is better than "alloweth" (Lange, Meyer), which rests only upon classical usage, because it comes nearer to the reflexive sense of παραδοῖ. Keil, p. 55; Morison, p. 108; Winer, p. 251.

way ... come. The ripened corn requires immediate attention, and the sickle is sent not at the end of time, (Meyer, Trench, Keil), for a human harvest is meant (Matt. 9 : 37, 38 ; John 4 : 35, 36), which is the ingathering of souls after faithful preaching. "Where God's word is rightly sown and accepted, it never remains without fruits of faith and godliness."—STARKE. The central truth of this parable, the gradual, independent development of God's kingdom, was to serve as a corrective against the Jewish expectation of a sudden revelation of a great kingdom of worldly power.

30–32. And he said, How shall we liken the kingdom of God? or in what parable shall we set it forth? It is like a grain of mustard seed, which, when it is sown upon the earth, though it be less than all the seeds that are upon the earth, yet when it is sown, groweth up, and becometh greater than all the herbs, and putteth out great branches; so that the birds of the heaven can lodge under the shadow thereof.

Ver. 30. And Christ said: **How ... forth?** The Saviour in condescension takes His disciples with Him in His search for an appropriate similitude, and by His double question arouses their eagerness and attention. After the picture of the slow development of the kingdom, that of its great extent follows to furnish a glimpse of its gloriousness. Ver. 31. **It ... seed,** the ordinary black mustard, which when sown is *less than all the seeds.* The mustard seed was often employed by the Jews for its minuteness as a picture of the very small.[1] This seed of the kingdom, Ver. 32, *when it is sown* and dies in its king (John 12 : 24), **groweth ... branches.** It is a fact

---

[1] Geikie, p. 359. Edersheim (I. p., 593) says it was used to "indicate the smallest amount, such as the least drop of blood, the least defilement, or the smallest remnant of sunglow in the sky." This minuteness alone and not the medicinal virtue (Trench) of the mustard seed is the basis of comparison.

still observed by travellers in the East, that among all garden-shrubs the mustard becomes the greatest.[1] **Even ... thereof** (Ezek. 17 : 23). Birds seek it not for food, but for shadow. The kingdom of God beginning in little Palestine with Jesus despised by the despised Jews, has grown to be a goodly tree, sheltering the nations. "By the little grain Christ bestows salvation on all humanity abundantly."—CLEM. ALEX. "The church has grown, the nations have believed, the princes of the earth have been conquered in the name of Christ."—AUGUSTINE.

33-34. And with many such parables spake he the word unto them, as they were able to hear it : and without a parable spake he not unto them : but privately to his own disciples he expounded all things.

Ver. 33. **With ... parables** (cf. Matt. 13) Christ **spake the word** to the people **as ... it.** In no other form were they able to receive it (ver. 12), nor could they bear more than a certain amount even of parabolic teaching. Ver. 34. **Without ... them.** This was henceforth His exclusive mode of instructing the people limited not only to that time.—WEISS. But **privately** *to his own* [2] **disciples**, to the closer circle of the twelve, *all things* were expounded, that they might tell it to others (ver. 21 sq.). "The mystery of the Lord is among those that fear Him" (Ps. 25 : 4).—STARKE.

35-41. And on that day, when even was come, he saith unto them, Let us go over unto the other side. And leaving the multitude, they take him with them, even as he was, in the boat. And other boats were with him. And there ariseth a great storm of wind, and the waves beat into the boat, insomuch that the boat was now filling. And he himself was in the stern, asleep on the cushion : and they awake him, and say unto him, Master, carest thou not that we perish? And he awoke, and rebuked the wind, and said unto the sea, Peace, be still. And the wind ceased, and there was

---

[1] Tristram, Nat. Hist. of the Bible, p. 472; Thomson II., p. 100.
[2] The word "own" is supported by ℵ, B, C, L, Δ.

a great calm. And he said unto them, Why are ye fearful? have ye not yet faith? And they feared exceedingly, and said one to another, Who then is this that even the wind and the sea obey him?

Ver. 35. **And . . . day**, on which he had taught the parables, *when even was come*, the time so well remembered by Peter, Jesus *saith unto them*, to the twelve:[1] **Let . . . side**, to the retirement offered by the eastern shore in its solitude.[2] Ver. 36. **Leaving . . . boat**. The disciples, who arrange everything, depart with Jesus, without His leaving the boat to dismiss the people[3] (Keil, Weiss). **And . . . him**. A small fleet of boats either of such, who to hear Jesus had entered boats and now accompanied Him some distance, returning as they saw the storm coming (Weiss), or of people from Peræa (3:8), who were on their homeward journey (suggestion of Keil). Ver. 37. **And . . . storm**, with terrible gusts of wind that drove everything before them, and with black clouds, that poured down floods of rain.[4] Such sudden storms are not infrequent in the sea of Galilee.[5] But so violent was this storm, that **the waves . . . filling**. The small fishing vessel was soon filled with water from the waves that broke over it, and the efforts of the disciples in bailing out the water seemed in vain. Ver. 38. Meantime Jesus

---

[1] Even though Matthew may have been called later (Luthardt, Synopt. Tabelle, but not Robinson), yet the larger number of the twelve were with Jesus. Grotius, Bleek, Meyer hold that more disciples are meant, while Nebe and Weiss include the twelve only.

[2] Stanley, Sinai and Palestine, p. 379.

[3] Lange, Trench, Meyer, Morison, interpret, without making further preparations for the journey.

[4] This is the meaning of λαῖλαψ (Trench. Syn, p. 277; Thayer, p. 368).

[5] Thomson, II., p. 33, says that these storms are due to the cold winds of the Lebanon, which having swept down the ranges of the Hermon, rush through the ravine of the Peræan hills that converge to the head of the lake, and act like immense funnels, and then strike the heated tropical air of the sea of Galilee, situated about six hundred feet below the sea-level.

himself . . . cushion.[1] In the extreme end of the stern there was a small low bench, where the steersman could sit if desired. Upon this bench the captain could rest when on quarter-deck, which was the place generally reserved for passengers of distinction. Here Jesus was *asleep* in the peaceful slumber of His unclouded conscience,[2] notwithstanding the storm and commotion of the disciples. Tired by the work of the day Christ paid tribute to the necessity of human nature. "He who never sleeps, sleeps; He who governs heaven and earth, sleeps."—ORIGEN. But the disciples *awake him*, for their faith deserts them as the danger increases; and not assured of the impossibility of the boat sinking that bore such a Saviour, they say: "**Master . . . perish?**" This exclamation full of unbelief as it is, still shows some faith, because the disciples approach Jesus. "Belief and unbelief are in wild commotion."—NEBE. Ver. 39. And Jesus *awoke* and "abandons His sleep for their sake, and concerns Himself about their trouble, as though it were His, and of free love helps them, without their merit." —LUTHER. He **rebuked . . . still.** In His dignity and majesty Christ arose, rebuked the wind as He did disease (Luke. 4 : 39), and muzzled the sea as He did a demoniac (1 : 25). Herein He proved Himself the Lord of nature[3] and mighty God by His direct command (Job

---

[1] προσκεφάλαιον may also mean a cushion to sit upon. (Stellhorn.) Therefore this cushion might have been "the steersman's wooden seat covered with leather." (Farrar.)

[2] Christ's sleep was "the reverse of Jonah." (Trench.) Jerome sees in Jonah's sleep a type of Christ's rest, but Jonah's presence brings danger, Christ's betokens deliverance.

[3] Athanasius (Letters XXIX.) says: "The Lord who rebuked it (the sea) was not a creature but rather its Creator, since a creature is not obedient to another creature. For although the Red Sea was divided before by Moses, yet it was not Moses who did it, for it came to pass, not because he

39 : 11 ; Ps. 65 : 7 ; 89 : 9), and prefigures the final triumph of His own over the powers of nature because of His presence.[1] "Christ is a mighty Lord, all that He wills He does in heaven and upon earth, in the sea and in the deep."—CRAMER, STARKE. **And . . . calm.** "The surge was straightway at an end, and not a trace of disturbance remained."—CHRYSOSTOM. The calm blue lake slumbered again in placid sweetness. "A great storm followed by a great calm ; so it is ever with God's consolations after trial."—CANSTEIN, LANGE. But now [2] Jesus said to His disciples, Ver. 40, **Why . . . faith ?** The storm of their hearts caused by unbelief is rebuked, and their abandonment of faith, that brought on fear, is censured. "Fearing is human, namely for fallen man in sin and fear of death ; but the faith in God shall expel this fear."—STIER. Ver. 41. **And . . . exceedingly** not from a disturbed heart, but in the calmness of a mighty awe before Christ's majesty. It is but natural for man to fear, whenever divine glory and power are revealed [3] (Luke. 2 : 10 ; 24 : 5). And the twelve **said . . . him ?** They who previously called Christ only "Master," now do not know what name to give Him, that will correspond to His great miracle. Almost approaching to the confession of His divinity, they do not

spake, but because God commanded. And if the sun stood still in Gibeon, and the moon in the valley of Ajalon, yet this was the work, not of the son of Nun, but of the Lord, who heard his prayer." Cf. also Luther, Erl. Ed. 1, 187.

[1] It is this presence of Christ, which justifies the figurative adaptation of the miracle to the Church. See Tertull. On Bapt. 12 ; Luther, Erl. Ed. 11, 77 sq.

[2] Matthew mentions the fact that Christ spoke to the twelve before rebuking the storm.

[3] How trivial is the conjecture of Weiss, that the disciples feared, because Christ was displeased.

ask like the people (1 : 27), "What is this?" but *Who then, what personality is He, that even the wind and sea obey him.* Not only demons are cast out by Him, but nature itself bows in immediate submission. "This is a stupendous miracle, one of those which test whether we indeed believe in the credibility of the miraculous or not; one of those miracles of power which cannot, like many of the miracles of healing, be explained away by existing laws."—FARRAR.

CHAPTER V.

1–20. And they came to the other side of the sea, into the country of the Gerasenes. And when he was come out of the boat, straightway there met him out of the tombs a man with an unclean spirit, who had his dwelling in the tombs: and no man could any more bind him, no, not with a chain; because that he had been often bound with fetters and chains, and the chains had been rent asunder by him, and the fetters broken in pieces: and no man had strength to tame him. And always, night and day, in the tombs and in the mountains, he was crying out, and cutting himself with stones. And when he saw Jesus from afar, he ran and worshipped him; and crying out with a loud voice, he saith, What have I to do with thee, Jesus, thou Son of the Most High God? I adjure thee by God, torment me not. For he said unto him, Come forth, thou unclean spirit, out of the man. And he asked him, What is thy name? And he saith unto him, My name is Legion; for we are many. And he besought him much that he would not send them away out of the country. Now there was there on the mountain side a great herd of swine feeding. And they besought him, saying, Send us into the swine, that we may enter into them. And he gave them leave. And the unclean spirits came out, and entered into the swine: and the herd rushed down the steep into the sea, *in number* about two thousand; and they were choked in the sea. And they that fed them fled, and told it in the city, and in the country. And they came to see what it was that had come to pass. And they come to Jesus, and behold him that was possessed with devils sitting, clothed and in his right mind, *even* him that had the legion: and they were afraid. And they that saw it declared unto them how it befell him that was possessed with devils, and concerning the swine. And they began to beseech him to depart from their borders. And as he was entering into the boat, he that had been possessed with devils besought him that he might be with him. And he suffered him not, but saith unto him, Go to thy house unto thy friends, and tell them how great things the Lord hath done for thee, and *how* he had mercy on thee. And he went his way, and began to publish in Decapolis how great things Jesus had done for him: and all men did marvel.

Ver. 1. **They**, Jesus and the twelve, came to the east

side . . . **Gerasenes,**[1] which is not the region about the well-known Gerasa, on the eastern boundary of Peræa (Jos. Wars, III. 3, 3; IV. 9, 18), near Arabia (Origen), but the tract about Kersa, whose ruins have been discovered directly on the eastern shore of the sea of Galilee.[2] Ver. 2. *And when* Jesus **was . . . tombs,** which are still to be seen in the immense mountain that rises directly above Kersa, **a man**[3] **. . . spirit** (1 : 24; EXCURSUS II., p. 31), Ver. 3, **who . . . tombs,** not merely because they offered excellent shelter, nor because the unclean spirits preferred tombs as unclean places (Matt. 23 : 27; Luke 11 : 44), nor for the reason that Satan has power of death (Hebr. 2 : 14); but the demons "acting on the existing consciousness, would lead the man, in accordance with his preconceived notions,[4] to select such places."—EDERSHEIM. **No man . . . chain,** for his strength in his demoniac rage was so great (cf. Acts 19 : 16). Ver. 4.

---

[1] This reading of א, B, D, is now generally preferred to "Gadarenes" of A, C, which is probably the correct word in Mt. 8 : 28. "Gergasenes" is due to the correction of Origen, who changed "Gadarenes" with a proper understanding of the locality but wrongly repudiated "Gerasa." It does not seem probable that Gen. 10 : 16; Deut. 7 : 1; Josh. 24 : 11, influenced the selection of "Gergasenes." Cf. Weiss, p. 171; Holtzmann, p. 151; Morison, p. 115; Robinson, p. 220.

[2] This discovery of Thomson (II., p. 34 sq.) has been almost universally accepted. It offers the clearest explanation of the gospel-record. Cf. Tristram, Land of Israel, p. 465; Porter, Syria and Palestine, p. 431; Farrar, p. 236.

[3] While Matthew (8 : 28) mentions two demoniacs, Mark and Luke speak of but one, who was "of superior notability and repute, and whose case was particularly lamented by that district, and for whose deliverance there was special anxiety." (Augustine, De. Cons. II., xxiv., 56.) Cf. also Robinson, p. 221.

[4] Jewish superstition held that demons sought lonely places and tombs (Edersheim, Ap. XIII., II., p. 760). The latter were preferred, because demons were held to be the spirits of departed wicked men. (Jos. Wars, VII. 6, 3.)

He ... fetters, i. e. shackles upon his feet to prevent escape, and **chains,** not necessarily manacles (Holtzmann); **the ... fetters,** which may have been stout cords (Keil), were **broken in pieces,** lit. rubbed together, until they gave way; **and ... him,** for he even endangered the life of men (Matt. 8 : 28). Ver. 5. **And ... crying out,** with fierce unearthly shouts, **and** *cutting himself with stones.* So terrible was the influence of the demons, that the afflicted man was constantly led to injure himself, a symptom of ordinary mania.[1] "As the devil raged mightily at the time of Christ's first coming, so also will he at the time of Christ's second coming, knowing that his time is short" (Rev. 12 : 12).—CRAMER, LANGE. Ver. 6. When the demoniac **saw Jesus from afar** on the heights **he ran** to the shore, **and worshipped him;** for the demons knowing Christ's power hoped against hope to escape present judgment by cringing worship. "All the kingdom of Satan is kept in check and under the government of Christ."—CALVIN. But noticing inwardly Christ's determination they would not brook interference, and compel the man to say, Ver. 6 : **What ...** (1 : 24) **God?** This unwilling confession of Christ's divinity is all the more glorious, because God is called the *Most High* (Gen. 14 : 18; Num. 24 : 16; Deut. 32 : 8; 2 Sam. 22 : 14; Ps. 57 : 2; 78 : 17; Dan. 4 : 17) as the one Lord of Heaven and earth.[2] "Who denies that Jesus is the Son of God is worse than the devil."—MAJUS, STARKE. In his par-

---

[1] Trench, p. 130; Morison, p. 117.

[2] "Most High God" (θεοῦ τοῦ ὑψίστου) the El Elyōn of the O. T. First used in patriarchal times it is an evidence of monotheism rising out of a former polytheism. Revelation finding a point of contact in this movement unveiled fully and clearly to Abraham the unity of the Almighty. (Delitzsch, Lectures on O. T. Theology, I. A. Par. 1, Note 1.) Oehler, O. T. Theology (Engl. Transl. Am. Ed.), p. 89.

oxysm one demon appeals from the Son to the Father, and as if intending to compel Christ through God says, **I . . . not.**[1] This spokesman of the demons would beg off not merely the casting out, but the beginning of the final judgment (Luke 8 : 31); for Satan and his ministers are afraid of God's decision. This fear led to the petition and adjuration, which the knowledge of the demons must have known to be unavailing. Ver. 8. For Christ then said, addressing the speaking demon, **Come . . . spirit,**[2] but He did not at once enforce His command, because the demons in their violent egress might have destroyed the man. In considerate wisdom Jesus therefore, Ver. 9, **asked . . . name?** so that by the recalling of his name, the man might be reminded of his self-consciousness, that had been almost lost.[3] And the disciples also are to receive clear evidence of the greatness of satanic power. The man saith, **My . . . many.** The plurality of the demons at once deprive the man of the "my," in which the individuality is beginning to awake. They call themselves *Legion* with a Jewish appellation for a great multitude, but they were not 6000, the number contained in a Roman legion. It was no hallucination of an insane man, when the demons said, *we are many*. In large numbers they had seated themselves in the various capacities of the soul. "How many a man is spiritually possessed of more than one devil; as many ruling sins as there are, so many evil spirits."—LANGE. The many find their unity of purpose in their leader,

---

[1] ὁρκίζω with double accusative (Acts 19 : 13; 1 Thess. 5 : 27) is derived from the Sept.

[2] The nominative of address here possesses its original harshness. Winer, p. 182.

[3] Trench refers to the fact mentioned by Schubert, that in somnambulism the calling of the name mostly awakens the sleep-walker.

who besought Christ much, Ver. 10, **that ... country**, not because they ruled in heathendom (Hilgenfeld), nor because there were mountains and tombs there (Keil), but because they desired to find another dwelling-place to prevent their being sent into the abyss. Ver. 11. Now, continues Mark with a descriptive diversion to aid vivid representation, **there ... mountain-side**, the fertile slope near Wady Semak,[1] **a ... swine**, unclean animals (Lev. 11 : 7). Ver. 12. **And they** (demons) **... them**. In Christ's presence the demons cannot even enter swine. "The devil's legion would not have had power over the herd of swine, unless they had got it from God."—TERTULLIAN. Their desire, prompted by the nearness of the swine, finds its explanation in the relation between Satanism and bestiality. In the swine they hope to remain temporarily,[2] but they are deceiving themselves. Therefore Jesus, Ver. 13, **gave them leave**, to punish the Jewish proprietors at the same time for their accommodation to their Gentile surroundings. And the unclean spirits coming upon the swine, **the herd** impelled by a furious power in wild panic **rushed**[3] **... the sea**,[4] for "the lake is so near the base of the mountain that the swine rushing madly down could not stop, but would be hurried into the water and drowned."—THOMSON. And thus the

---

[1] Morison, p. 121.

[2] It is impossible to suppose, that the demons knowing that the destruction of the swine would cause Christ's departure, desired it to hinder the work of Christ. This knowledge would include the cognition of their destruction, which they sought to avoid.

[3] Jerome (Life of St. Hilarion, 23), supposes that the vast number of swine corresponds to the "Legion," which he wrongly estimates at two thousand.

[4] Gregory Nazianzen (Orat. on Bapt. XXXV.), comparing the sea to the water of baptism, says of Satan : "He lights on baptized souls, whose sins the font has washed away. He fears the water; he is choked with the cleansing, as the Legion were in the sea."

demons meet the doom they wished to avoid, and the demoniac sees the powers that held him destroyed. "The devil is heard in his wish, but for his damnation." —AUGUSTINE. Ver. 14. **And they . . . them,** the swineherds, seeing what had happened, **fled** in every direction, and some **told** *it in the* **city,** Kersa, others **in** *the* **country,** in the nearest farms, probably to the owners of the swine. The report spreads rapidly. Where God will have His works announced, He quickly finds messengers. *And they,* that had heard, **came . . . pass.** The message is so marvellous, that they must see for themselves. "To come and see the wonders of God is necessary and profitable" (Ps. 46 : 8).—STARKE. Ver. 15. And they *behold* the demoniac **sitting** instead of raving about, **clothed,** although before he would suffer no clothes (Luke 8 : 27), and **in** *his right* **mind,** without a trace of possession. **And** *they were* **afraid,** "because the majesty of God shone brightly in Christ."—CALVIN. Ver. 16. And when the swineherds *that saw it declared* how all had happened, the people, Ver. 17, **began . . . borders.** Christ's holy power was not agreeable to these material men, "who were more concerned that Christ had given the swine to the devils, then that He had freed a man from the devil." —LUTHER. "Their prayer was heard (Ps. 78 : 29–31); for God sometimes hears His enemies in anger, even as He refuses to hear His friends in love" (2 Cor. 12 : 8, 9). —TRENCH. Ver. 18. And as Christ *was entering the boat* the healed demoniac **besought . . . him,** not because he feared that new demons would come in Christ's absence (Theophylact, Maldonatus), but from the sincere attachment of faith and gratitude. "The converted soul longs to be with Christ."—LANGE. Ver. 19. But Christ **suffered him not,** that it might not appear that He had sold His mercy, and desired this man as His servant

(Luther), **but ... thee.** The man, who was fitted for and needed such active evangelistic work, is sent to his own house (John 4 : 53) and friends, to declare the greatness of God's mercy as shown in His healing. "God uses every one as His wisdom sees will best subserve the interests of His kingdom."—CANSTEIN, LANGE. Ver. 20. And the man not only told his own house, but **began ... Decapolis** (Matt. 4 : 25 ; Mark 7 : 31), the region of the ten cities, all of which except Scythopolis were east of the Jordan, and east and southeast of the lake of Galilee. Pliny gives as the names of the other cities Hippos, Gadara, Pella, Philadelphia, Gerasa, Dion, Canatha, Damascus, Paphana. Josephus excludes Damascus, while Ptolemy includes Capitolias. Reland has demonstrated that Abila belonged to Decapolis. The last two names in the list of Pliny are therefore to be changed into Abila and Capitolias.[1] Even the people who had sent Christ away hear again *how great things Jesus had done.* "God sends preachers for a season even to the ungrateful."—OSIANDER. **And ... marvel.** They could not help being astonished, and though some remained simply surprised, yet to others " wonder may have been the first step to faith in Christ."—STARKE. "In the person of one man Christ has exhibited to us proof of His grace, which is extended to all mankind. Though we are not tortured by the devil, yet he holds us as his slaves, till the Son of God delivers us from his tyranny. Naked, torn and disfigured, we wander about, till He restores us to soundness of mind. It remains that, in magnifying His grace, we testify our gratitude."—CALVIN.

21-24. And when Jesus had crossed over again in the boat unto the other side, a great multitude was gathered unto him; and he was by the

---

[1] J. L. Porter in Smith's Bible Dict. sub. Decapolis ; Nebe, III., p. 229.

sea. And there cometh one of the rulers of the synagogue, Jairus by name; and seeing him, he falleth at his feet, and beseecheth him much, saying, My little daughter is at the point of death: I pray thee, that thou come and lay thy hands on her, that she may be made whole and live. And he went with him; and a great multitude followed him, and they thronged him.

Ver. 21. **And ... side**, the western shore, and had healed the paralytic, had called Levi and been at the feast (2 : 1 sq.),[1] a **great multitude** (3 : 7; 4 : 1) **was gathered unto him** (ἐπ'αὐτον), upon whom their desire was directed : and **he**[2] ... Ver. 22, **synagogue** at Capernaum, who, also called shepherds,[3] elders,[4] generally elected a chief, who received the specific name "Archisynagogus," here attributed to all. It was their duty to preside over and preserve order at services (Luke 13 : 14; Acts 13 : 15), to distribute alms, keep the buildings in repair, and even to punish by expulsion from the synagogue, by scourging and at times by death (Matt. 10 : 17; 23 : 34; Acts 22 : 19; John 9 : 22; 16 : 2).[5] This ruler was **Jairus**, a well-known O. T. name (Numb. 32 : 41; Josh. 13 : 30; Judg. 10 : 3; Est. 2 : 5), meaning "he will make bright"[6] (cf. also Jos.

[1] It is clear from all the synoptic gospels, that the feast must be connected with Levi's call. (Luthardt's Tabelle zur evang. Synopse as ag. Riddle in Robinson's Harmony, who separates the feast from the call.)

[2] It is here, therefore, and not in the house, where the feast was held (Meyer, Robinson), that Jairus approached Jesus (Keil, p. 63; Nebe, III., p. 434.

[3] Pātāsīm (ποιμένες).

[4] Z'Kēnīm (πρεσβύτεροι). Sometimes the name M'hūnīm (προστάτες) is used.

[5] Vitringa, De Syn. Vet. III. 17, p. 582 sq.; Schürer, Gesch. des Volkes Israel im Zeitaler Jesu Xti. II., p. 364; Winer's Reallexikon sub synagogue; Edersheim, I., p. 438; Nebe, III., p. 435.

[6] Ἰάειρος is doubtless the transliteration of Yāīr with Aleph, and not from an imaginary Yāīr with Ayin (he will awaken), upon which together with the coincidence of the age of the daughter of Jairus with the years of suffering of the woman having an issue of blood, Strauss, Volkmar, Keim, Holtzmann,

Antiq. V. 7, 6; Wars, VI. 1, 8). Ver. 23. *Seeing* Jesus, **he** *falleth at His* **feet**. Although a man of high station he bows down before the Saviour like men of low degree. "The cross teaches us to listen to the word and become humble."—HEDINGER, STARKE. He **beseecheth** Jesus *much* with the constantly repeated prayer, **My little**[1] **daughter** (7 : 27), a word of great tenderness for his only child (Luke 8 : 42), **is** . . . **death**,[2] in her last moments: **I pray thee**,[3] . . . **live**. In this request superstition is mixed with faith, as shown in the desire to have Jesus present bodily, that He might lay on His hands, which act was to Jairus not only symbolical of transference of power,[4] but thought of in a magical manner.[5] The word, of which it was but the visible medium (8 : 23 sq.; 10 : 16; Luke 13 : 12 sq.), was overlooked. But still Jairus holds Jesus to be "the true Messiah sent by God to help in such cases and perplexities, when no man can help, to free from the anxiety of death and the power of Satan, yea, to bring forth and give life out of death."—LUTHER. Because of this faith, Ver. 24, Jesus **went** *with* **him**, silently, to try and to strengthen his faith, for "God

---

build their supposition of the mythical character of these miracles (cf. Weiss, Com., p. 89; Markusev, etc., p. 184).

[1] θυγάτριον is one of Mark's favorite diminutives (5 : 41; 7 : 27; 8 : 7; 14 : 47).

[2] ἐσχάτως ἔχει, a Latinism for *in extremis est*.

[3] This insertion is demanded by ἵνα, which is not dependent upon παρεκάλει (Keil), but has an imperative force (Holtzmann), and is expressive of a wish (Nösgen). Winer, p. 315.

[4] The laying on of hands means giving what is our own to another, whether it be good or evil (Gen. 48 : 14; Lev. 4 : 15; 24 : 14); Nebe, III., p. 231.

[5] To prevent this magical misinterpretation Christ used the laying on of hands rarely (6 : 5; 8 : 23; 10 : 16; Luke 4 : 40; 13 : 13). It has risen again in that idea of ordination, which overstraining (1 Tim. 4 : 14) holds to a real transference of official dignity.

does not reject the weak in faith " (Isai. 42 : 3).—OSIANDER, STARKE. **And . . . followed,** and **thronged** (Tyndale), pressed close about Jesus.

25-34. And a woman, which had an issue of blood twelve years, and had suffered many things of many physicians, and had spent all that she had, and was nothing bettered, but rather grew worse, having heard the things concerning Jesus, came in the crowd behind, and touched his garment. For she said, If I touch but his garments, I shall be made whole. And straightway the fountain of her blood was dried up ; and she felt in her body that she was healed of her plague. And straightway Jesus, perceiving in himself that the power *proceeding* from him had gone forth, turned him about in the crowd, and said, Who touched my garments? And his disciples said unto him, Thou seest the multitude thronging thee, and sayest thou, Who touched me? And he looked round about to see her that had done this thing. But the woman fearing and trembling, knowing what had been done to her, came and fell down before him, and told him all the truth. And he said unto her, Daughter, thy faith hath made thee whole ; go in peace, and be whole of thy plague.

Ver. 25. **A woman . . . blood,** probably a chronic condition of hemorrhage for the long period of *twelve years.* " God has His own times and seasons ; He delays and yet helps."—QUESNEL, LANGE. Ver. 26. **And . . . physicians.** The state of medicine was very rude then,[1] but even modern science and excellent physicians at times aggravate instead of curing disease. " Medicines are not to be despised, but God does not always see fit to prosper them."—CRAMER, LANGE. **And . . . worse.** All her means were given to restore bodily health, but every cure increased the ailment.[2] " Men are not ready to do for the

---

[1] The Talmud mentions eleven remedies for this flux, of which about five are astringents and tonics, and the rest merely superstitious practices (Edersheim, I. 620). Mischna (Kidduschim, 4, 14) says: " The best of physicians deserves hell, and the most respectable of them is a brother of impious Amalek." See, also, the fierce gloss to this, Geikie, p. 193.

[2] This condition has been allegorically applied to heathendom, while the daughter of Jairus is supposed to represent Judaism. (Luther. Erl. Ed. 14, 331.)

healing of the soul, what they do for the cure of the body; many a one would not give for salvation what he expends upon his life and health."—QUESNEL, STARKE. Ver. 27. **Having . . . Jesus**, His wonderful cures and great power, **came . . . garment**, rather "the border of his garment" (Matt. 9 : 20), the Talith (cloak) with its fringes.[1] The secrecy of her approach was prompted by womanly delicacy, that would not permit her to speak of her disease before so many. Her position as a woman over against a Rabbi would also deter her. In addition "she was ashamed, accounting herself unclean,"—CHRYSOSTOM, (Lev. 15 : 25); and was humble withal. "She considers herself unworthy, that she should speak with Him or look upon Him; for she knows, that she has deserved nothing, and has never done anything for the Lord."—LUTHER. But faith urges her on, Ver. 28. **For . . . whole.** Her faith, like that of Jairus, contained an element of error. She supposed that external touch, but not of the holy fringes (Trench), was necessary to obtain the power of Jesus, which was conceived of physically as dwelling in the body of Christ, and not conditioned by His knowledge and will.[2] The truth of her faith was the confidence, "that in this man there must be divine, almighty force and power."—LUTHER. Ver. 29. **And . . . up**; in its very source, *and she* **felt** with joy **that** *she was healed of her* **plague** (3 : 10). "Faith is stronger than all earthly medicines," and "who touches Jesus rightly in faith will be cured if not in body, certainly in the soul" (3 John 2).—STARKE. Ver. 30. But **Jesus . . . forth.** Within

---

[1] For an interesting detailed account of the probable dress of Jesus, see Edersheim, I. 620 sq.

[2] Grotius has best expressed her error by saying, that like the philosophers she held that God does all things by nature, not by will (*Deum agere omnia φύσει οὐ βουλήσει*).

His soul, and therefore with absolute certainty, Jesus knew what the woman had done, for it had not occurred without His assent. "God does not need eyes to see, nor need He feel corporeally, but has in Himself the knowledge of all things."—AMBROSE. No blessings received are hidden from the Lord. He **turned ... garments?**[1] that the miracle might become evident and the woman led to confess not for His own glory, but to "exhibit her faith to all, and to provoke the rest also to emulation."—CHRYSOSTOM. The disciples think Christ's question unreasonable, not understanding how He could ask in the, Ver. 31, **multitude** *thronging* Him, *Who touched* **me?** They are not able to distinguish between the pressure of the crowd and the believing touch of an individual, as Christ can. He knows that "flesh presses, but faith touches."—AUGUSTINE. "Thus also in the church many approach Christ, receive the word of salvation with their outward ears, eat and drink with their mouths the sacrament of His very body and blood, yet receive no efficacy from it, and do not feel that flow of their sins stopping and drying up. Whence is this? Because they lack true faith, which alone from this fountain drinks grace upon grace." —CHEMNITZ. After His reply (Luke 8 : 46) Christ, Ver. 32, **looked ... thing,** that by her confession she might be assured, "lest being pricked by her conscience, as having stolen the gift, she should abide in agony."—CHRYSOSTOM. Ver. 33. **But** *the woman* caught by Christ's searching glance, *fearing and* **trembling** before the majesty of His omniscience, **came ... truth.** Thus Christ led her to receive the full blessing of faith, by a confession unto salvation. (Rom. 10 : 10). Ver. 34. **He ... Daughter**, a word of condescending love (2 : 5), **thy ... whole**

---

[1] Augustine attempts to explain the "seeming ignorance" of Christ by bold allegorizing. (Ag. Lying, 27.)

(Luke 7 : 50; 17 : 19; 18 : 42). It was not her faith as a moral quality, independent of Christ and of the reliance upon His power,[1] that had saved her; but trust as the receptive organ for His power. But Christ ascribes everything to her faith, the beginning of which marked the completion of her cure. "This He does to show us, how great a pleasure He has, if you hope everything good of Him, and seek help of Him."—LUTHER. This faith brings peace (Rom. 5 : 1). **Go in peace** *and be made* **whole,** The peace of God (Phil. 4 : 7) is to be the constant accompaniment of health bodily and spiritual.[2]

35-43. While he yet spake, they come from the ruler of the synagogue's *house*, saying, Thy daughter is dead: why troublest thou the Master any further? But Jesus, not heeding the word spoken, saith unto the ruler of the synagogue, Fear not, only believe. And he suffered no man to follow with him, save Peter, and James, and John the brother of James. And they come to the house of the ruler of the synagogue; and he beholdeth a tumult, and *many* weeping and wailing greatly. And when he was entered in, he saith unto them, Why make ye a tumult, and weep? the child is not dead, but sleepeth. And they laughed him to scorn. But he, having put

---

[1] Grass (Das Verhalten zu Jesus nach den Herrnworten, 1895) is correct in appreciating the inceptive element in the faith of those whom Jesus healed as "trust in Jesus as the worker of miracles." This beginning of faith, with its temporal and local color, is not, however, the core of faith. It only prepared for trust in the divine-human personality of Jesus.

[2] This woman, mentioned in the apocryphal gospel of Nicodemus (ch. 7), was supposed by Pseudo-Ambrose to be Martha, the sister of Lazarus. Eusebius (H. E. VII. 18) tells, that she had erected a statue to Christ at Cæsarea Philippi. It represented her "as kneeling before Him, with her hands stretched out, as if praying." A "strange plant," that grew about this monument, was said to heal all diseases. Sozomen and Philostorgius report that Julian destroyed this image. This tradition probably arose from the mistaken ascription to Jesus of a statue raised for an emperor. The word "Saviour" or "God" may have been used to designate the apotheosized emperor in an inscription of which the rest had become illegible. (Gieseler.) v. Ammon's supposition that the statue represented a person praying to her genius does not seem probable. (McGifford's Euseb., p. 304; Nebe, III., p. 442.)

them all forth, taketh the father of the child and her mother and them that were with him, and goeth in where the child was. And taking the child by the hand, he saith unto her, Talitha cumi; which is, being interpreted, Damsel, I say unto thee, Arise. And straightway the damsel rose up, and walked; for she was twelve years old. And they were amazed straightway with a great amazement. And he charged them much that no man should know this: and he commanded that *something* should be given her to eat.

Ver. 35. While Christ **yet spake**, and continued by His delay to try the faith of agonized Jairus, that patience might grow and the lesson of one miracle prepare for the next, messengers **come . . . dead**. This sudden announcement is to inform Jairus of the impossibility of any help. **Why . . . further?**[1] His way would be in vain, for thy daughter is beyond the reach of His power. "Reason despairs when it sees death (John 11 : 21, 32, 39, 40."—HEDINGER, STARKE. Ver. 36. But Jesus, whose "will it was that her death should be believed, that her resurrection might not be suspected,"—CHRYSOSTOM, **not . . . spoken**, i. e. not overhearing it (Ewald, Meyer, Klostermann), but hearing it incidentally (Weiss, Keil, Nösgen), *saith* to Jairus: **Fear . . . believe**. Let not the hopeless message cause despairing dread, only have faith. Fear and distrust will shut out help. The greater the fear, the less will be the possibility of faith. Jesus is anxious "that faith should hold on; He takes care, that where it is about to become weak, it does not cease."—LUTHER. If faith remain it shall receive abundant blessing, for never can it "be more extensive than the boundless power of God."—CALVIN. Ver. 37. And Jesus **suffered . . . John**. The miracle which Christ would do is to be hid from the people be-

[1] σκύλλω (Luke 7 : 6), originally meaning "to flay," has the secondary signification of "vexing, wearying," at times with reference to a journey. And no doubt it has this meaning here. "Why dost thou weary the master with this tedious way?" (Trench.)

cause of their unworthiness, and from the other disciples in their unpreparedness. The first prophetical evidence of Christ's resurrection-power is to be made known only to the chosen three, "the election within the election,"—CLEMENT ALEX., to prepare them to become more competent witnesses of the greatest glory (9 : 2 sq.) and the deepest humiliation (14 : 33) of their Lord while upon earth. "Let us learn of Christ to entrust only to a few elect the works of God that are to be done, that they may not be hindered."—QUESNEL, STARKE. Ver. 38. *And they come to the* **house,** before which and within which there was a **tumult,** *and many weeping and wailing* **greatly.** The noise was that of the professional female mourners, together with the flute-players (Matt. 9 : 23), of which in accordance with the rank of Jairus there was a large number. These mourners, also found among the Greeks and Romans, were introduced in Israel at an early period (Jer. 9 : 17). The mourning was to excite grief and to express wild hopeless despair, and was sometimes more than a business-like ostentation.[1] The death-cries are peculiar, indescribably plaintive, quavering, shrill, wild, weird sounds.[2] "To show sorrow over our dead is Christian, to howl and cry is heathenish."—STARKE. Ver. 39. When Christ *entered in* with Jairus and the three disciples (Luke 8 : 51)[3] He reproved the mourners for mourning where there was no cause; for **the . . . sleepeth.** That death is a sleep was not only known to the O. T. saints (2 Sam. 7 : 12; Job 3 : 13; Dan. 12 : 2), but even

[1] Thomson, I., p. 144.

[2] No two observers have described the death-cry alike. It is impossible to give an adequate idea of it in words. Trumbull, p. 148 sq.

[3] Meyer is wrong in finding a contradiction between the account of Luke and Mark in the separation of the disciples. Luke's words: "he suffered not any man to enter," refer to the crowd at the house, while Mark speaks of the multitude at the lake and the disciples.

the Greeks and Romans had a presentiment of the relation of sleep and death.¹ No one, however, before Christ applied this thought personally and demonstrated it by direct authority practically. Therefore to speak of those that die in Him as " they that have fallen asleep " (1. Cor. 7 : 39; 11 : 30; 15 : 6; 1. Thess. 4 : 14) is no poetry but absolute truth. Death is sleep because it is followed by awakening.² " This wisdom no philosopher could attain, though they have infinitely many opinions."—LUTHER. " Death is a sleep, a journey to peace, a gain, a laying aside of the earthly tabernacle."—CRAMER, STARKE. Ver. 40. And the people supposing bodily death to be real death **laughed . . . scorn.** Their derision, proving the superficiality of their mourning, arose from unbelief (Gen. 18 ; 12), for the world does not believe in resurrection as it sees only death everywhere. " God's wisdom is so exalted, that reason holds it to be pure folly, and all the world the dear Lord Jesus a fool."—LUTHER. But this mocking laughter was " an additional confirmation of the miracle, that those persons entertained no doubt whatever as to the maiden's death."—CALVIN. Christ, **having . . . forth,** because their boisterous presence was not to disturb the awful mystery, for " God's wonderous works require devout and attentive witnesses," —HEDINGER, STARKE ; **he . . . mother** with the three disciples **in** *where the child* **was,** into an inner chamber. " The house was now solitary and still. Two souls believ-

---

[1] They are called " brothers " and " twin-brothers " by Homer (Iliad, XIV. 231; XVI. 672), and Hesiod (Theog. l. 758). Virgil (Aen. IV. 244) says that the same rod of Mercury which sends sleep closes the eyes in death. Similar figures are found in Plutarch, Seneca, Galenus. Cf. Schubert, Geschichte der Seele (4th ed.) II. p. 353.

[2] " Sleeping is only the relative, death the absolute, antithesis to waking; dying is a falling asleep, but of such nature that it transcends the bounds of nature."—Delitzsch.

ing and hoping stand like funeral tapers beside the couch of the dead maiden—the father and mother. The church is represented in the three chiefs of its apostles."—TRENCH. Ver. 41. **And . . . hand**, and as prince of life touching death's prey, he simply saith **Talitha cumi**,[1] words that Mark relates as Peter told them in the Aramaic, that Christ spoke; **which . . . Arise**. With short command and without the struggle of an Elijah and Elisha (1 Kings 17:17 sq.; 2 Kings 4:18 sq.) Jesus speaks to the dead as to the living (Luke. 7:14; John 11:43), bidding them to **arise** (2:11; 3:3). "To God everything must live, to us everything is dead."—LUTHER. Ver. 42. **And . . . rose up** as in the morning, and **walked**, which proves the reality of her resurrection. She could walk, being no child ($\pi\alpha\iota\delta\iota\sigma\nu$, v. 41); **for . . . old**. Among the Jews a woman came of age at twelve years and one day.[2] *And they*, the parents, **were** *amazed with a great* **amazement** (2:12), for this was Christ's first raising of a dead person. Ver. 43. **And . . . this**, that He might not be sought as raiser of the dead, and that the maiden might not to her own harm become an object of curiosity and admiration (1:44; 7:36; 8:26). Finally Christ **commanded . . . eat**, not only "lest the resurrection should still be thought a deception,"—JEROME (Luke 24:41), but also to strengthen the maiden. In His true humanity Jesus well knew the necessity of the body, and could understand how refreshing food would be to the keen appetite of the maiden. "Even the child's mother was not so motherly as Jesus."—MORISON. The new life given by Jesus requires nourishment.

---

[1] Kūmī is Kūm in א, B, C, L, M, Σ, 33. This is not due to the accidental dropping of ī, for Kūmī occurs in later Aramaic. It is used in the Talmud (Shabb. 110 b.), where a woman suffering from bloody flux is addressed. (Edersheim, I., p. 631.)

[2] Edersheim, I., p. 618.

CHAPTER VI.

1–6. And he went out from thence; and he cometh into his own country; and his disciples follow him. And when the sabbath was come, he began to teach in the synagogue: and many hearing him were astonished, saying, Whence hath this man these things? and, What is the wisdom that is given unto this man, and *what mean* such mighty works wrought by his hands? Is not this the carpenter, the son of Mary, and brother of James, and Joses, and Judas, and Simon? and are not his sisters here with us? And they were offended in him. And Jesus said unto them, A prophet is not without honor, save in his own country, and among his own kin, and in his own house. And he could there do no mighty work, save that he laid his hands upon a few sick folk, and healed them. And he marvelled because of their unbelief.

And he went round about the villages teaching.

Ver. 1. Jesus **went** . . . **thence**, i. e. from Capernaum (Lange, Cook), but not necessarily the house of Jairus (Fritzsche, Meyer, Weiss), and **cometh** . . . **country**, or rather city,[1] by which Mark, differing from Matthew (9:1), designates Nazareth, as the city of His youth. This was His second visit,[2] and *his disciples followed him* (3:37). Ver. 2. And after having lingered a few days possibly with one of his sisters (ver. 3), **when** . . . **many** . . . **things?**[3] Contemptuously they ask whence Jesus, who had not been

---

[1] πατρίς means native city in later Greek (Jos. Ant. 10. 7. 3).

[2] Schleiermacher, Ohlshausen, Weiss, Volkmar, Holtzmann, Luthard accept but one visit of Christ in Nazareth, identifying Luke 4:16 with Matt. 13:54; Mark 6:1. But cf. Stier, 3. p. 51; Robinson, p. 213; Cook, p. 235.

[3] The article "the" (B, L) with "many" marks "the multitude as distinguished from few." (Keil.)

in any rabbinical school,[1] had learnt such marvellous truth (1 : 22). **What . . . man?** While the Nazarenes cannot gainsay Christ's superior knowledge, they question about it enviously, implying, from contempt of His person, that its character must suffer from its source. "It is common enough for those who would defeat the force of a sermon to criticise the preachers" (Acts 17 : 18).—STARKE. *Such mighty* **works,** powers,[2] **wrought** *by his* **hands?** It cannot be by His power! "Surely He has to do with the devil."—LUTHER. Ver. 3. **Is . . . carpenter?**[3] Jesus had, assisting His father,[4] learnt the trade of the carpenter; for every Jew, even though a rabbi, had to do manual labor.[5] Thus Paul was a tent-maker (Acts 18 : 3), worked (1 Thess. 2 : 9; 2 Thess. 3 : 8) and enjoined honest work (Eph. 4 : 28; 1 Thess. 4 : 11). But the trade of the carpenter seems to have belonged to those, which were in ill-repute for dishonesty.[6] When therefore the Naza-

---

[1] Holtzmann conjectures that Jesus had possibly not even passed through the ordinary schools. (Cf. Schürer, II. 353.)

[2] Trench well defines this designation of the miracles as "outcomings of that mighty power of God, which was inherent in Christ Himself that great power of God." (N. T. Syn., p. 344.) It is also used, Mark 5 : 30; 6 : 14; 9 : 39; Matt. 7 : 22; Luke 10 : 13. The other words for miracles are "signs," indicative of their divine instructive purpose (Mark 16 : 17, 20); "wonders" (13 : 22), a word never standing alone and describing the miracle from its effect; and the Johannine favorite "works" (John 6 : 28; 7 : 21; 10 : 25, etc.).

[3] This original word was soon conformed to Matt. 13 : 55. (Origen ag. Celsus VI., 36.)

[4] Not in the miraculous manner related in the apocryphal Gospel of the Infancy, Chap. XXV.

[5] For the high estimate of labor see in the Talmud, Aboth, 1 ; 10 ; Nedarim, 49b.; Kidduschim, 82b. In the sixty-three Talmudic tractates there is no commendation of trading and speculation, but many a passage against them, while manual labor is universally praised. See Delitzsch, Jüdisches Handwerkerleben zur Zeit Jesu, p. 23 sq.

[6] That carpenters were distrusted is evident from the rule laid down at the end of "Baba Kamma," "What the carpenter removes with the plane

renes called Jesus carpenter, it was not merely contempt for his unschooled past but also a sneer at his mean occupation. This was, as it still is, very primitive in tools and work.[1] By working Christ sanctified labor; He "was making ploughs and yokes, by which he taught the symbols of righteousness and an active life."—JUSTIN MARTYR. Is He not the **son of Mary**[2] . . . **James** (Acts 12:17; 21:18; 1 Cor. 15:7; Gal. 1:19; 2:9, 12), who was one of the bishops[3] at Jerusalem soon after 40 A. D. (Acts 15), and surnamed "the Just" for his great piety (Hegesippus, Memoirs, V.; Eus. II. 23, 4 sq.).[4] He probably wrote the epistle of James.[5] The other brothers, (3:32), **Joses, Judas and Simon,** are unknown, like the **sisters**, who were probably married, and lived in Nazareth (*here with us*), while Mary and the brothers dwelt in Capernaum. **And . . . him.** His humble youth, home and work was a stumbling-block, and they rejected His heavenly power. "The beggarly village pride of the Naz-

---

is his, what with the axe belongs to the owner; if he work in the owner's house even the shavings are the owner's." (Delitzsch, as above, p. 42.) This estimate, no doubt actuated the contemptible "carpenter-king" (Tertull. Answer to the Jews, X.), and called forth the sneer of Celsus. (Orig. ag. Celsus, VI., 36.)

[1] Cf. Geikie, p. 9, 155, 209, 437.

[2] This designation of Christ was probably due to the fact that Mary was a widow, for the Nazarenes would not have called Christ by a name, which marked His supernatural birth, even if they had known it.

[3] In the second century James is spoken of as the only bishop, because the developed episcopacy of that time is wrongly attributed to the primitive church. (Clement Alex. Hypot. VI. Eus. II. 1, 3; McGifford, p. 104.)

[4] Hegesippus ascribes an ascetic and essenic character to James, who was rather an earnest Jewish-Christian with a legalistic tendency. He suffered martyrdom about 61 A. D. by being first stoned and then beaten on the head by the club of a fuller. (Jos. Ant. XX. 9, 1; Clement, Hypot. VII.; Orig. I. 47; Eus. II. 1, 4; II. 23.)

[5] Nösgen (II. 47 sq.) argues that James, the son of Alphæus is the author of the epistle; but compare Weiss, Einleitung, p. 388 sq.

arenes cannot at all comprehend the humility of the Great One."—STIER. Christ's humiliation is an offence to the natural man. Ver. 4. **Jesus said,** citing a common proverb applicable to Himself, **A prophet,** one who having been granted a view of God's mysteries is their authorized proclaimer,[1] **is . . . country,** i. e. native city (ver. 1), **and . . . kin** (3 : 21), **and . . . house** (3 : 32). Christ, *the* prophet (Deut. 18 : 15), suffers the common lot of all prophets, even from those that are near, nearer, and nearest. "It is not proper to despise those, whom we have known from their youth, for God can have given gifts that we have not seen previously."—OSIANDER, STARKE. Ver. 5. And Christ **could . . . work,** except healing a **few sick folk,** not because of any inability of His own, but from the utter perverseness of the Nazarenes, who would have abused His grace. According to the small measure of the faith of the *few* He helped, but "the door was shut on the Saviour by the people's impiety." —CALVIN. Ver. 6. **And he . . . unbelief.** As Christ marvels at the greatness of the faith of the Gentile centurion (Matt. 8 : 10), He likewise marvels at the unreasonableness of the unbelief of the Nazarenes, who in this particular are a type of all Jews. Faith and unbelief stir up the amazement of Jesus.

7–13. And he called unto him the twelve, and began to send them forth by two and two; and he gave them authority over the unclean spirits; and he charged them that they should take nothing for *their* journey, save a staff only; no bread, no wallet, no money in their purse; but *to go* shod with sandals; and, *said he*, put not on two coats. And he said unto them, Wheresoever ye enter into a house, there abide till ye depart thence. And whatsoever place shall not receive you, and they hear you not, as ye go forth thence, shake off the dust that is under your feet for a testimony unto them. And they went out, and preached that *men* should repent. And

---

[1] Cremer, p. 292. προφήτης is the equivalent of Nāvî, on which see Ohler, O. T. Theology, p. 363.

they cast out many devils, and anointed with oil many that were sick, and healed them.

Ver. 7. Jesus *began to send forth* the twelve **by two and two**, not singly that they might sustain each other, and not in threes because the laborers were few (Matt. 9 : 37). In missionary work isolation is to be avoided for the sake of the messengers, and overcrowding because of the greatness of the field. Deputed with authority (3 : 15) Christ, Ver. 8, **charged . . . journey.** Without any preparation of provisions or clothing they were to depart, relying on what they would receive. "Ministers of the Word are worthy of their hire and bread."—HEDINGER, STARKE. They might take **a staff,** which they had, but they were not to provide one;[1] but *no bread, no* **wallet,** the leathern bag of shepherds (1 Sam. 17 : 40) or peasants used to carry provisions;[2] **no money,** i. e. copper money, not even the smallest coins[3] **in their purse,** the pocket of their girdle (Aphundah). Ver. 9. They were **to go . . . sandals,** having the ordinary coarse sandals of skin or palm-bark,[4] but no additional pair; and said He, **put . . . coats,** "inner garments" (Chaluq), which "lay close to the body and had no other opening than that round the neck and for the arms. To possess only one such coat was a mark of poverty."—EDERSHEIM. But "the servants of the gospel obtain, while they supremely regard the end, all the other equipments and resources."— LANGE. Ver. 10. **Wheresoever . . . thence.** The house,

[1] This is the readiest solution of the apparent contradiction with Matt. 10 : 10. That "staff" has various meanings (Augustine, De Cons. XXX. 71 sq.; Calvin), and that the staff prohibited was one for defence, not for travel (Bleek, Cook), is not indicated. Cf. Robinson, p. 221.
[2] Thomson, I., p. 532.
[3] "Even to-day the farmer sets out on excursions quite as extensive without a para in his purse." (Thomson, I., p. 533.)
[4] Morison, p. 146; Farrar, p. 211.

whose hospitality[1] was first extended to them, should remain their home, however humble it was. An easily satisfied and contented disposition should mark Christ's messengers. Ver. 11. **Whatsoever place** (region) . . . **you**, and the people **hear . . . them**. The testimony given by the symbolical act of shaking off the dust from the sandals was the breaking off of communion with those doomed to judgment (Luke. 10 : 11 ; Acts 18 : 6) by permitting nothing[2] banned to cleave even to the feet. " No crime is more offensive to God, than contempt of His word."—CALVIN. Ver. 12. And the disciples *went out and preached* repentance (1 : 15). Ver. 13. Casting out devils they **anointed . . . them** (James 5 : 14). The oil, frequently used as medicine (Isai. 1 : 6; Luke 10 : 34) by the ancients,[3] was the natural medium of the divine curative power through the word, like the spittle employed by Jesus (7 : 33; 8 : 23; John 9 : 6); but it was no necessary channel of the divine healing power (Acts 3 : 7; 9 : 34), nor did it impart spiritual grace.[4]

14-29. And king Herod heard *thereof:* for his name had become known : and he said, John the Baptist is risen from the dead, and therefore do these powers work in him. But others said, It is Elijah. And others said, *It is* a prophet, *even* as one of the prophets. But Herod, when he heard *thereof,* said, John whom I beheaded, he is risen. For Herod himself had sent forth and laid hold upon John, and bound him in prison for the sake of Herodias, his brother Philip's wife: for he had married her. For John said unto Herod, It is not lawful for thee to have thy brother's wife. And Herodias set herself against him, and desired to kill him ; and she could not; for Herod feared John, knowing that he was a righteous man and a holy, and

---

[1] Cf. Trumbull, in the Chapter on Hospitality in the East, p. 73 sq.

[2] " Anything that clave to a person was metaphorically called dust." (Edersheim.)

[3] Celsus (De Med. 2, 14, 17 ; 3, 6, 9, etc.) ; Jos. (Ant. XVII., 6, 5) ; Horace II., Satires, 1, 7.

[4] Tertullian (Ad. Scap. IV.) attributes to it only a bodily effect, but cf. Cyprian, Ep. LXIX. 2.

kept him safe. And when he heard him, he was much perplexed; and he heard him gladly. And when a convenient day was come, that Herod on his birthday made a supper to his lords, and the high captains, and the chief men of Galilee; and when the daughter of Herodias herself came in and danced, she pleased Herod and them that sat at meat with him; and the king said unto the damsel, Ask of me whatsoever thou wilt, and I will give it thee. And he sware unto her, Whatsoever thou shalt ask of me, I will give it thee, unto the half of my kingdom. And she went out, and said unto her mother, What shall I ask? And she said, The head of John the Baptist. And she came in straightway with haste unto the king, and asked saying, I will that thou forthwith give me in a charger the head of John the Baptist. And the king was exceeding sorry; but for the sake of his oaths, and of them that sat at meat, he would not reject her. And straightway the king sent forth a soldier of his guard, and commanded to bring his head: and he went and beheaded him in the prison, and brought his head in a charger, and gave it the damsel; and the damsel gave it to her mother. And when his disciples heard *thereof*, they came and took up his corpse, and laid it in a tomb.

Ver. 14. *And* **king Herod** heard of Christ. This was Herod Antipas, son of Herod the Great and Malthace the Syrian, the tetrarch ruling Galilee and Peræa until after Christ's ascension. Moved by his wife he went to Rome to seek the exclusive kingship, but was deposed by Caligula and banished to Lyons, where he died A. D. 39. He was ambitious, fond of pleasure and debauchery, cunning, superstitious and changeable. **He**[1] **said, ... dead,** which he maintained against other opinions (ver. 15, 16), fettered by a ghostly dread and evil forebodings in his conscience, that could not shake off the apparent evidence. **Therefore** *do these powers work in* **him.** Herod supposes that, owing to his wonderful return, John, who previously performed no miracles, has brought miraculous power from the unseen world. The carnal despot, who had not heeded the warning of the Word, becomes the slave of superstitious spiritualism. Ver. 15. **But ... Elijah.** Many of the people did not receive Christ as Messiah because of

---

[1] According to ℵ, A, C, L, Δ.

His lack of outward glory, but held Him to be the special forerunner, Elijah, whom by a misinterpretation of Mal. 4 : 5 they expected to return personally. **And others**, not valuing Christ as highly, **said . . . prophets**, an ordinary prophet like those of old. " The judgments of this world are always out of square, when they deal with spiritual things."—HEDINGER, LANGE. Ver. 17. **Herod . . . prison**, Machærus nine miles east of the northern end of the Dead Sea, **for the . . . her.** Herod Antipas while at Rome (Jos. Antiq. XVIII., 5, 1) the guest of his brother Philip, son of Herod the Great and Marianne, but not the ruler of Trachonitis, stole the heart of Herodias, his niece, daughter of Aristobulus, and abandoned his own faithful wife, the daughter of Aretas, king of Arabia, who for this cause made war upon Antipas and defeated him. Ver. 18. **John . . . lawful** (Lev. 18 : 16) **. . . wife.** John was as fearless before the tetrarch as before common soldiers (Luke 3 : 14), and truly faithful to his king.[1] " Whoever is in the ministry must not value his life, but do justice to his office, and without dread correct all that is offensive." —LUTHER. Ver. 19. *And* because of John's truthfulness *Herodias*, who had inherited her grandfather's unscrupulous cruelty, **set . . . him.** Her revengeful spirit sought the death of him, who dared to disturb her sinful indulgence. " They that are something special in office, money or property, suppose that because they do what pleases them, other people, especially preachers, should say what pleases them."—LUTHER. *But* Herodias *could not* obtain her wish; Ver. 20, **for Herod feared John**, partly because the people held him to be a prophet (Matt. 14 : 5),[2] but especially **knowing** *that he was a*

---

[1] Besser mentions the similar case of Frederick of Devon, nephew of Boniface, who censured the Emperor Louis for having his half-sister as wife.

[2] With this partial motive, related by Matthew, the account of Josephus

righteous **man** (Matt. 1 : 19), therefore acceptable to God, and **a holy,** a prophet of God (1 : 24). The wicked ruler fears his subject, who has such unimpeachable righteousness in his holy office. "Piety is still revered by the wildest children of the world."—HEDINGER, STARKE. And *when he heard* **him** having called him from prison at times to have him preach, **he** *was much* **perplexed;**[1] his worse and better self were in conflict, the one urging to revenge, the other under the impression of John's preaching reasserting itself. But still Herod **heard** *him* **gladly,** charmed by John's character and earnest eloquence, but he never decided for the truth (Acts 26 : 28). Ver. 21. **And when . . . come** for Herodias, the N. T. Jezebel, to vent her long-harbored hate, she grasped at it (ver. 24). **Herod** *on his* **birthday,** the celebration of which the Jews generally disapproved of,[2] *made a supper to his* **lords,** the highest civil officials, *and the* **high captains,** the high military commanders of a thousand men, *and the* **chief men of Galilee,** the most distinguished men of the district, but not in Herod's service ; Ver. 22, **the**[3] *daughter of* **Herodias,** Salome, who was born before Herodias left her first husband, and afterward married Philip, the tetrarch, **came** *in and* **danced** one of the voluptuous eastern dances, like an ordinary dancing-girl,[4] for "the unchaste Herodias had moulded her daughter to her own manner."— CALVIN. This **pleased . . . him,** because it was skilful and gratified their depraved sensual taste already

(Ant. XVIII. 5. 2) agrees, which describes the resultant of the common opinion upon Herod as jealousy of John in his popularity and fear of an insurrection.

[1] This is the better reading, supported by ℵ, B, L.

[2] Lightfoot, Exercit. on Matt. 14 : 6.

[3] Weiss holds "his" of ℵ, B, D, L, to be a mechanical repetition from the previous verse.

[4] Thomson, II., p. 345 sq.

inflamed by drink. "The festivities of the world are the best appointed tables of sin."—QUESNEL, LANGE. **And . . . damsel . . . thee.**[1] Herod in his drunken generosity makes a most extravagant promise as a reward for the gratification so unexpectedly provided. Ver. 23. *And he* **sware** that he would give her what she desired **unto the half of his kingdom.** Attempting to equal the royal munificence of Ahasuerus (Est. 5 : 3, 6), Herod in his revelrous braggadocio binds himself carelessly with an oath, that causes great evil. For the maiden, upon her mother's instruction (ver. 24), Ver. 25, **came . . . haste,** as if about to receive a joyous gift and said with unhesitating boldness : **I will** *that thou forthwith give me in a* **charger,**[2] a large platter, **the head of John the Baptist.** Her words and her eager demand are the echo of the short decisive answer of her mother (ver. 24), who will have no delay, that the king might not retract in his regard for John (ver. 20), whose head was to be actually presented that there should be no error, and that Herodias could gratify her long-pent-up vindictiveness. Ver. 26. **And the king** *was exceedingly* **sorry** for John's sake, **but for . . . her** The rash oath is wrongly kept in a mistaken constraint of royal honor, which Herod would not compromise because of those that were present ; and thus murder is added to careless swearing, for sin leads to sin. "The oath is sinful and therefore null, when it cannot be carried out except with sin and injustice."—QUESNEL, STARKE. Ver.

---

[1] Holtzmann, who arbitrarily fixes the birth of Salome from the recorded birth of her father and mother, claims that she must have been at least twenty years old and probably a widow ; but see for the contrary Jos. (Ant. XVIII. 5, 4), where Salome's wedding is mentioned subsequent to the marriage of Herodias, which is said to have taken place shortly after Salome's birth.

[2] "Charger" is derived from the French "charger" and Old English "charge," to load. It is that on which anything is laid.

27. **The king ... guard**[1] **... his head** to Salome, who presented it to her mother. "The Lord, in whose sight the death of His saints is precious, did not prevent this shameful death, that the fidelity of his witness might shine the brighter, who would rather lay his head upon the king's platter than sit at the king's table with a silenced mouth."—BESSER. Ver. 29. When John's **disciples ... tomb.** Fearlessly they confess their teacher by this loving service, and give him an honorable burial.[2] Even after death God will have the man honored, that honors him.

30-44. And the apostles gather themselves together unto Jesus; and they told him all things, whatsoever they had done, and whatsoever they had taught. And he saith unto them, Come ye yourselves apart into a desert place, and rest awhile. For there were many coming and going, and they had no leisure so much as to eat. And they went away in the boat to a desert place apart. And *the people* saw them going, and many knew *them*, and they ran there together on foot from all the cities and outwent them. And he came forth and saw a great multitude, and he had compassion on them, because they were as sheep not having a shepherd: and he began to teach them many things. And when the day was now far spent, his disciples came unto him, and said, The place is desert, and the day is now far spent: send them away, that they may go into the country and villages round about, and buy themselves somewhat to eat. But he answered and said unto them, Give ye them to eat. And they say unto him, Shall we go and buy two hundred pennyworth of bread, and give them to eat? And he saith unto them, How many loaves have ye? go *and* see. And when they knew, they say, Five, and two fishes. And he commanded them that all should sit down by companies upon the green grass. And they sat down in ranks, by hundreds, and by fifties. And he took the five loaves and the two fishes, and looking up to heaven, he blessed, and brake the loaves; and he gave to the disciples to set before them; and the two fishes divided he among them all. And they did all eat, and were filled. And they took up broken pieces, twelve basketfuls, and also of the fishes. And they that ate the loaves were five thousand men.

[1] σπεκουλάτωρ from the Latin, speculator, spy, watchman, and finally bodyguard, sometimes as executioner, in which latter sense it is used in the Talmud. (Shabb. 108a.)

[2] According to an old tradition John was buried in Samaria beside Elijah and Obadiah, but this cannot be verified.

Ver. 30. **And the apostles** (3 : 14), called thus by Mark only here, *gathered unto Jesus* on the western shore of the sea of Galilee, reporting about their mission (ver. 7 sq.), which was not without success, as the honorable title "apostle" proves. "We should thus wait on our ministry that we may joyously give account to Christ, the chief shepherd.—OSIANDER, STARKE. Ver. 31. **He saith, Come apart**, lit. privately (9 : 28; 13 : 3; Matt. 24 : 3; Luke 9 : 10), **into a desert place**, the uninhabited table-land on the eastern shore, and **rest a while** (1 : 35). Faithful labor deserves rest, but in Christ's vineyard it dare only be for a short time. Such rest the disciples could not find where they were, *for there were* **many coming and going.** The people on their passover journey to Jerusalem (John 6 : 4) came and went from Jesus in great crowds. Ver. 32. Jesus and the twelve **went . . . desert** near the eastern Bethsaida (Luke 9 : 10).[1] Ver. 33. **And . . . knew** (**them**[2]), i. e. understood that they were withdrawing; *they* (the multitude) **ran together** *on foot from all* **the cities,** wherever those that had seen Jesus depart spread the news on their journey by land around the lake, and all **outwent** Jesus. In their eager haste they easily travelled the twenty miles in less than the five hours it would take the boat (Cook). "Who is earnest about going to Christ will let no way and expense rue him."—HEDINGER, STARKE. Ver. 34. When Jesus *came forth* from the boat, and saw the multitude **he had . . . shepherd.** They were spiritually astray and famished (Matt. 9 : 36; Jer. 50 : 6; Ezek. 34 : 5, 6; Zech. 10 : 2, 3) because their shepherds not only were ignorant

---

[1] Jos. Ant. XVIII. 2, 1.
[2] "Them," αὐτοὺς and not αὐτοί (E, F, G, etc.), although found in ℵ, A, K, L, M, etc., is wanting in B, D, and seems to be an attempt to interpret the misunderstood "knew." (Cf. Weiss, p. 226; Keil, p. 74.)

of the true pasture (Ps. 23 : 2) but also fed themselves (Ezek. 34 : 2, 3). Therefore the good Shepherd, who came to seek and save the lost, is deeply moved, and *began to* **teach** *them* **many things** and heal (Matt. 14 : 14; Luke 9 : 11). The relaxation, which Christ and the twelve need, is given up in ministering to the people, whom Jesus taught all day. " The preaching of the Word should never be too long, the more the better " (Acts 20 : 7).—STARKE. Ver. 35. **When** . . . **came** in anxious care asking Jesus to dismiss the people, that they might go and buy food in the nearest villages (ver. 36). Ver. 37. *But He answered*,[1] **Give ye them to eat.** With this injunction Jesus tries their faith. It ought to have reminded them of 2 Kings 4 : 42, 43, and in view of their greater master produced a trustful petition to Him. But they say, **Shall** *we go and buy* **two hundred pennyworth**, a large sum [2] which we do not even possess, **of bread**, barley-cakes, which were considered mean food,[3] **and** *give them to* **eat?** Impossibilities hem in the disciples. In their doubting question they say, that not even enough of the coarsest fare can be bought for so large a sum. " They can calculate well, but they will not believe and see what a master they have in Christ."—LUTHER. Ver. 38. **He saith,** . . . **see.** Christ orders them to see what provisions can

---

[1] In connection with the words of Matthew (14 : 16), "they have no need to go away," which preceded the command, Augustine, to harmonize this account with John 6 : 6, well says : " We are to suppose that after these words the Lord looked at the multitude and spake to Philip in the terms which John records " (De Cons. II. 46). Cf. also Nebe, II., p. 190.

[2] The penny is the Roman denarius, about equal to 16 cents, and the ordinary day wage (Matt. 20 : 2). Two hundred pennies includes " the idea of a large amount " (Lightfoot).

[3] In the Talmud (Pesach. 3, 2) Rabbi Jochanan is reported to have said, Barley is good, whereupon he received the answer, Tell that to horses and asses (1 Kings 4 : 28). Nebe II., p. 194; Edersheim, I., p. 681.

be found among them. These He will use and bless, knowing, "I will divide and multiply otherwise than you."—STIER. *And when the disciples* **knew,** having found a lad (John 6 : 9), **they say,** *Five; and* **two fishes.** These dried or pickled were generally eaten with bread.[1] So small were the supplies, that the disciples might despair. But "although the place be a desert, yet He that feeds the world is here."—CHRYSOSTOM. Ver. 39. **He . . . down,** reclining upon their left fore-arm, **in companies** *upon the* **green grass.** The tall grass of early spring would, when turned down, form excellent couches for the people, who were to be arranged in groups. Christ ever adheres to the heavenly law of order (1 Cor. 14 : 33). Ver. 40. **And** *they* **sat down** in believing obedience and expectation, the new life of nature itself being prophetic, **in ranks,** lit. in flower-beds, to which they could aptly be compared in their bright variously-colored garments among the green grass. They sat **by hundreds, and by fifties,** i. e. not in respective parties of 100 and 50 (Fritzsche, Meyer, Keil, Weiss), but thus that if viewed from end to end, in rank, there were hundred, but if seen laterally, in file, there were fifty (Morison). Ver. 41. Jesus taking the bread and fish, **looking up** *to* **heaven** to the Giver of every good and perfect gift (James 1 : 17), **blessed**[2] God that He might bless the food, and in Jewish manner **brake** the bread. "Christ has taught us by His example, that we cannot partake of our food with holiness and purity, unless we express our gratitude to God, from whom it comes to us" (1 Tim. 4 : 5).—

---

[1] Edersheim (I., p. 682) says they were eaten like sardines, the pickled herrings of Holland and Germany, and the caviar of Russia.

[2] Possibly Jesus used the well-known Jewish table-prayer: "Blessed art Thou, Jehovah our God, King of the world, Who causest bread to come forth from the earth."

CALVIN. **Jesus gave . . , them.** While Christ was breaking and giving, the bread increased under His hands (Origen, Augustine, Jerome, Luther), but not as the disciples were distributing (Hilary, Ambrose, Calvin). Likewise **the two fishes** *were divided among them* **all.**[1] Christ was as well the Lord of the sea. This miracle, although analogous to the power by which God "every day out of a few seeds raises up on earth immense harvests,"— AUGUSTINE,[2] far transcends every natural process, not only in rapidity of multiplication but chiefly in the lifeless material in which it was wrought. It is a bodily type of the Lord's Supper. Ver. 42. **They . . . filled.** From smallest means Christ satisfied abundantly (Ps. 145 : 16). "We should learn to be pious and follow God's Word earnestly, believing that God will take care that we obtain food and clothing."—LUTHER. Ver. 43. **And they took . . . basketfuls** of the common wicker-baskets called in Jewish writings Kephiphah (Edersheim), *and also of the fishes.* God's gifts are never exhausted, and yet He allows no waste. Ver. 44. *They that ate were* **five thousand men,** without women and children.[3]

45-52. And straightway he constrained his disciples to enter into the boat, and to go before *him* unto the other side to Bethsaida, while he himself sendeth the multitude away. And after he had taken leave of them, he departed into the mountain to pray. And when even was come, the boat was in the midst of the sea, and he alone on the land. And seeing them distressed in rowing, for the wind was contrary unto them, about the fourth watch of the night he cometh unto them, walking on the sea ; and he would have passed by them : but they, when they saw him walking on

---

[1] Clem. Alex. (Strom. VI. 11) denies that the fish increased.

[2] In the 24th Tract. on John, Augustine again uses the comparison with natural growth, which has been much abused. (Trench. p. 211; Nebe, II., p. 204 sq.)

[3] For the allegorical interpretation of this miracle, see Luther, Erl. Ed. 11, p. 139.

the sea, supposed that it was an apparition, and cried out: for they all saw him, and were troubled. But he straightway spake with them, and saith unto them, Be of good cheer: it is I; be not afraid. And he went up unto them into the boat; and the wind ceased: and they were sore amazed in themselves; for they understood not concerning the loaves, but their heart was hardened.

Ver. 45. Jesus **constrained** *his disciples to enter* **the boat** to prevent their being carried away by the wrong messianic enthusiasm of the people (John 6 : 15). They were **to go** *before to* **Bethsaida**[1] (fish-town), near Capernaum, the town of Peter, Andrew and Philip (John 1 : 44), possibly the modern Ain Tabigah,[2] where " there is a slight bay, with abundant vegetation growing to the water's edge."—GEIKIE. Christ dismissing the multitude, Ver. 46, **departed** . . . **mountain**, the wild height at the slope of which He had been, **to pray** (1 : 35), probably for His disciples, as before He had set them an example (ver. 41). But Christ's prayer was also a necessity of His truly human nature. He sought communion with the Father (Luke 6 : 12), implored His aid (Mark 7 : 34; John 11 : 42), and petitioned for deliverance (Mark 14 : 35) in unswerving faith (Heb. 12 : 2). Ver. 47. **And . . . come**, the second evening from twilight to utter darkness, **the boat . . . land**. Jesus was not in the boat as in a former storm (4 : 35 sq.), but left the twelve to learn their weakness. But He kept them in His care. Ver. 48. **Seeing . . . contrary** They labored in vain against a northwestern hurricane. Christ allows them to struggle all night to arouse their faith, while looking upon them not

---

[1] Klostermann connects "to Bethsaida" with the dismissal of the multitude, accepting only an eastern Bethsaida. Lange, Thomson, Holtzmann, Riddle, Furrer, argue for one Bethsaida. But it is more than probable that there was a western one (Matt. 11 : 21; Luke 10 : 13). Cf. Keil, p. 89.

[2] Robinson, Later Researches, p. 358; Porter, Syria, p. 405; Geikie, p. 135.

as an idle spectator but in praying hope, ready to help. Jesus sees us when we think Him far off. **About** *the* **fourth watch of the night**, the morning watch[1] between 3 and 6 o'clock, **he cometh . . . sea**. The raging sea becomes a path (Ps. 77 : 19) as He treadeth upon the waves (Job 9 : 8) in the power of His divine (Prov. 30 : 4) and human (Ps. 8 : 6) sonship. His love, which generally found it necessary to restrain His extraordinary power, now needs it. **He . . . them**, walking not toward them but alongside as though to escape them, that they might call Him (cf. Luke 24 : 29). This is hardest to bear in trials that Jesus apparently passes by. Ver. 49. The disciples **supposed . . . troubled**. "The sight troubles them no less than the storm" (Chrysostom), because of their superstitious fear that it was a messenger of death. "This is the fault of our sin, that will not permit us to recognize His presence, but considers Him to be an apparition, yea, Satan. He appears otherwise than we think and keeps silence. In trial we hold that God is not God, but a terrible apparition, that will devour us in our troubles." —LUTHER. Ver. 50. But Christ said **Be of good cheer** (Act. 23 : 11) **. . . be not afraid**. (Gen. 15 : 1 ; 26 : 24; Matt. 28 : 5 ; Luke 2 : 10 ; Rev. 1 : 17). Thus the Lord reassures His disciples as they are brought face to face with His glory, exhibiting His "I" in grace. "That the majesty and miraculous presence of 'it is I' may not frighten, He surrounds it on both sides with a comforting assurance."—STIER. Ver. 51. And after Peter's petition, attempt and rescue (Matt. 14 : 28 sq.) **he . . . boat**[2] **. . .**

---

[1] The "watches" are evidently the Roman, of which there were four in the twelve hours of the night. The Jews generally had three watches, including nine hours, but later they adopted the Roman computation.

[2] The boat has often been compared to the Church tossed upon the waves of the world, but ever rescued by her Lord.

ceased. The storm becomes a calm (Ps. 107 : 29) before Christ. "Where Jesus is, there is peace."—Tüb. Bible, STARKE. Ver. 52. The disciples *were* **sore amazed in themselves.** Beyond themselves with wonder in their souls, they first kept silence, then confessed (Matt. 14 : 33). This confession was the clearing up of the amazement in which **they understood not** *concerning* **the loaves.** The lesson of this miracle had been lost on them; **their heart,** the very centre of their personal life,[1] **was hardened.** They were in a condition of non-receptivity for the mystery of Christ's divine power. This was not due to conscious obstinacy (3 : 5), but natural blindness. It is "a warning to us respecting the corruption of our understanding, that we may seek from the Lord new eyes." —CALVIN.

53-56. And when they had crossed over, they came to the land unto Gennesaret, and moored to the shore. And when they were come out of the boat, straightway *the people* knew him, and ran round about that whole region, and began to carry about on their beds those that were sick, where they heard he was. And wheresoever he entered, into villages, or into cities, or into the country, they laid the sick in the market-places, and besought him that they might touch if it were but the border of his garment: and as many as touched him were made whole.

Ver. 53. **They ... land**[2] **... Gennesaret,** the fertile crescent-shaped plain, mentioned only here and Matt. 14 : 34, northwest of the sea, about four miles long and one mile deep (1 : 38). In this region all knew Christ (3 : 7), and, Ver. 55 **ran .. sick** (2 : 4), **where** *they heard he* **was.** The afflicted were brought to Jesus where He could be found,

---

[1] Cremer, p. 495; Delitzsch, Bibl. Psychol. IV. par. 12; Öhler, O. T. Theol., p. 152.

[2] "To the land," omitted by A, D, M, seems original and corresponds with the meaning of γῆν, as distinguished from the sea. Before Gennesaret χώραν would be necessary.

and if He had departed from one place the carriers of the sick followed until they found Him. Ver. 56. **Whereso- ever . . . places,** the open centres through which Christ had to pass, and **besought . . . touched** in faith like the woman with the issue of blood (5 : 27) **were healed.** Notwithstanding the superstitious element in their faith, Christ " that He may not quench the smoking flax (Isai. 42 : 3) accommodated Himself to their ignorance. The weakness of those who, not knowing that Christ is God, desired to make a nearer approach to Him, was endured for a time."—CALVIN.

CHAPTER VII.

1–23. And there are gathered together unto him the Pharisees, and certain of the scribes, which had come from Jerusalem, and had seen that some of his disciples ate their bread with defiled, that is, unwashen, hands. For the Pharisees, and all the Jews, except they wash their hands diligently, eat not, holding the tradition of the elders; and *when they come* from the marketplace, except they wash themselves, they eat not: and many other things there be, which they have received to hold, washings of cups, and pots, and brazen vessels. And the Pharisees and the scribes ask him, Why walk not thy disciples according to the tradition of the elders, but eat their bread with defiled hands? And he said unto them, Well did Isaiah prophesy of you hypocrites, as it is written,

>This people honoreth me with their lips,
>But their heart is far from me.
>But in vain do they worship me,
>Teaching *as their* doctrines the precepts of men.

Ye leave the commandment of God, and hold fast the tradition of men. And he said unto them, Full well do ye reject the commandment of God, that ye may keep your tradition. For Moses said, Honor thy father and thy mother; and, He that speaketh evil of father or mother, let him die the death: but ye say, If a man shall say to his father or his mother, That wherewith thou mightest have been profited by me is Corban, that is to say, Given *to God;* ye no longer suffer him to do aught for his father or his mother; making void the word of God by your tradition, which ye have delivered: and many such like things ye do. And he called to him the multitude again, and said unto them, Hear me all of you and understand: there is nothing from without the man, that going into him can defile him: but the things which proceed out of the man are those that defile the man. And when he was entered into the house from the multitude, his disciples asked of him the parable. And he saith unto them, Are ye so without understanding also? Perceive ye not, that whatsoever from without goeth into the man, *it* cannot defile him; because it goeth not into his heart, but into his belly, and goeth out into the draught? *This he said*, making all meats clean. And he said, That which proceedeth out of the man, that defileth the man. For from within, out of the heart of men, evil thoughts proceed, fornications, thefts, murders, adulteries, covetings, wickednesses, deceit, lasciviousness, an evil eye, railing, pride, foolishness: all these evil things proceed from within, and defile the man.

Ver. 1. And during Christ's circuit in Galilee, *there are gathered together* with determined purpose *the Pharisees* (2 : 16) and *certain of the scribes* (2 : 6), *which had* **come** *from* **Jerusalem** (3 : 22). A special deputation of Jerusalem scribes, the most authoritative conservators of tradition, are sent to assist the Galilean Pharisees in finding testimony to accuse and condemn Christ. "As Christ and His disciples had their spies, even thus the pious are not without their detractors."—MAJUS, STARKE. Ver. 2. And the Galilean Pharisees *had seen*,[1] *that some of his disciples* on their missionary tour (6 : 7 sq.) **ate . . . hands.** Mark explains "defiled"[2] (common, Rom. 14 : 14) by ceremonially unwashed, and continues to relate to his Gentile readers the Jewish custom of ceremonial washings. Ver. 3. *The Pharisees* most especially, but also **all . . . diligently**,[3] i. e. lit. with the fist with which the hollow of the hand was rubbed, when the water was poured on [4]

---

[1] This new sentence is left unfinished because of the parenthetical interpolation of ver. 3 and 4.

[2] The Hebrew term is Tāmē (Delitzsch), and the later Rabbinic word Chōe.

[3] πυγμῃ (A, B, L, N, etc.) rather than πυκνά, of ℵ, Peshito, Itala and Vulgate, "crebro," which rests upon an emendation.

[4] The translation "diligently" is derived from the Peshito, which employs the same word here, as in Luke 15 : 8, for ἐπιμελῶς. The energy of the fist rubbing would serve to explain this, which is, however, not found elsewhere. The marginal interpretation "up to the elbow," first used by Theophylact, conceives of πυγμῃ as a measure of length. Lightfoot rendered " to the wrist," like Bengel and Edersheim, who supports it from Rabbinic usage, as Scaliger had Theophylact's rendering. It seems best to retain the literal meaning, which is not inconsistent with Rabbinic custom (Edersheim, II., p. 11), rather than the weakly supported "diligently," the questionable "up to the elbow," and the linguistically untenable "up to the wrist."

(Beza, Grotius, Calov. Fritzsche, Bleek, De Wette, Meyer, Klostermann, Weiss, Keil, Nösgen), *eat not*,[1] *holding the* **tradition of the elders**. The honorable name "elders" was applied in Christ's time especially to Hillel and Schammai, who had agreed on eighteen points concerning purification, which came to be universally accepted, and, as they had been solemnly re-enacted by the schools of the two elders, could not be modified. These laws, the omission of which was said to bring poverty,[2] or temporal destruction,[3] to make bread filth,[4] and excommunicated,[5] were put into force[6] shortly before Christ. They were placed above the Scriptures because they were oral ordinances of the scribes.[7] These men of tradition,[8] so scrupulous of "cleanness without, within were full of stains."—AUGUSTINE. Ver. 4. Coming from the *market-place, except* **they wash themselves**,[9] not by bathing (Meyer), but by an effusion or sprinkling (cf. Num. 8:7; 19:13, etc.; Ezek. 36:25; Hebr. 9:13; 10:22), to become clean from the defilement contracted by contact (Lev. 15:11) in the market-place. In like manner there are many other laws about *washings of* wooden [10] *cups and*

---

[1] It is related of Rabbi Akiba, that when in prison and furnished with only enough water to preserve life, he preferred to die rather than eat without ceremonial ablutions. Buxtorf, Syn. Jud., p. 236; Stier, II. 154; Farrar, p. 313.

[2] Shabb. 62b.   [3] Sota, 4b.   [4] Sota, 4b.
[5] Eduy. v. 6; Ber. 19a.   [6] Edersheim, II., p. 9 sq.
[7] Jer. Chag. 76d; Jer. Ber. 3b; Sanh. XI. 3; Erub. 31b; Edersheim, II., p. 15. Cf. also Jos. Antiq. XIII. 10, 6.

[8] For the similarity of the Romish doctrine of tradition to the Jewish, see Chemnitz, Examen Conc. Trid., Præf. Sect. III.

[9] The βαπτίσωνται of ℵ, B, is an interpretative substitution for the original ῥαντίσωνται of A, D, Γ, Π, etc.

[10] None of the vessels could be earthen, as these, when defiled, were to be broken (Lev. 15:12). The Talmudic tractate Kelim gives details. On all purifications, see Schürer, II. 401 sq.

pots, which latter, containing about a pint, were the Roman sextarii, sixths, being the sixth part of a congius; and **brazen vessels,** lit. coppers, large copper caldrons, and *reclining couches*,[1] which had been defiled by ceremonially unclean persons. Ver. 5. *The Pharisees and the scribes ask* Jesus, **Why . . . elders** (ver. 3), these holy precepts, but *eat* like Gentiles *with defiled hands?* A charge of irreverent transgression of religious law and custom is preferred. "With hypocrites the opinion and doctrine of men is esteemed more highly than God's word."—MAJUS, STARKE. Ver. 6. Jesus answered, **Well . . . hypocrites,** who in apparent zeal for God knowingly bind men by human tradition, that is contradictory to divine law; *as it is written* (1 : 2). Isai. 29 : 13, which is cited according to the Septuagint, and therefore includes the words "in vain" not in the Hebrew original, describes in the condition of the Israel of Hezekiah's time a constant state, greatly aggravated in Christ's day, for which judgment comes. **This** *people honoreth me* merely with their *lips, but their heart is far from* **me.** Their service is empty heartless profession and observance. Ver. 7. **In vain . . . teaching** not divine truth *as their doctrines,* but *human precepts.* Their worship is useless, since it is not according to divine revelation, but human invention. Ver. 8. **Ye . . . men,**[2] said Jesus, and continued with holy irony, **Full well** (beautifully) **. . . tradition.** The abandonment of divine law (ver. 8) has become conscious rejection, that only *your* tradition

---

[1] "Couches," although wanting in ℵ, B, L, Δ, is to be retained, for its omission is more probable than its addition. These couches, as well as the "coppers," show that βαπτισμοῖς cannot mean immersions.

[2] For the profane notions of God entertained in Jewish tradition, which portrays him wearing the Tallith, the phylactery, studying the Mishna, and in other still grosser anthropomorphisms, see Edersheim, II., p. 15 sq.

may be maintained. You only pretend to serve God, but follow your own will-worship (Col. 2 : 23). "This is the greatest evil before God, to transgress God's commandment for the precepts of men, for it means putting God below men."—LUTHER. Christ proves His charge. Ver. 10. **Moses said,** the mediator of the divine law acknowledged by Jesus (1 : 44) and His enemies, **Honor ... mother** (Exod. 20 : 12; Deut. 5 : 16). This commandment, cited according to the Septuagint, has the threat Ex. 21 : 17 (Lev. 20 : 9; Deut. 27 : 16) added, to show that an evil word against parents was deserving of death. The selection of the fourth commandment, with its severe threat rather than its gracious promise (Eph. 6 : 2), was prompted by the special injury it had received in tradition, which made void its fundamental importance, for it contains "the germs of all fear of God and love of the neighbor, all piety and morality in church and state."—STIER. Ver. 11, 12. Against it **ye say ... mother.** Christ mentions a real case,[1] for if any one would simply say "Corban"[2] (gift) which the R. V. renders "given to God," that over which it was pronounced was absolutely banned and considered as already on the altar; and although no actual gift was ever made the vow[3] was constantly binding against the parents, even when in need. Thus it encouraged selfishly disobedient wickedness against God and parents. Therefore the Pharisees, Ver.

---

[1] Nedarim IX. 1; VIII. 7, in which the very formula here used occurs: Körbān Shĕātāh Nĕhĕnĕh Lī. Edersheim, II., p. 21.

[2] Jos. Ant. IV. 44; Wars, II. 9, 4; C. Ap. I. 22.

[3] Although there are individual passages in the Talmud (Ab. III. 13; Nedar. 9a; 22a), which do not encourage promiscuous vowing, they are overbalanced by others, which were put into practice. Cf. Edersheim, II., p. 19 sq. The monastic vows of the Romish church have the same tendency of causing disobedience to the parents, as this was so clearly seen and

13, **were ... God** (Prov. 20 : 20 ; 28 : 24 ; 30 : 17) not only in this, but in *many such like things.* They were then the transgressors and not the disciples. Thus Christ revealed the hypocrisy of these hypocrites. Ver. 14. *And he called to him the multitude* (6 : 56) *again,* which had respectfully withdrawn when the scribes came, *and said,* **Hear** *me all of you and* **understand**. So important is the truth, that Christ will announce, that every one is called to hear (4 : 3), and inquire after the meaning, concealed as it shall be (4 : 12). Ver. 15. **There ... man.**[1] With Hebrew fulness of form Jesus unfolds the deeper significance of the Levitical law of defilement (Lev. 11 : 39 sq.; 12 ; 13), distinguishing between the unclean meats, which do not actually defile but only by symbolical legal enactment, and the real bodily defilement caused by what proceeds from man in birth, leprosy, death and decomposition. This is to teach that spiritual and moral defilement have their source within man. "It is as though He would say: Keep silence about *going in!* That which proceeds from the man is the whole impurity. If that which proceeds forth were pure, what entered in would not defile."—LUTHER. Ver. 17. *When* Christ *entered the house* in which He was staying at that place (6 : 10) to escape *the multitude, the disciples,* Peter being the spokesman (Matt. 15 : 15), **asked** *of him the* **parable**, which rests upon the double sense, the Levitical and moral, of entering and proceeding, clean and unclean. Ver. 18. Christ **saith ... also?** (cf. 6 : 52). Jesus is astonished that even His disciples, after the previous teaching and interpretation of parables (4 : 13), are to such degree unskilled

---

well expressed by Luther's father, in his citation of the fourth commandment. See J. Köstlin, Martin Luther, u. s. w. I. p. 84.

[1] Ver. 16 (4 : 9) is properly omitted according to ℵ, B, L, Δ. The word "parable" (ver. 17) may have caused its introduction.

in seeing the obvious meaning of His parable. The cause is the clinging to the outward (8 : 14 sq.), yet "the gentle teacher is not angered in accommodating Himself to the hardness of the hearing of His disciples."—BESSER. He said, **Perceive,** Ver 19, **clean ?**[1] All meats are really indifferent, as they enter the **belly** (Rom. 16 : 18), which with the meats is corruptible (1 Cor. 6 : 13). The laws of meats are therefore to pass away (Acts 10 : 14, 15), and while considerate love will bear the weak (Rom. 14 : 13 sq.) who still adhere to distinctions of meats, it is under no restrictions of these human precepts (Col. 2 : 22), which will become doctrines of demons (1 Tim. 4 : 1 sq.). The **heart** (6 : 52) is the living, eternal centre, for whose sake even the Levitical laws had been given. And therefore "an eating or non-eating had first to proceed from the heart." STIER. God can never be worshipped by meats; who does this "is merely as one, who has his belly for his lord." —NOVATIAN. What is eaten receives purification in a natural way, coming into the **draught,**[2] which as the place of refuse symbolizes the process preceding. Ver. 20. **That . . . man,** the natural man, *defileth.* Sin is the real defilement coming from our unclean Adamitic nature (Ps. 14 : 3). Ver. 21. **For . . . heart** (Prov. 6 : 14; Jer. 17 : 9) proceed **evil thoughts,**[3] inward reasonings of sin (Gen. 6 : 5; 8 : 21; Ps. 56 : 5; Rom. 1 : 21), the first-

---

[1] καθαρίζον (א, A, B, E, F) used by Origen is an anacoluthic nominative (Weiss, Winer, p. 532), and the whole clause is appositional (Winer, p. 624). This is more natural than the view of Chrysostom (Hom. LI. on Matt.) adopted by the revisers, that it is a parenthetical statement of Mark ; for Mark nowhere uses such a form.—Stier, 2, p. 167.

[2] ἀφεδρῶνα, a "barbarous term" (Suidas) for ἀφοδος (2 Kings 10 : 27), has a Rabbinic equivalent "Aphidra."

[3] διαλογισμός in the N. T. even without κακός has generally the signification of objectionable reasonings. The adjective, for whose exact meaning see Trench, Syn. p. 315, increases the force. Cremer, p. 575.

fruits of the heart, and the germs of the other sins; **fornications**[1] (1 Cor. 7 : 2); Ver. 22, **thefts** (Jer. 48 : 27), **murders** (Gal. 5 : 21; Rev. 9 : 21), **adulteries** (Jer. 13 : 27), **covetings**,[2] the desires after more, not only of money, but of every creature, that is beyond the individual. They are preceded as here by sins of impurity 1 Cor. 5 : 11; Eph. 5 : 3, 5; Col. 3 : 5, and followed as in Rom. 1 : 29 by **wickednesses**, which, found again in the plural only Acts 3 : 26, denote the wicked deeds strongly determined by the will directed toward evil,[3] and delighting in it (Luke 11 : 39; 1 Cor. 5 : 8; Eph. 6 : 12). With this term the six plurals, which have marked the many desires and acts[4] in which each peculiar sin has manifested itself, give way to six singulars, which emphasize the unity or habit of sin. **Deceit** (Rom. 1 : 29), cunning craftiness; **lasciviousness** (2 Cor. 12 : 21; Gal. 5 : 19; Eph. 4 : 19),[5] unbridled sensuality; **an evil eye** (Prov. 23 : 6; Matt. 20 : 15), frequently used in the East[6] for the envious look, which betokens the jealous heart; **railing** (blasphemy) (Eph. 4 : 31; Col. 3 : 8; 1 Tim. 6 : 4), the slander of men, not blasphemy of God (3 : 28); **pride** (Ps. 31 : 20), used only here as a noun in the N. T.,[7] is the self-conscious spirit, that

---

[1] The Authorized Version has "adulteries" first, but the order of the Rev. Version is preferable accdg. to א, A, B, L, Δ, Σ.

[2] See Trench, N. T. Syn. p. 81.

[3] Cremer, p. 810.   [4] Winer, p. 176.

[5] ἀσέλγεια (probably from ἀ privative and σέλγω, θέλγω, please) translated "wantonness," Rom. 13 : 13; 2 Pet. 2 : 18 originally meant lawless insolence, but later the meaning lasciviousness obtained.

[6] Thomson, I., p. 219. Fredrick Thomas Elworthy in "The Evil Eye" (1895) has shown that many superstitions were connected with the evil eye, and has traced them almost to prehistoric times. Christ, however, has put into a well-worn word true moral significance, giving both "evil" and "eye" no superstitious value, but actual lasting worth (Matt. 6 : 22, 23).

[7] The adjectival form occurs Luke 1 : 51; Rom. 1 : 30; 2 Tim. 3 : 2; James 4 : 6; 1 Pet. 5 : 5.

lifts itself above others, [1] (Uebermuth); **foolishness** (2 Cor. 11 : 1, 17, 21), the godless folly (Ps. 14 : 1 ; Rom. 1 : 22, 28, 31), placed last, " because it makes all the rest more incurable."—BENGEL. There is no principle of order, as with Matthew (15 : 19) who follows the decalogue, but the many sinful fruits of the heart, that defile, are enumerated in their multiplicity and variety.[2] " All the evil in the human heart cannot be sufficiently related, pitied and mourned for."—STARKE.

24-30. And from thence he arose, and went away into the borders of Tyre and Sidon. And he entered into a house, and would have no man know it: and he could not be hid. But straightway a woman, whose little daughter had an unclean spirit, having heard of him came and fell down at his feet. Now the woman was a Greek, a Syrophœnician by race. And she besought him that he would cast forth the devil out of her daughter. And he said unto her, Let the children first be filled : for it is not meet to take the children's bread and cast it to the dogs. But she answered and saith unto him, Yea, Lord: even the dogs under the table eat of the children's crumbs. And he said unto her, For this saying go thy way ; the devil is gone out of thy daughter. And she went away unto her house, and found the child laid upon the bed, and the devil gone out.

Ver. 24. *From* **thence**, the region near the sea of Galilee (6 : 56), Christ **arose** (cf. Gen. 31 : 13 ; 1 Sam. 23 : 16 ; Jonah 1 : 3), left, and **went . . . Sidon**.[3] He entered the district of these Gentile trading cities, not to convert the Gentiles (Matt. 15 : 24), but " like a private individual,"—CALVIN, to find temporary rest and refuge from Jewish enmity (Luke 4 : 24 sq.). *And he entered a* **house**, prob-

---

[1] Trench, Syn., p. 101.

[2] These words of Christ are the source of the Apostolic catalogues of sin (Gal. 5 : 19 ; Rom. 1 : 21), on which Ruskin aptly remarks : " There is evidently an intense feeling of the universality of sin ; and in order to express it, the Apostle hurries his words confusedly together, little caring about their order, as knowing all the vices to be indissolubly connected one with another."

[3] Sidon, which only D, L, Δ, among the uncials omit, is to be retained.

ably of some Israelite living there, whom He had healed (3 : 8), *and would have no man know it*, seeking seclusion (3 : 20; 4 : 35; 6 : 31): *and he could not* **be hid**, for His name and fame were too great. "A servant of the gospel must desire to remain hid, but without injury and neglect of what he owes his neighbor."—QUESNEL, STARKE. Ver. 25. **Straightway . . . daughter** (5 : 23) . . . **spirit** (1 : 23; EXCURSUS, II. p. 31), . . . **him** placed her hoping confidence on Him. "This report of God is a true gospel and word of grace. Out of it arose faith in this woman" (Rom. 10 : 17).—LUTHER. Trial ripened her faith. She *came* and followed Christ, "and made herself shameless by a goodly shamelessness."—CHRYSOSTOM. Not disturbed by His apparent unwillingness (Matt. 15 : 23), she finally entered the house after Him, *and* **fell** *down at his* **feet** (5 : 33). Her constant faith and clinging hope impelled her to implore Christ more eagerly and humbly, although He had not heard her; for she, Ver. 26, *was a* **Greek**, a Gentile in religion and no Jew (Rom. 1 : 16; Matt. 15 : 24); **a Syrophenician by race.** The addition "by race" shows, that the later mere geographical distinction of Syrophenicia from Libophenicia in Africa (Strabo, 17, 3; Juv. Sat. VIII. 59)[1] is not intended; but the original ethnic character of the woman is to be marked. She belongs to the accursed stock, which Israel ought to have destroyed but did not (Deut. 7 : 2; Judg. 2 : 2, 3). Her nationality is against her. "She is not of Abraham's seed, and has no right to ask anything."—LUTHER. But without a promise she throws herself solely upon grace, and brings honor upon her dishonored people. *She besought* Jesus again. Ver. 27. **And . . dogs.** Christ "vouchsafes no answer, but

---

[1] Sir G. Rawlinson in Smith's Bible Dict. maintains the geographical sense, as do most commentators.

smites the woman more sharply."—CHRYSOSTOM. He asserts that He is sent to give the bread of life **first**[1] (Rom. 1 : 16) to Israel (Rom. 9 : 4), **the children** of the kingdom (Matt. 8 : 12). Therefore *it is not* **meet** (Rom. 14 : 21 ; 1 Cor. 7 : 1 ; Col. 4 : 18), becoming and proper, to rob the children for the sake of the **dogs**, lit. little dogs. The Gentiles were called dogs to designate them as wild, lawless, unclean. But the diminutive "little dogs" is a beautiful modification of Christ, and turns the despised dogs of the street [2] into the little table dogs [3] of the home, which have some claim. Harsh as the Lord's words are, placing the Gentiles below the slaves and largely excluding them, they nevertheless offer hope. "All parts are stronger in *no* than *yes*, and yet there is more *yes* in them than *no :* indeed pure *yes* is in them, but deeply and secretly, and it appears but *no*."—LUTHER. Ver. 28. The woman *answered*, **Yea**, *Lord ;* it is as you say : but **even . . . crumbs.** The woman naturally quick, witty, and spiritually firm in faith, ceaseless in prayer, and truly humble, accepts Christ's position, but draws a wonderful conclusion from it. She "catches Christ in His own words."—LUTHER. In believing humble obedience she claims no place at the table with the children nor demands their bread, but simply asks for the crumbs, that will fall, so that *even* the dogs are filled from the abundant table of the great *Lord*. "What a mighty power is faith ; it takes Christ at His word,

---

[1] Weiss is wrong in affirming that Mark has removed the asperity of the original account as reported by Matthew. The distinction of time in Mark excludes present help, and is the harder by showing a future gift not now to be had. Matthew also has the tender term, "little dogs."

[2] Job 30 : 1 ; 1 Sam. 24 : 14 ; Prov. 26 : 11 ; 2 Peter 2 : 22. See Wood, Bible Animals, p. 40.

[3] That these dogs are table dogs is proved by ver. 28. The κύνες τραπέζης occur in Homer, Odys. 17, 309 ; Iliad, 22 : 69 ; 23, 173.

when He is most angry, and makes comfortable dialectic of His hard words."—LUTHER. Ver. 29. Christ *said*, after praising her great faith (Matt. 15 : 28), **For . . . daughter.** The strong assurance of faith and humble confession received the desired blessing. "What by continual crying she obtained not, she received by humble confession."—AUGUSTINE. Ver. 30. **And . . . bed,** not raving but quietly resting, *and the devil gone out.* Faith becomes sight for this woman. She and the centurion (Matt. 8 : 10) are the two believing Gentiles of the gospels, whose faith puts to shame the children of Israel. The woman's faith is however superior, not merely in its struggling prayer, greater than Jacob's (Gen. 32 : 25 sq.), and surmounting the greatest hindrance not from without (2 : 4), nor of men (10 : 48), but from Christ Himself; but chiefly in its deep humility.

31-37. And again he went out from the borders of Tyre, and came through Sidon unto the sea of Galilee, through the midst of the borders of Decapolis. And they bring unto him one that was deaf, and had an impediment in his speech; and they beseech him to lay his hand upon him. And he took him aside from the multitude privately, and put his fingers into his ears, and he spat, and touched his tongue; and looking up to heaven, he sighed, and saith unto him, Ephphatha, that is, Be opened. And his ears were opened, and the bond of his tongue was loosed, and he spake plain. And he charged them that they should tell no man: but the more he charged them, so much the more a great deal they published it. And they were beyond measure astonished, saying, He hath done all things well: he maketh even the deaf to hear, and the dumb to speak.

Ver. 31. Jesus *went out from the borders of Tyre* to avoid the people crowding about Him to be healed; and since it is too soon to return to Galilee, *came through* **Sidon,** the ancient (Gen. 10 : 19; Josh. 11 : 8; Judg. 1 : 31), wealthy merchant city of Phenicia, on the plain between the Lebanon and the Mediterranean, originally more powerful than Tyre, the old rock-city, which was most prosperous in Christ's day.[1] Thence, possibly keeping along the base of the Lebanon on the road toward Damascus, Christ turned southward, approaching the sea of Galilee on the east, and from the north entered the *borders of Decapolis* (5 : 20), through which He passed. Ver. 32. Some people in the "love that bears another's care,"—LUTHER, **bring . . . speech**.[2] Burdened with an organic defect (ver. 35) this man could not speak rightly, but was not absolutely dumb. *They beseech* Christ *to lay his* **hand** *upon* **him** (5 : 23). But Jesus cannot heal thus; He must awaken personal faith in the man, most afflicted in being deprived of hearing, the noblest sense[3] for receiving the mysteries of the kingdom. "Most people can both hear and speak, but how common is spiritual deafness and dumbness."—ZEISIUS, LANGE. Ver. 33. Christ **took him aside** (8 : 23). The process of healing, which is so circumstantial and visible because thus only could Jesus treat with the man, begins with taking the deaf one privately, not that the people might not

---

[1] Thomson, I., p. 127 sq.; 143 sq.; 154-157; 159; 161. For Tyre espec., p. 260 sq.

[2] μογιλάλος, which together with ςαγάδος is used in the Sept. for Ilêm, dumb (Isai. 35 : 6; Ps. 38 : 13), also expresses "slow of tongue" (Exod. 4 : 11, Theodotion, Aquila, Symmachus), and is equivalent to βατταρίζειν, stutter, wherefore the Peshito has Pakn. The meaning adopted by the Revisers is also confirmed by "spoke right" (ver. 25).

[3] Nebe (III. 232) quotes this excellent account of Steinmeyer (die Wunder, p. 119): "All honor to the eye, but the ear is more important. The superiority of the latter over the former is settled even in the domain of the natural senses. The eye can be closed, if it is so willed; it is so constructed that it may be shut; in sleep it closes of itself. The ear on the contrary can be shut up only by mechanical, unnatural force; even in sleep it is open, and, therefore, the ever-present medium of chasing away sleep. But it is still more evident, that spiritual apperception is mediated rather by the ear than the eye. To the hearing the gospel is addressed. Blessed are they that hear the Word! Where there is no hearing, there is no salvation; for faith comes by hearing."

crowd (Bleek), nor be moved to new demands (Lange, Weiss), but that the man seeing but Jesus might concentrate his whole attention upon Him. (Stier, Keil, Nebe, Nösgen, Cook.) "How graciously does the Lord descend to the peculiar necessity of each one, and does exceeding abundantly above all that we ask and pray."—STIER. Spiritual cure demands isolation with Jesus. *He thrust his fingers into* **his ears,** to show that He knew the source of the evil, which had to be removed first. Speech would not help, if hearing was wanting. The finger (Luke 11:20) of Jesus would pierce the obstacle of the ear. **And . . . tongue.** Christ did not spit upon the deaf man's tongue (Meyer), but wetting His finger moistened the tongue as He did the eyes of the blind (8:23; John 9:6). This was no mere external sign of an invisible efficacy (Grotius), pointing to the truth that what proceeds from the mouth of Jesus His word can heal; but the spittle through the word[1] to be uttered was the bearer of the power (6:13). "Two things belong to a Christian, that his ears be opened and his tongue loosened."—LUTHER. Ver. 34. Jesus **looking** *up to* **heaven** (Matt. 14:19; John 11:41) to show the dumb man that the Father must assist (John 5:17) and to encourage him to pray; and praying Himself (6:46) *he* **sighed** in sadness of spirit (8:12; John 11:33) over the wretched condition of this man, which, like death (John 11:38), represented the natural condition of men. "It is a common sighing over all tongues and ears, yea, over all hearts, bodies and souls of men from Adam even unto the last."—LUTHER.

---

[1] If Nebe objects to the spittle being the medium, and emphasizes the word alone, he is as wrong as Ohlshausen, Meyer, Weiss, Keil, who undervalue the word. It is true here as in the sacrament, "Verbum accedit ad elementum et fit sacramentum."

Then Christ saith: **Ephphatha**[1] ... **opened**. He that calls the things that are not as though they were (Rom. 4 : 17), opens the ear by this word (cf. ver. 33). "Who is mightier than the Lord, who can do with His word, what no one can effect."—STARKE. Ver. 35. **And his ears**, lit. his hearings, the closed passages, **were ... loosened**, which is no figurative term (Weiss, Keil), but tells the actual healing of the tongue-tied man (Nebe). The third feature of this miracle was, *he* **spake plain**, at once, and was not compelled to learn slowly. "They who are healed by Christ and endued by his Spirit, should speak rightly to God's pleasure."—STARKE. Ver. 36. Jesus *charged* the people not to tell (5 : 43), desiring to be hid; **but ... it**. The people, whose hearing has not been opened, have not learnt obedience. They sin, and "unaccustomed to the doctrine of Christ are carried away by an immoderate zeal, when it is not called for." —CALVIN. Ver. 37. **They ... astonished**. Suddenly as some of these people had before (5 : 19) rejected Jesus, others are now carried beyond themselves in wonder of His work, and confess, **He** *hath done all things* **well**. The complete healing of the deaf man is a sign of the accomplishment of all things unto salvation by Christ. The hyperbolic language of the excited people has become sober truth in Jesus the great re-creator (Gen. 1 : 31). **He ... speak**. His finished act shows itself in the present condition of the healed man, which praises Him. What Satan has destroyed, Christ has restored forever.

---

[1] ἐφφαθά is the Aramaic Imperat. Ethpael of Patach used passively. In the transliteration of Ĕthpătăh the Dagesh emphat. in Tau becomes θ.

CHAPTER VIII.

1-10. In those days, when there was again a great multitude, and they had nothing to eat, he called unto him his disciples, and saith unto them, I have compassion on the multitude, because they continue with me now three days, and have nothing to eat: and if I send them away fasting to their home, they will faint in the way; and some of them are come from far. And his disciples answered him, Whence shall one be able to fill these men with bread here in a desert place? And he asked them, How many loaves have ye? And they said, Seven. And he commanded the multitude to sit down on the ground: and he took the seven loaves, and having given thanks, he brake, and gave to his disciples, to set before them; and they set them before the multitude. And they had a few small fishes: and having blessed them, he commanded to set these also before them. And they did eat, and were filled: and they took up, of broken pieces that remained over, seven baskets. And they were about four thousand: and he sent them away. And straightway he entered into the boat with his disciples, and came into the parts of Dalmanutha.

Ver. 1. *In those days,* while Jesus was passing through Decapolis (7 : 31), *there was again*[1] *a great multitude,* that " doubtless had done nothing else than followed the word and desired to hear it."—LUTHER. When the people had nothing to eat Jesus said to His disciples, Ver. 2, *I have* **compassion** (1 : 41; 6 : 34; 9 : 22) *because they continue with me now three days, and have nothing to eat;* Ver. 3, *and if I* dismiss them, *they will faint in the way; and some of them are come from far.* As in the former feeding[2] (6 : 31 sq.). Christ was moved by the bodily need of

---

[1] This is the reading of ℵ, B, D, G, L, etc., and is to be preferred to $\pi\alpha\mu\pi\dot{o}\lambda\lambda o\nu$ (A, E, F, H, etc.).

[2] Although this miracle is considered as identical with the feeding of the five thousand by Schleiermacher, Credner, Fritzsche, Strauss, DeWette.

the people, who do not forget Christ on account of bread as many to-day (Stier.) He sees more clearly the great difficulties, the long stay (3 days) that exhausted the supplies, the desert place, the great distance that some have come. All this "He is concerned about, before they think of asking Him."—LUTHER. He takes counsel with, Ver. 4, *his disciples*, who, not remembering the former lesson (6 : 52), ask, **Whence . . . place?** They show no greater confidence than formerly (ag. Nebe), but are just as helpless and disregard Christ's power. They possess a short memory of the heart for divine benefits, and have not the faith, that "argues from the past to the future and truly derives confidence from God's former dealings of faithfulness and love" (1 Sam. 17 : 34 sq.; 2 Chron. 16 : 7).—TRENCH. "If our counsels were to be considered, God would never do a work that would befit Him as God, therefore it is better that He does everything without our counsel."—LUTHER. The Lord asks the disciples about the means present (ver. 5), and after all are seated in order (ver. 6), blesses bread and fish (ver. 6, 7), which

Hase, Neander, Ewald, Volkmar, Beyschlag, Wendt, Weiss, Holtzmann, and others; it is clearly distinct, as maintained by Augustine, Chrysostom, Jerome, Luther, Calvin, Grotius, Calov, Bengel, Paulus, v. Ammon, Ohlshausen, Lange, Ebrard, Stier, Klostermann, Keil, Nebe, Meyer, Nösgen.

The *locality* of this miracle is further south on the eastern shore. The *time* is toward fall, for the people cannot sit on the grass (6 : 39), but on the bare ground (ver. 6). The *stay* of the people is three days, while in the other miracle but one day (6 : 35). The *means* are greater, seven loaves and a few fish, instead of five loaves and two fish (6 : 41). The *number of persons* is less, four thousand, and not five thousand (6 : 44). The *broken pieces* fill only seven *baskets*, which have a different name. These last three particulars are clearly contrasted in ver. 19, 20. The *fish* are here blessed separately (ver. 7). The *symbolism of the numbers* (Augustine, Sermon XLV.; Edersheim, II., p. 64) is distinct, 5 and 12 pointing to the five books of the law and the twelve tribes ; 4 and 7, the world-number and the holy number, indicating a Gentile audience to be sanctified. See, also Augustine, De Cons. II. 50, par. 105; Nebe, III., p. 135.

multiply in his hands (6 : 41); and there remain of broken pieces, Ver. 8, seven **baskets**,[1] large wicker baskets, that might hold a man (Acts 9 : 25), which the disciples had taken because of the long journey. The whole [2] miracle teaches "the less you think of the earthly, the more Christ thinks of it and cares for it."—MÜLLER. After Jesus dismissed the people, Ver. 10, **he** . . . **Dalmanutha**, which, although otherwise unknown, must have been on the western shore,[3] possibly at Ain-el Bârideh, but probably near the modern Minje (Magadan Matt. 15 : 39) [4] at the northern end of the plain of Gennesaret.[5]

11-13. And the Pharisees came forth, and began to question with him, seeking of him a sign from heaven, tempting him. And he sighed deeply in his spirit, and saith, Why doth this generation seek a sign? verily I say unto you, There shall no sign be given unto this generation, and he left them, and again entering into *the boat* departed to the other side.

Ver. 11. *The Pharisees*, with the Sadducees (Matt. 16 : 1) *came forth* from their homes (Meyer, Keil, Holtzmann, Nösgen), *and began to* **question**, dispute, with Jesus probably about His messianic claim, and in order not to yield to the truth, demand a **sign from heaven**, *tempting him*. They are not satisfied with the strong evidence of the miracles, that had been performed, but seek some signal

---

[1] σφυρίδας as distinguished from κοφίνους.
[2] On a fuller exposition, see 6 : 35 sq.; Nebe, III., p. 135 sq.; Luther Erl. Ed. 2 : 457 sq.; 13 : 197 sq.; 206 sq.
[3] Robinson (Res. III., p. 514, 530) places it on the eastern side, identifying with it the modern village Dehemija. Thus also Volkmar, Weiss. Thomson points to Dalhamia (II., p. 60).
[4] Magadan (א, B), and not Magdala, must not be identified with Dalmanutha, as by Augustine, De Cons. II. 51, par. 106.
[5] Cf. Tristram, Land of Israel. p. 425; Holtzmann, Com., p. 184; Edersheim, II., p. 68. On the whole subject the monograph of M. Schultze, "Dalmanutha. Geographisch-linguist. Untersuchung z. Marc. 8 : 10 u. Matth. 15 : 39." (1884.)

manifestation from heaven, like the manna of Moses, the standing still of the sun in Gibea, thunder and rain as ordered by Samuel and Elijah, as testimonials of the messianic time (Joel 2 : 30). In this request they act as true Pharisees,[1] but in spiteful spirit, **tempting him.** It is their purpose to incite Jesus to attempt a sign, in which they expect Him to fail. In this temptation they are tools of the great Tempter. Ver. 12. And Christ **sighed ... spirit** (2 : 8). In the inwardness of His self Jesus is moved by holiest indignation at their perversity, and with pitying grief at their self-injurious blindness, and **saith, ... sign?** (6 : 2). It was characteristic of the Jewish **generation,** not as contemporaries, but as one in spirit,[2] while denying the real wonders of Jesus in unbelieving hypocrisy to seek signs (1 Cor. 1 : 22). "They do not estimate His (Jesus) signs; God should do as they wish or not be God."--LUTHER. Therefore Christ says, **verily ... (3 : 28),**[3] **There ... generation.** This absolute refusal, not contradicting Matt. 12 : 39,[4] confirmed by an oath, was due to their wicked unbelief. Therefore in just severity Christ, Ver. 13, *left them, and departed to the* eastern *side.*

[1] When teaching was disputed, and to substantiate Messianic prophecies the Pharisees asked for heavenly signs (Edersheim, II., p. 69).

[2] This ethical meaning of γενεά is frequent in the N. T. From the association with the Jews it has received a bad sense (Matt. 11 : 16; 12 : 39, 41, 42; 17 : 17; Mark 8 : 38; 9 : 19; Luke 9 : 41; 11 : 29, 30, 32; 16 : 8; 17 : 25, etc.). Cf. Nebe, III., p. 168.

[3] In the literal rendering, "if there shall be a sign given," the *if* (ἐἰ corresponds to the Hebrew im and marks a denying oath (Hebr. 3 : 11; 4 : 3), there being an aposiopesis of the apodosis (Winer, p. 500).

[4] Neither Meyer, who claims that Mark omitted the real point, nor Weiss, who holds that this word, originally in a different connection, is not altogether appropriate, is correct. Christ refused the specific sign from heaven, and then added the peculiar Messianic sign of Jonah, which Mark, to emphasize the force of the denial, has omitted. Even the sign vouchsafed according to Matthew was a virtual refusal. (Cf. Augustine, De Cons. II. 51. par. 106.)

14-21. And they forgot to take bread; and they had not in the boat with them more than one loaf. And he charged them, saying, Take heed, beware of the leaven of the Pharisees and the leaven of Herod. And they reasoned one with another, saying, We have no bread. And Jesus perceiving it saith unto them, Why reason ye, because ye have no bread? do ye not yet perceive, neither understand? have ye your heart hardened? Having eyes, see ye not? and having ears, hear ye not? and do ye not remember? When I brake the five loaves among the five thousand, how many baskets full of broken pieces took ye up? They say unto him, Twelve. And when the seven among the four thousand, how many basketfuls of broken pieces took ye up? And they say unto him, Seven. And he said unto them, Do ye not yet understand?

Ver. 14. In their hasty departure the disciples **forgot** *to take bread; and* as Peter the eye-witness well remembers, they had but *one loaf.* " The forgetfulness becomes an occasion of new instruction : therefore even the faults of believers must serve for their good" (Rom. 8 : 28).—QUESNEL, STARKE. Ver. 15. And Jesus **charged them** (5 : 43 : 7 : 36; 9 : 9) earnestly with a double command, **Take heed** (see ye), *beware* (look away), because of the **leaven** which, forbidden in the sacrifice of thanksgiving (Lev. 2 : 4; cf. Amos 4 : 5) and at Passover (Ex. 12 : 15), is always, except Matt. 13 : 33, Luke 13 : 20, 21, representative of hidden and permeating evil.[1] (1 Cor. 5 : 6, 7, 8; Gal. 5 : 9). This leaven of *the Pharisees* was pious hypocrisy (Luke 12 : 1), and of *Herod*[2] and his party worldly hypocrisy. Opposite as Pharisees and Herodians were, the former being the orthodox nationalists, the latter the

---

[1] It occurs in the same sense in Rabbinic literature (Ber. 17a; Rosh ha Shanah, 4a). Stier, II. 188; Edersheim, II., p. 70).

[2] The Sadducees (Matt. 16 : 6) are omitted by Mark, not because Herod was a Sadducee, but for the reason that the Herodians, although a political party, represent the Sadducean tendency of liberalism and were often joined with the Pharisees against Christ (3 : 6; Matt. 22 : 16). Mark has adopted the stronger term in the antithesis, Christ having joined " Sadducees " with " Herod."

broad servants of Rome, they are one in the evil spirit of opposition against Christ, and show, " unbelieving hypocrisy and hypocritical unbelief in their inmost unity, as it must betray itself in the inimical communion against God's truth in Christ."—STIER. Against this power of hypocrisy, so dangerous to truth and so seductive, the disciples, and in them, all believers are warned. Ver. 16. *They reasoned one with another, saying,*[1] **We have**[2] **no bread.** The twelve suppose that Christ used their lack of bread to warn them against eating any bread made by Pharisees and Sadducees, or being at table with them. This would necessitate their leaving the world.[3] They are so bound up in the outward that they do not see the spiritual. The weaker the faith, the greater is the care of bodily things. Ver. 17. *Jesus perceiving* their reasoning said, **Why . . . yet** (1 Cor. 3 : 2; Hebr. 12 : 4) **perceive**, do you after all your opportunities not notice with your heart (John 12 : 40) the application of my words, *neither* **understand** by reflection their meaning? *have ye your heart* **hardened?** (6 : 52) has it become so impervious to spiritual suggestions? Ver. 18. **Having eyes,** or better, ye have eyes and see not, ears and hear not. You possess spiritual receptive organs, which you do not use. **Do** *ye not* **remember?** The memory of former help should have led them to look beyond the external. Therefore

---

[1] λέγοντες (א, B, D) is opposed by A, C, L, N, and was probably supplied from Matthew. The following ὅτι serves the same purpose.

[2] ἔχομεν is to be retained against ἔχουσιν of B. It is found in A, C, L, N, etc.

[3] The interpretation of Klostermann, Weiss, that the disciples thought that Jesus would have them guard against leaven, possibly poisoned, which the Pharisees might attempt to smuggle into their midst; and the supposition of Edersheim, that they supposed they should seek a sign, are both strained and fanciful.

Christ questions them (ver. 19, 20[1]) about the broken pieces left after the two miracles of feeding, and finally asks, Ver. 21, **Do ye ... understand?** Recalling the miracle do ye still cling to the bread? Then they understood (Matt. 16 : 12). Although "they have been very forgetful of the favor, which they have but lately received,"—CALVIN, and Christ must rebuke them strongly, He does so in "great mildness."—CHRYSOSTOM. " What patience He has with the ignorance of the apostles, and with their weakness of faith. He does not go and leave them as the Pharisees; but He bears and corrects their folly in the most pleasant manner and must explain Himself over against them, as against children, with clearest words about what He has said, and accommodate Himself to their capacity. And they do not reject the love, the confidence and honor toward Him, but as upright disciples suffer the chastisement of their master gladly and are thereby bettered."—LUTHER.

22-26. And they come unto Bethsaida. And they bring to him a blind man, and beseech him to touch him. And he took hold of the blind man by the hand, and brought him out of the village; and when he had spit on his eyes, and laid his hands upon him, he asked him, Seest thou aught? And he looked up, and said, I see men; for I behold *them* as trees, walking. Then again he laid his hands upon his eyes; and he looked stedfastly, and was restored, and saw all things clearly. And he sent him away to his home, saying, Do not even enter into the village.

Ver. 22. *And they*, Jesus and His disciples, **come unto Bethsaida** on the northeastern coast of the lake (Grotius, Griesbach, Meyer, Klostermann, Lange, Keil, Nösgen), which was greatly improved by Philip the tetrarch and called Julias in honor of the daughter of the Emperor Augustus. The people (7 : 32) *bring unto him a* **blind man**, who had

---

[1] For the two Greek words for "basket" referred to in the margin of the Rev. Version, see note to ver. 8.

become blind by disease, *and beseech* Christ *to touch him*, with a magical idea of the power proceeding from Jesus (5 : 23, 27). Human weakness would ever prescribe to Christ, but He knows the true way. Ver. 23. **He ... village** to be alone with him (7 : 33). "To the blind man receiving sight the view of heaven and divine works in nature would be more joyful than that of human works in the village."—BENGEL. *When he had* **spit**[1] *on his eyes*, which had "a sacramental import,"—COOK, (6 : 56; 7 : 33), *and laid his hand upon him* (5 : 23) *he asked*, **Seest thou aught?**[2] This question, making the saliva and touch healing by the word, is directed toward calling forth the effort of the man, who, Ver. 24, **looked ... walking.** Remembering before his blindness how men looked, this man recognizes them; but his vision is still so unschooled, that they seem in height as trees while their motion proves them men.[3] "The eyes of the understanding, that have been opened, do not see all truths at once, but in the beginning we must bear with weakness" (2 Cor 4 : 6).—HEDINGER, STARKE. Ver. 25. *Then again* Jesus *laid his hands upon his eyes.* " He laid on His hands that He might show that His flesh was the instrument through

---

[1] The story of Tacitus (Hist. 4 : 81), adopted by Suetonius and Dio Cassius, that Vespasian, upon request, healed a blind man by his spittle, is used by Holtzmann to discredit Christ's miracle. But Holtzmann forgets to state that the physicians previously pronounced the man not incurable, and accepts, without criticism, an account told with an evident purpose to exalt the emperor. He does not notice the probable collusion of the physicians. (Cf. Morison, p. 219.)

[2] The "if" (εἰ) introduces a direct question, therefore the Rev. Vers. is preferable to the indirect rendering of the Auth. Ver. (Winer, p. 509).

[3] That blind men when couched first see unclearly and are especially mistaken as to distance and magnitude is proved by the well-known case of Chesselden, as well as later ones. (See Berkley, Principles of Human Knowledge, ed. by Dr. Krauth, p. 323.) But Mark has not related this to show his knowledge of physiology. (Bauer.)

which and with which He, the eternal Word, performed all works of vivification."—CHEMNITZ. The blind man then *looked* **steadfastly** through the apparent veil, *was restored* (3 : 5) *and saw all things* **clearly**, lit. glistening in the distance.¹ This progressive healing, found only in Mark, who alone has reported the parable of progressive growth (4 : 26 sq.), is told not so much to exhibit the full liberty of Christ in His method of procedure (Calvin), but to show the loving kindness of the Lord, who condescends to the weakness of the faith of the blind man, and leads him gradually to sight and faith. It is symbolical of the progress of the disciples from blindness (ver. 21) to true, distinct vision (ver. 29). "Knowledge in spiritual things is gradual."—STARKE. Ver. 26. Christ *sent* the man *to his home* in another village, saying, **Do²** *not even enter the* **village** of Bethsaida through which you were led, for rumor will injure your soul (1 : 44 ; 7 : 36 ; 9 : 30). Christ desires of those, whom He helps, that they should in solitude consider His gracious love.

27–9: 1. And Jesus went forth, and his disciples, into the villages of Cæsarea Philippi : and in the way he asked his disciples, saying unto them, Who do men say that I am? And they told him, saying. John the Baptist : and others, Elijah ; but others, One of the prophets. And he asked them, But who say ye that I am? Peter answereth and saith unto him, Thou art the Christ. And he charged them that they should tell no man of him. And he began to teach them, that the Son of man must suffer many things, and be rejected by the elders, and the chief priests, and the scribes, and be killed, and after three days rise again. And he spake the saying openly. And Peter took him, and began to rebuke him. But he turning about, and seeing his disciples, rebuked Peter, and saith, Get thee behind me, Satan : for

---

¹ τηλαυγῶς (A, B, D) and not δηλαυγῶς (C, L), which emphasizes rather the distinctness (δῆλος) than the distance. (τῆλε, afar.)

² The words "nor tell it to any in the town" (Auth. V.), which follow, and have given such difficulty to some interpreters, are justly omitted accdg. to ℵ, B, L. They contain an explanatory gloss.

thou mindest not the things of God, but the things of men. And he called unto him the multitude with his disciples, and said unto them, If any man would come after me, let him deny himself, and take up his cross, and follow me. For whosoever would save his life shall lose it; and whosoever shall lose his life for my sake and the gospel's shall save it. For what doth it profit a man, to gain the whole world, and forfeit his life? For what should a man give in exchange for his life? For whosoever shall be ashamed of me and of my words in this adulterous and sinful generation, the Son of man also shall be ashamed of him, when he cometh in the glory of his Father with the holy angels. And he said unto them, Verily I say unto you, There be some here of them that stand by, which shall in no wise taste of death, till they see the kingdom of God come with power.

Ver. 27. From Bethsaida **Jesus . . . Philippi,** which, called Philippi to distinguish it from the Cæsarea of Palestine (Strabo's Tower), received its name from the tetrarch Philip, who changed the original *Paneas*, an appellation due to a cave dedicated to Pan, to Cæsarea in honor of the emperor (Jos. Antiq. XVIII. 2, 1; Wars, II. 9, 1). It belonged to Syria, and was situated in a quiet well-watered mountain-gap, near the source of the Jordan, among the southern spurs of Mt. Hermon, about 120 miles north of Jerusalem. Its population was largely Gentile. Later its old name revived as Banias.[1] Not into this city but its surrounding villages Jesus came, **In the . . . am?** "The design of Christ was to confirm His disciples fully in the true faith, that they might not be tossed about amidst various reports."—CALVIN. Ver. 28. *And they told him, saying,* some following the opinion of Herod (6 : 16), *John the Baptist ; others Elijah* (6 : 15); *but others, one of the prophets* (6 : 15). All these various opinions honor Christ, but not fully. Ver. 29. Therefore **he . . . am?** This question was the aim of the former. By it, those who have been with Him and know His words and works are

---

[1] Holtzmann, p. 190; Robinson, Res. III., p. 360; Lat. Res., p. 404; Porter, Damascus, I., p. 317; Thomson, I., p. 343 sq.; Tristram, Land of Israel, p. 585 sq.

to "be led to a sublimer notion, and not to fall into the same low view as the multitude."—CHRYSOSTOM. And *Peter,* "the ever-fervent, the leader of the apostolic choir," —CHRYSOSTOM (1 : 29), **saith ... Christ** (1 : 1). In this confession, which concluded with the acknowledgment of divine Sonship (Matt. 16 : 16), all former confessions (John 1 : 49; Matt. 14 : 33; John 6 : 69) are summed up most fully and clearly in the proclamation of the Messiahship of Jesus and His divine-human personality. Even the short form of Mark includes this in the light of O. T. prophecy. "In these words the whole Apostle's creed is included."—LUTHER. "Here the one true Catholic faith is originally confessed, and because we heartily hold the same faith, we are indeed the right Catholics."—CHEMNITZ. Ver. 30. **And**[1] **... him,** because the false messianic expectations in Israel would be attached to Him. "Truths have their time in which they are to be discovered; at times silence is better than speaking."—QUESNEL, STARKE. Ver. 31. Jesus began *to teach* His disciples, that "His kingdom is not temporal or earthly,"—LUTHER, for *the Son of man* (2 : 10) **must suffer** *many things.* The sufferings of Christ in their variety and greatness were *necessary* because prophesied (Luke 24 : 46), for the perfection of Jesus (Hebr. 2 : 10) and for the deliverance of men (Is. 53 : 4; Matt. 8 : 17). He had also *to be* **rejected** (Ps. 118 : 22 ; Mark 12 : 10) *by* **the elders** of the Sanhedrim, who were the non-clericals, probably chosen for their standing and political influence. These with **the chief-priests,** the men of high-priestly

---

[1] The omission of the praise of Peter (Matt. 16 : 17 sq.), while proving that it was not absolutely essential (Beza), cannot be accounted for on the ground of its having no "independent meaning" (selbständige Bedeutung) (Weiss) here; but it is due rather to the character of the readers (Meyer, Keil) and Peter's humility.

families, and **scribes** (2 : 6), the official interpreters of law and tradition, were the constituents of the national religious assembly of the Seventy.[1] These leaders would necessarily reject Christ, as He sees, for His truthful opposition to their error and hypocrisy. He would also be **killed** by this enmity,[2] but for the salvation of men (Rom. 5 : 6; 2 Cor. 5 : 15; Hebr. 9 : 12): and **after three days**[3] **rise** again (16 : 6). The rising, necessary according to Scriptures (1 Cor. 15 : 4), was to be the proof of the acceptance of Christ's atoning death and His inherent life-power (Rom. 4 : 25 : John 14 : 19). While John mentions the early consciousness of Jesus about His sufferings (John 2 : 19, 22 ; 3 : 14, 15 ; 6 : 51, etc.), the synoptical gospels, beside the figurative indication (Luke 12, 49, 50), mention four distinct announcements, of which this is the first. (2) 9 : 30; (3) 10 : 33; (4) Matt. 26 : 2.[4] There is a progress in these announcements, beginning with this declaration of the necessity of suffering. In 9 : 31 the action of the enemies is indicted as going beyond the circle of the Jews ("delivered up into the hands of men"), preparing for the third declaration (10 : 33), which introduces the Gentiles and describes the details of the suffering most fully. Everywhere the resurrection is attached. Therefore "the glory of Christ's

---

[1] Holtzmann, p. 48; Edersheim, I., p. 93, 96, 263. "Sanhedrim" in Smith's & Schaff's Bible Dict.; Nebe, Leidensgeschichte, I., p. 11.

[2] Schnedermann (II. 137) fixes upon Christ's opposition to the Jewish Sabbath-laws as *the* cause of His crucifixion. But the real cause was the bitter enmity of a detected and censured hypocrisy, which sought apparent and real transgressions of the traditional law, not of the Sabbath alone, and finally found blasphemy as the condemning charge.

[3] This characteristic expression of Mark is not in contradiction with "on the third day" and the actual facts; for the three days are not reckoned with mathematical exactitude, but spoken of with popular latitude, which counts part of a day as a day.

[4] Schmid's N. T. Theol., p. 215; Nösgen, I., p. 395.

resurrection should be always exhibited in connection with the ignominy of His death."—CALVIN. Ver. 32. **And he . . . openly,** not in a parable (2 : 20 ; Matt. 12 : 40), but with " great boldness " (2 Cor. 3 : 12) to prepare His disciples. *And Peter took him* aside, *and* **began to rebuke him** (cf. Matt. 16 : 22). Peter is sorely scandalized."—LUTHER. It is not only adverse to his thoughts, that He whom he has a little while before confessed as God should die as if but a man (Augustine), but he sees in this death a failure of the Kingdom, and would therefore restrain Jesus. But Peter's intentions, pious as they seemed, were utterly wrong. " If reason undertakes to judge God's mysteries it will always err and fail " (1 Cor. 2 : 12 sq.).—QUESNEL, STARKE. Ver. 33. But Christ *turning about* away from Peter, *and seeing his disciples,* in their presence and hearing, **rebuked Peter,** who " while he rebukes merits rebuke,"—BENGEL, which is administered, that no other disciple may ever venture to dictate to Christ, if His way be different from their thoughts. Christ **saith, . . . Satan.** In this severe rebuke Peter is not called Satan,[1] but behind Peter's words is the Adversary, who urges the same abandonment of suffering as in the former temptation (cf. Matt. 4 : 10), but in a different mode. He uses Peter's flesh and blood (Eph. 6 : 12) to dissuade Jesus from being obedient, who as a man was not without dread of His suffering (Luke 12 : 50 ; Mark 14 : 36). " This unsinful feeling Satan touches to move the obedient servant of God to a sinful will."—BESSER. Christ repels him, and then says to Peter: **for . . . men.**

---

[1] Augustine refers "Satan" to Peter, because he goes before rather than follows (Ps. XXXV. 5; LVI. 6; On John, Tract. XXVII. 8; Enchir. C. 101; Ag. Faustus VIII. 2 ; XXVI. 8). Thus also Chrysostom, Hom. LIV. 6 on Matt.; Luther, Walch, VII. 297; Calvin, Harm. of Matt. Mark, Luke. II., p. 302.

Thy thoughts are not, as in thy confession, of the Father (Matt. 16 : 17), but human.[1] And these human ideas against the cross, natural and innocent as they seem, are opposed to God's plan and agreeable to Satan. "The human is often the profane."—STIER. "This rebuke was not lost on Peter, for, after his correction and full preparation, he preached even to his own death the truth of the death of Christ."—AUGUSTINE. Ver. 34. *And Jesus called unto him the multitude*, that had gathered even in that Gentile region, *with his disciples, and said*, turning from His cross to that of His followers, and "openly indicating and presupposing His own cross in theirs,"—STIER, **If . . . cross.** The free desire to follow Christ necessitates the denial of the old, sinful "I": otherwise Christ is denied. After Him each one is to bear *his* **cross**, which, as shameful as it is painful, is not every suffering, but that borne willingly for Christ's sake. It dare not be self-imposed, but must be divinely ordered. Every one has **his** cross. Christ "does not teach that we should carry the cross He bore. For every one a cross is prepared, i. e. after the measure of the strength of every one (for we cannot suffer the same things, because we are not alike in faith and power of the Spirit)."—LUTHER. But without cross, no Christian. "None can be reckoned to be the disciples of Christ unless they are true imitators of Him, and are willing to pursue the same course."—CALVIN. Ver. 35.[2] **For . . . save it.** The life[3] of man, derived from the life-giving

---

[1] Augustine, Ps. LVI. 14; Luther, Walch, VII. 299.

[2] This saying is uttered again three times: Matt. 10 : 39; Luke 17 : 33; John 12 : 25. (Maclear.)

[3] The original meaning of ψυχή (něphěsh) is life in its specialization in the individual, particularly man. It involves "the conception of a person living, but not self-living. It marks the person of a man, but not man as a per-

spirit (Gen. 2 : 7), which as the divine principle was to
assert itself in man, has through sin become divorced
from the spirit (Gen. 6 : 3), and enslaved by the body.
To save this life, thus sinfully determined, by avoiding
the cross, is to lose true life eternally. To surrender
this life for Christ's sake and **the gospel's**—in the proclamation and life of which the suffering for Christ's sake
is to be endured as it is the message of Him—would *save*
the real life, which Christ as the vivifying spirit imparts
(1 Cor. 15 : 45). " Let him that is afraid of losing only
think what he shall find."—CANSTEIN, STARKE. Ver.
36. **For . . . life?** What advantage is it to gain the
world, if it were possible, with its fulness of wealth, power,
pleasure, and thereby forfeit true eternal life? "Why
does man seek so much the drops of peace, or the little
parts of the world, if the whole world full of goods would
conduce to eternal condemnation?"—LUTHER. Ver. 37.
For . . . life? As infinite as is the value of true life, so
impossible is it for man to give anything as price of exchange for his life (Ps. 49 : 7). This can only be done by
the divine Son of man (10 : 45). If He be rejected there
is no price. "A lost soul cannot be redeemed again, but
the certain law remains, that in hell there is no redemption except through Me. But those are lost without Me,
not for My sake; therefore they have not the ransom,
i. e. Me, and thus they are lost eternally without hope."
—LUTHER. Ver. 38. **For . . . me**, the suffering son of

---

son." (Delitzsch.) From this idea "soul" has been derived. (Cf. R. v.
Raumer concg. "Geist u. Seele" in Delitzsch's Bibl. Psychol., p. 145.) The
translation "life" is, however, preferable here and in the next verse, for while
it does not express the idea of individuation included in ψυχή, it approaches
nearer to its wideness than "soul." Cf. Öhler, O. T. Theol., p. 149; Hofmann, Weiss. u. Erfüll., I. 17 sq.; Delitzsch, Bibl. Psychol. (2 ed.), p. 96 sq.;
119 sq.; 233 sq.; 258 sq.; 281 sq.; Cremer, p. 949, and in Herzog-Plitt,
Realencyc. V. 1 sq.

man, **and . . . generation** (ver. 12). This refers primarily to the Jews, **adulterous** in breaking the spiritual marriage between Jehovah and themselves (Isai. 54 : 5 ; Jer. 3 : 14 ; 31 : 32 ; Hos. 2 : 2 ; 3 : 1 ; 9 : 1), and in consequence **sinful** in every way. Who cannot even bear the reproach of Christ from such a generation, whose mockings are really an honor, of him **the . . . cometh** to judgment *in the* **glory of his Father** (John 17 : 5 ; Hebr. 1 : 3), the bright effulgence of divine essence imparted by the Father to the only-begotten Son (1 : 11);[1] *with his* **holy angels** (Matt. 24 : 31 ; 2 Thess. 1 : 7), the glorious, heavenly servants, mighty in strength (Ps. 103 : 20). What folly to be ashamed of the humble Christ and to lose the participation in His glory! Chap. 9 : 1,[2] Christ said : **Verily . . . power.** As a pledge of the final coming with glory a near approach within the life-time of some disciples is announced. This revelation of the Kingdom with power took place in the destruction of Jerusalem, which is the first stage of the final judgment preparatory to the consummation of the Kingdom (ch. 13). Such a beginning of the second Advent would prove that Christ was sitting at the right hand of God, in glory and power.

[1] On δόξα see Cremer, p. 312.
[2] The connection of this verse with the ninth chapter by Hugo à St. Caro is evidently wrong (Matt. 16 : 27, 28). Possibly it was due to the interpretation of Origen, Hilary, Jerome, Theophylact, Leo the Great, which refers these words to the Transfiguration.

CHAPTER IX.

2–8. And after six days Jesus taketh with him Peter, and James, and John, and bringeth them up into a high mountain apart by themselves: and he was transfigured before them: and his garments became glistering, exceeding white; so as no fuller on earth can whiten them. And there appeared unto them Elijah with Moses: and they were talking with Jesus. And Peter answereth and saith to Jesus, Rabbi, it is good for us to be here: and let us make three tabernacles; one for thee, and one for Moses, and one for Elijah. For he wist not what to answer; for they became sore afraid. And there came a cloud overshadowing them: and there came a voice out of the cloud, This is my beloved Son: hear ye him. And suddenly looking round about, they saw no one any more, save Jesus only with themselves.

Ver. 2. *And* **after six days**, the exact time since the announcement of His sufferings (8 : 31), designated by Luke (9 : 28) in a general way as eight days,[1] **Jesus . . . John,** to show them the glory, that had previously (5 : 37) made Him master of death, and would be His as victor after His humiliation (14 : 33), that their faith might be confirmed; *and bringeth them up into a* **high mountain,** which was not Tabor,[2] but the high peak of Mount Her-

[1] Thus Lightfoot, Fritzsche, Godet, and Nebe harmonize rather than in the manner accepted since Augustine, who supposes that Matthew and Mark "regarded simply the intermediate days." He is followed by Jerome, Chrysostom, Luther, Calvin, Erasmus, and most of the later commentators. (Cf. Augustine, De Cons. II. C. LVI. 113; Luther, Walch, VII., p. 321b.)

[2] The traditional view, accepting Mt. Tabor in Galilee about six miles south-east of Nazareth, which is found in Origen, Jerome, and Cyril of Jerusalem, is untenable because of the existence of a city on the top of Tabor. Robinson (Res. III. 222 sq.), after the lead of Lightfoot and Roland, has thoroughly disproved the traditional view, and his position is adopted by almost all modern exegetes.

mon,¹ whose solitude was best fitted for prayer (Luke 9 : 28), and which in its grandeur best corresponds to the revelation to be made of Christ. **He . . . them.** In view of the elect three Jesus was changed from the form of servant (Phil. 2 : 7) to the form of God (Phil. 2 : 6). This was not due to God's special appearance (Exod. 34 : 29), but was made possible by Christ's inherent divine life and essence, whose glory shone out from Him as majesty (2 Pet. 1 : 16), predicting His future eternal glory, which was His in past eternity (John 12 : 16; 17 : 5, 22, 24). The actualization of the transfiguration was however not the independent deed of Christ, but a gift of the Father granted upon prayer (Luke 9 : 28). It was no myth (2 Pet. 1 : 16), but a real occurrence, proving that Christ as light (John 1 : 7) and life (John 14 : 6) would not be conquered by death, but as life-giving spirit (1 Cor. 15 : 45) would permeate even the mortal body, and bring about the resurrection and transfiguration of believers (2 Cor. 3 : 18; Matt. 13 : 43; Phil. 3 : 21).² " It was something wonderful that Christ was transfigured in the mortal body, still subject to suffering, and has shown the glory of immortality while yet in mortality."—LUTHER. Ver. 3. **His . . . glistering,**³ *exceeding white ; so as no fuller on earth can whiten them.* The glory rested not only upon the countenance (Matt. 17 : 2; Luke 9 : 29) of Jesus, but came forth from His whole body, whose brightness made the garments so wondrously light and white as to sur-

---

¹ The low spur Panium, suggested by Hasæus, Lightfoot, Kuinoel, Thomson, is excluded by the explicit mention of the ascent and height. Therefore, the Hermon itself is the most probable spot, as claimed by Paulus, Michaelis, Ammon, Porter, Cook, Nebe, Ebers, Guthe.

² Cf. especially v. Hofmann, Schriftbeweis, 2, 1, 518; Nösgen, I., p. 423 sq.

³ Glistering is an old form for glistening. (See Spenser's Hymn of Heavenly Beauty, ver. 17.)

pass the greatest skill of the fuller.[1] With light was Jesus divinely clad (Ps. 104 : 2; Hab. 3 : 4), whose heavenly glory is incomparable to the greatest human beauty and art. Ver. 4. **And . . . Moses.** This appearance of Elijah and Moses was no spiritual vision [2] or dream (Luke 9 : 32), but a real visible fact. The disciples knew the O. T. saints, either because Jesus addressed them as such (Nösgen), or more probably by "extraordinary revelation."—CALVIN. Elijah, mentioned first because most prominent in the Jewish messianic expectations, appeared with Moses. The latter as the law-giver and "moulder" (Tertullian), the former as the "reformer" (Tertullian) of the theocracy by the institution of prophecy, testify to Jesus as the representatives of law and prophecy, not only by their past activity but by their miraculous end (2 Kings. 2 : 11; Deut. 34 : 6; Jude 9), which pointed to the future completion of their work in a real antitype.[3] *They,* proving "that the dead are not dead,"—LUTHER, *were talking with Jesus* of His decease

---

[1] This comparison of Mark testifies to the ability of the fullers, who, having their fields (2 Kings 18 : 17; Isai. 7 : 3; 36 : 2) outside of the city because their trade was considered unclean, used lye, natron (Prov. 25 : 20; Jer. 2 : 22), and soap (Mal. 3 : 2), possibly the juice of some plant. They not only prepared new cloth, but washed clothing. Because they were brought into relation with women their occupation was not highly valued. (Cf. Delitzsch, Jüd. Handwerkerleben zur Zeit Jesu, p. 41; Geikie, p. 203.)

[2] Tertullian (ag. Marcion, IV. 22) is the father of the modern visionary theorists of mental visions.

[3] The position of Nösgen (I. 428), that the appearance of Moses and Elijah was to assure Jesus of the pleasure of God and of all true members of the kingdom in His work, and to confirm Him against Jewish enmity, which appealed to these witnesses, imparts a defensive tinge to the transfiguration, after the manner of Chrysostom (Hom. on Matt. LVI. 3). It is, however, unwarranted by the text, and imported from the conversation (ver. 11 sq.), which was caused by the appearance of Elijah, but is not offered as an explanation of it.

(Luke 9 : 31), in which with the resurrection following law and prophecy were fulfilled (Luke 24 : 44). Ver. 5. *And Peter*, impulsive as ever, *said to Jesus*, when he saw Elijah and Moses about departing (Luke 9 : 33), **Rabbi**, Master, Teacher, the highest Jewish title of honor and authority[1] (Matt. 23 : 7, 8), *it is* **good** *for us to be here;* for you and us it is advantageous (9 : 42, 43; 14 : 21; 1 Cor. 7 : 26) to be in such a place and in such company; *let us make three* **tabernacles**, booths of boughs as those of the feast of Tabernacles. Peter thinks it better to remain here in glory, than to descend into suffering, and would build dwellings for Elijah, " who brought down fire on the mountain, and Moses who entered into the thick darkness and talked with God."—CHRYSOSTOM. But while thus attempting to save Jesus from suffering, and desirous of a kingdom of glory without a cross, Peter dishonors Christ by honoring Elijah and Moses equally. But, Ver. 6, **he wist**[2] . . . **afraid.** The great fear common to all moved Peter to speak so foolishly and propose earthly homes for heavenly beings. Ver. 7. **And there . . . them.** God answers Peter by sending His own tabernacle to Moses and Elijah. It was the bright (Matt. 17 : 5) cloud of His gracious presence (Exod. 16 : 10; 24 : 18; 40 : 34; 1 Kings 8 : 10, 11) full of glorious majesty, and by its effulgent intensity " dark with excess of light,"—MILTON (1 Tim. 6: 16). The disciples " were not yet prepared for beholding the brightness of the heavenly glory. For, when the Lord gave tokens of His presence, He employed, at the same time, some coverings to restrain the arrogance of the human mind."—CALVIN. **And . . . voice** (1 : 11; John 12 : 28) . . . **him.** These words, ut-

---

[1] Cf. Edersheim, II., p. 381, 407 sq.

[2] Wist (knew) is the preterite of the Anglo-Saxon verb witan (German, wissen).

tered at Christ's baptism before His temptation, are repeated to attest His divine Sonship and the Father's pleasure (Matt. 17: 5) in the greater obedience, soon to be manifested in His sufferings (Hebr. 5 : 8). The psalms, prophets and the law are cited (Ps. 2 : 7 ; Isai. 42 : 1 ; Deut. 18 : 15) to show that Moses and the Prophets are heard when Christ is listened to, whom the disciples are therefore bidden to hear. He is " the only Teacher, that on His mouth alone it may depend."—CALVIN. Ver. 8. **And . . . themselves.** When the three recovered from the dread of the voice (Matt. 17 : 6, cf. Exod. 20 : 19; Hab. 3 : 2, 16; Hebr. 12 : 19), and looked up and around from the ground on which they had been prostrate on their faces (Matt. 17 : 6; cf. Exod. 3 : 6; 1 Kings 19 : 13) they saw Jesus alone. He remains after the shadows of the O. T. (Col. 2 : 17) have disappeared. "We must only hold to Christ for He is all, and in all" (Col. 3 : 11). —STARKE.

9-13. And as they were coming down from the mountain, he charged them that they should tell no man what things they had seen, save when the Son of man should have risen again from the dead. And they kept the saying, questioning among themselves what the rising again from the dead should mean. And they asked him, saying, The scribes say that Elijah must first come. And he said unto them, Elijah indeed cometh first, and restoreth all things: and how is it written of the Son of man, that he should suffer many things and be set at naught? But I say unto you, that Elijah is come, and they have also done unto him whatsoever they listed, even as it is written of him.

Ver. 9. As they descended Christ **charged them** (7 : 36) **. . . the dead.** Only after the resurrection could the transfiguration be announced, because the other disciples as well as the people would be aroused to false hopes of a glorious outward kingdom and be scandalized by Christ's sufferings, if they believed the message, which they might doubt. "The glory of the resurrection would render the previous glory more credible."—BENGEL. Ver. 10. The three **kept** (Luke 2 : 51) within their hearts **the saying,** Christ's injunction; but were **questioning . . . mean.** Their dispute is not about the general resurrection, but about Christ's. Although told shortly before (8 : 32) they could not comprehend how Jesus could rise, because they do not see how the Christ just transfigured could die. And further, Ver. 11, **they**[1] **. . . come.** Probably recalling Christ's earlier assertion that John the Baptist was the Elijah that was to come (Matt. 11 : 14), the disciples are now in doubt remembering John's death and having seen Elijah (ver. 4). Are not, they reason, the scribes then correct in holding to the bodily re-appearance of Elijah[2] *before* the day of the Lord (Messiah) as stated Mal. 4 : 5, 6? But now Jesus has come before Elijah has appeared; has then this messianic sign been rightly fulfilled? Can John be said to have effected what is foretold Mal. 4 : 6? Jesus answered, Ver. 12, **Elijah . . . things.** Christ confirms the position of the scribes as far as the coming first[3] of Elijah according to the Scriptures is concerned, and speaks of his preparatory (Luke 1 : 17) restorative work (Mal. 4 : 6) in its universality of God's intention (John 1 : 7), which

---

[1] The marginal reading, following Beza, Grotius, De Wette, Lachmann, Meyer, Keil, Holtzmann, is ὅ τι. But ὅτι, "recitative," is more in accord with Mark and more tenable in N. T. Greek (Winer, p. 167, 457). It is accepted by Bleek, Ewald, Klostermann, Weiss, Nösgen.

[2] Lightfoot, Hor. Hebr. on Matt. 17 : 10, 11; Edersheim, II. App. VIII., p. 706, " Rabbinic Traditions about Elijah, the Forerunner of the Messiah."

[3] Justin Martyr admits to Trypho (C. XLIX.) the appearance of Elijah before the second Advent. This is also taught by Tertullian (De Anima, 35; De Resurr. Carnis. 22), Origen (Com. on Matt. and John), Jerome (on Matt. 11 : 15), Augustine (De Civ. Dei, 20 : 29; St. John, Tract. IV., 5, 6), Chrysostom (Hom. LVII. on Matt.).—Luther (Walch, VII., 328 sq.) and Calvin dispute it. There is certainly no proof for it in the words of Christ, however Malachi may be interpreted.

Israel's sin hindered (Luke 7 : 30). A complete restitution of all things is not taught (cf. Acts 3 : 21). The apparent contradiction of John's work and death with this promise, Christ solves with the question, **and how . . . Son of man** (2 : 10) **. . . naught?** If the O. T. shows a Messiah suffering (espec. Ps. 22 ; Isia. 53)[1] and *set at naught*, counted as nothing (Isai. 53 : 3), who shall restore (Isai. 61 : 1 sq.), dare the sufferings of the precursor be used to discredit his labor? Ver. 13. **But . . . come.** John, although not Elijah (John 1 : 21), was the Elijah of the N. T., like unto him of old in dress (2 Kings. 1 : 8) in fiery, earnest spirit, in penetrating power and reformatory work (Luke 1 : 17). Unto him *they*, the Jews, **have also done** *whatsoever* **they listed** (desired, German, Lust). They heeded not his words nor liberated him from Herod, but secretly concurred through their leaders in his death, *even as it is written*, 1 Kings 19 : 1 sq., which typifies John's end. What was done to John was a prophecy of what would be done to the Son of man. "Be not astonished that the servants of Christ are badly treated, for it is clearly told in the Scriptures" (Matt. 10 : 17 sq.).—QUESNEL, STARKE.

14–29. And when they came to the disciples, they saw a great multitude about them, and scribes questioning with them. And straightway all the multitude, when they saw him, were greatly amazed, and running to him saluted him. And he asked them, What question ye with them? And one of the multitude answered him, Master, I brought unto thee my son, which hath a dumb spirit; and wheresoever it taketh him, it dasheth him down: and he foameth, and grindeth his teeth, and pineth away: and I spake to thy disciples that they should cast it out; and they were not able. And he answered them and saith, O faithless generation, how long shall I be with you? how long shall I bear with you? bring him unto me. And they brought him unto him: and when he saw him, straightway the spirit tare him grievously; and he fell on the ground and wallowed foaming. And he

---

[1] Öhler's O. T. Theol., p. 531 sq.

asked his father, How long time is it since this hath come unto him? And he said, From a child. And oft-times it hath cast him both into the fire and into the waters, to destroy him: but if thou canst do anything, have compassion on us and help us. And Jesus said unto him, If thou canst! All things are possible to him that believeth. Straightway the father of the child cried out, and said, I believe; help thou mine unbelief. And when Jesus saw that a multitude came running together, he rebuked the unclean spirit, saying unto him, Thou dumb and deaf spirit, I command thee, come out of him, and enter no more into him. And having cried out, and torn him much, he came out: and *the child* became as one dead; insomuch, that the more part said, He is dead. But Jesus took him by the hand, and raised him up; and he arose. And when he was come into the house, his disciples asked him privately, *saying*, We could not cast it out. And he said unto them, This kind can come out by nothing, save by prayer.

Ver. 14. *And when they*, Jesus and the three disciples, came to the others, **they . . . them.** The scribes used the helplessness of the disciples to impugn their Master. Therefore when, Ver. 15, *the multitude saw him*, they *were* **greatly amazed**, not because His face still shone (Exod. 34:29), but because He came so unexpectedly to prove His power when the scribes had conquered. The crowd *running to him* **saluted** *him* with eager, grateful delight. Upon His authoritative question in defence of His disciples, Ver. 17, **one . . . spirit**, not a demon causing dumbness, but one not speaking through the possessed (on Demoniacs, see EXCURSUS II., p. 31). This spirit, Ver. 18, *wheresoever it* **taketh** *him*, at whatever place it comes upon him, **dasheth him down**, throws him into convulsions: *and he*, the boy, **foameth** at the mouth, **grindeth his teeth,** and as a result of these attacks, **pineth away,** wastes away (4:6; 11:21). I *spake to thy disciples* to cast it out; *and they were* **not able.** The help I seek they could not give. Ver. 19. *And Jesus answered*, O **faithless,** unbelieving (John 20:27; 1 Cor. 7:12) *generation* (8:12, 38). Christ is filled with deep sadness and holy indignation because of this generation, in which

Deut. 32 : 5, 20 is fulfilled anew. His complaint is against all, the scribes in their perverse unbelief, the father in his doubt, and the undecided disciples, who have dishonored His name. He asks, **how long** *shall I be with you* until you believe, *and bear with you?* **bring him unto me.** With this command end words, which reveal Jesus again in the pain and long-suffering of His divine mercy, and the patience of His human love. Ver. 20. As the people brought the lad, the demon, *when he saw* Jesus, convulsed the boy, and **he . . . foaming.** "In proportion as the grace of Christ is seen nearer at hand, and acts more powerfully, the fury of Satan is the more highly excited."—CALVIN. Jesus, to elicit faith, Ver. 21, *asked the father* how long his son was thus, and, Ver. 22, **he** said, *From a* **child.** This shows that the possession was not due to special sin (cf. John 9 : 2). The father again describing the terrible malady, how the demon casts his child into fire and water to kill it, asks, almost despairing and remembering the failure of the disciples, **but . . . us.** In deepest fatherly sympathy the man identifies himself with his son, and asks for deliverance from their common torture; but he doubts Christ's power, and does not possess the confidence of the leper (1 : 40). Ver. 23. **Jesus** *said unto him, If thou* **canst.**[1] Thou hast said "if thou canst," if *thou* canst: the possibility is not on my side, but thine. **All . . . believeth** (Matt. 17 : 20: Luke 17 : 6). The believer will obtain everything that is to his real benefit. The measure of faith is the measure of blessings. "By faith man is lord of all things."—LUTHER. Ver. 24. **Straightway . . . said**[2] **. . . belief.** Upon the word of promise the father's faith struggles into existence, but it is still so weak that the incipient believer

---

[1] "Believe" is rightly omitted according to ℵ, B, C, L, Δ, etc.
[2] "With tears" is wanting in ℵ, A, B, C, L, Δ.

recognizes it to be but unbelief in comparison with what Christ demands, and prays for deliverance from it. As much as faith lacks, unbelief rules. But a soul "destitute of faith, yet terrified at scepticism" would not pray thus, for only in faith is unbelief recognized and felt as an evil. "As our faith is never perfect, we are all partly unbelievers."—CALVIN. Ver. 25. Jesus, prevented from developing the father's faith by the *multitude that came running together*, **rebuked** (1 : 25) the demon, calling him also **deaf**, because this with his silence[1] (ver. 17) characterized him. But Christ made even the deaf demon to hear, saying, **I . . . him**. The cure shall be immediate and lasting. The demon, who had come from time to time (ver. 18, 22), shall never return (Matt. 12 : 45). But he came out, Ver. 26, causing such convulsions, that the lad appeared and was by most called dead. Ver. 27. **But . . . hand** (5 : 41 ; Dan. 10 : 9, 10 ; Rev. 1 : 17), *and* **raised him up.** The touch of Jesus is life-giving. Ver. 28. *When Jesus was come into the house*, where He was staying, **his . . . saying**[2] **. . . out.** They cannot understand why, when acting on Christ's order (6 : 7) and in reliance upon their previous experience (6 : 13), they should fail. Ver. 29. Christ censuring their little faith (Matt. 17 : 20) *said*, **This kind**, this sort of demons, for there is a gradation among demons (Eph. 6 : 12), **come . . . prayer.**[3] Prayer alone, not as an exercise but as a result of faith, will help. Who truly prays believes, and believing prayer will show its power (11 : 23, 24 ; John 15 : 7). "The faith that has a sharp taste will arouse the spirit of prayer."—LUTHER.

---

[1] The crying out, which Luke (9 : 39) mentions, is that of the boy as the demon comes upon him, and does not contradict Mark's account of the demon as not speaking.

[2] ὅτι is again recitative and not interrogative. See v. 11.

[3] "And fasting" omitted by ℵ, B, is very probably a later addition.

30-32. And they went forth from thence, and passed through Galilee; and he would not that any man should know it. For he taught his disciples, and said unto them, The Son of man is delivered up into the hands of men, and they shall kill him; and when he is killed, after three days he shall rise again. But they understood not the saying, and were afraid to ask him.

Ver. 30. Jesus *passed through Galilee; and he would not that any man* **should know it,** that He might be alone to teach His disciples. Ver. 31, how the *hands of* **men** would abuse *the* **Son of man** (2 : 10; 8 : 31 sq.) Ver. 32. *But* the disciples *understood not* (ver. 10) *and* **were afraid to ask,** because they had a presentiment of some sad occurrence. But their Jewish idea of the kingdom prevented them from comprehending the clear words of the Lord. "A confused principle of piety, rather than a clear knowledge of the truth, kept them attached to Christ, and prevented them from leaving His school."—CALVIN.

33-37. And they came to Capernaum: and when he was in the house he asked them, What were ye reasoning in the way? But they held their peace: for they had disputed one with another in the way, who *was* the greatest. And he sat down, and called the twelve; and he saith unto them, If any man would be first, he shall be last of all, and minister of all. And he took a little child, and set him in the midst of them: and taking him in his arms, he said unto them, Whosoever shall receive one of such little children in my name, receiveth me; and whosoever receiveth me, receiveth not me, but him that sent me.

Ver. 33. **They . . . Capernaum** (1 : 21), and when Jesus *was in the house* of Peter (2 : 1) He inquired of their disputings on the way. Ver. 34. *But they* first **held their peace** (3 : 4) being ashamed, and then asked (Matt. 18 : 1) about their debate, **who** *was the* **greatest.** Moved by the selection of the favored three, and impelled by Jewish prejudices which made great distinctions of rank in the messianic age,[1] the twelve, led by the announcements

[1] Edersheim, II., p. 116.

(8 : 32 ; 9 : 30) of Jesus to expect a near revelation of the kingdom, disputed who of them would be greater than the others. They did not in honor prefer one another (Rom. 12 : 10). "Pride reigns in almost all conditions."—QUESNEL, LANGE. Ver. 35. Jesus **sat down** (2 : 14; 4 : 1) deliberately, to solemnly teach *the twelve* (3 : 14), whom He *called* to Himself, *and* **saith . . . all.** This word, repeated later (Matt. 20 : 26; 23 : 11; Luke 22 : 26), announces as the principle of the kingdom, that the lowest place of service is the highest rank. But the last place shall not be sought to attain the first (Luke 14 : 10), but to serve all (John 13 : 4 sq.). "In this kingdom we are not to become great, but to become small."—LUTHER. Ver. 36. *And he took a little child*, probably a son of Peter,[1] **and . . . midst** to be seen by all (cf. 3 : 3) as a living lesson of childlike humility: *and* **taking** *him into his* **arms,** to show his hearty reception by loving embrace (Luther: herzete), *said*, Ver. 37. **Whosoever . . . children,** humble, simple and helpless, **in my name,** upon the authority (13 : 6; Matt. 7 : 22), power (Luke 10 : 17) and faith in My name (John 14 : 14; 16 : 23), **receiveth me** (Matt. 25 : 40): **and . . . me** (Matt. 10 : 40; John 13 : 20). The ready acceptance of all children, literal and spiritual, which is possible only by humble (ver. 35), faith, is the receiving through Christ of the Father, whose authorative representative He is (cf. John 5 : 23, 24, 30). To receive the weakest and humblest for Christ's sake, is the entertainment of God Almighty.

38–50. John said unto him, Master, we saw one casting out devils in thy name: and we forbade him, because he followed not us. But Jesus said, Forbid him not: for there is no man which shall do a mighty work in my

---

[1] An untrustworthy tradition of the 9th century claims this honor for St. Ignatius, because he calls himself θεοφόρος, which was construed passively instead of actively (Cook, On Matt. 18 : 2).

name, and be able quickly to speak evil of me. For he that is not against us is for us. For whosoever shall give you a cup of water to drink, because ye are Christ's, verily I say unto you, he shall in no wise lose his reward. And whosoever shall cause one of these little ones that believe on me to stumble, it were better for him if a great millstone were hanged about his neck, and he were cast into the sea. And if thy hand cause thee to stumble, cut it off: it is good for thee to enter into life maimed, rather than having thy two hands to go into hell, into the unquenchable fire. And if thy foot cause thee to stumble, cut it off: it is good for thee to enter into life halt rather than having thy two feet to be cast into hell. And if thine eye cause thee to stumble, cast it out: it is good for thee to enter into the kingdom of God with one eye, rather than having two eyes to be cast into hell; where their worm dieth not, and the fire is not quenched. For every one shall be salted with fire. Salt is good: but if the salt have lost its saltness, wherewith will ye season it? Have salt in yourselves, and be at peace one with another.

Ver. 38. John, thinking about the authority of the name of Christ, relates a case in which he holds this name to have been abused. He said, **Master** (ver. 5), . . . **not us.** This man, whom the disciples saw, was no Jewish exorcist (Matt. 12 : 27), nor had he the covetous aim of Simon (Acts 8 : 18 sq.) and the impure motives of the sons of Sceva (Acts 19 : 13 sq.); but the name of Jesus, so widely known, was used by him as a real power to perform miracles, although he was no direct follower of Jesus and the disciples. Because he was not in their outward communion they forbade him after the spirit of Joshua (Num. 11 : 28). Ver. 39. **But . . . of me.** Christ, having in the highest degree the mind of Moses (Num. 11 : 29) and inspiring Paul to the same spirit (Phil. 1 : 18), affirms that whosoever performs such deeds must have experience enough of His power to be unable to change so quickly as to blaspheme His name (cf. 1 Cor. 12 : 3). Although His name may be used to perform mighty works without faith (Matt. 7 : 22), yet the exorcist that John tells of probably had a germ of faith, that might develop and was not to be disturbed by intolerant zealousness for visible communion with the disciples. But while Christ does not forbid, He does not enjoin activity outside of the pale of the church. The disciples are to learn that "God has a marvellous method in the dispensation of His graces and gifts, and we must not be ready to reject what is not yet perfectly pure and flawless." —HEDINGER, STARKE. Ver. 40. **For . . . us.** He whose activity is not directed against our work really works for us. This is no contradiction of Matt. 12 : 30, where inactive neutrality is called decision against Jesus; for here the non-opposed activity, although without the apostolic circle, is designated as decision for Him. Christ "distinguishes between the worldly neutrality and the neutrality of weakness."—AUGUSTINE. "He is with Christ, who though he does not outwardly follow Christ, yet is not against His doctrine, like Nicodemus, Joseph of Arimithea and other secret disciples of Jesus Christ." —STARKE. This word of Christ absolutely repudiates the position, that beyond a certain communion there is no salvation.[1] Ver. 41. **For . . . reward** (Matt. 10 : 42). Not only great activity, but also the least service rendered a disciple for Christ's sake, shall receive its appropriate reward from God. The value of this last act shows how highly the inclination toward Christ by working in His name is appreciated. The smallest favor done for Christ's sake is often a sign of incipient faith. To hinder this deserves as great punishment, as the least act of love deserves reward. Ver. 42. **And . . . ones**, children literally and spiritually, *that believe on me*[2]

---

[1] Augustine (On Baptism, ag. the Donatists, Bk. VII., C. 30. 77) well says: "But there may be something Catholic outside the Catholic Church, just as the name of Christ could exist outside the congregation of Christ, in which name he who did not follow with the disciples was casting out devils."

[2] "On me," omitted by ℵ, Δ, is supported by A, B, L, Σ.

(1 : 15) **to stumble** (4 : 17; 6 : 3), be entrapped away from faith, **it . . . sea**. This punishment of having not an ordinary millstone turned by hand (Matt. 24 : 41; Luke 17 : 35), but the immense stone moved by an ass hanged about the neck[1] and to be drowned, was not only a Roman,[2] but also a Greek, Syrian and Phenician custom. It was considered one of the severest modes of punishment. Such terrible earthly punishment is preferable to being a spiritual rock of offence to the least of the believers and receiving divine punishment. Therefore we should, by self-renunciation, avoid offending others, and becoming a stumbling stone to ourselves. Ver. 43. **And . . . off** Matt. 5 : 30). The **hand**, the **foot** (ver. 45), the **eye** (ver. 47), the first as the member of activity, the second of our walk, the third of guidance to direct work and walk and through which temptation enters most readily (Gen. 3 : 6; Matt. 6 : 23) and lust shines out (Matt. 5 : 28; 1 John 2 : 16), are to be **cut off**, i. e. " tamed through the Spirit, that they do not what sin will have."— LUTHER. They are not to be instruments of unrighteousness (Rom. 6 : 13). **It is good** *for thee to enter life* eternal **maimed, halt** (ver. 45), **with one eye** (ver. 47), having had these members as offending and sinful become inactive with their lusts, *rather than having* them unrestrained in sin, and *go into* **hell** (Gehenna). Gehenna is derived from the valley of Hinnom, also called Topheth (2 Kings 23 : 10; Isai. 30 : 33), which, situated south of Mount Zion (Josh. 18 : 16), is a gloomy ravine enclosed by bleak hills. Used during the reign of Ahaz and Manasseh for the idolatry of Molech and Chemosh, to appease whom the

---

[1] Although the Talmud (Kidd. 29b) contains this expression, it is as a figure for insurmountable difficulties. Edersheim. II., p. 120.

[2] The Romans inflicted it upon some of the leaders of the insurrection under Judas of Galilee.

Israelites cast their children into the red-hot arms of a huge brazen statue (2 Kings 16 : 3 ; 2 Chron. 28 : 3 ; Jer. 7 : 31), it was profaned by Josiah (2 Kings 23 : 10 sq.) to stop the abomination of such idolatry by scattering human bones and other corrupting matter. It became the place of burial (Jer. 7 : 32), and finally the common cesspool,[1] and was regarded with detestation. Thus it arose to be the expression for the final place of torment, which Christ further calls **unquenchable fire**,[2] taking up the word of John the Baptist (Matt. 3 : 12) and confirming the eternity of punishment and its character. Ver. 48. **Where . . . quenched.** Isaiah's expression (66 : 24) is adopted by Christ as His. With it He affirms, by the picture of the **worm**, the inner decay of the dead (Job 17 : 14 ; 21 : 26 ; Isai. 14 : 11), and by **the fire** to destroy outwardly the wicked and idolaters (Isai. 1 : 31 ; 27 : 4 ; 47 : 14), the endless pains of conscience of the eternally dead and the unceasing action of the holiness of God (fire) (Isai. 10 : 17 ; Rev. 14 : 11 ; 20 : 10) against them. The fire is not quenched, because the worm dies not. It is the unchanging perversity which necessitates endless punishment. How can any dare to doubt hell and its damnation, after Christ has so plainly asserted it. Ver. 49. **For . . . fire**[3] **. . . salt.** Whoever would escape unquenchable fire, must now be *salted*, receive the preservative result of the *fire* of self-renunciation (ver. 43 sq.) and divinely sent tribulation (1 Pet. 4 : 12 ; Hebr. 12 : 6 sq.). Thus he will be an acceptable offering (Isai. 66 : 20 ; Mal.

---

[1] Plumptre, Thomson, II., 494 sq.; Porter, Syria, p. 92.

[2] The omission of v. 44 and 46 is upon the authority of א, B, C, L, Δ, etc.

[3] "And every sacrifice," etc., referred to in the margin by the Revisers, is wanting in א, B, L, Δ, and eleven cursives, and is found in A, C, D, etc., and the majority of uncials. As it presents a real difficulty, it is more probable that it was original.

1 : 11; Rom. 12 : 1) and received after the type of the O. T. sacrifice, both meat-offering (Lev. 2 : 13) and burnt-offering (Ez. 43 : 23, 24), because he is purified and made incorruptible by *salt*, which is parallel with fire. For "fire is salt and salt is fire."—STILLING. Both penetrate and separate the corruptible, and preserve what is sound. Ver. 50. **Salt . . . it?** *Salt* pictures not, as Matt. 5 : 13, the disciples in their power of preserving the decaying world, but the spirit, which makes them such salt. This is the inward spirit of grace, that works self-sacrifice and sanctification, and is **good**, life-preserving and saving. But if the Christian has lost this spirit, he is as useless as salt without saltness,[1] fit to be cast out (Matt. 5 : 13). Therefore Christ adds, **Have** *salt in yourselves, and be at peace one with* **another** (1 Thess. 5 : 13). The possession of salt in the heart, the right spirit of grace, will season words and deeds (Eph. 4 : 29; Col. 4 : 6), and must lead to peace and not emulation as to rank (ver. 34), honor, or any other matter among Christians. The salt keeps humble and peaceful. "As the salt is not to salt the salt, but what is unsalted, thus the life-power of the children of God should not be wasted in contention among themselves, but be applied to give life to the world."—OHLSHAUSEN.

---

[1] Thomson (II. 42 sq.) tells of a merchant, who, having stored up salt in houses with earthen floors, found his salt near the ground entirely spoilt. It was literally thrown into the street and trodden under foot.

CHAPTER X.

1–12. And he arose from thence, and cometh into the borders of Judæa and beyond Jordan: and multitudes come together unto him again; and, as he was wont, he taught them again. And there came unto him Pharisees, and asked him, Is it lawful for a man to put away *his* wife? tempting him. And he answered and said unto them, What did Moses command you? And they said, Moses suffered to write a bill of divorcement, and to put her away. But Jesus said unto them, For your hardness of heart he wrote you this commandment. But from the beginning of the creation, Male and female made he them. For this cause shall a man leave his father and mother, and shall cleave to his wife; and the twain shall become one flesh: so that they are no more twain, but one flesh. What therefore God hath joined together, let not man put asunder. And in the house the disciples asked him again of this matter. And he saith unto them, Whosoever shall put away his wife, and marry another, committeth adultery against her: and if she herself shall put away her husband, and marry another, she committeth adultery.

Ver. 1. Christ *arose from* **thence**, Capernaum (9 : 33), and *cometh into the borders of Judæa*, on His way toward Jerusalem (ver. 32). This is the first Judæan journey reported by the Synoptists, although they presuppose others (Matt. 23 : 37; Luke 13 : 34). Entering from the south, He visited also the borders of *beyond Jordan*, i. e. Peræa (3 : 8).[1] And *multitudes*, that gathered (3 : 7, 8), were no longer shunned as in Galilee (9 : 30), but taught. Ver. 2. **And . . . wife?**[2] This question was one much

---

[1] This interpretation of Klostermann and Weiss is not generally accepted. Most commentators, e. g. Ewald, Meyer, Lange, Keil, Nösgen, Morison, Cook, etc., regard "and beyond Jordan" as designating the way of approach.

[2] The addition of Matthew (19 : 3) " for every cause " defines the point of discussion more closely; but Mark's general statement is not contradictory.

disputed in the Rabbinic schools. The stricter school of Schammai permitted divorce only for unchastity, while the laxer school of Hillel allowed a man to send away his wife for almost any reason,[1] both starting from Deut. 24:1 ("unseemly thing," lit. matter of nakedness).[2] Schammai was more in the right than Hillel, who used an exegetical possibility to the detriment of morality.[3] In this matter the Pharisees sought Christ, **tempting him**; that declaring Himself for Schammai He might fall into disfavor with the majority of the people in their loose practice, or taking Hillel's side He might be declared lax, and in contradiction with His own former utterances (Matt. 5:32; Luke 16:17, 18), that were more severe than Schammai. Ver. 3. **He** *answered, What did Moses*[4] *command* **you**? and approved of no school, but appealed to the Scriptures, leading back beyond the mooted question (Matt. 19:4 sq.). But the Pharisees in opposition revert again to Deut. 24:1, saying, Ver. 4, **Moses . . . away.** They claim the legal right of divorce, if properly

---

[1] In Gitt. 90a, the tractate on divorce, the spoiling of a dinner is given as a sufficient ground of divorce. Rabbi Akiba taught that a man might divorce his wife if he saw a more attractive woman. Although many of the better Rabbis discouraged such ideas, the objectionable advice of the liberals obtained. (Edersheim, II., p. 332 sq.)

[2] Ërräth Dābār.

[3] See Farrar, p. 444, who has well summed up Stier's remarks.

[4] Mark reports Christ as arguing from the Mosaic to the paradisaic law, and not conversely as Matt. But neither Matt. (Stier, Meyer, Baur, Holsten) nor Mark (Bleek, Lange, Volkmar, Weiss, Holtzmann) has the original order exclusively; nor is Mark determined by the character of his readers. (Kiel.) The accounts of the two witnesses can be combined, if v. 3 of Mark is placed before Matt. 19:4: "Have ye not read, etc.," and the assertion Mark v. 4 before the question Matt. v. 7, and v. 6 sq. of Mark after v. 8 of Matt. Christ's double question is then followed by an answer and objecting question of the Pharisees, which Christ meets, and closes up his thought, in the circular manner so frequently found in John, by reasserting strongly his second question. (Cf. Augustine, De Cons. II. LXII. 122.)

done by a written *bill of divorce*, which could not be given suddenly in anger but only after endorsement by a Rabbi. Ver. 5. **But . . . commandment.** The law to which you appeal, supposing that a Mosaic enactment cannot be sinful, has simply permitted existing conditions, as e. g. blood-revenge (Deut. 19 : 1 sq.), restricting them as much as possible. Such permission was necessary **for your hardness of heart,** to which the Law (Exod. 32 : 9; 33 : 3; Deut. 9 : 6, 27; 10 : 16) testifies and which the prophets confirm (Jer. 9 : 26; Ezek. 3 : 7). Sin makes certain concessions necessary in law to avoid greater evils; but sufferance does not mean divine approval. This Jesus shows by appealing to God's original law. Ver. 6. **But** *from the beginning of creation* (2 Pet. 3 : 4), *Male and Female made he* **them.** Christ, to explain the later law of Moses, begins with the divine order of creation, as reported by Moses in his historic foundation-chapters, and cites Gen. 1 : 27b according to the Septuagint. The creation of the woman has not yet been told, but in Adam she had been potentially made. The duality, so necessary as complement and counterpart, began in unity. Ver. 7. **For . . . cleave** (be glued—Petter) **to his wife.** Ver. 8. **And . . . flesh.** The words of Adam (Gen. 2 : 24) are adopted by Christ, because they prophetically spoke the divine mind on the closeness of the marriage-bond, which transcends in its demand the filial relation and finds its foundation in the unity of two, male and female, and not more (Mal. 2 : 14 sq.), in oneness of flesh. Two persons are one person within the limits of the bodily-sexual life (1 Cor. 6 : 16, 17; 7 : 4; Eph. 5 : 28 sq.). "Have they become one flesh, they cannot be divided."—LUTHER. Ver. 9. **What . . . asunder.** God's joining together of male and

---

[1] This clause omitted in ℵ, B, is found in A, C, D, L, N.

female in the creation of Adam[1] furnishes the constant sanction of marriage. Because the union is God's, man should not in violation of divine purpose separate. Therefore divorce is not originally lawful (ver. 2). Ver. 10. *And*, as Mark reports more accurately, in . . . **matter** of divorce and subsequent marriage. Ver. 11, 12. **And** . . . **adultery**. This principle for the Church of the N. T. does not exclude the exception Matt. 19 : 9. It makes of an unauthorized second marriage an act of adultery against the forsaken part, and places the woman in an equal position, against the custom of the Jews, which permitted only the husband to dissolve the marriage-bond (Jos. Antiq. XVI. 7, 10). Marriage, a type of Christ's relation to the Church (Eph. 5 : 32), should have the same permanence.[2]

[1] Cf. von Hofmann, Weissag., Mann u. Weib, p. 65 sq.
[2] 1 Cor. 7 : 15 is no relaxation of this word of Christ. It is an exception caused by sin like Deut. 24 : 1; and "Christ gives the cause to *seek* the apostle to *suffer* divorce." (Gerhard.) The inspired apostolic permission, together with the declaration of Christ, justify the Luth. Church in holding that, "unjust is the tradition which forbids an innocent person to marry after divorce" (Sm. Art. App., p. 351, 78), while firmly maintaining with Luther (Erl. Ed. 51 : 47) that there should be no divorce for difference of faith. (Form. Con. C. XII., Epit. 531, 19; Sol. Decl. 669, 24.) The position of Luther, who restricted divorce to the two causes, adultery and malicious desertion, which are scripturally sanctioned, obtained at first in the Luth. Church. (Sermon vom ehl. Stand (1519) Erl. Ed. 16 : 49 sq.; Ausleg. des 7 Kap. des 1 Cor. Br. (1523) 51 : 36 sq.; Walch, VIII. 1056 sq.; Ein Predigt vom Ehestand (1525) 17 : 116 sq.; Letter to the council and ministers at Domitsch (Aug. 1525) 53 : 326; De Wette, III. 22; Von Ehesachen (1530) 23 : 144 sq.; Ausleg. von Matt. 5 : 31 (1532) 43 : 120, Walch, VII. 452; Pred. über Matt. 19 : 1-19. (1537) 44 : 131 sq.; Walch, VII. 961 sq.). The laxer view of Melanchthon, which included cruelty, gained acceptance after the close of the 17th century.—Cf. Chemnitz Exam. (Ed. Preuss, p. 496 sq.; Gerhard, Loci (Ed. Preuss) VII. 369, espec. Sec. III. 1, p. 571 sq.; Harless, Die Ehescheidungsfrage; Ethics, p. 441 sq.; Martensen, Ethics, III. 50 sq.; Frank, Chrl. Sittl. II. 400 sq.; Richter, Kirchenrecht, p. 635; Walther, Amer. Pastoraltheol. (3d ed.) 242 sq.

13–16. And they brought unto him little children, that he should touch them: and the disciples rebuked them. But when Jesus saw it, he was moved with indignation, and said unto them, Suffer the little children to come unto me; forbid them not: for of such is the kingdom of God. Verily, I say unto you, Whosoever shall not receive the kingdom of God as a little child, he shall in no wise enter therein. And he took them in his arms, and blessed them, laying his hands upon them.

Ver. 13. *And*, while Jesus was still in the house (ver. 10), **they,** fathers and mothers, *brought unto him little children* and infants (Luke 18 : 15), **that . . . them,** by laying on hands (Matt. 19 : 13), so that the children might receive of His blessed power. Children are unblessed without Jesus. **And . . . them**, not only because they did not wish to be disturbed in their conversation with Jesus, but also because they thought it inconsistent with the dignity of Christ. Ver. 14. **But . . . indignation,**[1] because His disciples so little knew His mind, and so soon forgot the previous instruction (9 : 36; Matt. 18 : 3). He **said . . . not.** With this double antithetic command, that sharply rebukes the disciples, Christ grants approach "to those who are not yet of age to know how much they need His grace."—CALVIN. *For of* **such,** little children and those like them in true simplicity, humility, and helplessness, *is the kingdom of God* (1 : 15), not by natural possession (John 3 : 3, 5) but by non-obstructive receptivity for redeeming grace. Ver. 15. **Verily** (3 : 28) **. . . therein.** Child-nature is the proper state for obtaining the kingdom, and even adults who enter must become as children in spirit (Matt. 18 : 3). "If Christ will not save any one, except he become a child, how much more does He save those who are children before."—LUTHER. Therefore, Ver. 16, *he took them in his arms* (9 : 36), *blessed them* individually, **laying his hands** *upon them,*

---

[1] This severe word (ἠγανάκτησεν) is nowhere else attributed to Jesus.

which was the channel of His words of blessing (5 : 23). This was a real invoked (Matt. 19 : 13) blessing, not dependent upon nor commensurate with the understanding of the children. It was not instituted as a rite, but forms the spiritual, although not historic, foundation of infant-baptism, and is its justification.[1] " Infants are renewed by the Spirit of God, according to the capacity of their age, till that power which was concealed within them grows by degrees, and becomes fully manifest at the proper time."—CALVIN.

17-22. *And as he was going forth into the way, there ran one to him, and kneeled to him, and asked him, Good Master, what shall I do that I may inherit eternal life? And Jesus said unto him, Why callest thou me good? none is good save one, even God. Thou knowest the commandments, Do not kill, Do not commit adultery, Do not steal, Do not bear false witness, Do not defraud, Honour thy father and mother. And he said unto him, Master, all these things have I observed from my youth. And Jesus looking upon him loved him, and said unto him, One thing thou lackest: go sell whatsoever thou hast, and give to the poor, and thou shalt have treasure in heaven; and come, follow me. But his countenance fell at the saying, and he went away sorrowful; for he was one that had great possessions.*

Ver. 17. *And as* Jesus *was going forth* **into the way**, out of the house (ver. 10), on the road of journey, *there ran* eagerly *to him* a young man (Matt. 19 : 22), the ruler of a local synagogue (Luke 18 : 18), who **kneeled** in reverence for Christ (cf. 3 : 11 ; 5 : 6), and **asked . . . life?** The ruler addresses Jesus as **good**, not in compliment or flattery, but in truth, because he believes the high attribute of goodness attainable by man. Therefore he asks what good thing (Matt. 19 : 16) he must do to gain eternal life. This was a question often asked of rabbis; and it combines with the memory of the kingdom as an allotted gift (inherit), the pharasaic notion of

---

[1] Cf. Luther, Walch, VII. 983 sq.

obtaining by a special meritorious act **life eternal**, which conception was known more clearly only to the later Jews (Dan. 12 : 2 ; Ecclus. 2 : 23 ; 15 : 3),[1] although life as the highest and best of all possessions was always emphasized (Deut. 34 : 4, 7 ; Ps. 27 : 13 ; 34 : 12 ; Prov. 6 : 23 ; 8 : 35). This life eternal, as the absolute antithesis to death, receives its highest fulfilment and blessing with the coming of salvation in Christ (Rom. 6 : 23 ; Col. 3 : 4 ; 2 Tim. 1 : 10), and therefore is not only a future one as the Synoptists[2] show (Matt. 19 : 16; Mark 10 : 30; Luke 10 : 25 ; 18 : 18), but a present one as confirmed by John (3 : 13, 16 ; 5 : 39, 40 ; 17 : 3) and Paul (2 Cor. 2 : 16 ; 4 : 11 ; Phil. 2 : 16). The question after life eternal is a blessed one if asked not in work-righteousness, but in reliance upon divine grace in Jesus. Ver. 18. He said to the ruler, **Why . . . good**[3] **. . . God.** Christ refuses to be called good, not because He was not thus, nor to suggest a development necessary for Himself, nor to contrast His perfect human consciousness with God, nor to lead to the confession of His divinity. Good is repudiated as connected with " Master,"[4] because applied

---

[1] Delitzsch (Lect. on O. T. Theol. Par. 27 Hades) says that the O. T. apocrypha show that "the religious consciousness, from premises which revelation offers, gradually drew the conclusion, that man trusting upon God attained through death, what could not be reached without death, namely, the perfect life in communion with God. But only the N. T. fact of redemption offers certainty and puts an end to the wavering." Cf. also Öhler, O. T. Theol., p. 169, 174, 514, 551, 559.

[2] The synoptists, while not applying the term life eternal to the present, know of the present blessedness of this life as is shown by the blessings of the Sermon of the Mount. See Nösgen, I., p. 283.

[3] Matt. 19 : 17. " Why askest thou me concerning that which is good ? " must be inserted after the question of Mark.

[4] Stier (II. 325) notes that this is different from John 10 : 11, " I am the good shepherd," which is to be interpreted by the sense of " good " in this passage.

so superficially to sinful man. God alone is good, because He alone has the full inner harmonious perfection. Man even at the best can receive goodness but imperfectly. "The Saviour will not suffer this word 'good,' because the Pharisee does not direct it toward God."—LUTHER. To his good-will (Rom. 7 : 12) Christ refers, when He says, Ver. 19, **Thou . . . commandments**, for whose observation life is promised (Lev. 18 : 5 ; Deut. 30 : 19). In holding up the required standard of the law, without any rabbinic tradition, Christ establishes no righteousness of the law (Rom. 10 : 5), but only vindicates its sufficiency, if kept. "What God hath commanded must be better than all commandments of men, even though they were the most beautiful."—LUTHER. The second table is cited, because it could more readily bring to the consciousness of the self-righteous man (cf. Luke 18 : 11, 12) his defect of love (Matt. 19 : 19), that would prove a want of piety. The commandments are mentioned in order from the fifth to the tenth, which is combined with the ninth after the manner of Lev. 19 : 13 ; Deut. 24 : 14 ; Mal. 3 : 5, because with the rich young man coveting would take the form of withholding what was due and defrauding (1 Cor. 6 : 7, 8 ; 1 Tim. 6 : 5 ; James 5 : 4). The fourth commandment is the last because the fundamental one (7 : 10), and apt to be regarded by the young ruler as no longer applicable to himself. Thus Christ departs from the recognized order of the commandments not in arbitrary freedom, but in wise pastoral application to the young man, who, Ver. 20, **said . . . youth**. The young ruler in his atomistic (these things) self-righteousness answers at once, asserting especially in answer to the fourth commandment his complete observance since earliest youth (2 Tim. 3 : 15). He was truthful, but confounds blamelessness "touching the righteousness, which is in the law" (Phil. 3 : 6), with true goodness and love. Ver. 21. **And ... him.** Despite blind self-righteousness the young man had an eager, earnest longing for the spiritual. For this he received Christ's love of appreciation, and for his blindness the love of compassion. Therefore Christ said, **One ... lackest** (Luke 10 : 42), but in it shall thy whole love be tested: **go ... heaven,** glory and honor before God (Matt. 6 : 2), and recompense from the believing poor (Luke 16 : 9): **and ... follow me.** This urgent invitation to discipleship was the motive for the preceding command, which demands no supererogatory work nor sanctions communism, but sought to deliver the young man from the love of riches by their complete surrender, the only help in this individual case. Riches must not hinder salvation (1 Tim. 6 : 17). They affected this in the young ruler, for, Ver. 22, **his ... fell,** became gloomy, **and ... sorrowful,** "Through the overpowering love of what was valueless, he lost the possession of what was of greatest price."—AUGUSTINE.

23–31. And Jesus looked round about, and saith unto his disciples, How hardly shall they that have riches enter into the kingdom of God! And the disciples were amazed at his words. But Jesus answereth again, and saith unto them, Children, how hard is it for them that trust in riches to enter into the kingdom of God! It is easier for a camel to go through a needle's eye, than for a rich man to enter into the kingdom of God. And they were astonished exceedingly, saying unto him, Then who can be saved? Jesus looking upon them saith, With men it is impossible, but not with God: for all things are possible with God. Peter began to say unto him, Lo, we have left all, and have followed thee. Jesus said, Verily I say unto you, There is no man that hath left house, or brethren, or sisters, or mother, or father, or children, or lands, for my sake, and for the gospel's sake, but he shall receive a hundredfold now in this time, houses, and brethren, and sisters, and mothers, and children, and lands, with persecutions; and in the world to come eternal life. But many *that are* first shall be last; and the last first.

Ver. 23. **Jesus ... about** on His disciples, **and saith**

... **God**, in its eternal consummation (1 : 15). Ver. 24. When **the disciples** ... **amazed** at the great danger of riches, **Jesus** ... **again**, addressing them in affectionate solicitude, **Children** (2 : 5 ; 5 : 34 ; John 13 : 33), and confirms the danger of having riches to be the trusting[1] in them (Ps. 52 : 7 ; 62 : 10 ; Prov. 11 : 28 ; Matt. 6 : 21 ; 1 Tim. 6 : 17). As so many do this, Ver. 25, **It** ... **God**. With a proverbial[2] expression, which is not to be weakened by reading cable (κάμιλον) for camel (κάμηλον) and by supposing the needle's eye to be a narrow gate, Jesus asserts the impossibility of the rich (cf. Isai. 53 : 9) being saved. Ver. 26. The disciples **were** ... **saved?** In greatest astonishment the disciples, who know how all men both rich and poor seek possessions (1 Tim. 6 : 9) and notice some desire in their own hearts, ask, who, if it be so impossible, can be saved. "Salvation is not to be taken as such an easy and small matter, for then we will not be concerned about it. What we hold difficult, we seek earnestly" (Phil. 2 : 12).—CANSTEIN, STARKE. Ver. 27. **Jesus** ... **God.** Christ now speaks as a "pleasant, faithful teacher,"—LUTHER, and "after men have been bowed down teaches them to rely on the grace of God alone."—CALVIN. Men cannot free themselves from the dangerous power of riches, but God, who can accomplish all things not inconsistent with His holiness, wisdom, and love, grants the prevenient and preserving grace, imparting to all-powerful faith (9 : 23) its inward strength (Col. 2 : 12 ; 1 Peter 1 : 5). The greatest comfort to us weak, sinful men is that God is greater than our heart (1 John 3 : 20). Ver. 28. Then **Peter**, forgetting what God had

---

[1] "For them that trust in riches," wanting in ℵ, B, Δ, is to be retained accdg. to A, C, D, N. (Keil, p. 109.)

[2] Cf. a similar proverb about the elephant in the Talmud, Ber. 55b, and in the Koran, Sur. 7 : 38.

done for the twelve, in self-complacency compares their denial with the rich young man (ver. 22), and says, **Lo . . . followed thee.** The disciples had truly forsaken all they had (1 : 20) for Christ, but Peter recounts it in a spirit of boastfulness and asks for the reward (Matt. 19 : 27). What was all in comparison with Christ? "All which? O blessed Peter, the rod, the net, the boat? the craft? These things dost thou tell me of as all."—CHRYSOSTOM. Ver. 29. **Verily . . . no man** (cf. Tim. 4 : 8) **. . . house,** the dear ones of the family, **or . . . gospel's** (8 : 35), Ver. 30, **but . . . hundredfold,** the completest[1] recompense, **now . . houses** of friends that receive him, spiritual **brethren . . . sisters** (1 Tim. 5 : 1, 2), **mothers** in Christ to care for him (Rom. 16 : 13), but no fathers, for there is but one spiritual father (1 Cor. 4 : 15), and **children,** as many as he begets by the gospel (1 Cor. 4 : 15), **and lands** through the common possessions of believers (Acts 2 : 44; 4 : 32). Thus, though poor, the believers possess all things (2 Cor. 6 : 10) and all are theirs (1 Cor. 3 : 22), **with persecutions,** which are added as a special blessing (Matt. 5 : 10; Rom. 5 : 3; 2 Cor. 12 : 10; Phil. 1 : 29; 2 Thess. 1 : 4; 2 Tim. 3 : 11; 1 Peter 1 : 6; 3 : 14; 4 : 12; Hebr. 12 : 6); **and . . . come,** the glorious future age in which the messianic reign is complete (1 Peter 4 : 11; Hebr. 1 : 8; 9 : 26; Rev. 1 : 6, 8; 4 : 9, 10, etc.), **eternal life** (ver. 17), " the all-embracing unity, consummation, fulness, and depth of all-compensating retribution."—LANGE. " How faithful is God! and how richly He rewards the duty that we owe Him without all recompense" (Hebr. 11 : 6).—HEDINGER, STARKE. Ver. 31. **But,** adds Christ, **many . . . first** (Luke 13 : 30). This word of warning, which the parable of the laborers in the vine-

---

[1] Ten, the number of perfection, ten times.

yard (Matt. 20 : 1 sq.) unfolds, is directed against the wrong spirit of seeking reward, by which those first in this life in honor, work, gifts, self-denial, shall be last in eternity; while the last here, who have relied upon grace, shall be first. Grace is the law of God's kingdom, and even reward is of grace (cf. Luke 17 : 10).

32-34. *And they were in the way, going up to Jerusalem; and Jesus was going before them: and they were amazed; and they that followed were afraid. And he took again the twelve, and began to tell them the things that were to happen unto him, saying, Behold, we go up to Jerusalem; and the Son of man shall be delivered unto the chief priests and the scribes; and they shall condemn him to death, and shall deliver him unto the Gentiles; and they shall mock him, and shall spit upon him, and shall scourge him, and shall kill him; and after three days he shall rise again.*

Ver. 32. **In the way** (ver. 17) leading to Jerusalem, **Jesus . . . going before** the disciples with bold and calm resolve; **and they,** the twelve, **were amazed** (ver. 24) at the calm majesty with which their Lord proceeded toward the city, where they knew great enmity awaited Him; and **they that followed,** other disciples, **were afraid,** in dread of things to come. "What a scene, Jesus walking in lonely majesty toward death, and behind Him in awful reverence and mingled anticipations of dread and hope," —FARRAR, His disciples. **And he . . . twelve** closely to Himself, and began to tell of His sufferings (8 : 31), their place, His deliverance by betrayal to the chief priests (14 : 10), who would deliver Him to the Gentiles (15 : 1 sq.), the mocking (15 : 20), spitting (15 : 19), scourging (15 : 15), ending with death by crucifixion (Matt. 20 : 19) and resurrection. "He came to His passion, and willing it, not in ignorance nor by constraint."—CHRYSOSTOM.

35-45. *And there come near unto him James and John, the sons of Zebedee, saying unto him, Master, we would that thou shouldest do for us whatsoever we shall ask of thee. And he said unto them, What would ye* that I should do for you? And they said unto him, Grant unto us that we may sit, one on thy right hand, and one on *thy* left hand, in thy glory. But Jesus said unto them, Ye know not what ye ask. Are ye able to drink the cup that I drink? or to be baptized with the baptism that I am baptized with? And they said unto him, We are able. And Jesus said unto them, The cup that I drink ye shall drink; and with the baptism that I am baptized withal shall ye be baptized; but to sit on my right hand or on *my* left hand is not mine to give: but *it is for them* for whom it hath been prepared. And when the ten heard it, they began to be moved with indignation concerning James and John. And Jesus called them to him, and saith unto them, Ye know that they which are accounted to rule over the Gentiles lord it over them; and their great ones exercise authority over them. But it is not so among you; but whosoever would become great among you, shall be your minister; and whosoever would be first among you, shall be servant of all. For verily the Son of man came not to be ministered unto, but to minister, and to give his life a ransom for many.

Ver. 35. **There . . . John** (1 : 19), who, through their mother[1] (Matt. 20 : 20), to whose desire they acquiesce against their better knowledge (9 : 35; 10 : 31), ask for the promise to have a favor granted before announcing it. Ver. 36. But Jesus **said . . . you?** not because He is ignorant of their thoughts (2 : 8), but that in speaking them out they may be laid open to themselves and all, to be corrected. Ver. 37. *They said,* **Grant . . . glory.** This high aspiration of the sons of Zebedee, showing their character (3 : 17), was prompted by the promise Matt. 19 : 28, and their peculiar election (5 : 37; 9 : 2). The petition for places next to Christ in honor and power, while indicating faith in His glorious kingly rule, is full of self-seeking pride and desires glory, though Christ has just spoken (ver. 34) of suffering. "The flesh always desires to become glorious before it is crucified, to become exalted sooner than it is humbled."—LUTHER.

[1] Mark's omission of the mother is no contradiction, for, "who acts through another person, acts through himself." (Cf. Matt. 8 : 5 and Luke 7 : 3; John 3 : 22 and 4 : 1.) Robinson, Harm, 219; Tertull. on Bapt. C. XI.; Augustine, De Cons. II. LXIV. 124.

Ver. 38. **But ... seek.** You are ignorant of what your request includes for you. "They sought the exaltation, but they did not see the step."—AUGUSTINE. Therefore Christ says, **Are ... that I drink?** The **cup**, designating here the inner experience of suffering willingly received, is in its full sense for Christ not the partaking (Ps. 16 : 5) of the cup of rejection (Ps. 75 : 8; Ezek. 23 : 31; Rev. 14 : 10), although it is the taking of "the cup of fury and staggering" (Ps. 60 : 3; Isai. 51 : 17) as punishment (Jer. 49 : 12) in tasting God's wrath even unto death (14 : 36), which Christ underwent vicariously (Isai. 53 : 5; 2 Cor. 5 : 21) changing the cup of fury into the "cup of salvation" (Ps. 116 : 13). To the cup is added **the baptism**, which, looking to the suffering as endured (Luke 12 : 50), expresses it under the picture of the floods that go over the soul (Ps. 42 : 7; 69 : 2; 124 : 4¶). In these Christ died and arose (Rom. 6 : 4). These James and John promise to undergo, saying, Ver. 39, **We ... able**, hastily like Peter (John 13 : 37). Christ, recognizing their willing (14 : 38) love, foretells that they shall suffer with Him, which James experienced first and John last. All that are Christ's must drink His cup (2 Cor. 4 : 10; Gal. 6 : 17; 1 Pet. 4 : 13) before coming to His glory (Rom. 8 : 17). Ver. 40. **But ... prepared.** Not even the Son can by His own preference or of Himself alone (John 8 : 28) give special glory (1 Cor. 15 : 41) above that of all saints (2 Tim. 2 : 11, 12; 1 John 3 : 2; Rev. 3 : 21), but the Father (Matt. 20 : 23), according to whose appointment the Son gives the kingdom (Luke 22 : 29), and to whom the Son is finally subjected (1 Cor. 15 : 28) has prepared it (Matt. 25 : 34) in His eternal purpose. Ver. 41. **When ... indignation** (ver. 14) because of equal ambition and jealousy (9 : 34). "There was not one of them who would willingly yield to others, but each one secretly cherished within himself the expectation of the primacy."—CALVIN. Ver. 42. Therefore *Jesus called them to Him* (9 : 35) *and* **saith ... accounted,**[1] recognized, **to rule ... them.** The disciples are bidden to recall how in the worldly kingdoms those received as rulers and called great overrule (Acts 19 : 16; 1 Peter 5 : 3) the will and interests of their subjects according to their arbitrary sovereignty. The ruling ambition is characteristic of all Gentile kingdoms. Ver. 43. **But .. you.** The kingdom of Christ has a different law of greatness. **Whosoever ...** Ver. 44, **... all** (9 : 35). Greatness in Christ's kingdom consists in service, the primacy in being a bondservant (1 Cor. 9 : 19). Under the one Lord and Master (John 13 : 13), the head of the Church (Eph. 1 : 22; Col. 1 : 18), even the spiritual power to be exercised through the word (Matt. 16 : 19; 18 : 18; 2 Cor 10 : 8; 13 : 10) is no lordship over faith and life (2 Cor. 1 : 24; 1 Peter 5 : 3). Those who have rule (1 Cor. 12 : 28; Hebr. 13 : 17) as shepherds (Acts 20 : 28) are to use their office for service (2 Cor. 4 : 5; Phil. 1 : 1): "My office is only a service, which I should perform freely for all."—LUTHER. Ver. 45. **For ... the Son of man** (2 : 10) **... minister.** The king himself was a servant who, as prophesied (Isai. 43 : 24, 25), came not for rule and judgment (John 3 : 17) but as a "deacon" of all (Luke 22 : 27; John 13 : 1 sq.). His highest service was to **give ... many.** The giving of life by the Son of man was not only an example of love (John 10 : 12, 18; 15 : 13) for men (1 John 3 : 16), but especially a price of redemption freeing from punishment (Exod. 21 : 30; Numb. 31 : 30; Prov. 11 : 8; 21 : 18) and the atoning sacrifice (Lev. 17 : 11; Ps. 49 : 7, 8; Isai. 53 : 10, 12; Mark 14 : 24; Rom.

---

[1] For this sense of διακονῶντες, see Luke 22 : 24; Gal. 2 : 6, 9. Winer, p. 613.

3 : 25 ; 1 Cor. 11 : 24, 25). Redeeming from sin (14 : 24 ; 2 Cor. 5 : 19; Tit. 2 : 14; 1 Pet. 2 : 24), death (Hebr. 5 : 7, 8) and Satan (Hebr. 2 : 14), its value was not only that of the man Christ Jesus (1 Tim. 2 : 6), in obedience (Rom. 5 : 19; Heb. 9 : 14) shedding His blood (Eph. 1 : 7; 1 Peter 1 : 19), but it was the blood of God (Acts 20 : 28 ; 1 John 1 : 7) offered in the form of a servant (Phil. 2 : 7). It was a ransom primarily as an equivalent,[1] and then a substitution for the **many**, the sinful mass of men (Rom. 5 : 15, 19). "The death of Christ is the complete atonement of the world (Rom. 5 : 10; 1 John 2 : 2)."— STARKE.

46–52. *And they come to Jericho : and as he went out from Jericho, with his disciples and a great multitude, the son of Timæus, Bartimæus, a blind beggar, was sitting by the way side. And when he heard that it was Jesus of Nazareth, he began to cry out, and say, Jesus, thou son of David, have mercy on me. And many rebuked him, that he should hold his peace : but he cried out the more a great deal, Thou son of David, have mercy on me. And Jesus stood still, and said, Call ye him. And they call the blind man, saying unto him, Be of good cheer : rise, he calleth thee. And he, casting away his garment, sprang up, and came to Jesus. And Jesus answered him, and said, What wilt thou that I should do unto thee ? And the blind man said unto him, Rabboni, that I may receive my sight. And Jesus said unto him, Go thy way, thy faith hath made thee whole. And straightway he received his sight, and followed him in the way.*

Ver. 46. **They . . . Jericho**, which, about six hours from Jerusalem, lay southeast of the ancient Jericho of the Canaanites in the valley of the Jordan. It was a garrison city, a beautiful wealthy resort amid palm-groves and balsam gardens, of mildest climate even in winter, "the Eden of Palestine, the very fairyland of the old world."—EDERSHEIM.[2] As Christ **went . . . multitude**,

---

[1] ἀντί does not express vicariousness, but it implies it. Luthardt, Comp. (7th ed.) 219; Frank, Charl. Wahr. II. 181.
[2] II. 394; Thomson II. 439 sq.; Porter, Syria, 184.

who, on the passover journey to Jerusalem, banded together for common protection (Luke 10 : 30), the **son of Timæus**, whose common Aramaic name was **Bartimæus**, a patronymic like Bartholomew (3 : 18), and who was later well known as a disciple (ver. 52), but then **a blind**[1] **beggar . . . way.** Ver. 47.[2] **When . . . Nazareth**, the name told him by the people (1 : 24), **he . . . me** (Matt. 9 : 27; 15 : 22). With the plea for help in bodily distress Bartimæus connects the believing confession, that the day of sight for the blind (Isai. 29 : 18; 35 : 5) has now come in **the son of David.** This was the prominent Jewish name for the Messiah and the basis of all their expectations, starting from prophecies like 2 Sam. 7 : 12, 13; Isai. 7 : 13 sq.; Ezek. 34 : 23 sq. Jesus was the son of David by actual descent on Mary's side[3] and

---

[1] For the frequency of blindness in the East, see Geikie, p. 187.

[2] There is a harmonistic difficulty here. Matthew (20 : 30) mentions two blind men, Mark and Luke (18 : 35) but one. Matthew and Mark speak of the healing when Christ leaves Jericho, Luke as he enters. It is not necessary with most modern scholars to ascribe an error to one of the evangelists, although the explanation of Augustine, Lightfoot, Osiander, which claims three different healings, is not tenable. The discrepancy in number cannot be solved only by Le Clerc's principle : "Who names more, embraces fewer; who recounts fewer does not deny more." It must be combined with the apparent contradiction of place, which is not explained by changing "drew nigh" (Luke), to "be near" (Grotius, Robinson), nor by accepting two Jerichos (Macknight), but rather by supposing with Bengel, that one man called on Christ as He entered, and finding another in the city, they were both healed as Christ left. Luke mentions the man met first, and without specializing the place of healing tells of it. Mark mentions the more prominent, and together with Mattthew, who is fullest, is exact as to place. August. De Cons. II. LXV. 125, 126; Trench, Mir. 339; Robinson, 221, 235.

[3] von Hoffmann (Erfüll. 34 sq.) traces the Davidic descent of Jesus to Joseph alone ; and Delitzsch (Mess. Weiss, p. 62) points to the fact that in Jewish law descent came through the father, but he admits the possibility of the Davidic origin of Mary. This admission, together with the necessary virgin-birth (Isai. 7 : 14) of Christ, which must not be obscured by human

through Joseph by adoption. Ver. 48. Not hindered by the people, who wrongly *rebuke* him, Bartimæus prays more urgently. Ver. 49. **And Jesus . . . still**, had the blind man called, who, as Mark describes graphically, Ver. 50, cast away **his garment** (abbas), outer cloak, *sprang up, came to Jesus*, upon whose question he answered, Ver. 51. **Rabboni**[1] (John 20 : 16), the highest title of respect, **that . . . sight**, lit. look up. "The most blessed desire of men is, that God may enlighten them to eternal life (Eph. 1 : 18)."—STARKE. Ver. 52. **Jesus . . . whole** (5 : 28 ; 6 : 56). This word was immediately fulfilled, and Bartimæus became a disciple. "Faith is counted of such high dignity that salvation is ascribed to it, although the work of God."—LUTHER.

law, and also Luke 1 : 32; Rom. 1 : 3; Gal. 4 : 4, vindicate the direct Davidic blood of Jesus. Nösgen, I. 99.

[1] ῥαββουνει, whose suffix has lost its personal force as it became a title, is a superlative of honor for "master" (Rab, Rabbi, Rabboni). It was a common term, possibly a Galilean provincialism. (Kautzsch.) Cf. Keil, p. 113.

CHAPTER XI.

1-10. And when they drew nigh unto Jerusalem, unto Bethphage and Bethany, at the mount of Olives, he sendeth two of his disciples, and saith unto them, Go your way into the village that is over against you: and straightway as ye enter into it, ye shall find a colt tied, whereon no man ever yet sat; loose him, and bring him. And if any one say unto you, Why do ye this? say ye, The Lord hath need of him; and straightway he will send him back hither. And they went away, and found a colt tied at the door without in the open street; and they loose him. And certain of them that stood there said unto them, What do ye, loosing the colt? And they said unto them even as Jesus had said: and they let them go. And they bring the colt unto Jesus, and cast on him their garments; and he sat upon him. And many spread their garments upon the way; and others branches, which they had cut from the fields. And they that went before, and they that followed, cried, Hosanna; Blessed *is* he that cometh in the name of the Lord: Blessed *is* the kingdom that cometh, *the kingdom* of our father David; Hosanna in the highest.

Ver. 1. **And**, having spent the sabbath at Bethany and being at a festal meal outside of the village (Nebe), at the house of Simon the leper, where Mary anointed Jesus (14 : 3 sq. ; Matt. 26 : 6 ; John 12 : 1, 3), **they . . . Bethphage**[1] **. . . Bethany.** In the enumeration of these villages, which are named as the point of starting (Bethany) and the place where the preparations for the entry began (Bethphage), the order, reverse to their actual position on the journey, is determined by their nearness to Jerusalem. **Bethphage** (house of figs), which is no district,[2] but a small village near Jerusalem, not men-

---

[1] D, the Itala, and Origen omit "Bethphage," but it is well attested by the MSS.

[2] This is claimed by Lightfoot and Caspari (Leben Jesu, p. 162).

tioned elsewhere in the Scriptures and unknown to-day, was known to the writers of the Talmud, to Origen, Eusebius, and Jerome. East [1] of it lay **Bethany** (ver. 1; John 11 : 18), the modern El-Azariyeh,[2] about two miles (15 stadia, John 11 : 18) from Jerusalem on the road to Jericho, and on the southeastern slope of the **mount of Olives**. This mountain, also called Olivet (Acts 1 : 12), had many olive-groves on its sides. Elevated 3,000 feet above the sea-level, and 2,000 feet above the temple-mount, it is a ridge with four peaks distant five stadia (two-thirds of a mile) from Jerusalem (Jos. Ant. XX. 8, 6) on its eastern side, from which it is separated by the brook and valley of Kidron (Jos. Jew. Wars, V. 2, 3).[3] It is mentioned by the O. T. prophets as the place of the coming of the Lord in glory and to judgment (Ezek. 43 : 1 sq.; Zech. 14 : 4). Where the Lord comes to judge, He appears first in mercy. Near Bethphage **he sendeth . . . disciples**, Peter and John (cf. 14 : 13 and Luke 22 : 8), with the command, Ver. 2, **Go . . . you**, some unknown place,[4] **straightway . . . him**. In this order, which with the following directions shows the divine prescience and lordship of Christ, the disciples are commanded to bring the colt of an ass,[5] which, because it was never before used, was suitable for the sacred act contemplated (Numb. 19 : 2; Deut. 21 : 3; 1 Sam. 6 : 7; 2 Sam. 6 : 3). The ass, frequent in the East, was originally an animal

---

[1] Robinson (Res. II. 103) places Bethany west of Bethphage, contrary to uniform ancient tradition.

[2] Thomson, II. 599; Schaff, Bible Lands, 276.

[3] Robinson, I. 348 sq.; Thomson, II. 464 sq.; 599 sq.

[4] Neither Bethany (Origen, Weiss, Holtzmann) nor Bethphage (Knincel, Fritzsche, Bleek, Klostermann, Meyer, v. Hofmann, Nebe, Morison, Keil, Nösgen) is clearly indicated.

[5] Mark mentions the foal alone, because it was used. (Cf. Matt. 21 : 2.)

of honor in Israel (Judg. 5 : 10; 10 : 4; 2 Sam. 17 : 23; 19 : 26); but after the Jews came in contact with other people it lost this position. Its use by Jesus in fulfilling Zech. 9 : 9 pointed to His lowliness, poverty and peacefulness. He, to further assure His disciples, adds, Ver. 3, **And . . . send** [1] **him back** [2] **hither.** The demand of the **Lord,** a word which designates Christ's superior power (5 : 19; 10 : 51; Matt. 7 : 21; 8 : 2, 6, 8, etc.) as the Messiah (1 : 3), is united with a human promise of immediate return. As in the use of the colt sacredness and lowliness are seen, thus in these words divinity and humanity appear. The disciples, Ver. 4, *went away*, and as Peter well remembers, **found . . . door without,** the entrance to the inner court, **in . . . open street,** i. e. the road which ran round about the house. Ver. 5. **And certain . . . stood there,** probably servants of the owner of the colt, at first hinder and then permit, as soon as the disciples speak what the Lord told them. Their believing obedience is rewarded, and they learn the power of the word of the Lord. Ver. 7. **And . . . garments,** the outward cloaks, serving their Master with their own in thoughtful love and reverencing honor; **and he sat . . . him.** Jesus approaches Jerusalem as king in obedience to the divine word (Zech. 9 : 9), and not in mistaken enthusiasm. He openly declares His kingship and its character by His appearance (ver. 2). Ver. 8. **And many** of the people, thronging toward Jerusalem for the passover, are attracted by the action of the larger band of disciples (Luke 19 : 36), imitate it and **spread . . . way.** This was a sign of enthusiastic reverence (2 Kings 9 : 13), that laid offerings at the feet of Jesus. Its source as with the disciples was God's

---

[1] The present is preferable accdg. to ℵ, A, B, C, D, Δ.
[2] "Again" is found in ℵ, B, C, D.

Spirit, who used the people as babes to perfect the praise of the Son (Matt. 21 : 16). **Others** of the multitude spread **branches,** lit. leafage, palm-branches (John 12 : 13), and still others approached with leaves, twigs, etc., twisted together, *which they had cut from the fields.* Thus they showed their homage of Christ as a royal victor,[1] to whom they would give their hearts. Ver. 9. **And . . . cried,** as the disciples had begun (Luke 19: 37), **Hosanna.** (Give salvation indeed!) This acclamation and prayer for salvation, taken from Ps. 118 : 25, was used at the feast of tabernacles, when the altar of burnt-offering was joyously surrounded, especially on the seventh day. It was this joyousness and the messianic hope attached to the 118th Psalm which formed the starting-point of the triumphant cry : **Blessed . . . Lord** (Ps. 118 : 26). The Messiah fulfils the commission of Jehovah as His messenger (Hebr. 3 : 1) and revealer (John 12 : 45). Ver. 10. **Blessed . . . David.** In the son of David (10 : 48) has come the realization of the promise given to David of an eternal kingdom (2 Sam. 7 : 16; Jer. 33 : 17) with its glory and power. **Hosanna . . . highest.** May the prayer of salvation be heard in the highest heaven (Luke 2 : 14). This joyous acceptance of their king by Israel, so soon followed by rejection, will be the greeting of re-acceptance (Matt. 23 : 39). Meantime it is the confession of the Israel of the N. T. of their king in whose presence there is joy and salvation.

11. And he entered into Jerusalem, into the temple: and when he had looked round about upon all things, it being now eventide, he went out unto Bethany with the twelve.

Ver. 11. Entering Jerusalem Jesus went at once **into**

---

[1] It is this well-known meaning of strewing branches rather than the waving of the branches at the feast of tabernacles which is here intended.

... **temple**, His Father's house (Luke 2 : 49); and **when ... things**, not with the astonishment of a stranger, but with the eyes of the holy judge noticing the profanation of the temple (ver. 15), *it being now* **eventide ... Bethany**. This He did every evening (ver. 19) until Thursday for the sake of rest and safety.

12-14. And on the morrow, when they were come out from Bethany, he hungered. And seeing a fig tree afar off having leaves, he came, if haply he might find anything thereon: and when he came to it, he found nothing but leaves; for it was not the season of figs. And he answered and said unto it, No man eat fruit from thee henceforward for ever. And his disciples heard it.

Ver. 12. **On the morrow**, Monday of passion-week, *when they were come out from Bethany* (ver. 11) Christ **hungered**. This real want of Jesus, in which He took upon Himself and sanctified our infirmity (Hebr. 4 : 15), was also a figure of His spiritual desire after good works in Israel,[1] and offered the opportunity of the following miracle to teach the disciples. Ver. 13. Seeing a **fig tree**, of which there were many on this road,[2] **afar off**, standing on some rocky eminence in the fields, **having leaves**, a full promising foliage, **he came ... thereon**, for the leaves of the fig tree, which are later than the fruit-buds, seemed to point to fruit. **And ... leaves**. In this Christ was not actually deceived, because He judged from His Galilean experience, which taught Him the later appearance of figs; nor did He mislead others. His act was a parable. Such " symbolic act is done as real, as professing to mean something; and yet, although not meaning the thing which it professes to mean, is no deception, since it means something infinitely higher and

---

[1] Cf. the similar double sense of " I thirst " (John 19 : 28).
[2] Stanley, Sinai and Palestine, p. 422; Geikie, p. 212.

deeper, of which the lower action is a type, and in which the lower is lost, transfigured and transformed by the higher, whereof of it is made the vehicle."—TRENCH.[1] "Jesus seeks fruit upon the tree, of which He knew that it had no fruit, because He asks fruit of the man, whom He knows as unfruitful."—AUGUSTINE. For such instruction this tree was especially fitted, **for . . . figs.** While in general the fig-season, which began at the end of June,[2] had not yet come, this one tree augured an extraordinary advancement,[3] and promised that the fruit-buds had become the early figs (bokkoroth), which were much desired (Isai. 28 : 4; Jer. 24 : 2; Hos. 9 : 10; Nah. 3 : 12).[4] And even had they not appeared, some figs of last year (kermuses)[5] should have remained. But the tree was altogether barren.[6] It was a picture of Israel, of whose unfruitfulness as testified by the prophets (Ezek. 17 : 24; Hos. 9 : 10; Joel 1 : 7) Christ had previously spoken (Luke 13 : 6 sq.), and to which He again referred Luke 23 : 31. By its many leaves of profession Israel promised what it did not have. Its sin was not being

---

[1] Miracles p. 344 sq. Augustine often discussed this difficulty and solved it. Ennar. Ev. II. 51; Serm. XXVI. 7; XXXIX. 3 sq.; XLVIII. 3. Cf. also Morison, p. 309.

[2] Sometimes the first crop was earlier. It was followed by a second crop in August and a third in September, of which some figs hung on all winter. Therefore Jos. (Wars, III. 10, 8) says that ripe fruit was found ten months (April and May being the exceptions) in good localities.

[3] Thomson (I. 538) tells of a large green-colored fig ripening early, which he plucked in May on Mt. Lebanon, 150 miles north of Jerusalem, where trees are nearly a month later.

[4] The Mishnah (Shebh. IV. 7) and Talmud (Jer. Shebh. 35b) state that unripe fruit was eaten as soon as it received a red color. Edersheim, II., p. 375.

[5] Keil argues for these alone, while Farrar rightly includes the bokkoroth.

[6] The abnormity of the tree was not the great foliage (Ebrard, Wichelhaus, Meyer, Klostermann, Weiss), but the lack of fruit with such foliage. Farrar. p. 119; Trench, p. 347; Morison, p. 310.

barren but being false.¹ Therefore Christ cursed it in its type, saying, Ver. 14, **No . . . ever.** The blighting of the tree, the symbolical counterpart to the ratification of the Levitical priesthood by the budding of the rod of Aaron in one night (Numb. 17 : 8), was the cursing of Israel which should have been a blessing (Gen. 12 : 2) and a light (Isai. 60 : 1). This it would henceforth cease to be ; and even in its final conversion when it would live again (Rom. 11 : 15) after divine ingrafting (Rom. 11 : 23 sq.), it would have no occasion of giving fruit to men, because of the immediate coming of the last day (13 : 28, 29). *And his disciples* **heard it,** with deep attention, and remembered it as a constant warning against hypocritical profession.

15-18. And they come to Jerusalem : and he entered into the temple and began to cast out them that sold and them that bought in the temple, and overthrew the tables of the money-changers, and the seats of them that sold the doves ; and he would not suffer that any man should carry a vessel through the temple. And he taught, and said unto them, Is it not written, My house shall be called a house of prayer for all the nations? but ye have made it a den of robbers. And the chief priests and the scribes heard it, and sought how they might destroy him: for they feared him, for all the multitude was astonished at his teaching.

Ver. 15. Coming to Jerusalem Jesus *entered the temple,*² **and . . temple.** The outer court of the Gentiles had for the convenience of the people been changed into a mart for the buying of sacrificial animals, oil,

---

¹ As a further commentary on this miracle Trench refers to the epistle to the Romans, espec. 2 : 3, 17, 27 ; 10 : 3, 4 ; 11 : 7, 10.

² This cleansing of the temple, not a third repetition (Starke), is placed by Matthew on the previous day. In this he is not more exact than Mark (Aug. De Cons. II. LXVIII. 131, Calvin), but the latter is more definite, connecting what is temporally and really connected. (Luthardt, Keil.) It was a second act not to be confounded with the same deed at the beginning of the ministry of Christ. (John 2 : 13 sq.) Aug. De Cons. II. LXVII. 129; Robinson, p. 212.

incense and other things needed in the sacrifices. With trade the haggling spirit of the East had entered. Jesus **overthrew . . . money-changers,** who, in changing Roman and foreign coins into the half-shekel of the temple, with which alone purchases for temple-purposes could be made, the temple-tax paid and free-will offerings given, went beyond the permitted percentage.[1] He also overthrew **the seats . . . the doves,** which, necessary for purification and the sacrifices of the poor (Lev. 5 : 7 ; 12 : 6 ; 14 : 22 ; 15 : 14 ; Numb. 6 : 10), were sold beyond their value. The priests, who, as suggested by ver. 18, were probably financially interested,[2] would in their examination refuse animals bought beyond the temple precincts. A further abuse Christ stopped. Ver. 16. **He . . . temple.** The bazaar-like court had been made a common thoroughfare, which the people used in their daily errands of business. This, too, Christ caused to cease in holy zeal (John 2 : 17) for God's house. His forcible acts are a constant example to His servants to rid the church of profaning abuses without regard of men. Ver. 17. Christ **taught . . . robbers.** With a reference to Isai. 56 : 7, cited according to the Septuagint, Christ justifies His purification of the temple. The promise of Isaiah, to which the Lord imparts the character of a command, shows how the obligation of all nations to make the temple a house of prayer rests the more strongly upon Israel, which has now made the very court of prayer for other nations a *den of robbers,*[3]

---

[1] Edersheim, I., p. 367 sq.

[2] Edersheim I., p. 371 sq. Luther (Walch, VII. 1062 sq.) holds that the greed of the priests had added offerings not scripturally sanctioned. Cf. also Calvin, III. 12.

[3] "Robbers" and not "thieves" is the proper translation. (Cf. Matt. 21 : 13; 26 : 55; 2 Cor. 12 : 20.) Trench, Syn., p. 157. Luther's rendering "Mördergrube" is a just inference from Jer. 7 : 11. Stier, 2, p. 385.

as intimated by Jer. 7 : 11 (Sept.). The holy place has become a cave of brigands by the dishonest robbery of unjust trade. How terrible the desecration which turns the house of prayer and salvation into the house of destruction! "There God's honor was stolen and robbed, and the souls of men killed."—LUTHER. Ver. 18. **And . . . scribes** (10 : 33), the leaders of the Sanhedrim **heard** of Christ's deed, **and sought . . . destroy him**, and carry out their long-cherished decision (John 5 : 16; 7 : 32; 10 : 31; 11 : 45 sq.), which was strengthened by Christ's recent act. But as yet they could not, **for . . . teaching** (1 : 22, 27; 4 : 2). The leaders at Jerusalem saw and feared the superior authority of Jesus over the people by His teaching. The impossibility of taking Him now by violence was clear to them (14 : 1, 2; Matt. 26 : 5). "The wicked would always injure the pious, but they cannot always, for God is their protection."— STARKE.

19. And every evening he went forth out of the city.

Ver. 19. See ver. 11.

20–25. And as they passed by in the morning, they saw the fig tree withered away from the roots. And Peter calling to remembrance saith unto him, Rabbi, behold, the fig tree which thou cursedst is withered away. And Jesus answering saith unto them, Have faith in God. Verily I say unto you, Whosoever shall say unto this mountain, Be thou taken up and cast into the sea; and shall not doubt in his heart, but shall believe that what he saith cometh to pass; he shall have it. Therefore I say unto you, All things whatsoever ye pray and ask for, believe that ye have received them, and ye shall have them. And whensoever ye stand praying, forgive, if ye have aught against any one; that your Father also which is in heaven may forgive you your trespasses.

Ver. 20. As the disciples **passed by** on Tuesday morning, *they saw the fig tree* (ver. 13), that **had** begun to wither the previous day (Matt. 21 : 19), **withered away from the roots.** The sudden judgment, which Christ had miraculously performed on a tree and not on man, upon whom only miracles of grace were then bestowed, had progressed to its completion. " Because the tree would not bear fruit, its leaves also died."—GERHARD. Ver. 21. **And ... away.** Peter expresses the astonishment of all at the wonderful effectiveness of Christ's curse. "The cursing of sinners can make the pious fearful."—CANSTEIN, STARKE. Ver. 22. **Jesus answering** unfolded the power of the curse as the result of His faith, and said, **Have ... God.** After the example of their Master, the Captain of faith (Hebr. 12 : 2), the disciples are bidden to direct their trust toward no creature but toward God.[1] Such faith which leads to faith in Christ (John 14 : 1) is power over creation. Nothing is mightier and more invincible than faith. Ver. 23. **Verily ... you** (3 : 28) **... heart,** be inwardly divided by a conflict between trust and distrust (James 1 : 6), **but ... it.** This word, uttered previously Matt. 17 : 20, uses the Mount of Olives and the Mediterranean Sea in graphic picturesqueness to assert that faith will succeed against hindrances almost insurmountable[2] (cf. Isai. 40 : 4). Because it holds the Almighty it can perform His miracles. But "Christ does not give a loose rein to the wishes of men, that they should desire anything at their pleasure."— CALVIN. Consequently he adds, Ver. 24. **Therefore ... them** in God's will (Isai. 65 : 24), and **ye shall have them** (Job 22 : 27; Ps. 145 : 19; Matt. 7 : 7 sq.; 1 John 3 : 22; 5 : 14, 15 ; James 5 : 15). As Christ received His power

---

[1] θεοῦ is objective genitive as in Acts 3 : 16; Gal. 2 : 20.

[2] Besser (Vol. X., p. 617), upon the basis of Zech. 4 : 11; Ps. 46 : 3; Dan. 7 : 3; Rev. 18 : 21, interprets the mountain as the Roman power in distinction from the fig tree, the Jewish people.

during prayer (John 11 : 41, 44), thus our command of faith must be prayerful; for prayer offered in Christ's name (John 14 : 13) will receive everything, although sometimes differently and at other times than it desires (Acts 12 : 15; 2 Cor. 12 : 8 sq.), according to God's higher purpose (Eph. 3 : 20). " Prayer is the language of faith, and faith is the soul of prayer."—RAMBACH. Ver. 25. **And . . . stand praying** (Luke 18 : 11, 13) . . . **trespasses**[1] (Matt. 6 : 14, 15). The prayer of faith dare not be used to curse any one (Luke 9 : 54 sq.), as Christ has done with the fig tree, but it must be offered after having freely forgiven all that have offended us (1 Tim. 2 : 8). Then the **Father,** a term which even in the O. T. (Deut. 32 : 6; Isai. 63 : 16; Jer. 3 : 19, etc.) denotes not the natural but the covenant relation, and in the N. T. marks the adoption through Christ (Matt 5 : 16, 45, 48; 6 : 1, 4, 6, 8, etc.; 7 : 11, 21; Luke 6 : 36; 12 : 30), as **your** *father,* whose fatherhood over you is different in kind from His relation to Christ (John 20 : 17); a father, **which . . . heaven** (Matt. 6 : 9), and therefore has heavenly power, finding you in the proper condition for receiving His forgiveness, as shown by your forgiving, will forgive **you your trespasses,** the oversteppings of the law with their consequent results, for which there is no reasonable excuse.[2] "We must have a brotherly heart toward our neighbor, if God is to have a fatherly heart toward us."— STARKE.

27-33. And they come again to Jerusalem: and as he was walking in the temple, there come to him the chief priests, and the scribes, and the elders; and they said unto him, By what authority doest thou these things? or who gave thee this authority to do these things? And Jesus

[1] Ver. 26 is wanting in ℵ, B, L, Δ, and was probably inserted from Matt. 6 : 15.
[2] Cremer, p. 778.

said unto them, I will ask of you one question, and answer me, and I will tell you by what authority I do these things. The baptism of John, was it from heaven, or from men? answer me. And they reasoned with themselves, saying, If we shall say, From heaven; he will say, Why then did ye not believe him? But should we say, From men—they feared the people: for all verily held John to be a prophet. And they answered Jesus and say, We know not. And Jesus saith unto them, Neither tell I you by what authority I do these things.

Ver. 27. Christ when again in Jerusalem, *walking* and teaching (Matt. 21 : 25) *in the temple*, is approached by the *chief priests, scribes and elders* (8 : 31), who said, Ver. 28, **By . . . things?** This question about Christ's authority, to which is added the further question as to His commission, was asked in memory of the recent purification of the temple (ver. 15). Although these representatives of the Sanhedrim had a right to ask Christ, they did so hoping to compel Christ to a reply, which might be charged against Him as revolutionary or blasphemous (14 : 63, 64 : Luke 23 : 1, 2) to His destruction (ver. 18). Ver. 29. **Jesus . . . things.** With direct power Christ proves His authority, making the inquisitors the questioned. He asks about, Ver. 30, **the baptism of John, . . . men?** The baptism of John, as his characteristic work (1 : 4; Acts 1 : 22; 10 : 37; 13 : 25), about which the scribes had themselves formerly asked (John 1 : 25), was referred to primarily because Christ knew that it would ward off His enemies, but also because its answer would lead to Christ and establish His authority. Ver. 31. And the scribes **reasoned . . . him?** It was not the desire of these men to seek the truth, but to entrap Jesus. But now Christ has caught them, and they see clearly that the acknowledgment of John's baptism as divine would bring upon them the charge of unbelief. Although they must now know themselves to be unbelieving, they would not have it appear before the people.

They will not say, Ver. 32, **From . . . prophet.** John was not only a prophet, but more than a prophet (Luke 7 : 26, 28). The high regard in which the people hold John keeps the scribes from calling his work only human. Men-servants as they are, they slavishly dread the displeasure of the people. Ver. 33. **And they . . . know not.** They, who pride themselves with their knowledge, would rather in hypocrisy appear ignorant, because "they feel the truth to be opposed to their wicked desires."— CALVIN. " Miserable case, when the men of light use their knowledge of the truth to oppose that truth."— QUESNEL, LANGE. Jesus **saith, . . . things.** The truth is not given them, because they have shown that they would wilfully reject it. Nor has the time come for the testimony of Christ, which would be used to kill Him. He does not answer, because a lie cannot demand an answer.

CHAPTER XII.

1-12. And he began to speak unto them in parables. A man planted a vineyard, and set a hedge about it, and digged a pit for the winepress, and built a tower, and let it out to husbandmen, and went into another country. And at the season he sent to the husbandmen a servant, that he might receive from the husbandmen of the fruits of the vineyard. And they took him, and beat him, and sent him away empty. And again he sent unto them another servant; and him they wounded in the head, and handled shamefully. And he sent another; and him they killed; and many others; beating some, and killing some. He had yet one, a beloved son: he sent him last unto them, saying, They will reverence my son. But those husbandmen said among themselves, This is the heir; come, let us kill him, and the inheritance shall be ours. And they took him, and killed him, and cast him forth out of the vineyard. What therefore will the lord of the vineyard do? he will come and destroy the husbandmen, and will give the vineyard unto others. Have ye not read even this scripture:

> The stone which the builders rejected,
> The same was made the head of the corner:
> This was from the Lord,
> And it is marvellous in our eyes?

And they sought to lay hold on him; and they feared the multitude; for they perceived that he spake the parable against them: and they left him, and went away.

Ver. 1. And Christ **began** now in Jerusalem as formerly in Galilee (4 : 11, 33) **to speak . . . them**, the representatives of the Sanhedrim (11 : 27 sq.), in the hearing of the people (Luke 20 : 9) **in parables** (3 : 23), like those of the two sons (Matt. 21 : 28 sq.) and the marriage of the king's son (Matt. 22 : 1 sq.), of which Mark relates the central and severest one. **A man . . . vineyard.** Jesus, in using an illustration from life,[1] adopts the O. T.

[1] Geikie, p. 171, 366.

image of the vineyard so frequently applied to God's people (Deut. 32 : 32 ; Ps. 80 : 8 sq.; Isai. 27 : 2 sq.; Jer. 2 : 21; Ezek. 15 : 1; 19 : 10; Hos. 10 : 1) with a special reference to Isai. 5 : 1–7. The vineyard is a fit symbol of God's kingdom, because the vine represents the inward power of the king (Gen. 49 : 11; John 15 : 1) and the spreading of the kingdom (Ps. 80 : 9; cf. Mark 4 : 30), and the whole vineyard receives divine care,[1] for which large returns are reasonably to be expected (Song of Songs, 8 : 11, 12). **Planted** by God Himself (Exod. 15 : 17; Ps. 44 : 2; Isai. 60 : 21; 61 : 3) under Moses and Joshua (Deut. 32 : 12), **he set . . . it.** As the owner of a vineyard would build an enclosure of loose stone (Numb. 22 : 24; Prov. 24 : 31; Isai. 5 : 5), to keep out jackals, foxes (Song of Songs, 2 : 15; Neh. 4 : 3) and wild boars (Ps. 80 : 13), thus God separated Israel by their land[2] and law from all people (Numb. 23 : 9; Isai. 27 : 3; Zech. 2 : 5; Eph. 2 : 14). He **digged . . winepress.** The **pit,** a lower trough (yekeb), which is here used for the whole press, was excavated out of rock or earth and laid with masonry. Into this smaller lake (lacus, the Roman name) the juice flowed through a spout from the upper press (gath) (Neh. 13 : 5; Isai. 63 : 2; Lam. 1 : 15), in which the grapes had been placed, and were trodden out by the feet of persons amid singing and rejoicing (Judg. 9 : 27; Isai. 16 : 10; Jer. 25 : 30). He **built a tower,** which was a temporary booth (Job 27 : 18) or cottage (Isai. 1 : 8; 24 : 20), where the keepers watched and the workmen lived during the vintage (Isai. 5 : 2). The tower and pit are only picturesque details,

---

[1] Augustine, Serm. XXXVII. 1.

[2] Palestine, central as it was, was hedged in on the west by the Mediterranean Sea, on the north by Libanus and Anti-Libanus, on the east by the river Jordan, and on the south by the wilderness of Idumæa.

and cannot be pressed in the application:[1] they show that God had done everything. "He left no means untried for granting to His Church all necessary protection."—CALVIN. He **let it . . . husbandmen**, vinedressers, who represent the leaders of Israel (Ezek. 34 : 2 ; Mal. 2 : 7); **and went . . . country**, "for a long time" (Luke 20 : 9). This denotes the withdrawal of God after the primal revelation at Sinai, that in His longsuffering He might see how Israel would keep the law. "He bore long with them, not always bringing the punishment close upon their sins."—CHRYSOSTOM. Ver. 2. **And . . . season**, of vintage, **he sent . . . a servant**, a prophet or extraordinary messenger in distinction from the husbandmen, the ordinary servants (Bengel), **that . . . vineyard**, i. e. the householders' share as rent, symbolizing the fruits of righteousness sought by God. The more grace we receive, the more fruit is demanded. Ver. 3. And the husbandmen *took* the servant, *beat him, and sent him empty away*; Ver. 4, **another**, perhaps more eminent, *they wounded in the head*,[2] *and handled shamefully ;* Ver. 5, another **they killed**. This was the climax of the constantly increasing outrages upon successive servants. **Many others**, they treated thus, **beating . . . some**. How true this description is, is proved by the slaying of the prophets by Jezebel (1 Kings 18 : 13), the casting into prison of Micaiah (1 Kings 22 : 24), the threat against Elijah (1 Kings 19 : 2), the stoning of Zechariah (2 Chron. 24 : 21) and Jeremiah in Egypt, according to tradition, which also mentions the sawing asunder of Isaiah (cf. Hebr. 11 : 37, 38, and Jer. 7 : 25, 26 ; 11 : 7, 8 ;

---

[1] Luther (Walch, VII. 1095), has interpreted the pit as God's word, and the tower as God's protection by men and angels.

[2] This is now almost universally accepted as the rendering of ἐκεφαλίωσαν after the Vulgate. (In capite vulnerant.)

Zech. 1 : 4; Acts 7 : 52; 1 Thess. 2 : 15). Ver. 6. The lord of the vineyard **had . . . beloved son** (1 : 1, 11; Hebr. 1 : 2), **he sent . . . last**, as the crowning effort of his mercy, **saying . . . my son** (John 5 : 23), who as the appearance of myself (John 14 : 9) is above all servants in dignity (Hebr. 3 : 5, 6). With this word, which dare not be used to contradict God's prescience, Christ paints in human colors the great mercy and long-suffering of God. But the greater His mercy, the more the enmity of the husbandmen grew. Ver. 7. They **said . . . heir**. Christ is heir of all things (Hebr. 1 : 2) as Son of Man (Eph. 1 : 20 sq.; Phil. 2 : 9 sq.). " The Lord Christ is heir of all things not as God, but as man; for as God He is maker of all."—THEODORET. **Let . . . ours**. The hating, envious brethren of the true Joseph (Gen. 37 : 19) conspire against the Son to obtain absolute control over the theocracy. "What God had founded they would fain possess without God and against God."—TRENCH. Ver. 8. **They . . . vineyard**, adding outrage to murder. Christ died "without the gate" (John 19 : 17; Hebr. 13 : 12, 13), but the wicked husbandmen only fulfilled God's purpose and defeated themselves (Acts 3 : 18; 4 : 27 sq.). " That they might possess they killed Him; and because they killed Him they perished."—AUGUSTINE. This Christ brings home to His hearers, asking, Ver. 9, **What . . . do?** Repeating the answer of some (Matt. 21 : 41), Jesus tells of the destruction of Jerusalem and the giving of the gospel to the Gentiles. Confirming His parable by the Scriptures, He adds, Ver. 10, 11, **Have . . . eyes?** From the psalm (118 : 22), which was applied to Him in His entry into Jerusalem (11 : 9 sq.), Jesus convicts the chief men of Israel as those unwise (1 Cor. 3 : 10) builders, who reject the precious corner-stone (Isai. 8 : 14; 28 : 16; Acts 4 : 11; Eph. 2 : 20; 1 Peter 2 : 6), **the** foundation of a new spiritual temple (Eph. 2 : 21 ; 1 Peter 2 : 4). But God, whose counsel will prevail, makes the rejected one the great accepted one. This is the great miracle. "God sends His Only-begotten into the flesh to sinners—highest *grace !* The sinners crucify Him—terrible *sin !* And yet grace triumphs over sin, prepares from it the *salvation* of the world."—STIER. Ver. 12. The scribes *sought to lay hold* on Jesus, but **feared . . . multitude**, who greatly reverenced Him. They knew that the parable was against them: and **they . . . away.** "The world despite its efforts cannot execute its malice and wickedness sooner than God from hidden reasons permits (Luke 22 : 53)."—STARKE.

13-17. And they send unto him certain of the Pharisees and of the Herodians, that they might catch him in talk. And when they were come, they say unto him, Master, we know that thou art true, and carest not for any one: for thou regardest not the person of men, but of a truth teachest the way of God: Is it lawful to give tribute unto Cæsar, or not? Shall we give, or shall we not give? But he, knowing their hypocrisy, said unto them, Why tempt ye me? bring me a penny, that I may see it. And they brought it. And he saith unto them, Whose is this image and superscription? And they said unto him, Cæsar's. And Jesus said unto them, Render unto Cæsar the things that are Cæsar's, and unto God the things that are God's. And they marvelled greatly at him.

Ver. 13. **And** the Pharisees after a private council (Matt. 22 : 15) send as spies (Luke 20 : 20) **certain . . . Herodians** (3 : 6) **. . . talk.** As they could do nothing by violence (ver. 12), they seek to entrap Jesus by stratagem. "Because they cannot suppress the gospel with the fist and violence, they set themselves against it with evil designs and poisonous tricks."—LUTHER. Ver. 14. **When . . . God.** Not sincerely like Nicodemus (cf. John 3 : 2), but with designing flattery, which was nevertheless an unconscious testimony to the truth, they address Christ as **Master.** "Thou art a master and dost offer to teach every one and give answer; therefore Thou must not leave us without an answer, nor refuse us. They act as though they were His dear disciples."—LUTHER. They call Him **true** (John 14 : 6; Rev. 1 : 5), fearless, without regard of **person** (lit. countenance), not showing favor to any one, even the highest in rule, for which they use the old figure of the lifting up of the face granted by a king to those prostrate before him (1 Kings 2 : 16, 17, 20; Ps. 72 : 2; Prov. 18 : 5; Mal. 2 : 9). His teaching of the **way of God** (1 : 2) is acknowledged as true. After this attempt to win the favor of Christ they propose the crucial question, **Is . . . give?** This was a great debate ever since Pompey (63 B. C.), after deciding the contention between Hyrcanus and Aristobulus, began to tax the Jews (Jos. Antiq. XIX. 4, 4), on whom Augustus, after the death of Herod, laid an additional personal tax. The Pharisees, appealing to Exod. 30 : 13, held the view of the mass of the people, that in Israel taxing was a divine prerogative, while the Herodians stood for the claim of the Romans. If Jesus decided for the Pharisees, the Herodians could accuse Him as a revolutionist and His fate might be that of Judas the Gaulonite (Acts 5 : 37; Jos. Antiq. XVIII. 1, 1; XX. 5, 2); if He decided for the Herodians the people would reject Him. The cunning plotters had thought, " if He says we shall give tribute to the emperor, the Jews will take Him. If He says, tribute shall not be given to the emperor, the Gentiles will take Him."—LUTHER. Ver. 15. *But he*, **knowing . . . hypocrisy** (cf. 2 : 8), " because His Spirit was a discerner of hearts,"—CALVIN, " showed Himself to be true, as they had said,"—BENGEL, when He said, **Why . . . penny** (6 : 37), *that I may see it*. Ver. 16. **And . . . brought it.** How authoritatively does Christ treat those who came to ensnare Him, and how obediently they bring from the money-changers (11 : 15) the penny with which Christ would give them an ocular demonstration of the truth. He asks, **Whose . . . superscription?** The coin which Christ had was not of the special coinage made for Judæa, in which palms, lilies, grapes, took the place of the picture of the emperor, which the Jews regarded as idolatrous; but it was a regular silver penny containing the beautiful head of wicked Tiberius, encircled by a laurel wreath and bound with the sacred fillet. Underneath was his name. About this and the image Christ asked the Pharisees, **and they said . . . Cæsar's.** The apparently simple question which the Pharisees answer so readily ensnares them, the ensnarers. For it was a principle, admitted even in the day of the Maccabees,[1] that the right of coinage involved the right of taxation. Ver. 17. **Jesus . . . God's.** The Pharisees are reminded that the actual rule of the emperor involves duties toward him, which are, however, circumscribed by his sphere, a truth that the Herodians are to take to heart and to give God His dues in His special covenant relation, of which the temple coins are an evidence. "To the emperor thou shalt give money, but thyself to God, for what remains for God, if all belongs to the emperor."—TERTULLIAN. And the Pharisees are likewise to learn to "give to God that which has the image and superscription of God, the soul (Luke 15 : 8 sq.)."—ERASMUS. Christ lays down a principle, which maintains "a clear distinction between spiritual and civil government,"—CALVIN, but also asserts a higher unity, for obedience to the powers that be (Rom. 13 : 1 sq.) and to every human ordinance is for the Lord's sake (1 Peter 2 : 13).[2] "God will

---

[1] Later Judaism openly proclaimed this law, holding that Abigail pleaded with David that Saul's coin was still in circulation. Edersheim. II. 385.

[2] The Lutheran Church has ever held the duty of passive submission to

have the heart, the body and the possessions are the state's."—LUTHER.

18-27. *And there came unto him Sadducees, which say there is no resurrection; and they asked him, saying, Master, Moses wrote unto us, If a man's brother die, and leave a wife behind him, and leave no child, that his brother should take his wife, and raise up seed unto his brother. There were seven brethren: and the first took a wife, and dying left no seed; and the second took her, and died, leaving no seed behind him; and the third likewise: and the seven left no seed. Last of all the woman also died. In the resurrection whose wife shall she be of them? for the seven had her to wife. Jesus said unto them, Is it not for this cause that ye err, that ye know not the scriptures, nor the power of God? For when they shall rise from the dead, they neither marry, nor are given in marriage; but are as angels in heaven. But as touching the dead, that they are raised; have ye not read in the book of Moses, in the place concerning the Bush, how God spake unto him, saying, I am the God of Abraham, and the God of Isaac, and the God of Jacob? He is not the God of the dead, but of the living: ye do greatly err.*

Ver. 18. *And there come,* with the hope of bringing Christ to ridicule, **Sadduccees, . . . resurrection.** The Sadducees, originating at the time of Jonathan, the Maccabee (160-143 B. C.) and representing the general reaction of rationalism against the extreme Pharisaism, doubted not only resurrection, but "denied the immortality of the soul, and the punishment and rewards of the state, reserving only the right of conscience in religious belief. It is equally distant from Romish hierarchical suppression of the state, and the Reformed misapplication of the theocratic principle, as it appears typically in the lives of Zwingle, Calvin and Knox. Luther has fully stated and maintained, especially in the revolution of the peasants, the power and independence of the state. For his position, which is virtually that of the Lutheran Church, see Gospel for the twenty-third Sunday after Trin., Housepostil (Erl. Ed. 3 : 170). Churchpostil (14 : 295); An den chrl. Adel, etc. (1520) (21 : 281 sq.); Eine Vermahnung sich zu hüten vor Aufruhr (1522) (22 : 43 sq.) Von weltl. Obrigkeit (1523) (22 : 68 sq.); Wider die himml. Propheten (1524) (29 : 146 sq.); Ob Kriegsleute auch selig sein können (1526) (22 : 248 sq.); Krieg wider die Türken (1529) (31 : 35 sq.); Verantwortung des Aufruhrs (1533) (31 : 236 sq.); Ausleg. des 72 Ps. (1540) (20 : 272 sq.); Op. Ex. Ps. CXXVII. 20 : 48.

Hades" (Jos. Wars, II. 8, 14). They demanded proof from the clear letter of the Law, for the doctrine, which was only a hope in the O. T. (10 : 17) and had been fancifully exaggerated by the Pharisees. From the Law they start, saying, Ver. 19, **Master, . . . seed.** This law (Deut. 25 : 5, 6), with the addition of the last clause from Gen. 38 : 8 modified after Gen. 19 : 32, 34, was cited to show the necessity of the case to be related. It is no proof of an original remnant of polyandry (Morison), but was given for the preservation of the families, because they formed integral parts of the theocracy.[1] Ver. 20. *There were* **seven brethren**, who all had the same wife and left no seed. Ver. 22, 23. **Last . . . wife.** This case, which might have happened,[2] and which is graphically spread out by the Sadducees, receives its force from the assumption, also adopted by modern materialism, that the conditions of the present life are necessary in the hereafter, and therefore a future life is impossible. Ver. 24. **Jesus . . . God?** The error of the Sadducees was due to their ignorance of Scripture as the product of the Spirit (2 Peter 1 : 20, 21), whom they knew not. Therefore they were ignorant of the **power of God**, which cometh with the Spirit (Luke 24 : 49 ; Acts 1 : 8 ; 1 Cor. 2 : 4), and by which He, who alone hath immortality (1 Tim. 6 : 16), maketh alive (Acts 26 : 8 ; Rom. 4 : 17 ; 8 : 11). Beginning with the results of this power, Jesus says, Ver. 25, **For . . . heaven.** When rising **from the dead**, which is the privilege of those obtaining eternal life[3]

---

[1] Öhler, O. T. Theol., p. 235.

[2] Although the Talmud (Yeb. 64b) laid down that if a woman had lost two husbands she should not marry a third, yet in Jer. Yebam. 6b, there is a story of a man who was induced to wed the twelve widows of his twelve brothers.

[3] The ἐκ before νεκρῶν shows this (Luke 20 : 35 ; Acts 4 : 12 ; 1 Peter 1 : 3). Cf. also ἐξανάστασις (Phil. 3 : 11).

(Dan. 12:2), the present material relation ceases, because the bodies are spiritual (1 Cor. 6:13; 1 Cor. 15:39 sq.). Men shall be **like angels,** not identical, but similar to them, in glorious heavenly corporeity. With this last assertion Jesus openly contradicts the Sadducees, who denied the existence of angels and spirits (Acts 23:8). Then coming to the Scripture, He adds, Ver. 26, 27, **Have . . . Moses** (Exod. 3:2, 3, 4), which you accept, *in the* **place . . . living.** Referring in Jewish manner to the title of the section cited, as "The Bush,"[1] Christ uses a very word of God to Moses. It is the fundamental covenant promise, renewed to Moses at the time when God revealed His unchangeable character in the name Jehovah (Exod. 3:14), upon which Moses was to rely in the establishment of the Israelitish commonwealth. Such renewal if the patriarchs were dead would invalidate God's eternal life, because as *their* God (Heb. 11:13 sq.), who gave them what was His, He would be the God of them that had been. And being a dead God, the covenant and privileges of Israel would be void. God as God must be the God of the living (Hab. 1:12). "Because God says, he is a God of Abraham, Abraham must be something and live."—LUTHER. Therefore **ye do greatly err.** With this repeated warning (ver. 24), Jesus shows the Sadducees the greatness and danger of their error, which was not only of the head. Doubt of the resurrection is subversive of all faith in God.

28-34. And one of the scribes came, and heard them questioning together and knowing that he had answered them well, asked him, What commandment is the first of all? Jesus answered, The first is, Hear, O Israel; The

---

[1] Similarly 2 Sam. 1:17-27 was called "The Bow," Ezek. 1:15-28 "The Chariot." Rom. 11:2 refers to the section "Elias." Maclear, p. 135. Delitzsch, Paulus des Ap. Brief an die Römer, hebr. übersetz. (Leipzig, 1870), p. 12.

Lord our God, the Lord is one: and thou shalt love the Lord thy God with all thy heart, and with all thy soul, and with all thy mind, and with all thy strength. The second is this, Thou shalt love thy neighbour as thyself. There is none other commandment greater than these. And the scribe said unto him, Of a truth, Master, thou hast well said that he is one; and there is none other but he: and to love him with all the heart, and with all the understanding, and with all the strength, and to love his neighbour as himself, is much more than all whole burnt offerings and sacrifices. And when Jesus saw that he answered discreetly, he said unto him, Thou art not far from the kingdom of God. And no man after that durst ask him any question.

Ver. 28. *And one of the scribes* (2:6) **came,** sent by the Pharisees to tempt Christ,[1] and **heard** the Sadducees disputing with Jesus, **and knowing . . . them well** (lit. beautifully), and having approved Christ, **asked . . . all?** This was a much mooted question among the scribes, who placed their own enactments about circumcision, fringes, phylacteries, etc., above the Scriptures. The total number of commandments was 613, the number of letters in the Decalogue; 248, as many as the members of the body, were affirmative, and 365, the number of veins and arteries and the days of the year, were negative. Out of this maze, in which the Pharisees sought to entangle Christ, the scribe honestly desired help. Ver. 29. **Jesus . . . one.**[2] Christ quotes Deut. 6:4,[3] which, called Shema from its initial word, was the beginning of the

---

[1] Although Mark makes no mention of this, he does not contradict Matthew. For the latter gives the public import of this interview, while the former shows the inward spirit of the scribe, who in his innocence was used as a tool. He was well disposed from the beginning, and not changed by Christ's word. (Augustine, Chrysostom.) Stier, II. 466; Nebe, III. 330.

[2] This rendering rather than that of the margin brings out the prominent thought of Deut. 6:4.

[3] Keil well says that the original text and the Septuagint are both heard. In the commandment itself "with all thy mind" is added from the Sept. to "heart, soul, strength" of the original. "Strength" is $\mathrm{\mathit{ἰσχύς}}$ instead of $\mathrm{\mathit{δύναμις}}$ of the Sept.

morning and evening prayer of every Israelite, stood at the head of the Jewish division of the commandments, was contained in the phylactery, the small leather prayer-box tied on the forehead, and was found in the Mezumah, the little box with extracts of the law, which was nailed to the door-posts. Its very use showed its fundamental character.[1] Therefore Christ began with it, because it is the beginning and foundation of all law, and the basis of its unity. Then, as on a former occasion (Luke 10 : 27), He says, Ver. 30, **Thou shalt love**, with the free deep love of reverence, as the direction of the will,[2] **the Lord** (Jehovah, the Unchangeable) as **thy God, with** (lit. out of) **all thy heart**, the inmost part of thy nature (2 : 6; 3 : 5, etc.), **with all thy soul**[3] (8 : 35), the self-conscious individuality, **with all thy mind**, the full moral reflection,[4] *and* **with all thy strength**, which sums up the fulness of love in its inward power. This commandment is "the kernel of the law."—LUTHER. Ver. 31. **The . . . neighbor** (Luke 10 : 30 sq.) **as thyself**. This second commandment, taken from Lev. 19 : 18, according to the Sept., is no separate one. It rests upon the first, which must be exemplified by it (Rom. 13 : 8 sq.; Gal. 5 : 14; 1 John 4 : 7 sq.). Its measure is that of true self-love. "Whosoever serves his neighbor, serves not only his neighbor, but God in heaven."—LUTHER. **There . . . these.** All

---

[1] Delitzsch (Lect. on O. T. Theol. § 1b) says this is "the fundamental principle of the religion of Israel, which in this respect was without equal in antiquity." He protests against the rendering of many modern scholars, "Jehovah is a unique one," and defends "Jahve est unus."

[2] The word is $\dot{\alpha}\gamma\alpha\pi\dot{\eta}\sigma\epsilon\iota\varsigma$. See Cremer, p. 9; Trench, Syn., p. 41.

[3] Weiss argues from v. 33 that Mark uses "soul" and "heart" synonymously, but in truth the scribe's answer, like his apprehension, is not as full and exact as that of Jesus.

[4] Luther's translation "Gemüth" adds an element of feeling, that expresses the power but obscures the intellectual coloring of $\delta\iota\dot{\alpha}\nu o\iota\alpha$.

commandments are great only as they rest on these, in which "God does not look at what men can do, but at what they ought to do; since in this infirmity of the flesh it is impossible that perfect *love* can obtain dominion."—CALVIN. Ver. 32. The scribe commends Jesus, and repeats[1] the commandment, adding, Ver. 33, **it is . . . sacrifices.** This confession, a true echo of 1 Sam. 15 : 22 ; Ps. 51 : 15 sq.; Hos. 6 : 6; Micah 6 : 6 sq., rightly asserts the superiority of the moral law over all ceremonial enactments. All ceremonies without love are but a hypocritical cloak. Ver. 34. *When Jesus saw* that the scribe *answered* **discreetly,** with intelligent insight, He **said, . . . God.** The scribe was almost a disciple, but not quite (cf. Acts 26 : 28). "If thou art not far off, enter; better otherwise to have been far off."—BENGEL. In this effect of Christ upon the deputy of the Pharisees, He had gained a victory. **And . . . question.** The wisdom and power of Jesus had overcome the daring of His plotting enemies.

35-37. And Jesus answered and said, as he taught in the temple, How say the scribes that the Christ is the son of David? David himself said in the Holy Spirit,
> The Lord said unto my Lord,
> Sit thou on my right hand,
> Till I make thine enemies the footstool of thy feet.

David himself calleth him Lord; and whence is he his son? And the common people heard him gladly.

Ver. 35. *Jesus*, after having first asked (Matt. 22 : 42), **answered** a number of Pharisees, who had probably gathered to discuss further plans, *as he taught in the* **temple,** where the previous words had been spoken from

---

[1] "Understanding" (σύνεσις), which in Mark 12 : 33 takes the place of "soul" (ψυχή) of the original, is here put for "mind" (διάνοια) of v. 30. It marks the apprehensive power. See also note on "soul" v. 30.

ver. 1 onward. **How . . . son of David?** (10 : 48). Jesus does not deny His descent from David, but shows the Pharisees how their constant messianic title does not fully express the character of the Christ. "They saw one part of what He was, they knew not the other."—AUGUSTINE. Therefore Christ would lead them to a full knowledge, which would be the complete answer to the question about the greatest law. "You can never from your whole heart, from your whole soul, from your whole mind love God, unless you rightly understand Christ and know who He is."—LUTHER. Ver. 36. **David . . . Spirit,** through whom he spoke (2 Tim. 3 : 16; 1 Peter 1 : 11; 2 Peter 1 : 21), **The Lord . . . footstool**[1] **of thy feet.** This word of the 110th Psalm, which was accepted as messianic by Jews and is more frequently cited in the N. T. than any other word of the O. T. (Acts 2 : 34, 35; 1 Cor. 15 : 25; Hebr. 1 : 13; 5 : 6; 7 : 17, 21), was used by Christ to prove His divinity rather than Ps. 45 : 7, 8; Isai. 7 : 14; 9 : 6; Jer. 23 : 6; Micah 5 : 2, because it is David who acknowledges the Messiah as **Lord,** whom God seats at **his right hand** (cf. Dan. 7 : 13, 14), i. e. gives equal power and majesty (Exod. 15 : 6; Ps. 17 : 7; 18 : 35; 20 : 6; 60 : 5; 63 : 8; 98 : 1; Isai. 41 : 10; Lam. 2 : 3), until, in the picture of a victorious king, His feet are on the neck of the conquered enemies (Josh. 10 : 24; Ps. 8 : 6; 18 : 38; 45 : 5; 47 : 3). After this announcement of the victory of the divine Messiah, Jesus asks, Ver. 37, **David . . . son?** With this inferential question Jesus teaches His divine and human nature. This is "the mystery how He is David's son and David's Lord; how one person is both man and God; how in the form of man He is less than the Father, in the form of God equal with the Father."—AUGUSTINE. **And . . . gladly,** in His won-

---

[1] "Underneath" (ὑποκάτω) is best attested by ℵ, A, L, Δ.

derful teaching of power, especially about the divine dignity of the Messiah. The simple people have a better desire for the truth than those wise in their own conceit (Matt. 11 : 25 ; 1 Cor. 1 : 26, 27).

38-40. **And in his teaching he said, Beware of the scribes, which desire to walk in long robes, and** *to have* **salutations in the marketplaces, and chief seats in the synagogues, and chief places at feasts: they which devour widows' houses, and for a pretence make long prayers ; these shall receive greater condemnation.**

Ver. 38. *And in his* **teaching,** reported fully Matt. 23, *he* **said, . . . robes,** the cloaks (tallith) with the sacred fringes ; **and . . . marketplaces** (Matt. 23 : 7), deferential greetings by their honorable title "Rabbi," Ver. 39, **and . . . feasts** (Matt. 23 : 6 ; Luke 14 : 7), the highest position in the house of worship and in the homes. The Lord rebukes them not "because they hold such places, but because they love them."—AUGUSTINE. Ver. 40. **They . . . houses,** by being supported by them (cf. 1 Kings 17 : 9 ; 2 Kings 4 : 8 ; Luke 8 : 2 sq.), and in the unjust administration of their property, while **for a pretence** they make **. . . prayers.** They do not really pray, but stand to be admired, making many words like the heathen (Matt. 6 : 7 ; Luke 18 : 11 sq.). **These . . . greater,** more abundant (1 Cor. 12 : 23) **condemnation,** for their pride, rapacity, dead formality, and because of their hypocrisy. God hates all pretence.

41-44. **And he sat down over against the treasury, and beheld how the multitude cast money into the treasury: and many that were rich cast in much. And there came a poor widow, and she cast in two mites, which make a farthing. And he called unto him his disciples, and said unto them, Verily I say unto you, This poor widow cast in more than all they which are casting into the treasury: for they all did cast in of their superfluity; but she of her want did cast in all that she had,** *even* **all her living.**

Ver. 41. Jesus **sat down . . . the treasury.** Probably Jesus sat on one of the flight of steps rising from the "court of women." In the colonnades surrounding this stood thirteen **trumpet-shaped chests (Shopharoth),** of which according to their inscriptions nine were for temple-tax and sacrifice-tribute, and four for wood, incense, temple-decorations, burnt-offerings and free-will gifts. At one of the latter Christ **beheld** with spiritual eyes, how of the multitude, **many . . . cast in much** money, large handfuls of copper coins; for the Jews were so liberal that a law had to be enacted against giving too much to the enormously wealthy temple-treasury. At the time of Pompey it contained nearly $2,500,000 in money alone. But still the eyes of the Lord that are upon all offerings saw no sacrifice among the large gifts. Ver. 42. **And . . . mites** (lepta), the smallest coins, **which . . . farthing** (fourthling), the Roman quadrans, ¼ of an as, about 2 mills. Although in required gifts it was not allowed to contribute less, yet in her free-will offering the widow could have kept one mite, but she did not. Ver. 43, 44. Then Christ **called . . . living,** her whole present means of subsistence. Poor as she was, she was richer than Crœsus and all Israel (Jerome). " How she must have fixed her trust on God, and not have cared for the morrow; since she did to-day what to-day brought with it."—BRAUNE.

CHAPTER XIII.

1-2. And as he went forth out of the temple, one of his disciples saith unto him, Master, behold, what manner of stones and what manner of buildings! And Jesus said unto him, Seest thou these great buildings? there shall not be left here one stone upon another, which shall not be thrown down.

Ver. 1. As Christ **went . . . temple,** "paying, as it were, His last adieu,"—CALVIN, **one . . . disciples** probably Peter, **saith . . . buildings!** Jesus, who had left through the "Golden Gate," on the east side of the temple, was asked to look upon the immense polished and bevelled marble-blocks of the temple-wall, some of which were 25 cubits[1] long, 8 cubits high and 12 cubits broad (Jos. Antiq. XV. 11, 3), while others were 45 cubits in length, 5 in height and 6 in breadth[2] (Jos. Wars, V. 6, 6). And how magnificent was the sculpture and adornment of the temple with its buildings, cloisters, halls, terraces, etc.[3] Its solidity and grandeur, which filled the disciples with amazement, seemed to prove its permanence. But, Ver. 2, **Jesus . . . down.** As Jerusalem and the temple had once before been destroyed (2 Kings 25:13) according to prophecy (Micah 3:12; Jer. 26:18), thus, as Christ had previously said (Matt. 23:37 sq.), it would occur again, but more

---

[1] A cubit is equivalent to 18 inches.
[2] Geikie (p. 33) says: "The stones used were of great size, a whole row still seen on the south-east corner measuring nineteen feet, or even more, in length, and four feet in height; one of them, twenty-two feet above the present surface, weighing, it is believed, over a hundred tons."
[3] For an excellent description, see Farrar, p. 516; Geikie, p. 34 sq.

thoroughly. After 40 years the whole surroundings of the temple were "so thoroughly levelled and dug up that no one visiting the city would believe it had ever been inhabited" (Jos. Wars, VII. 1, 1). Even Titus, astonished at the great buildings, saw in his triumph the hand of God (Jos. Wars, VI. 9, 1). It was God, who, breaking down what He had built (Jer. 45 : 4), made this desolation (Ps. 46 : 8).

3–8. *And as he sat on the mount of Olives over against the temple, Peter and James and John and Andrew asked him privately, Tell us, when shall these things be? and what shall be the sign when these things are all about to be accomplished? And Jesus began to say unto them, Take heed that no man lead you astray. Many shall come in my name, saying, I am he; and shall lead many astray. And when ye shall hear of wars and rumors of wars, be not troubled: these things must needs come to pass; but the end is not yet. For nation shall rise against nation, and kingdom against kingdom: there shall be earthquakes in divers places; there shall be famines: these things are the beginning of travail.*

Ver. 3. As Jesus **sat . . . mount of Olives** (11 : 1) over against the temple, **Peter . . . Andrew** (1 : 29), named according to their prominence (3 : 19) in the early apostolic period, for James takes precedence of John, **asked privately,** apart from the other disciples, Ver. 4. **Tell . . . accomplished?** The disciples, who connect the coming of Christ and the end of the world with the downfall of Jerusalem (Matt. 24 : 3), seek the time and sign of the completion of **all** the last things. The uniting of these eschatological features, parallel to the connection of Christ's first and second coming in the prophets (Isai. 40 : 3 sq.; 61 : 1 sq.; Mal. 4 : 4 sq.), and founded upon previous announcements of Jesus (9 : 1; Matt. 10 : 15; 11 : 22; 12 : 36, 41, 42), is wrong only as it is temporal. Jesus Himself used the destruction of Jerusalem, as *an* end typifying *the* end, and passes from the former to the latter.¹ God's judgments like His mercies are one. Ver. 5. **Jesus . . . astray**. Christ does not enter upon the question of time (ver. 4 and 32), but begins with a warning, that occurs again ver. 9, 23 and 33. The whole import of this discourse is practical. "The purpose of our asking after Christ's coming must not be inquisitiveness, but the desire to remain steadfast with Him until then."—STIER. Ver. 6. For **Many . . . in** (lit. on, relying on) **my name . . astray** (ver. 22). This sign, presenting "an essential point of view for all eschatology,"—LANGE, was as previously foretold (John 5 : 43) fulfilled among the Jews, who, as in the time of exile they were led astray by false prophets (Jer. 14 : 13; 29 : 8, 9; Ezek. 13), shall again be deceived by false Messiahs. Such were Theudas (Acts 5 : 36, 37; Jos. Antiq. XX. 5, 1) and others (Jos. Antiq. XX. 5, 2 ; Wars, VI. 5, 2). But the disciples shall beware. Ver. 7. **When ye . . . wars** close by, and **rumours of wars** in the distance, **be not troubled** (lit. cry not out ; Matt. 24 : 6 ; 2 Thess. 2 : 2): **these . . . pass**, because of the wickedness of the Jews; **but the end . . . yet**. Among the preliminary occurrences, that are pictures of the final end, were the internal Jewish fights, the rising against Nero, and on the border of the empire the war with the Parthians, after 58 A. D. Ver. 8. **Nation . . . kingdom** (cf. Isai. 19 : 2). The contentions of the Syrians and Jews in the cities (Jos. Wars, II. 17, 10 ; 18 : 1 sq.),

---

¹ This takes place at v. 24, although all the previous verses about Jerusalem's end await a re-fulfilment. It is not therefore true, as Luther says that Matt. and Mark confuse the two ends, and do not keep the proper order like Luke. They do not "cook it in one pap." Still less foundation is there for finding two different original sources, which have been combined in this account, as Wendt (Lehre Jesu, Göttingen, 1886, Erster Theil, p. 1 sq.) arbitrarily does ; or for denying the connection of the fall of Jerusalem with the Parousia (Erich Haupt.).

and the rising of the emperor Otho against Vitelius were first fulfilments of these words, that await a fuller accomplishment. **There . . . places.** This happened in the valley of the Jordan and Asia Minor, where in the time of Tiberius twelve cities were thus visited, in Laodicea (A. D. 61) and in Pompeii (A. D. 62). **There . . . famines** and pestilence (Luke 21 : 11), like those threatened and fulfilled of old (2 Chron. 20 : 9 ; Jer. 14 : 12 ; 21 : 7). Some occurred under Claudius (Acts 11 : 28) and Nero. Before the "new earth" is born, famines shall also occur. "What God's goodness gave men for the use of life was misused to their guilt, therefore God uses these things for their punishment."—GREGORY THE GREAT. **These travail** (Isai. 26 : 17 ; Jer. 22 : 23 ; Hos. 13 : 13). The birth-woes of the destruction of Jerusalem, as the beginning of a new period of the kingdom (9 : 1), are a prophecy of the travailing (Rom. 8 : 22 ; 1 Thess. 5 : 3), of the final regeneration (Matt. 19 : 28).

9–13. But take ye heed to yourselves: for they shall deliver you up to councils; and in synagogues shall ye be beaten; and before governors and kings shall ye stand for my sake, for a testimony unto them. And the gospel must first be preached unto all the nations. And when they lead you *to judgment*, and deliver you up, be not anxious beforehand what ye shall speak; but whatsoever shall be given you in that hour, that speak ye; for it is not ye that speak, but the Holy Ghost. And brother shall deliver up brother to death, and the father his child; and children shall rise up against parents, and cause them to be put to death. And ye shall be hated of all men for my name's sake: but he that endureth to the end, the same shall be saved.

Ver. 9. **Take heed,** says Christ, repeating Matt. 10 : 17, 18 ; **for . . . councils,** sanhedrims, judicial assemblies, which soon took place (Acts 4 : 3 ; 5 : 18, 27 ; 23 : 1): and *into synagogues,* where ye shall be **beaten.** This punishment, carried out by the minister (Chazzan) of the synagogue, was experienced by Paul (2 Cor.

11 : 24). It was generally inflicted with leathern thongs, the condemned lying on the ground (Exod. 21 : 20; Lev. 19 : 20; Deut. 22 : 18; Prov. 10 : 13; 12 : 20). **Before governors** (proconsuls, proprætors, procurators) **and kings ... testimony** of the gospel **unto them.** Paul was accorded this privilege, for he stood before Felix and Festus (Acts 24 : 10 sq.; 25 : 1 sq.), and Agrippa (Acts 26 : 1) and Nero (2 Tim. 4 : 16). Many Christians in the persecutions stood before emperors. But they were not to seek but only to suffer this. "As the snakes know by nature that there is enmity between them and men, and they therefore slyly beware of men, thus the saints of God shall, wise as serpents, take heed of the men, whose natural character is enmity against God."—LEYSER. Amid such persecutions, Ver. 10, **the gospel must first, before the end, be preached ... all the nations.** The apostles beginning at Jerusalem came unto "the uttermost part of the earth" (Acts 1 : 8; Col. 1 : 6, 27) as then known, to Italy, Illyricum and Spain (Rom. 15 : 19, 24, 28). This activity was the beginning of the missionary activity of the Church, which must finally reach all people, whether they hear or forbear (Ezek. 2 : 5) "That is the character of the Church; it blooms, when persecuted; it grows, when suppressed; it prospers, when despised; it conquers, when it bleeds; it stands, when it seems to succumb."—HILARY. Ver. 11. *And*, Christ continues, recalling Matt. 10 : 19, 20; Luke 12 : 11, 12, **when they lead you** under arrest **and deliver you up to** Gentile tribunals, **be not ... Holy Ghost.** This promise, that God through His Spirit, as the Spirit of glory (1 Peter 4 : 14), would give the words (cf. Exod. 4 : 12) to those, whose whole work rested upon the Spirit (John 15 : 26, 27), is applied only to compulsory appearance before judges. Although the whole sufficiency of

the servants of Christ is from God (2 Cor. 3 : 5), yet they must ordinarily meditate and prepare (1 Tim. 4 : 13). Ver. 12. **Brother ... death** (Matt. 10 : 21). The closest bonds of consanguinity between brothers, parents and children shall not prevent persecution against disciples, which shall reach the terrible climax of children having their own parents killed, an actual experience in the early persecution[1] and in those of the Reformation.[2] Ver. 13. **And ye shall be hated ... my name's sake** (Matt. 10 : 22), although you are the best of men (cf. Acts 26 : 9). Wherever the name of Jesus is, there must be hatred of the world (1 John 3 : 13). **But ... saved** (Matt. 10 : 22). Endurance, "the queen of virtues,"— CHRYSOSTOM, the opposite to agreement with the world, if it last unto the end (Rev. 2 : 10), assures of salvation (Col. 2 : 6 sq.; Hebr. 3 : 6, 14; 10 : 35 sq.; 2 Pet. 3 : 17; 1 John 2 : 24 sq.). Those "that die for the truth, live with the truth."—AUGUSTINE.

14–23. *But when ye see the abomination of desolation standing where he ought not (let him that readeth understand), then let them that are in Judæa flee unto the mountains: and let him that is on the housetop not go down, nor enter in, to take anything out of his house: and let him that is in the field not return back to take his cloke. But woe unto them that are with child and to them that give suck in those days! And pray ye that it be not in the winter. For those days shall be tribulation, such as there hath not been the like from the beginning of the creation which God created until now, and never shall be. And except the Lord had shortened the days, no flesh would have been saved: but for the elect's sake, whom he chose, he shortened the days. And then if any man shall say unto you, Lo, here is the Christ; or, Lo, there; believe it not: for there shall arise false Christs and false prophets, and shall shew signs and wonders, that they may lead astray, if possible, the elect. But take ye heed: behold, I have told you all things beforehand.*

[1] Tertullian, Scorpiace, X.; Luther, Walch, VII., 1291.

[2] Petter tells of Woodman, the Sussex martyr of Queen Mary's time, who was "betrayed and taken by means of his own father and brother and other friends."

Ver. 14. **But . . . not**, in the holy place (Matt. 24 : 15). The sign of the **abomination**, prophesied by Daniel (9 : 27; 11 : 31; 12 : 11),[1] is not the standing of the image of an emperor[2] in the temple, nor primarily the Roman armies with their ensigns,[3] but the diseased[4] condition of all Israel, apparent in the profanation of the temple (11 : 15 sq.), and the outrageous deeds of the zealots there (Jos. Wars, IV. 3, 7, 12; 6, 3; VI. 2, 1), which caused the desolation by the Roman armies (Luke 21 : 20). Seeing such a condition (**Let him . . . understand**). The disciples, to whom this injunction of Christ is addressed, are attentively to search and understand the prophecy, which Israel neglected. The great abomination of sin must be studied from the divine word for our salvation. **Let . . . mountains.** As Lot fled (Gen. 19 : 17), thus the disciples at the impending doom are bidden to escape at once to the surrounding mountains. In the common flight of the Jews (Jos. Wars, II. 9 : 16)

---

[1] Keil is formally correct in claiming that Christ's words are taken only from Dan. 11 : 31; 12 : 11, which is the position of Calvin; but Dan. 9 : 27 as the basis of the more detailed prophecy ought not be excluded.

[2] That the abomination was such an image finds support in the passages of Daniel, which were first fulfilled in the days of Antiochus Epiphanes (1 Macc. 1 : 54; 2 Macc. 6 : 2), and in the fact that "abomination" is in the Sept. specially applied to idols (1 Kings 11 : 5; 21 : 26; 2 Kings 16 : 3; 21 : 2). But as no such image is known to have "stood" in the temple before the destruction of Jerusalem, for an attempt was stopped (Jos. Wars, II. 9, 2), the idolatrous abomination in its completion outwardly must refer to the Roman ensigns, to which sacrifices were offered (Jos. Wars, VI. 6, 1). It has never been settled by those exegetes, who argue for the image, whose image it was. Jerome, Eusebius, Theodoret, Theophylact, think of Tiberius, Luther of Caligula, Clemens Alex. of Nero, and Chrysostom of Titus.

[3] Thus Origen, Chrysostom, Grotius, Bengel, Kuinoel, Ebrard, Lange, Godet, Weiss, etc.

[4] βδέλυγμα means originally a foul thing causing a stench. (Cf. Luke 16 : 15; Rev. 17 : 4, 5; 21 : 27.)

the Christians came to Pella,[1] about 100 miles distant in Peræa. Ver. 15. **Let him . . . house.** So sudden would be the necessity of the flight, that those on the house-tops resting must not, by the inside steps, enter their house to take even the necessary clothing and provision, but hurry along the tops of the houses to the city wall, using the outside steps of the houses (cf. 2 : 4) to descend. Ver. 16. **Let , . . cloak.** Those at work in the fields, without their outer garments as was usual, should immediately betake themselves to the mountains and leave behind the mantle so necessary as a covering. When God's judgments come, we should not shrink back (Luke 17 : 32), but take our life as prey (Jer. 45 : 5), and in faith save our souls (Hebr. 10 : 39). Ver. 17. **But . . . days!**[2] In deepest compassion Jesus bewails the helpless women, who cannot flee quickly, and to whom the blessing of children would then be a curse (Luke 23 : 29). Ver. 18. **And pray . . . winter,** for then the ways would be hard to travel and the mountains inhospitable. The prayer of believers can change the season of the judgments in God's power, and therefore the Roman armies came in spring when the weather was favorable for travelling. "How does the dear Lord encourage us so affectionately, that we should pray for the relief of His unavoidable judgments."—GERHARD. Ver. 19. **For . . . shall be**, a prophecy for whose literal fulfilment Jos. Wars, VI. 9 : 3 vouches. In Jerusalem, crowded at the Passover with about three million people, pestilence arose and famine followed, during which men killed themselves and sprang into the fire. In despair

---

[1] Stanley, Sinai and Palestine, p. 330. Eus. (H. E. III. 5, 3) followed by Epiphanius (De pond. et mens. 15) tells of this flight.

[2] For the figurative interpretation of these words, see Augustine, Ps. XCVI. 14.

mothers sought food for their children; and one mother killed, roasted and ate her own child. Cruelty was rampant, and frequent were the outbursts of violence in the internal struggles of various factions. The Romans had taken 97,000 captives, and during the whole siege 11,000,000 souls had perished. "Such terrible tribulation we should look at closely and see industriously, what sin is, which brings such suffering, that we may beware of it."—LUTHER. Ver. 20. **Except . . . days.** If God had not determined to shorten the time of tribulation for the sake of the Christians, who in relation to the mass of the Jews (flesh) were the elect remnant (Isai. 1 : 9; 10 : 22), all Israel would have been eradicated. Titus, eager from the first to make a quick siege, surrounded the city with a wall, which he fortified with thirteen garrisons in three days, and thus the city besieged by Nebuchadnezzar sixteen months, was taken in five. The despised Christians were the cause of this mercy, which shall again appear at the final end. "It conveys wonderful consolation to the godly, that God will never allow His wrath to proceed so far as not to provide for their safety."—CALVIN. Ver. 21, 22. **Then . . . there** (cf. Matt. 24 : 26); **believe . . . elect.** Many false Messiahs and prophets arose in Judæa before the destruction of Jerusalem (Jos. Wars, VI. 5, 4), who performed deceptive miracles[1] (Jos. Wars, II. 13, 4), especially an Egyptian (Jos. Wars, II. 13, 5).[2] They might have deceived the elect, if this were possible; but it is impossible, because God holds them (Matt. 16 : 18; 1 Cor. 10 : 13), and will do so in the lying wonders of the last days (2 Thess. 2; Rev. 13). Ver. 23. **But . . . beforehand.** The comprehensive prophecy of

---

[1] Tacitus (Hist. 5 : 13) also mentions that the Jews were deceived by signs.

[2] Eusebius (H. E. II. 21) connects this Egyptian with Acts 21 : 38.

Christ was the guide of His disciples, whose watchfulness was the condition of God's saving power. "Who will not permit himself to be warned, but is nevertheless deceived, is lost by his own fault."—STARKE.

24-27. **But in those days, after that tribulation, the sun shall be darkened, and the moon shall not give her light, and the stars shall be falling from heaven, and the powers that are in the heavens shall be shaken. And then shall they see the Son of man coming in clouds with great power and glory. And then shall he send forth the angels, and shall gather together his elect from the four winds, from the uttermost part of the earth to the uttermost part of heaven.**

Ver. 24. **In those days** of the end of the world, **after . . . tribulation** (ver. 19) of Jerusalem, which is prophetically connected in God's manner (2 Peter 3 : 8) with the end, the **sun . . . darkened**. The darkening, a figure of great sorrow (Isai. 5 : 30; 13 : 10; Jer. 15 : 9; Ezek. 32 : 7, 8; Amos 8 : 9; Micah. 3 : 6), will be an actual physical one, and therefore **the moon . . . light**, and, Ver. 25, **the stars . . . heaven**, i. e. sink behind the horizon. The **powers . . . heavens**, moving and upholding the universe, **shall be shaken**; for as the prophets foretold (Joel 2 : 30; Haggai 2 : 6, 21; Isai. 34 : 4) and the N. T. confirms (Hebr. 12 : 26, 27; 2 Peter 3 : 10 sq.; Rev. 6 : 12; 21 : 2), the regeneration of the world (ver. 8) occurs in the advent of the eternal Light and Power, at whose death the sun became dark. Ver. 26. **Then . . . glory** (8 : 38; 14 : 62). He, who was once lowly, shall appear, as prophesied (Dan. 7 : 13), **in clouds**, the chariots of God (Ps. 104 : 3; Isai. 19 : 1), even as He ascended (Acts 1 : 11). He comes to judgment (John 5 : 22, 27; Rev. 1 : 7) **with great power** to recreate the world (Isai. 65 : 17; 66 : 22; Rev. 20 : 11; 21 : 1), and **with glory** not of grace (John 1 : 14) concealing His brightness, but in the

fulness of eternal heavenly majesty (John 17 : 5). This is his full revelation (1 Cor. 1 : 7; Col. 3 : 4; 2 Thess. 1 : 7; Tit. 2 : 13; 1 Peter 1 : 7; 4 : 13). Ver. 27. **Then . . . angels** (8 : 38) *to gather* (Matt. 13 : 41) at first (1 Thess. 4 : 16, 17) **his elect,** whom they have always ministered to (Hebr. 1 : 13, 14), **from the four winds,** the four main points of the compass, **from . . . heaven,** i. e. those living, and those whose souls are in Paradise. " That will be a great grandeur and glory, greater than of all emperors and kings on earth. Then the whole air will be full of elect angels and holy men, everywhere surrounding the Lord in the clouds; they shall be brighter than the sun, and He, the Lord, and all saints with Him, will pronounce judgment on the condemned."
—LUTHER.

28-37. Now from the fig tree learn her parable: when her branch is now become tender, and putteth forth its leaves, ye know that the summer is nigh; even so ye also, when ye see these things coming to pass, know ye that he is nigh, *even* at the doors. Verily I say unto you, This generation shall not pass away, until all these things be accomplished. Heaven and earth shall pass away: but my words shall not pass away. But of that day or that hour knoweth no one, not even the angels in heaven, neither the Son, but the Father. Take ye heed, watch and pray: for ye know not when the time is. *It is* as *when* a man, sojourning in another country, having left his house, and given authority to his servants, to each one his work, commanded also the porter to watch. Watch therefore: for ye know not when the lord of the house cometh, whether at even, or at midnight, or at cockcrowing, or in the morning; lest coming suddenly he find you sleeping. And what I say unto you I say unto all, Watch.

Ver. 28. **Now . . . nigh** (Song of Songs 2 : 12, 13). In this beautiful comparison Jesus not only offers His disciples a most cheerful picture of promise and consolation amid the tribulation of the last days,[5] but foretells

---

[5] Luther, Walch, VII. 1498.

the final conversion of Israel (11 : 14; Matt. 23 : 39; Rom. 11 : 26) as a great sign of the end. "No man, reason or wisdom on earth can speak and explain this, that redemption and joy shall come, where only death and destruction is seen."—LUTHER. Ver. 29. By this sign **ye know ... these things** (ver. 24-27) ... **doors** as judge (James 5 : 9), but bringing to you the kingdom (Luke 21 : 31). Ver. 30. **Verily ... generation** (8 : 12) of Israel, a type of all unregenerate, **shall ... accomplished.** "Now we see with our own eyes the fulfilment of His words."—AMBROSE. "Israel rejecting Me shall remain until it calls Hosanna in truth! The withered fig tree shall stand, until it puts forth leaves."—STIER. Ver. 31. **Heaven ... away.** What is affirmed of the word of God (Ps. 119 : 89, 96; Isai. 40 : 8) Christ claims for His words, because He is divine. The earth and heaven will be changed (Ps. 102 : 26, 27; Isai. 51 : 6; 2 Peter 3 : 7, 10), but the words of Jesus are firm and eternal. "Heaven and earth, called into being out of nothing, carry the possibility of not-being within themselves; but Christ's words, descended from eternity, can never cease to be."—HILARY. How certain then is a salvation founded upon such words. Ver. 32. **But ... heaven**, although they know many things (cf. 1 Peter 1 : 12), **neither the Son ... Father.** The Son, although one with the Father (John 10 : 30), being the eternal Word (John 1 : 7 sq.), that made and upholds the world (Col. 1 : 17; Hebr. 1 : 3), who knows all things (John 21 : 17), and is therefore not subordinate, has yet in the form of the servant (Phil. 2 : 5 sq.), in which He became poor and laid aside heavenly glory (2 Cor. 8 : 9; John 17 : 5), limited His power by His love. He knew not the hour, because it was not necessary for His work and for men.[1] Ver. 33. **Take ... pray.**[2] With "endure" these warnings are "the four moral keynotes of the discourse of the Last Things."—FARRAR. Ver. 34. **It is ... watch.** This comparative picture, which is formally without an apodosis, teaches the duty of every Christian to work for Christ in his place (cf. Matt. 20:1 sq.) under the guidance of those called as watchmen (Isai. 21:6, 11, 12). As "bodily oversight and watchfulness in a house are necessary, much more spiritual watchfulness (1 Peter 5:8)."—STARKE. Ver. 35. **Watch ... cometh** (Matt. 24:45), **whether at even,** shortly after sunset in the first watch, **at midnight,** the end of

---

[1] On this passage Augustine holds, that Christ always knew in the Father (Serm. XLVII.), but He knew it not for "disclosure" (On Ps. X. 15), "because it was no part of His office as our Master that through Him it should become known to us" (On Ps. XXXVI. 16). He was ignorant "as making others ignorant" (On Trin. C. 12, 23). Chrysostom believes that Christ used this word to stop inquiry (Hom. on Matt. LXXVII.). Athanasius, who cites it as abused by the Arians (Disc. III. C. XXVI. 26), says: "It is not the Word's deficiency, but of that human nature, whose property it is to be ignorant" (Disc. III. C. XXVII. 43). In this position he is followed by Gregory Naz. (4th Theol. Orat. XV.). Basil (Letters CCXXXVI.) thinks, after comparing this passage with Matt., that it means: "No man knoweth, neither the angels of God; nor yet the Son would have known unless the Father had known." (On further views of the Fathers, see Gore, Bampton Lect. VI. 163, and p. 267, notes.) The view of Athanasius was adopted by Luther, who says (Walch, XII. 209): "The humanity of Christ has, just as another holy natural man, not always thought, spoken, willed, remembered all things, as some make an almighty man of him, confuse the two natures and their work unwisely." In like manner the other older teachers of the Lutheran Church placed the limitation in the human nature, which by "communicatio idiomatum" had the possession, but not always the use of divine attributes. Modern Lutheran theologians, since Thomasius (Christi Person u. Werk., 2. ed. 2, p. 156), with the exception of Philippi (Kirchl. Glaubenslehre, 2. ed. IV. 2, p. 422), regard the self-limitation one of divine love in the unity of the theanthropic person of Christ. (Luthardt, Compendium, 7th ed., p. 190; Frank, Chrl. Wahr. II. p. 143.)

[2] "Pray" is wanting in B, D, although otherwise well attested.

the second watch, **at cockcrowing** (14 : 30), between midnight and morning, **or in the morning,** at the end of the fourth watch (see 6 : 48). This warning for the special porters was given, Ver. 36, *lest* the Lord **coming find** them **sleeping,** which would entail punishment[1] (cf. Matt. 25 : 1 sq.). "The more uncertain the time of the coming of the Lord is, the more care is demanded to watch and be ready."—STARKE. Ver. 37. **And . . you,** apostles, types of all porters, **I say unto all** believers, **Watch.** The last word emphasizes the condition of Christians necessary at all times, in view of Christ's coming. "Who desires to stand before the Lord and not to be afraid of His advent, must watch constantly (Luke 21 : 36)."—STARKE.

[1] Edersheim says of the temple-guards on duty in the night: "Any guard found asleep when on duty was beaten, or his garments were set on fire—a punishment, as we know, actually awarded."

CHAPTER XIV.

1–2. Now after two days was *the feast of* the passover and the unleavened bread: and the chief priests and the scribes sought how they might take him with subtilty, and kill him: for they said, Not during the feast, lest haply there shall be a tumult of the people.

Ver. 1. **Now after two days,** counting from Tuesday evening, **was the feast of the passover,** which began on the evening of the 14th of Nisan, **and the unleavened bread,** which commenced on the 15th and lasted seven days (Jos. Antiq. III. 10, 5). These festivals, originally distinct (Exod. 12 : 14 sq. ; Lev. 23 : 5, 6 ; Numb. 28 : 16, 17), soon became one, and the name Passah, designating God's passing over (Exod. 12 : 13), was applied to the seven days of unleavened bread, that emphasized a religious custom (Deut. 16 : 1 ; 2 Chron. 35 : 16 sq.) ; and conversely (Jos. Antiq. II. 15, 1 ; XI. 4, 8 ; Wars, V. 3, 1). The **chief . . . take** Jesus, as the Pharisees had long ago (3 : 6) determined and incited the Sanhedrim (John 7 : 32, 45, 51 ; 11 : 53 ; 12 : 42). But they would do so **with subtilty,** since force was impossible (11 : 18 ; 12 : 12). Ver. 2. **For . . . people,** who are now enthused for Him (11 : 8). These men fear "not the ills from God, neither lest a pollution should arise to them from the season, but in every case the ills from men."—CHRYSOSTOM. But their counsel shall not prevail ; our passover (1 Cor. 5 : 7) must be slain on the feast, " that the ancient figure might give place to the only sacrifice of eternal redemption."—CALVIN.

3-9. And while he was in Bethany in the house of Simon the leper, as he sat at meat, there came a woman having an alabaster cruse of ointment of spikenard very costly; *and* she brake the cruse, and poured it over his head. But there were some that had indignation among themselves, *saying,* To what purpose hath this waste of the ointment been made? For this ointment might have been sold for above three hundred pence, and given to the poor. And they murmured against her. But Jesus said, Let her alone; why trouble ye her? she hath wrought a good work on me. For ye have the poor always with you, and whensoever ye will ye can do them good: but me ye have not always. She hath done what she could: she hath anointed my body aforehand for the burying. And verily I say unto you, Wheresoever the gospel shall be preached throughout the whole world, that also which this woman hath done shall be spoken of for a memorial of her.

Ver. 3. **While,** on the previous Sabbath, Jesus **was in Bethany** (11 : 1) **in the . . . Simon the leper** (1 : 40), not a Pharisee (Luke 7 : 36), but a friend[1] of Lazarus, healed by Jesus, to whom **as he . . . meal,** the festive Sabbath dinner, **there came a woman,** Mary, the sister of Martha (John 12 : 3),[2] **having . . . alabaster cruse,** a small sealed bottle made of alabaster,[3] which contained twelve ounces (John 12 : 3) of *nard genuine*[4] and **very**

---

[1] Paulus and Hengstenberg would make Mary the wife of Simon, Bleek and Lange his widow, and Ewald his daughter, Simon being deceased.

[2] This Mary is not to be identified with Mary Magdalene (Augustine, Hengstenberg), who in turn is made the woman, "a sinner" (Luke 7 : 37), so that there is but one unction (Clement Alex., Tertullian, Origen, Chrysostom); for this anointing is clearly different from that of Luke 7. But no two unctions took place at Bethany, one six days before the passover and the other two days (Jerome, Theophylact, Osiander, Lightfoot), but only one is reported by Matt., Mark and John (Augustine, Luther, Calvin, Gerhard, Bengel, Meyer, Keil, Godet, Nösgen, etc.). Nebe, Leidensgeschichte, I. 20 sq.

[3] This is, however, not absolutely necessary, for the name "alabaster," originally applied to flasks from Alabastron, Egypt, and then to the white stone of which they were made, was finally used for all vessels containing perfume. Maclear, p. 152.

[4] The much disputed "πιστικῆς" cannot refer to a place Piste (Augustine), supposed to be mentioned by Æschylus (Persæ, V. 1) as a city of

costly. Nard, an aromatic plant (Song of Songs 1 : 12 ; 4 : 13, 14), of which the best-known species is the nardus spicata, although found in Gaul, Syria and Assyria, is especially at home in India. From its dried leaves with a part of the root the ointment, which was very expensive,[1] was prepared. Mary **brake the cruse** in its narrow neck, and **poured it** lavishly over the *head* of Jesus, and anointed His feet (John 12 : 3). Him she honored in deep love and reverence as high priest (Ps. 133 : 2) and king (Song of Songs 1 : 12), although unwittingly. Ver. 4. But there were **some** disciples (Matt. 26 : 8) incited by Judas (John 12 : 4 sq.), who, indignant among themselves, said, **To . . . made?** Ver. 5. **It . . . pence** (6 : 37), $48, an immense sum, **and given . . . poor.** And they **murmured** strongly **against her.** The disciples not knowing the purpose of Judas (John 12 : 6) were influenced by his apparent interest for the poor, and caught the infection of his malicious tongue. They condemn Mary, and call that anointment wasted, which is given to God's great Anointed (Ps. 45 : 7). "Nothing is wasted upon Christ. Miserable parsimony, if we refuse Him anything."—HEDINGER, STARKE. Ver. 6. He said, **Let . . . me.** The reproach against Mary and the interference with her is reproved, because her deed proceeding from living faith (Rom. 14 : 23) is good. It was also the result and representation of that thankfulness for the love of Jesus by the retributive love (1 John 4 : 19), which is the "rich source and living seed of all other

---

Persia, because Persia is never mentioned as producing ointment. Nor can it be liquid, for, though nard mixed with wine and water was used, πιστικός never stands for πιστός. The best derivation supported by later Greek is from πίστις: therefore faithful, trustworthy, genuine and not pseudo-nard. Nebe, Ldg. I., p. 33 sq; Morison, p. 379 sq.

[1] It is mentioned among the precious gifts sent to Cambyses by the Ethiopians.

love acceptable before God."—BESSER. Ver. 7. **For . . . you** (cf. Prov. 22 : 2), **and whensoever . . . good.** Many are the opportunities for charity, where there is a desire to help. **But . . . always,** for I go to the Father (John 14 : 12, 28); therefore do now what ye can. Ver. 8. **She . . . she could** totally and fully and **anointed . . . . . . for the burying.** Her act was prophetically the last service of love. Ver. 9. **And . . . preached** her deed **shall . . . memorial of her.** Wherever the name of Jesus is spoken of in the wide world Mary is remembered as the first and best example of that love, which in humility and with great self-sacrifice brings the costliest gifts to the Saviour. Without such love the gospel would not be spread.

10-11. And Judas Iscariot, he that was one of the twelve, went away unto the chief priests, that he might deliver him unto them. And they, when they heard it, were glad, and promised to give him money. And he sought how he might conveniently deliver him *unto them.*

Ver. 10. **And** in contrast with the love of Mary **Judas Iscariot** (3 : 19) **that . . . the twelve,** "of the first company of those selected as the best,"—CHRYSOSTOM, **went . . . Christ.** The motive of Judas was not revenge for the correction at Bethany (Aquinas, Gerhard, Bynæus), nor the hope that Christ would thus be compelled to free Himself and would then establish the desired earthly messianic kingdom (Thiess, Paulus, Winer, Hase); nor despair in Christ's Messiahship (Neander, Bleek, Ewald, Schenkel, Keim, Holtzmann). But avarice, against which he had heard many warnings (10 : 25; Matt. 6 : 19; 13 : 22; Luke 16 : 11; John 6 : 70), and into the service of which he placed his energy, sagacity, and financial ability (John 12 : 6), that Christ had seen in him, was the root of evil (1 Tim. 6 : 10). By this he opened his heart to Satan¹ (Luke 22 : 3), and the presence of the heavenly Goodness became a savor of death (2 Cor. 2 : 16) unto a terrible end (Matt. 27 : 3 sq.; Acts 1 : 16 sq.).² Ver. 11. The priests *when they heard* the desire of Judas **were glad** that they could attain their purpose (ver. 1); and as children of darkness rejoice in such wickedness. **They . . . money**, which Judas bargained for (Matt. 26 : 15). He received 30 pieces of silver (30 shekels—$15), as prophesied Zech. 11 : 12. This sum, equivalent to four months' wages, was the price of a slave (Exod. 21 : 32). The servant (Phil. 2 : 7) is sold for a servant's price. Judas **sought . . . conveniently**, without arousing the people, and when Jesus was not among friends at Bethany, *deliver him*. "The children of the world are wiser than the children of light, but in wickedness and evil plans."—STARKE.

12-16. And on the first day of unleavened bread, when they sacrificed the passover, his disciples say unto him, Where wilt thou that we go and make ready that thou mayest eat the passover? And he sendeth two of his disciples, and saith unto them, Go into the city, and there shall meet you a man bearing a pitcher of water: follow him; and wheresoever he shall enter in, say to the goodman of the house, The Master saith, Where is my guest-chamber, where I shall eat the passover with my disciples? And he will himself shew you a large upper room furnished *and* ready: and there make ready for us. And the disciples went forth, and came into the city, and found as he had said unto them: and they made ready the passover.

Ver. 12. *On the first day of* **unleavened bread** (ver. 1), Thursday evening,³ **when** in the temple **they sacrificed**

¹ The apocryphal Gospel of the Infancy (C. 35) has invented the fable that Judas, when a boy, was healed by Jesus of a demon, who came out "in the shape of a dog."

² Nebe, Ldg. I., p. 59 sq.; Geikie. p. 274 sq.; Edersheim, II., p. 471 sq.; Farrar, p. 526 sq.

³ The synoptists clearly state, that Jesus ate the passover at the regular time, but John (13 : 1; 18 : 28; 19 : 14, 31) seems to contradict. That,

... **passover**, which was at the going down of the sun (Deut. 16:6), between the two evenings (Exod. 13:6; Lev. 23:5; Numb. 9:3, 5),[1] **the ... passover?** Perhaps they supposed that Jesus would eat in the seclusion of Bethany, which for religious purposes was reckoned a part of Jerusalem. Ver. 13. **He .. two**, Peter and John (Luke 22:8), **and saith ... him**. The same prescience of Jesus that directed the disciples to the colt (11:2) again gives minute orders, which begin with the command to follow a slave bearing water (Deut. 29:11; Josh. 9:21). Christ "chose to direct them by a miracle that afterward their faith might remain firm."—CALVIN. Ver. 14. They were to say **to the goodman**[2] **... house**,[3] which the slave entered, *The Master saith*, to thee a disciple, **Where ... disciples?** Jesus in His modesty asks for the **guest-chamber** (inn, Luke 2:7), where beasts of burden were allowed, and shoes, staff, and garments laid off. He that was born in an inn would hold His last meal just as humbly. Only the inn (kataluma, khan) must be His alone (*my*). No other company, as was customary, is to be there; for in the days of passover general hospitality prevailed. Christ and His disciples would form a proper company, which could not be less than ten persons, nor more than that each could have a

however, John, whose words can and have been brought into agreement with the synoptists, was of the same opinion is attested by Polycarp, who ate the passover with John on the 14th of Nisan. (Robinson, Harm., p. 243 sq.; Schaff, Hist. of Christ, ch. I. 134.) Against this view, cf. Farrar, Excursus X., p. 671 sq. See Appendix, p. 285 sq.

[1] For a description of such passover sacrifice among the Samaritans, see Trumbull, p. 371 sq.

[2] "Goodman" is a relic of olden time, in which the esteem towards the head of the household was thus expressed (Morison).

[3] This man was not Joseph of Arimathaia, but the father of Mark (ver. 51). (Ewald, Lichtenstein, Edersheim.)

small portion of the paschal lamb. The goodman, continued Christ, Ver. 15, **will . . . room.** This was the best and most secluded room (2 Sam. 18:33; Dan. 6:10), to which there was an outer entrance. It was often used for prayer (2 Kings 23:12; Acts 1:13; 20:8), as sickroom (1 Kings 17:19) and death-chamber (Acts 9:37, 39), but also for honored guests (2 Kings 4:10). The disciples would find it **furnished,** the reclining couches with tapestry set about the table, **and ready,** the lamps and dishes placed, and all ceremonial requirements fulfilled. It was thus; and the disciples, Ver. 16, **made . . . passover.** The preparation included not only the final preparation of the lamb, which, purchased on the tenth of Nisan, had to be slain and made ready in the temple about the time of the evening sacrifice,[1] but also the obtaining of the unleavened cakes (Exod. 12:18), the bitter herbs, the wine for the cups, which was mixed with water.

17-21. And when it was evening he cometh with the twelve. And as they sat and were eating, Jesus said, Verily I say unto you, One of you shall betray me, *even* he that eateth with me. They began to be sorrowful, and to say unto him one by one, Is it I? And he said unto them, *It is* one of the twelve, he that dippeth with me in the dish. For the Son of man goeth, even as it is written of him: but woe unto that man through whom the Son of man is betrayed! good were it for that man if he had not been born.

Ver. 17. *When it was* **evening,** the second evening after the setting of the sun, Jesus *cometh with the twelve.* Ver. 18. *And as they* **sat** (lit. reclined) after the washing of the feet (John 13:1 sq.), *and* **were eating,**[2] *Jesus,* beginning as told John 13:13 sq., said, **Verily . . . me.**

[1] See Edersheim, II. 487 sq.
[2] They were now in the passover celebration at the third part, the setting out of the bitter herbs, which is preceded by the "cup of consecration," and the washing of hands, for which Jesus substituted the washing of feet.

When Jesus utters this word He is not only conscious that it is a prophecy (Ps. 41 : 9), but He seeks in great sadness (John 13 : 21) of love to warn the lost child, previously warned (John 13 : 10). "The world would love betrayal and despise the traitor. Christ despises betrayal and seeks to save the traitor, whose soul He loves."—GERHARD. Ver. 19. The disciples **began, . . . Is it I?** Overwhelmed by surprise and sorrow they ask, surely it is not I: for they are at once conscious of their innocence and fear their weakness. And Judas, the hypocrite, follows and deceives them. Peter, not satisfied, beckons to John (John 13: 24 sq.), who, reclining at the right of Jesus, asks him. Ver. 20. Jesus *said*, **It is . . . dish.** The sign is to be the dipping with Jesus into the dish, which after a blessing is the fourth part of the passover feast. Into this dish, containing the Chasoreth, the sauce of vinegar, water, almonds, figs and spice, which symbolizes the fruits of the Holy Land as a gift after the delivery from Egypt; the bitter herbs, as lettuce, endive, succory and horehound, representing Israel's bondage, are dipped. This Judas does, and Christ gives him the piece dipped in (John 13: 26). But the effrontery of Judas still deceives the rest. Ver. 21. Jesus says, **The Son of man** (2: 10) . . . **written of him** (cf. 8 : 31 ; Ps. 22 ; Isai. 53) . . **born.** The necessity of Christ's death, which on His part is a free going in obedience to the divine purpose, does not abate the guilt of Judas. Not because God foresaw the deed of Judas did he sin ; but when God foresaw it, He foretold it. "Though God by His righteous judgment appointed for the price of our redemption the death of His son, yet nevertheless Judas in betraying Christ brought upon himself righteous condemnation, because he was full of treachery and avarice. In short, God's determination that He would save the redeemed, does not at all interfere with Judas being a wicked traitor."—CALVIN. But Christ in His love desired, if such were possible, that Judas had never been born. "This is the last call of love, stronger than the howling of hell, a love which accompanies the lost even to the boundaries of misery, where it must leave them."—STIER.

22–25. *And as they were eating, he took bread, and when he had blessed, he brake it, and gave to them, and said, Take ye: this is my body. And he took a cup, and when he had given thanks, he gave to them: and they all drank of it. And he said unto them, This is my blood of the covenant, which is shed for many. Verily I say unto you, I will no more drink of the fruit of the vine, until that day when I drink it new in the kingdom of God.*

Ver. 22. **As . . . eating,** being now at the seventh part[1] of the passover, the taking of unleavened cakes, breaking and distributing them after the blessing: " Blessed be thou, O Lord our God, Thou king of the universe, who bringest forth fruit out of the earth " (1 Cor. 10:16). *Jesus,* making the passover of fulfilment out of the passover of promise, **took bread,** one cake, as there was to be one gift to be given to the one body of believers (1 Cor. 10:17). **And when . . . blessed it,** not only as was generally the custom (6:41), but with special grace, that it might be a true Eucharist, and "the germ and beginning of a *blessing* of divine miraculous power[2] upon all communion-bread,"—STIER; He **brake** it, simply to divide it (6:41), but not as a symbol.[3] " Figures and

---

[1] Since the dipping into the Chasoreth, the Haggadah or "shewing forth" (1 Cor. 11:26), i. e. the telling about the delivery from Egypt according to the law (Ex. 12:27; 13:8); and the filling of the second cup and its drinking after the inquiry, "What mean ye by this service?" by a child or proselyte; and the singing of the first part of the Hallel (Ps. 113, 114) had taken place. Maclear, p. 157.

[2] Gerhard compares this blessing with that of fruitfulness given at creation.

[3] The apparent support of the symbolical meaning of breaking is 1 Cor.

signs in the N. T. belong to the O. T. among the Jews, and who confesses that he has the figure or sign of the N. T., he confesses that he does not yet possess the N. T., and has retrograded, denied Christ and become a Jew."—LUTHER. Then Christ **gave it . . . them,** whether into the hand or mouth is not certain, and said, **Take ye;** eat (Matt. 26 : 26): **this is my body.** In this most wonderful eating, the mouth takes the bread as the communion (1 Cor. 10 : 16) of the very *body*[1] of Christ, which is not simply flesh (John 6), but flesh and blood, permeated by the living spirit. It is the body about to be given into death (Luke 22 : 19), but miraculously glorified, because it is the body of the Godman. "Christ has not only given Himself to us as brother, friend, surety; that was not enough for His love, He gave Himself to us as meat."—TAULER. Ver. 23. **And,** at the eighth part of the passover, the "cup of blessing" (1 Cor. 10 : 16), Jesus **took a cup,** and having thanked, **gave** it to the disciples: **and . . . it,** as directed (Matt. 26 : 27); for all are to have personal participation in the full power of Christ's life. All are given the blood, in which is the life of the body (Lev. 17 : 11). Ver. 24. And He said, **This . . . covenant,**[2] The covenant of the O. T. (Exod. 24 : 8) instituted with blood of oxen, for every covenant requires blood (Hebr. 9 : 18), is

11 : 24. But the best MSS. (ℵ, A, B, C) omit "broken," and the Rev. Version properly reads: "This is my body which is for you." The breaking of bread would be a very inapt picture.

[1] For the impossibility of a figure in "is" or "body" see Krauth, The Conservative Reformation, etc., p. 608 sq. Grass (Verhalten zu Jesus. etc., p. 112) states as the clear result of uninfluenced exegesis: "The eating of the bread is identical with the eating of His body, and the drinking of the wine is identical with the drinking of His blood."

[2] The reading of Luke, "the new covenant in my blood" (cf. also 1 Cor. 11 : 25), is not contradictory. While emphasizing the *newness* of the covenant more strongly, as Matt. and Mark its uniqueness (*the* covenant), it makes the cup equally with Matt. and Mark a carrier of the blood.

as a shadow (Col. 2 : 17; Hebr. 10 : 1) now supplanted by *the covenant*, which is the eternally new (Jer. 31 : 33, 34; Hebr. 8 : 8, 13; 9 : 15) in Him that maketh all things new (2 Cor. 5 : 17). His **blood**, as that of the blameless lamb of God (John 1 : 29; 1 Peter 1 : 19; Hebr. 9 : 14), **shed** for the remission of sins (Matt. 26 : 28; Hebr. 9 : 20) **for many** (10 : 45), the whole mass of men (1 Tim. 2 : 6; 2 Cor. 5 : 14; Hebr. 2 : 9; 1 John 2 : 2), is, glorified like the body (ver. 22), given in the Lord's supper. "In the O. T. those that sacrificed could eat of the sacrifice, and thereby became certain of the gracious acceptance of their offering by God. Thus we partake of Christ's sacrifice in the sacrificial meal of the new covenant for the assurance that it has truly been accepted for us by God, and that we are reconciled with Him. Here we receive the good thing, an established heart (Hebr. 13 : 9, 10), well comforted with the remission of sins."—LUTHER.[1] Then Christ said,[2] Ver. 25, **Verily I say . . . the kingdom of God.** Jesus will no more on earth drink of wine making glad (Ps. 104 : 15), until the *kingdom of God* in its glorious consummation (1 : 15; Matt. 13 : 36 sq.; Luke 22 : 30) on the new earth (2 Peter 3 : 13; Rev. 21 : 5) will be the supper of the lamb (Rev. 19 : 9). Then He will partake of the glorified spiritual-bodily gifts of joy.

26. And when they had sung a hymn, they went out unto the mount of Olives.

Ver. 26. After singing the rest of the Hallel (Ps. 115–118) Jesus and His disciples go to the Mount of Olives (11 : 1).

[1] For an excellent exposition of the Lord's Supper, see Besser, Leidensg., p. 69 sq.

[2] In all probability Jesus repeated this word, which He had spoken at the beginning, at the time of the "cup of consecration" (Luke 22 : 15 sq.), with its prayer: "Blessed be Thou, Jehovah our God, Thou king of the universe, who hast created the fruit of the vine."

27-31. And Jesus saith unto them, All ye shall be offended: for it is written, I will smite the shepherd, and the sheep shall be scattered abroad. Howbeit, after I am raised up, I will go before you into Galilee. But Peter said unto him, Although all shall be offended, yet will not I. And Jesus saith unto him, Verily I say unto thee, that thou to-day, *even* this night, before the cock crow twice, shalt deny me thrice. But he spake exceeding vehemently, If I must die with thee, I will not deny thee. And in like manner also said they all.

Ver. 27. **Jesus . . . be offended** I shall be a stumbling-block to you. "They saw Him handled as a child of the devil, therefore they doubted whether He was the Son of God; they saw that He did not help Himself, therefore they doubted whether He was the Saviour; they saw Him treated like the most rejected enthusiast, therefore they doubted whether He was the truth; they saw Him led to death, therefore they doubted whether He was life."—BRENZ. This was as foretold Zech. 13 : 7, **I will smite . . . scattered abroad.** The good shepherd (John 10 : 4) over men (Ezek. 34 : 31) will be smitten of God (Isai. 53 : 4), and His flock scattered (ver. 50). But the helpless sheep are to know that "God does not cease to recognize as His sheep those who are driven out and scattered in every direction for a time."—CALVIN. Ver. 28. **Howbeit . . . up** (8: 31) through the glory of the Father (Rom. 6 : 4 ; cf. also 7 : 4 ; 8 : 11), **I . . . Galilee** (16 : 7 ; Matt. 28 : 7, 16 ; John 21 : 1 sq.), as a shepherd to gather you the "little ones" (Zech. 13 : 7). "You will desert Me, but I will not desert you." —STIER. Ver. 29. **But Peter . . . I.** The ardent confessor (John 6 : 68) is honest, but in proud self-reliance, lowering others, overestimates himself. The most dangerous condition is presumptuous self-confidence (1 Cor. 10 : 12). Ver. 30. **But . . . cock crow twice** (13 : 35), **. . . thrice.** Mark most fully and clearly reports this word with its climax. Before morning the rock shall have become a shaking reed (ver. 66 sq.). Ver. 31. But Peter spake **exceeding vehemently** with the full resistance of his fiery nature, **If I must die** ... **they all**, not to be outdone by Peter's strong assertion. "Having no reliance on the promise and neglecting prayer, they advance with inconsiderate haste to boast of a constancy which they did not possess."—CALVIN.

32–42. And they come unto a place which was named Gethsemane: and he saith unto his disciples, Sit ye here, while I pray. And he taketh with him Peter and James and John, and began to be greatly amazed, and sore troubled. And he saith unto them, My soul is exceedingly sorrowful even unto death: abide ye here, and watch. And he went forward a little, and fell on the ground, and prayed that, if it were possible, the hour might pass away from him. And he said, Abba, Father, all things are possible unto thee; remove this cup from me: howbeit not what I will, but what thou wilt. And he cometh, and findeth them sleeping, and saith unto Peter, Simon, sleepest thou? couldst thou not watch one hour? Watch and pray, that ye enter not into temptation: the spirit indeed is willing, but the flesh is weak. And **again** he went away, and prayed, saying the same words. And again he came, and found them sleeping, for their eyes were very heavy; and they wist not what to answer him. And he cometh the third time, and saith unto them, Sleep on now, and take your rest: it is enough; the hour is come; behold, the Son of man is betrayed into the hands of sinners. Arise, let us be going: behold, he that betrayeth me is at hand.

Ver. 32. **They** ... **Gethsemane** (oil-press), a garden (John 18 : 1) whither Jesus was wont to go (John 18 : 2), at the foot of Olivet. It probably contained an oil-press, and has, since the fourth century, been placed about a hundred yards east of the bridge across the Kedron in a spot containing very old trees, which cannot, however, go back to the time of Christ, since Titus in the siege of Jerusalem cut down all the trees.[1]

---

[1] Stanley, Sinai and Palestine, p. 455; Wilson, Bible Lands, I., p. 481; Nebe, Ldg. I., p. 231. Thomson (II., p. 483) argues against the traditional site.

"It was proper that in a garden the blood of the physician should be shed as medicine, because in a garden the sickness of the sick originated."—AUGUSTINE. At the entrance He said **to his . . . I pray.** With this word, recalling Gen. 22 : 5, Christ, though mentioning His purpose, conceals the mystery of His obedient suffering from the eight disciples, that were not yet able to bear it. Ver. 33. **He . . . and John** (5 : 37 ; 9 : 2). . . . **began** actively to suffer, and *to be* **greatly amazed**, lit. thoroughly terrified *and* **sore troubled**, almost beyond Himself in sorrow. The sadness of Jesus increasing to awful terror. "although much too high for us, because the person that suffers is too high and above all,"—LUTHER, is in part revealed by Him, when, Ver. 34, **he . . . soul** (8 : 35), . . . **death**. The very depth of the individual life of Jesus with its wonderfully delicate sensitiveness, as He is the Sinless and Living One, is overwhelmed by a sorrow that hurries Him almost to death. It is not a trembling because of the bodily suffering to come, but the dread of the Holy One before death (Heb. 5 : 7), as the wages of sin, with its power of condemnation (Isai. 53 : 8). "Such sorrow and terror is a proof that Christ is true man, for otherwise such sorrow could not have held Him ; yet again it is testimony that He is true God, because He endured and conquered such sorrow. Upon His neck lay the sin of the whole world, that such death, which He was to suffer, was a death of sins, and a death of the wrath of God."—LUTHER. To the three, Christ further said, **abide . . . watch.** Ye cannot help Me, I must do My work alone (Isai. 63 : 3), but you can be near as witnesses (1 Peter 5 : 1), that seeing you for whom I suffer I may be consoled. Ver. 35. **And he went forward** *a little*, further into the centre of the garden about a stone's cast (Luke 22 : 41), and **fell on the ground** in deepest humiliation

(Ps. 22:6) and **prayed** with crying (cf. Ps. 18:6; 22:2; 69:13; 109:4) and tears (Heb. 5:7). "This word is repeated so often in this account, as though the evangelists had agreed to give us no peace, until we notice this praying of the Lord Jesus."—RAMBACH. Seeking freedom from this *hour* of agony, Ver. 36, **he ... Abba, Father,** repeating the Aramaic (Abba) in Greek to testify strongly His affection toward the Father, although under His judgment. If we have the spirit of adoption and of the Son, we can also cry thus (Rom. 8:15; Gal. 4:6). **All ... thee** (10:27) ... **cup** (10:38) of suffering and judgment (Jer. 25:15) **from me ... wilt.** The Son would have the Father use His almighty power not to break the eternal promise of salvation (Heb. 6:18), which Christ Himself knows must be fulfilled (8:31), but to take away what in His human nature He dreaded before (John 12:27), this terrible present agony. Yet even now, learning obedience (Heb. 5:8), His meat is the Father's will (John 4:35) although it be tears (Ps. 42:3). "The will of God must always be dearer to us than our own, cost what it may to fulfil it (Heb. 10:36)."—QUESNEL, STARKE. Ver. 37. And Christ *cometh and findeth* the three **sleeping** "for sorrow" (Luke 22:46), because they did not pray. This was "an additional aggravation of His sufferings, that even they forsook Him,"—CALVIN, and had no word of consolation for Him (Ps. 69:20). Therefore He *saith* especially *unto* **Peter,** who had made so firm a promise (ver. 31), **Simon** (1:29; 3:16), thou old natural man, not a Peter (rock) now, **sleepest ... hour?** In work thou didst wake all night (Luke 5:5), with Me thou canst not conquer thy weakness one hour? What shall come in the other hours? "If thou art not faithful in the least, what, wilt thou be faithful in much?"—RAMBACH. And then addressing the others like Peter

(Matt. 26 : 40), Jesus continued, Ver. 38, **Watch and pray** (1 Peter 5 : 8 ; 1 Thess. 5 : 6); ye, who would watch rightly, must watch prayerfully with your heart (Song of Songs 5 : 2) and spirit (Isai. 26 : 9) ; and would ye pray properly ye must watch, *that ye* **enter not** and fall (1 Tim. 6 : 9) in *temptation*, which is so near (ver. 29 sq.). The **spirit** *indeed*, the original divine life-power of God, as renewed in believers,[1] *is* **willing** (Rom. 7 : 18, 22), *but the* **flesh**, the lower nature, which, sinfully determined, is directed against the spirit [2] (Rom. 7 : 17, 18, 23 ; Gal. 5 : 17), **is weak** in temptation and yields readily. This word, for believers alone, is no excuse, but should sharpen watchfulness. Ver. 39. **And . . . words** (cf. Rom. 12 : 12), but more submissively (Matt. 26 : 42). Ver. 40. **And . . . heavy; and**, as Mark adds graphically, **they wist not . . answer him** (9 : 6). They continue in their weakness, but Christ's mercy does not cease (Isai. 42 : 3). Ver. 41. **He . . . rest**, while yet you may. And after some time, He says, *it is* **enough**, the time for sleep is past. **The hour** of darkness (Luke 22 : 53) *is come*, **Behold . . . the hands of sinners.** The sinless one is given over to those one with the traitor in wickedness. Ver. 42. **Arise . . . going** toward the entrance of the garden ; the traitor *is* **at hand.** Jesus has seen the lights, and as a good shepherd will not desert the other disciples in the coming danger.

43–50. And straightway, while he yet spake, cometh Judas, one of the twelve, and with him a multitude with swords and staves, from the chief priests and the scribes and the elders. Now he that betrayed him had given them a token, saying, Whomsoever I shall kiss, that is he ; take him, and lead him away safely. And when he was come, straightway he came to him, and saith, Rabbi ; and kissed him. And they laid hands on him, and took him. But a certain one of them that stood by drew his sword,

---

[1] Cremer, p. 787. [2] Cremer, p. 827.

and smote the servant of the high priest, and struck off his ear. And Jesus answered and said unto them, Are ye come out, as against a robber, with swords and staves to seize me? I was daily with you in the temple teaching, and ye took me not: but *this is done* that the scriptures might be fulfilled. And they all left him, and fled.

Ver. 43. *Straightway, while* Jesus *yet spake* what is told ver. 42, *cometh Judas* (3:19; 14:10), and *with him a* **multitude**, a detachment of the Roman temple-cohort (John 18:12), *with swords*, and men of the Levitical temple-guard and a motley crowd of servants of the priests with *staves*, sent from the Sanhedrim (8:31; 11:27). "Judas was called by Christ to lead the multitude of nations to faith in Jesus to be saved by Him; but behold, he brings the multitude to destroy Christ, and receives eternal condemnation."—BRENZ. Ver. 44. *He*, having given the armed band as a token that he would kiss Christ, adds in his wicked eagerness, *take him, and lead him away safely*. Ver. 45. And *straightway he came to* Jesus, *and saith* reverently, **Rabbi,** and **kissed him** with many kisses (Luke 7:45; 15:20, Acts 20:38). The kiss in the East was not only a sign of friendship and love, given when meeting or parting (Gen. 29:13; 33:4; Ruth 1:14; 2 Sam. 20:9), but also a token of reverence (1 Sam. 10:1; 1 Kings 19:18; Ps. 2:12; 72:9; Isai. 49:23; Micah 7:17). Judas desires to deceive his Master with this special show of reverence and love, feigning sorrow that the enemies have come. But among all kisses of enemies (Prov. 27:6), this, far more outrageous than that of Joab (2 Sam. 20:9, 10), is the most terribly wicked. Jesus suffers this too, and in love reproved Judas (Matt. 26:49). Ver. 46. Then the band **laid hands** *on him* roughly, and **took him** (Ps. 22:16). Ver. 47. **But a certain one,** Peter (John 18:10), **drew his sword** (Luke 22:38), **and** . . . pet **servant** (Malchus, John 18:10) *of the high priest,* *and struck off his* right (Luke 22:50) **ear**. Peter, whose name the early gospels do not mention in this connection, to save him this additional disgrace (cf. ver. 66 sq), in his good intention acted in a manner most dangerous for Christ. "It is one of the most foolish things, agreeable to Satan, to defend the gospel with the sword."—LUTHER.[1] The Christian's sword is spiritual (Eph. 6:17). Jesus, after correcting Peter (Matt. 26:52 sq.; John 18:11), *said* to His captors, Ver. 48, *Are ye come out as against a* **robber**, which I am not, though I permit Myself to be taken. Ver. 49. **I . . . temple** (Luke 19:47) **teaching** openly, and ye **took me not** (John 7:30, 44; 8:20), although you had every chance. But that you succeed now is only *that the* **Scriptures . . . fulfilled** (Isai. 53:12). "The agreement of the prophetical predictions with the sufferings of Jesus should assure us that He is the Saviour of the world (Luke 24:46)."—STARKE. Ver. 50. *And all* the disciples *left him and fled* (ver. 27). Now they abandoned all hope in Him as Messiah (Luke 24:21.)

51-52. And a certain young man followed with him, having a linen cloth cast about him, over *his* naked *body;* and they lay hold on him; but he left the linen cloth, and fled naked.

Ver. 51. **A . . . young man**. This is now universally supposed to be Mark.[2] Aroused by the armed band of the captors of Jesus, he had followed from his father's house (ver. 14), where Judas sought Jesus, who was supposed still to be at the passover meal. Mark even now, after the disciples had fled, **followed with** Jesus, because

---

[1] Walch, VIII., p. 871; Erl. Ed. 2, p. 45 sq.

[2] Since Ohlshausen this supposition has gained general acceptance among all commentators. Epiphanius, relying upon the account of Hegesippus about the clothing of James the Just (Eus. H. E. II. 23), points to the latter; Chrysostom, Ambrose, and Gregory the Great think of John; Ewald suggests Paul, and Grotius a workman in Gethsemane.

he desired to see what would happen. He had a **linen cloth**, a fine[1] linen wrapper, **cast . . . his naked body**, or rather over his inner tunic; for to be clothed in this alone was considered nakedness (1 Sam. 19:24; Job 24:10; Isai. 20:2). Ver. 52. When the soldiers *laid hold* of Mark, *he left the linen cloth and fled* in his under-garment. This incident, long remembered by Mark, shows the eagerness and boldness of his character, as well as the instability of his youthful self-confidence.[2]

53-65. And they led Jesus away to the high priest: and there come together with him all the chief priests and the elders and the scribes. And Peter had followed him afar off, even within, into the court of the high priest; and he was sitting with the officers, and warming himself in the light *of the fire*. Now the chief priests and the whole council sought witness against Jesus to put him to death; and found it not. For many bare false witness against him, and their witness agreed not together. And there stood up certain, and bare false witness against him, saying, We heard him say, I will destroy this temple that is made with hands, and in three days I will build another made without hands. And not even so did their witness agree together. And the high priest stood up in the midst, and asked Jesus saying, Answerest thou nothing? what is it which these witness against thee? But he held his peace, and answered nothing. Again the high priest asked him, and saith unto him, Art thou the Christ, the Son of the Blessed? And Jesus said, I am: and ye shall see the Son of man sitting at the right hand of power, and coming with the clouds of heaven. And the high priest rent his clothes, and saith, What further need have we of witnesses? Ye have heard the blasphemy: what think ye? And they all condemned him to be worthy of death. And some began to spit on him, and to cover his face, and to buffet him, and to say unto him, Prophesy: and the officers received him with blows of their hands.

Ver. 53. **They . . . priest**, first to Annas for a preliminary non-official questioning, then to Caiphas, his son-in-law, the ruling high priest (John 18:13 sq.);[3] and *there*

---

[1] σινδών is used for precious, costly linen (Matt. 27:59; Mark 15:46; Judg. 14:12).

[2] See Introduction, p. ix.

[3] Both high priests, as Euthemius suggested, lived in different wings of

come together the sanhedrists (ver. 43 ; 8 : 31), who had previously been summoned to an extraordinary night-session in the palace of Caiphas, and not in a temple-chamber, the only legal place. Thus the judge of all the world stands accused before the wicked. Ver. 54. **And Peter . . . off,** partly in the self-reliant desire to keep his word (ver. 31) against Christ's warning (cf. also John 13 : 36), partly from love. "That he followed was love ; that he followed afar off arose from fear. Love draws him, fear keeps him back."—GERHARD. But he came **even within,** *into the court of the high priest,* through the intervention of John (John 18 : 15), who was probably known to the servants by his sale of fish (Luthardt). Peter *was sitting with the* **officers,** the servants of the high priest and the temple-guard (ver. 43), **and warming . . . fire,** for the night was chilly.[1] Peter's faith and love were getting cold in this place of danger. Ver. 55. **Now . . . council,**[2] assembled in full number with the exception of Nicodemus and Joseph of Arimathæa (15 : 43), **sought . . . death.** The very beginning of this trial was illegal, because in capital accusations the accused had the right of defence first ;[3] but Jesus had no such opportunity,

the same palace, that had a common courtyard. This will solve the apparent contradiction between the synoptists and John as to the place of Peter's denial.

[1] Augustine (Tract. on John CXIII. 3) has expressed, what travellers have since confirmed: "Though it was not winter it was cold: which is sometimes wont to be the case even at the vernal equinox."

[2] The council could not have been a smaller tribunal, that of three judges or of twenty-three, but it must have been the seventy-one, because they alone had the power of pronouncing death.

[3] Beside this regulation there were others for the conducting of trials. The judges, appointed by and from the Sanhedrim, who sat in a semi-circle, probably under a presiding judge (Nasi) and a vice-president, were to have shorthand writers to take down the testimony. Each one of the members of the council had his special place, and if one had spoken for the

for at once witnesses were sought who, without being legally cautioned, were expected to tell what would be sufficient to pronounce the judgment beforehand determined upon. The chief priests "wished to invest this plot with the appearance of a court of justice."—CHRYSOSTOM. But they *found* no true testimony. Ver. 56. **For . . together.** Despite all attempts no case was made out; for the witnesses, of whom according to Deut. 17:6 at least two had to be accordant, did not agree (cf. Ps. 55:9). "As the sun gives its brightest rays when breaking forth from behind clouds, thus the innocence of Christ, when clouded by false testimonies, shines in its brightest light."—GERHARD. Ver. 57, 58, 59. **And . . . together.** Referring to Christ's word in the temple (John 2:19), which He applied to Himself, they would have it spoken against the temple. But their report does not coincide; for not only do they change " Break ye " into " I break," but one claims that Christ had asserted the power (" I am able," Matt. 26:61), the other the purpose (" I will ") of destroying; and they add " with hands " and " without hands." Ver. 60. **And . . . thee?** The high priest rises in apparent indignation because Jesus, who was expected to incriminate Himself by some unguarded or angry answer, does not reply to such accusations. " He insinuates that Christ is not free from blame, because witnesses speak against Him."—CALVIN. Ver. 61. *But* Jesus **held . . . answered nothing,** because an answer

panel he might not speak against it. " Not guilty " might be pronounced in the same day, but for "guilty " a day had to intervene. But in cases of profanation it is at least doubtful if judgment was not rendered at once. The voting began with the younger members, that they might not be influenced by the older. The hours of trial were after morning service, but never in the night except to complete a case. On the Sabbath or festivals or their eves no trial could take place. All these regulations were violated in the trial of Jesus. (Edersheim, II., p. 555 sq.; Nebe, Ldg. I., p. 324 sq.)

would be an acknowledgment of the charge, which had not been sustained. Besides " His whole life and conduct among the Jews was a better refutation than any answer to the false testimony."—ORIGEN. He desired to keep silent and suffer (Ps. 38 : 13 ; Isai. 53 : 7). " When Jesus did not answer, He kept silent as a lamb. When He answered, He taught like a shepherd. He had to hold His peace in His passion, who shall not keep silent in judgment, for He had come to be judged, who shall come to judge."—AUGUSTINE. Our silence of guilt before God (Matt. 22 : 12 ; Rom. 3 : 19) has been borne by Jesus, that we might say : " Who is he that shall condemn ? " (Rom. 8 : 33). *Again the high priest asked him*, administering the oath (Matt. 26 : 63), **Art . . . Blessed ?** This question was possibly suggested to the high priest by the claim of Christ about building the temple (ver. 58), which according to Zech. 6 : 12 was expected of the Messiah. It was put with inward venom to force an answer, but with great outward solemnity. Christ is asked about His divine Sonship as Messiah, because thus, it is hoped, a case of blasphemy may be made out against Him, who asserts to be **the Son of the Blessed,** whose very name according to Rabbinic custom the high priest fears to utter. " This pretended reverence for God was intended to become a heavier charge against Christ."—CALVIN. Ver. 62. He, although knowing what His answer must involve, because He is the truth (John 14 : 6 ; 18 : 37) and no liar like His accusers (John 8 : 44), and in obedience to the powers that be (Rom. 13 : 1), wicked as they are, **said . . . right hand** (12 : 36) **. . . heaven** (13 : 26). With a triumphant announcement Jesus tells how He the lowly one will begin (9 : 1) and continue to come in heavenly power in clouds of judgment (Ps. 18 : 10 ; 97 : 2 ; 104 : 3 ; Dan. 7 : 13 ;

Rev. 1 : 7) until His final revelation. It is a call of judgment to the wicked judges, when He says: "In flesh and blood I will be eternal, Almighty God and rule over all, until I come at the last day, to judge the quick and the dead."—LUTHER. Ver. 63. **And . . . clothes** from the neck downward, which, not allowed him in mourning for the dead (Lev. 10 : 6; 21 : 10), was permitted in cases of blasphemy, as a testimony against it (2 Kings 18 : 37).[1] Of this he accuses Jesus by his action and saith, Ver. 64, **What . . . blasphemy** (2 : 7): **what think ye?** Without examining the truth of the words of Jesus according to the test Deut. 18 : 21 sq., the high priest sets aside all corroborative testimony, and illegally pronounces judgment before the vote is taken (see note on ver. 55). *And all* acquiescing in such injustice, *condemn* Christ **worthy of death.** The formal question was: "What think ye, gentlemen,' for life' or 'for death'?" And they answered: "for death." "The guilty escapes and the innocent is beaten; the ungodly abuses and the pious is condemned; what the wicked has deserved, the good suffers; what the servant contracted, the Lord pays; what man was guilty of, God endured; the source of all life is found worthy of death."—GERHARD. Ver. 65. *And* the priests leave their seats in wild confusion, and *some began* **to spit** on Christ, which was the greatest insult possible (Numb. 12 : 14 : Deut. 25 : 9; Isai. 50 : 6). It was however a fulfilment of prophecy (10 : 34; Ps. 69 : 7 sq.; Isai. 50 : 5 sq.). "Bearing shame and spittle He washes our face clean and beautiful."—JEROME. **And . . . Prophesy,** who is

---

[1] Rending of clothes, as a token of consternation, mourning, etc., was a general custom among the Jews as among the Greeks and Romans (Gen. 37 : 34; 44 : 13; Judg. 11 : 35; 1 Sam. 4 : 12; 1 Kings 21 : 27; Isai. 36 : 22, etc.).

he that struck thee (Matt. 26 : 68). Thus contempt was shown for Christ as a prophet, who, when blindfolded, could not tell who smote Him. By the endurance of all the blows Christ "has restored to us that image which has been disfigured and almost effaced by sin."—CALVIN. *And*, when the councillors had finished, *the officers* (ver. 54), the guards, *received him* **with blows of their hands.** "What can be equal to this insolence? On that face, which the sea when it saw it had reverenced, from which the sun, when it beheld it on the cross, turned away its rays, they did spit and struck it with the palms of their hands."[1]—CHRYSOSTOM. "What did God the heavenly Father? Could He keep silent? Could He not have destroyed this band through fire from heaven? They would have deserved it. But the Father would now rather see the obedience of His Son, than reveal His majesty."—BRENZ.

66–72. And as Peter was beneath in the court, there cometh one of the maids of the high priest; and seeing Peter warming himself, she looked upon him, and saith, Thou also wast with the Nazarene, *even* Jesus. But he denied, saying, I neither know, nor understand what thou sayest: and he went out into the porch; and the cock crew. And the maid saw him, and began again to say to them that stood by, This is *one* of them. But he again denied it. And after a little while again they that stood by said to Peter, Of a truth thou art *one* of them; for thou art a Galilæan. But he began to curse, and to swear, I know not this man of whom ye speak. And straightway the second time the cock crew. And Peter called to mind the word, how that Jesus said unto him, Before the cock crow twice, thou shalt deny me thrice. And when he thought thereon, he wept.

Ver. 66. *And as Peter,* while the Sanhedrim was in session above, was *beneath in the court* (ver. 54), *there* **cometh** to hear and talk about the news **one of the maids . . . high priest,** the porteress (John 18 : 17), who had admitted Peter. Ver. 67. **Seeing . . . himself,** some-

---

[1] See also Luther, Erl. Ed. 2, p. 61.

thing uneasy in his manner attracted her attention, and *she* **looked upon him** with intent gaze, recognized him as a stranger, remembers his admission (ver. 54) *and saith,* **Thou ... this** outcast **Nazarene** (John 1 : 46), *Jesus.* Children of God cannot remain hid among worldly people. Ver. 68. *But Peter denied* his master (Luke 22 : 57) and his discipleship (John 18 : 17), and said, **I ... sayest.** The strong Peter, conquered by a woman's accusation, claims to be so loyal a Jew as not even to be able to know, nor, think as he will, to understand such a charge. The fear of endangering his life (cf. ver. 31) has prompted him (cf. ver. 47). "The pillar of strength has at a single breath of air trembled to its foundation. Where is now all that boldness of the promise, and his overweening confidence in himself beforehand?"—AUGUSTINE. Then Peter *went out into the* **porch,** the covered archway leading to the gate, for he would escape from this dangerous place. *And the* **cock crew.** This was the first warning that he had denied the Holy and Righteous One (Acts 3 : 14). Ver. 69. *And the maid* **saw him** slowly edging out, *and began to say to them that stood by: This is one of* those followers of Jesus, which was taken up and repeated by others (Matt. 26 : 71 ; Luke 22 : 58). And Peter returned and **denied again** with an oath (Matt. 26 : 72). The noble confessor (John 6 : 68) fails utterly. "We shall never cease to fall if the Lord do not stretch out His hand to uphold us. When the vigor of the grace of Christ was extinguished in Peter, whoever might afterward meet him, and interrogate him about Christ, he would have been ready to deny a hundred or a thousand times."—CALVIN. Ver. 70. *After a* **little while,** about an hour (Luke 22 : 59), the servants around the fire **said ... them** (ver. 69) ... **Galilean.** Since the last denial Peter had probably mingled more boldly among the men, and to disarm all suspicion had spoken freely. But in this recklessness his speech betrayed him as a Galilean, who pronounced many letters differently.[1] To save himself, Ver. 71, *he began to* **curse**, *and* even **to swear, I know . . . you speak.** Peter adopts the cursing language of his company, and speaks in a despising manner of his Master. The denial of Christ leads from sin to sin. But the goodness of the Lord will not abandon Peter, for, Ver. 72, **straightway . . . crew** (ver. 30, 68), and Jesus looked upon Peter (Luke 22 : 61). *And Peter called to mind the word* of his Lord (ver. 30), and *when he thought thereon*, went out (Matt. 26 : 75) and **wept** bitterly (Matt. 26 : 75). The " tears which he shed in secret testified before God and the angels that his repentance was true."—CALVIN. He had no remorse like Judas (Matt. 27 : 3 sq.), but a sincere godly repentance (2 Cor. 7 : 10), which found consolation in the promise Luke 22 : 32. This consolation grew, though small at first, until at Easter all terror was overcome. Peter, a warning in his denial, is a rock for us in the assurance that God forgives our sins. " If I could paint Peter, I would write on every hair of his head, ' Remission of sins,' because he is an example of this article of forgiveness of sins."—LUTHER.[2]

[1] The Galilæans could not distinguish א and ע, א, ע and ה. They confused ת and ת. All gutturals were pronounced deeply and darkly. (Nebe, Ldg. I., p. 369.)

[2] Cf. also Walch, VIII., p. 886 ; Erl. Ed. 2, p. 68 sq.

CHAPTER XV.

1–5. *And straightway in the morning the chief priests with the elders and scribes, and the whole council, held a consultation, and bound Jesus, and carried him away, and delivered him up to Pilate. And Pilate asked him, Art thou the King of the Jews? And he answering saith unto him, Thou sayest. And the chief priests accused him of many things. And Pilate again asked him, saying, Answerest thou nothing? behold how many things they accuse thee of. But Jesus no more answered anything; insomuch that Pilate marvelled.*

Ver. 1. *Straightway in the morning* the various classes of the Sanhedrim (8 : 31), *and the whole council* **held a consultation**, not to correct the illegality of the night-trial (14 : 55), but to find an accusation to bring before Pilate, that he, having the power of execution (John 18 : 31 sq.), might be compelled to put Jesus to death; for blasphemy (14 : 64) was no cause before him. **They bound Jesus**, whose fetters had been taken off during the trial, again; *and* **carried him away** up Mount Zion to the tower of Antonia, which is on the north side of the temple area (Jos. Wars, I. 5, 4 ; 21, 1 ; V. 3, 8; Ant. XV. 11, 4).[1] In the palace of the tower the Roman governor, whose usual headquarters were at Cæsarea (Acts 23 : 23), remained during the festival to quell disturbances, which so often arose (Jos. Wars, I. 4, 3 ; Ant. XVII. 9, 3 ; XX. 5, 3). To him they **delivered up** Jesus, who was thus rejected by His own people (Luke 17 : 25 ; John 1 : 10, 11),

---

[1] This, the position of Ewald, Lange, Kraft, Caspari, Godet, etc., is not accepted by others, who claim that Pilate was in the palace of Herod, for the description of which see Jos. Wars, I. 21, 1 ; V. 4, 4.

and delivered to the Gentiles (10 : 33; Luke 18 : 32) in the person of **Pilate**. The first name of Pontius Pilate seems to indicate that he was descended from the Roman gens of the Pontii, who had come from the Samnites and were known by C. Pontius Telesius, the great general. The cognomen, Pilate, means "armed with a javelin." Pilate was the fifth procurator of Judæa, appointed after Valerius Gratus, by Tiberius (Jos. Ant. XVIII. 2, 2). He was under the proprætor of Syria, whose frequent absence gave him the full power of a "legatus." Attired in military dress and attended by a guard (Matt. 27 : 27), he had assessors in council (Acts 25 : 12) when sitting as a judge upon the portable tribune (Bema), that was erected on the tessellated pavement (Gabbatha. John 19 : 13) always found in Roman courts. In character, he was cruel, unscrupulous, and regardless of the religious privileges granted Israel, as shown by the killing of the Galileans (Luke 13 : 1, 2); by the bringing of the images of the emperor to Jerusalem, which were only removed because of the firmness of the Jews, who preferred death to acquiescence (Jos. Wars, II. 9, 2; Ant. XVIII. 3, 1); by the using of the temple-money to build a canal, and having the Jews, who resisted, killed most treacherously and brutally (Jos. Wars, II. 9, 4; Ant. XVIII. 3, 2). The Samaritans also complained of his cruelty (Jos. Ant. XVII. 4, 2). But when Pilate found these attempts unavailing, he gave way to the Jews for the sake of his safety and position, especially in the trial of Jesus, which seemed of no vital importance to him. The sense of justice in conflict with his own advantage caused his vacillation; but the selfish interests prevailed. Upon complaint of Vitelius, proprætor of Syria, he was summoned to Rome. He found Tiberius dead, was deposed by Caius and banished to Vienne in Gaul, where he committed suicide (Eus. H. E. II. 7).[1] Ver. 2. *Pilate*, after he had gone out and heard the accusation of the Jews (John 18 : 29 sq.), *asked* Jesus, *Art thou* **the king . . . Jews?** The charges which the Sanhedrists brought were not what they had ascertained by their examination (14 : 53 sq.), but sedition, prohibition of the payment of tribute-money (Luke 23 : 2), and assumption of the title " King of the Jews " in a political sense. But Pilate, seeing that all the charges were really contained in the last, interrogates Jesus, who was altogether innocent (cf. 12 : 17; John 6 : 15), on the last point. It seems impossible that this poor Jew, with nothing royal about him, should be a king. But Jesus **answering**, made a good confession (1 Tim. 6 : 12) of the character of His kingdom (John 18 : 33 sq.), and said, **Thou sayest.** Christ is " an eternal, almighty king, God's Son, who delivers us from the power of Satan, of sin and eternal death, not bodily death, for here upon earth we must suffer and die, as our King Himself has suffered and died. Who knows this character of the King and of His kingdom, willingly submits to the cross, for he knows, that though here there must be suffering, there in eternity there shall be joy and glory."—LUTHER. Ver. 3. *And* when Pilate went out to tell the Sanhedrists that he found no fault in Christ (Luke 23 : 4; John 18 : 38), **the . . . things.** The priests, who know Pilate and their former power over him (ver. 1), claim that Jesus was "stirring up the people " and " teaching falsely, beginning in Galilee " (Luke 23 : 5). Galilee is especially mentioned, because the Galileans were noted for their seditious character. Ver. 4. *And Pilate again asked* Jesus to answer to these charges.

---

[1] A later tradition reports that Pilate lived on the mountain in Switzerland, which still bears his name, and committed suicide by casting himself into Lake Lucerne.

Ver. 5. **But . . . thing**, because Pilate knows how unproved these last accusations are, and the priests would not listen to any answer. But this silence was also due to Christ's suffering obedience (14 : 61). *Pilate* **marvelled**, for he knew how readily Jesus could refute the charges made against Him. The wonderful patience, meekness and calmness of Jesus impress the hardened Roman sceptic. " Pilate does not know the divine majesty of Christ, and yet marvels at His silence. How much more is it proper for us, who believe in His eternal Godhead, to marvel at His silence, His beatings and scourgings, His shame and His cross."—GERHARD.

6-15. Now at the feast he used to release unto them one prisoner, whom they asked of him. And there was one called Barabbas, *lying* bound with them that had made insurrection, men who in the insurrection had committed murder. And the multitude went up and began to ask him *to do* as he was wont to do unto them. And Pilate answered them, saying, Will ye that I release unto you the King of the Jews? For he perceived that for envy the chief priests had delivered him up. But the chief priests stirred up the multitude, that he should rather release Barabbas unto them. And Pilate again answered and said unto them, What then shall I do unto him whom ye call the King of the Jews? And they cried out again, Crucify him. And Pilate said unto them, Why, what evil hath he done? But they cried out exceedingly, Crucify him. And Pilate, wishing to content the multitude, released unto them Barabbas, and delivered Jesus, when he had scourged him, to be crucified.

Ver. 6. *Now at* **the feast**, not at every feast, but only at the passover (John 18 : 39), **Pilate . . . prisoner**, *whom they asked of him*. This custom was probably originally Jewish, and not imported from Rome in imitation of the amnesty granted at the Lectisternia and Bacchanalia. It represented the release of Israel from the bondage of Egypt. Ver. 7. **And . . . Barabbas**[1] (son of a

---

[1] Some minor MSS. and Origen make his name in Matt. Jesus Barabbas, which was probably an error of a transcriber, although Fritzsche, Bleek, De Wette, and Meyer see in the omission of "Jesus" a design.

Rabbi),[1] *bound with them that had made* **insurrection**, which was not that recorded Luke 13 : 1 or in Jos. Ant. XVIII. 3, 2 (see ver. 1), but one of the many later uprisings in which Barabbas **had . . murder.** Barabbas was no simple misguided zealot, who fought for the glory of Israel, but he used the insurrection for his own purpose of robbery (John 18 : 40). Ver. 8. *And the multitude*, who up to this time had not been at the trial of Jesus, **went up** to Pilate's palace (ver. 1) and asked for their privilege (ver. 6). Ver. 9. *And Pilate*, whose attempt to transfer the case of Jesus to Herod had failed (Luke 23 : 6 sq.), now saw a favorable opportunity of avoiding a decision against Jesus, by enlisting the people for Him. He said, **Will . . . Jews?** Sly as was Pilate's purpose his method was unfortunate. It did not give the people free choice (ver. 6), and declared Jesus guilty *de facto*, a legal misstep, which involved all that Pilate was forced to. The addition of the messianic title, spoken perhaps with a sarcastic inflection, was also calculated to arouse not sympathy but antipathy. Still Pilate attempted to throw the decision on the people. Ver. 10. **For . . . delivered** Jesus. Their envy, parallel to that of the brothers of Joseph, was not only kindled by the superior wisdom of Jesus, His powerful, truthful preaching, His wonderful deeds and blameless righteousness, but above all by His influence over the people (11 : 18 ; 12 : 37), which injured their absolute rule. Ver. 11. But, while Pilate was listening to the message from his wife (Matt. 27 : 19), the *chief priests* went around among the multitude and **stirred** them *up* to ask for Barabbas. They led the blind astray (Deut. 27 : 18) to prefer a murderer (Acts 3 : 13, 14) to the Righteous One. Ver. 12. *And*

---

[1] Some interpret "son of a father," according to the gospel of the Hebrews, and refer either to John 8 : 44 or Matt. 23 : 9.

Pilate, in pity for Jesus, to whom he should have rendered justice, **again . . . Jews** (ver. 9). And the people more enraged by Pilate's imputation that they have called Jesus Messiah, Ver. 13, **cried . . . Crucify him.** In fulfilment of Ps. 69 : 26; Mark 12 : 8, they cast Jesus from them (see also *delivered*, ver. 1), counting Him unworthy of any punishment at their hands, and demanding the most outrageous punishment that the despised Gentiles can give. The cross that Barabbas had deserved is for Jesus. "The Jews would sooner have asked for the release of the devil himself, than they would have released the Son of God. The nobler the treasure and gift which God gives, the more inimical are the world and the devil against such treasure and gift."—LUTHER. Ver. 14. *Pilate*, although he might have known the stubbornness of the Jews (see ver. 1; Jos. Ant. XVIII. 3, 1), **said . . . done?** With this appeal to the sense of justice of the Jews, Pilate condemns himself for unjustly retaining an innocent prisoner. But the innocence of Jesus is again asserted, that we should learn its lesson. "He is God's Son, holy and without sin; therefore He should be free from curse and death. We are sinners, under the wrath of God; therefore we should justly bear death and condemnation. But God turns it about; He that has no sin must become a curse and bear the punishment of sin. Through Him we are in grace and children of God."—LUTHER. But the Jews **cried out exceedingly** in wildest commotion like beasts thirsting for blood, **Crucify . . .** Ver. 15. **. . . multitude**, offers simply to scourge Jesus (Luke 23 : 22), but the people are not satisfied. Then Pilate dramatically attempted to clear himself of guilt (Matt. 27 : 24 sq.), but **released . . . him.** This scourging, that always preceded crucifixion, was performed by the soldiers, since Pilate as procurator had no lictors. For it there was used a scourge of leathern thongs, into which pieces of lead and small sharp-pointed bones were plaited. The condemned had to bare their breast and back, and were tied with their hands to a low post; and so severe was the scourging among the Romans that death frequently followed. Christ was wounded for our transgressions (Isai. 53 : 5). "For me Christ is scourged, that He might redeem me from the scourges of future wrath; for me He is wounded, that He might heal me."—BERNARD.

16–20. And the soldiers led him away within the court which is the Prætorium; and they call together the whole band. And they clothe him with purple, and plaiting a crown of thorns, they put it on him; and they began to salute him, Hail, King of the Jews! And they smote his head with a reed, and did spit upon him, and bowing their knees worshipped him. And when they had mocked him, they took off from him the purple, and put on him his garments. And they lead him out to crucify him.

Ver. 16. The soldiers led Jesus *within* **the court,** *which* served as the **Prætorium,** the guard-room (Phil. 1 : 13),[1] *and they call together* **the whole band,** not the whole cohort, but a maniple, to have cruel sport with Jesus, which Pilate wrongly permits. Ver. 17. **They . . . purple,**[2] with some cast-off soldier's mantle as a satire upon His kingship. The color is however typical of Christ's work (Isai. 63 : 1). "Christ is clothed with purple, which He reddens with His blood, that He might obtain for us the garment of righteousness."—GERHARD. They plait **a crown of thorns,** which are brought from outside the city, and *put it on him* to show that the attainment of His kingship is only thorns. But thorns, which the curse of sin brought (Gen. 3 : 18), and which God selected as the

---

[1] Weiss remarks aptly that Mark added Prætorium to offer his Roman readers a comparison with the castra prætoriana of Rome.

[2] Matt. (27 : 28) calls it "scarlet," for antiquity did not clearly distinguish these colors. (Horace, Satires, VI. 100.) Nebe, Ldg. II., p. 115.

symbol of Israel to whom He still showed grace (Exod. 3:2), are now the crown of "the lily among thorns" (Song of Songs 2:2). "Upon His head a crown of thorns is imposed, because the sting of our sins, through whose atonement His royal praise arises, is similar to the pricking of dry thorns."—AUGUSTINE.   Ver. 18.   *They began to salute him*, **Hail, King of the Jews!** The messianic name, which they heard, is used to mock Jesus and the Jews, who had made themselves despicable by the rejection of their true king. Little did these Roman soldiers dream that their empire would once bow before this king. Ver. 19. **They . . . reed**, which they had previously given Him as a sceptre (Matt. 27:29), and thus by driving the thorns into His head increased His pain. They **spit upon him** (14:65), and **bowing . . . him.** Even this mockery the Lord suffered. "There was no ignominy to which He refused to submit for our salvation."—CALVIN. Ver. 20. *And* after Pilate had once more tried to arouse the sympathy of the Jews (John 19:4 sq.), they replaced His garments, and **lead him out**[1] **. . . him.** The Jews like the Romans had their executions outside of the cities (Numb. 15:35; 1 Kings 21:13; Acts 7:58). Jesus, the true **sacrifice**, had to suffer without the gate (Heb. 13:12).

21-32. And they compel one passing by, Simon of Cyrene, coming from the country, the father of Alexander and Rufus, to go *with them*, that he might bear his cross. And they bring him unto the place Golgotha, which is, being interpreted, The place of a skull. And they offered him wine mingled with myrrh: but he received it not. And they crucified him, and part his garments among them, casting lots upon them, what each should take. And it was the third hour, and they crucified him. And the superscription of his accusation was written over, THE KING OF THE JEWS. And with him they crucified two robbers; one on his right hand, and one on his

---

[1] Tradition has not only attempted to vouch for the exact road taken, but it has also invented seven stations and presumed to count 1,220 steps.

left. And they that passed by railed on him, wagging their heads, and saying, Ha! thou that destroyest the temple, and buildest it in three days, save thyself, and come down from the cross. In like manner also the chief priests mocking *him* among themselves with the scribes said, He saved others; himself he cannot save. Let the Christ, the King of Israel, now come down from the cross, that we may see and believe. And they that were crucified with him reproached him.

Ver. 21. *And* as Jesus in exhaustion succumbs under the cross, the soldiers **compel**, impress into service[1] *one passing by*, **Simon of Cyrene,** a hellenistic Jew, born in Cyrene, Africa, but now dwelling in the **country** near Jerusalem, where the Jews of Cyrene had two synagogues (cf. Acts 2:10; 6:9). He was converted by this sudden service imposed on him, and became well known to the Christians at Rome, through his sons **Alexander**[2] **and Rufus** (Rom. 16:13). To his constant honor he "is a picture of all Christians, for they must bear the cross after the Lord here on earth."—LUTHER. Ver. 22. *They bring* Jesus **unto . . . skull.** It received this name from its rounded summit,[3] and not because skulls lay around[4] (Luther, Kuinoel, Ohlshausen, Tholuck). It was outside but near Jerusalem (Heb. 13:12; John 19:20), on a country road (Luke 23:26), in a garden (John 19:41). Whether the traditional site on which the church of the Sepulchre stands is the true spot cannot be determined.[5]

[1] This right of requisition was originally Persian, and was used to expedite the delivery of royal messages.

[2] The identification of Alexander with the Alexander mentioned Acts 19:33, or 1 Tim. 1:20, or 2 Tim. 4:14, is without foundation, like the supposition that Simon is Symeon, called Niger (Acts 13:1).

[3] This has become the most accepted interpretation since Calov.

[4] The fathers, Origen, Chrysostom, Athanasius, Epiphanius, Theophylact, supposed that the first Adam was buried where the second Adam suffered.

[5] That the present church is on the same spot as that mentioned by Eusebius (Vita Const. III. 26; cf. also Socr. H. E. I. 17; Sozomen, H. E. II. 1) seems clear, but not that the original church is in the right place. Nebe, Ldg. II., p. 194.

Ver. 23. **And ... it not.** This drink, which received its stupefying quality from the myrrh, was given to those to be executed, because of a Rabbinic gloss on Prov. 31:6. Jesus refuses it, because He wishes to remain clearly conscious in the suffering still to be borne, and able to utter the words yet to be spoken. Ver. 24. **And ... him.** The cross, which was the so-called crux immissa (†),[1] was first erected,[2] and then Jesus stepped on the projection (sedile), which was but a few feet above the ground,[3] stretched out His hands, which with the feet[4] were nailed to the cross (Luke 24 : 39, 40). Crucifixion, extremely painful,[5] and the greatest shame, was borne by Christ in His great obedience (Phil. 2 : 8) to take away the curse of the law (Gal. 3 : 13). "Christ has broken the ban of human disobedience, which began on wood; having become obedient unto the death of the cross, He has healed through the stretching out of His hands the sickness, which through the extended hand of Adam came upon us."—IRENÆUS. *And*, after Christ's first word (Luke 23 : 34), they **part his garments,** the outer cloak, turban, girdle, sandals, **casting lots ... should take,** as prophesied Ps. 22 : 18; and then they cast lots for the tunic without seam (John 19 : 23 sq.), which one received. It

[1] For full arguments, see Nebe, Ldg. II., p. 169 sq.

[2] Although Friedlieb and Langen suppose that sometimes the criminal was first fastened to the cross, which was then erected, there is no testimony in antiquity for this mode. Nebe, Ldg. II., p. 197.

[3] The common conception of the crucified hanging very high is an error. The crosses of the ancients were generally low. That it must have been thus in the case of Jesus is proved by the sponge of vinegar being given to him on a hyssop-reed (John 19 : 29).

[4] In the 18th century it was denied that the feet had been nailed. It was supposed that they had been bound, and even Tholuck in the first edition of his Commentary on John thought thus. But this positon has been altogether abandoned. Cf. also O. Zöckler, Das Kreuz Christi (1875), p. 484 sq.; H. Fulda, Das Kreuz und die Kreuzigung (1878), p. 347 sq.

[5] Schaeffer, Luth. Com. II., p. 372.

was customary for the executioners to receive the possessions of the criminals, but Jesus had only His clothes. He " was poor in birth, poorer in life, poorest in death," —BERNARD, to enrich us (2 Cor. 8 : 9). " God determined that His own Son should be stripped of His garments, that we, clothed with righteousness, may appear in boldness in company with the angels."—CALVIN. Ver. 25. **And . . . hour,** nine o'clock.[1] Christ had six hours of suffering before Him, but the Father had counted them. Ver. 26. *And the* **superscription of his accusation,** which, written on a gypsum tablet, that was generally carried around the neck by the criminal on the way to execution and then fastened to the cross, was **The King of the Jews.** This superscription in Latin (Rex Judæorum), Aramaic, Greek (John 19: 20), was not removed by Pilate, though desired by the Jews, who felt its reproach (John 19 : 21, 22). In this Pilate was unwittingly " a herald of Christ in the same sense that Caiphas (John 11 : 49) was a prophet."—CALVIN. Ver. 27. *And with* Christ *they crucify* **two robbers,**[2] who had possibly been companions of Barabbas, *one on his right hand, and one on his left,*[3] fulfilling Isai. 53 : 12. Christ is among the rejected, that we might be among the accepted of God. Ver. 29. *And* the Jews **that passed by railed on him** (cf. Ps. 22 : 6), suppressing every human instinct in their malignant hate. And **wagging their heads,** a sign of rejoicing, passionate

---

[1] John 19 : 14 apparently contradicts this, but the sixth hour may be according to the later Roman computation 6 o'clock. Augustine (Tract. on John CXVII. 1) thinks that Mark refers to the crucifying by the tongues. (Cf. also Ps. LXIV. 5; De Cons. III. XIII. 40 sq.) Eusebius, Theophylact, correct John. (Cf. also Robinson, p. 261.) Many accept a transcriber's error in John. Cf. Nebe, Ldg. II., p. 155 sq.

[2] The apocryphal Acts of Pilate call them Testas and Dysmas.

[3] Ver. 28 is wanting in ℵ, A, B, C. D, X, and was probably inserted from Luke 22 : 37.

insult (2 Kings 19 : 21 ; Isai. 37 : 22 ; Lam. 2 : 15 ; Ps. 44 : 14 ; 109 : 25), they say, **Ha!**[1] in derision, **thou that destroyest . . . Ver. 30 . . . from the cross.** What had passed at the trial before the Sanhedrim (14 : 58) was told to the people possibly by the false witnesses themselves, and they call on Jesus to use His claimed power of building for His own rescue. They did not know that Christ was even then laying the foundation of an eternal spiritual temple (Eph. 2 : 20). Ver. 31. *In like manner the* **chief priests**, forgetting their position and dignity, **mocking him** *among themselves with the scribes*, assured that they have now triumphed, **said . . . save.** His miracles, as is now evident, are magical deceptions, otherwise He could help Himself. But the very act of not-saving Himself was the saving of the world (Heb. 2 : 10, 14). Ver. 32. **Let . . . Israel**, this self-constituted Messiah, **now . . . believe.** These men, so little understanding their own scriptures (cf. 8 : 31 ; Isai. 53 : 2), demand sight and a sign for faith (John 4 : 48). Even when the sign of resurrection was given they believed not. They have insulted in Christ, and His trust in God (Matt. 27 : 43), the Father Himself, whom Christ by His obedience was glorifying (John 12 : 28). **And . . . him**, and one afterward blasphemed Christ (Luke 23 : 39), while the other was converted by the words and humble meekness of Jesus.[2] "These circumstances carry great weight ; for they place before us the extreme abasement of the Son of God, that we may see more clearly how much our salvation cost Him, and that, reflecting that we justly deserved all the punishments which He endured, we may be more and more excited to repentance."—CALVIN.

[1] αἰα is equivalent to the Latin Vah.
[2] This, the position of Origen, Ambrose, Cyril, Jerome, Chrysostom, is better than supposing that Mark has by enallage put the plural number for

33-41. And when the sixth hour was come, there was darkness over the whole land until the ninth hour. And at the ninth hour Jesus cried with a loud voice, Eloi, Eloi, lama sabachthani? which is, being interpreted, My God, my God, why hast thou forsaken me? And some of them that stood by, when they heard it, said, Behold, he calleth Elijah. And one ran, and filling a sponge full of vinegar, put it on a reed, and gave him to drink, saying, Let be; let us see whether Elijah cometh to take him down. And Jesus uttered a loud voice, and gave up the ghost. And the veil of the temple was rent in twain from the top to the bottom. And when the centurion, which stood by over against him, saw that he so gave up the ghost, he said, Truly this man was the Son of God. And there were also women beholding from afar: among whom were both Mary Magdalene, and Mary the mother of James the less and of Joses, and Salome; who, when he was in Galilee, followed him, and ministered unto him; and many other women which came up with him unto Jerusalem.

Ver. 33. **And . . . hour,** twelve o'clock noon, **was . . . hour,** three o'clock. This darkness over all Palestine, which could not have been caused by an eclipse, for it was then full moon, was a miracle (Amos 8 : 9). The very noon became night, as in the birth of Christ the night was turned into day, to show that nature, so intimately bound up with man (Rom. 8 : 19 sq.), is still more closely connected with the Son of Man (Ps. 8 : 6) and the Creator and Lord of nature, who has previously shown His power (4 : 36 sq.). The sun not only hid its face from the wickedness of men, giving a sign of judgment (Isai. 5 : 30; 13 : 10; Joel 2 : 10; Mark 13 : 24; Rev. 6 : 12; 7 : 16; 9 : 2), but it signalled the going down of the sun of righteousness. Ver. 34. **At . . . voice,** which showed His agony and yet His strength, **Eloi, Eloi,**[1]

the singular. Augustine (De Cons. III. XVI. 53), Calvin, Beza, Kuinoel, Ebrard, Stier, Keil.

[1] ἐλωί, for which Matt. has ἠλί, is the Aramaic form of Ēlī. It cannot be translated as "My power," the rendering of the apocryphal gospel of Peter (5), of which the Peshito shows a trace. This translation was heretical, indicating the Valentinian speculation that the "Sophia" was now abandoned by the "light" (Iren. Ad. Hær I. 4, 1; 4, 5; 8, 2). Th. Zahn, Das Ev. des Petrus (1893), p. 30 sq.

lama[1] sabachthani,[2] which . . . My God . . . forsaken me? This fourth word[3] of Jesus on the cross, the first verse of the 22d Psalm, which Jesus did not pray completely, marks the deepest point in the suffering of the Godman, who cannot now call God Father as at the beginning and conclusion of His seven words (Luke 23 : 34, 46), because He feels the utter forsakenness by God, experiencing fully all such words as Ps. 18 : 4 sq.; 40 : 12; 42 : 7 sq.; 69 : 1 sq.; 88 : 3 sq.; 89 : 46, as He stands for sinful men, who have forsaken God (Jer. 2 : 13). Nevertheless in His faith He remains in God, whose greatest judgment of wrath He undergoes in death, and calls Him His, even though God does not now show Him the reason (John 5 : 20) of this abandonment, which is so hard to bear for the Son, in constant communication with the Father. This struggle is far more difficult than that in Gethsemane (14 : 34 sq.). "Here begins the contest and the conquering of eternal hell and despair of God. Here God contends with God. In the Garden Christ had a God, who was gracious to Him, for no misfortune is so great, we can bear it, where there is the consolation that we still have a gracious God, may our suffering be what it will. But here God was against Him."—LUTHER. Ver. 35. **And . . . Elijah.** The cry "Eli," which they understood and whose power they

[1] Matt. has λιμα.

[2] Säbäktänī is the Chaldaic, used by the Targum of Jonathan for the original Hebrew Äsärtänö, which Luther employed following the Vulgate.

[3] The first word (Luke 23 : 34), spoken immediately after the crucifixion, was an intercession for the murderers; the second (Luke 23 : 43), uttered some time after the mocking of the Jews, was a promise of salvation to the penitent robber; the third (John 19 : 26, 27), before the beginning of the darkness, was a word of care of the son Jesus for His mother. The fourth word was soon followed by the fifth (John 19 : 28), the word of thirst, the sixth (John 19 : 30), the completion of the work, and the seventh (Luke 23 : 46), the commending of the soul to the Father.

felt, was in derision interpreted as an appeal of the false Messiah to Elijah, who was expected to come with the Messiah (6:15; 9:11). They imply that because God will not help Him, He puts His trust in man (Jer. 17:5). This mockery was an intrigue of Satan, who "impelled the wicked enemies of Christ basely to turn His prayer into derision, intending by this stratagem to strip Him of His chief armor."—CALVIN. Ver. 36. *And* after Jesus had said "I thirst" (John 19:28), *one* of the soldiers *ran, and filling a sponge full of* **vinegar**, the sour wine-and-water (posca) of the soldiers, *put it on a* **reed** of hyssop (John 19:29), and *gave him* **to drink,** fulfilling Ps. 69:21. Then, though the Jews would hinder him (Matt. 27:49), he says, **Let be,** permit me; this will not prevent Elijah's coming. Now *let us see whether Elijah cometh to take him down.* Ver. 37. *Jesus uttered* in *a loud voice* the last two words (John 19:30; Luke 23:46) *and* **gave up the ghost,**[1] the principle of life (cf. 2:8; 8:12) and breathed it out freely (John 10:18); for if He had not willed thus, death could not have held Him (Acts 2:24). "Not against His will did the Spirit leave the flesh of Jesus, but because He wished, and when He wished, and how He wished."—AUGUSTINE. Now life dies. Ver. 38. *And the* **veil** . . . **temple,** the heavy costly curtain of purple and gold, scarlet and hyacinth, inwrought with figures of cherubim, 20 feet long and 30 feet broad, which separated the Most Holy from the Holy (Jos. Wars, V. 5, 4), **was** . . . **bottom.** God, by opening the Holiest, shows that the time of shadows is past, since the true high priest has entered by His blood into the eternal Holiest (Hebr. 10:19). "The right sacrifice has been offered, and in

---

[1] The idea of breathing underlies ghost, Anglo-Saxon gâst, Ger. Geist, as it does spirit.

future there shall be an end of the law and the sacrifices of the law, which were but types of this sacrifice."—LUTHER. There was also an earthquake (Matt. 27 : 51). Ver. 39. **And . . . centurion,**[1] who, commanding the twelve soldiers, four for each cross, *stood over against Jesus*, and had closely watched His actions and words, saw that He **so**[2] *gave up the ghost*, died with such power and calmness, and amid such signs, *he said*, **Truly . . . God.** He does not regard Jesus as some son of a god or heathen demi-god, but trusting upon the word he had heard (John 19 : 7), went beyond all the Jews, in confessing Christ as *the Son of the God*, becoming at once monotheist and Christian. Together with the centurion of Capernaum (Matt. 8) and Cornelius (Acts 10), he forms the "triumvirate of believing Gentile soldiers."—MACLEAR. Now Christ attracts all (John 12 : 32). Ver. 40. **And . . . off,** for after the third word of Jesus (John 19 : 27), when probably they were near the cross, they had again to retire by order of the soldiers. Among them were **Mary Magdalene.** Mary of the city of Magdala (Migdal-el, Josh. 19 : 38), situated on the south-east corner of the plain of Gennesaret, who is not to be confused with the woman, a sinner (Luke 7 : 37; Mark 14 : 3), was a follower of Jesus, who had healed her of seven demons (16 : 9; Luke 8 : 2). She was present from the beginning of the crucifixion (John 19 : 25; cf. also Mark 16 . 1, 9). And so was **Mary, the mother of James, the Less,** who was thus called for his stature to distinguish him from James, the son of Zebedee, and James, the son of Alphæus (see 3 : 18). She was also the mother of **Joses,** not the brother of Christ (3 : 31), and

---

[1] Tradition has named him Longinus, and German commentators love to think of him as a German, because a German legion was then in Palestine.

[2] "Cried out" is wanting in ℵ, B, L.

the wife of Clopas, who is not the same as Alphæus (3 : 18).
And **Salome**, wife of Zebedee, mother of John and James,
sister of Mary, the mother of the Lord (John 19 : 25),
likewise followed Jesus, although at first mistaking the
nature of His kingdom (Matt. 20 : 20 ; Mark 10 : 35).
When Jesus was in Galilee, these women, Ver. 41, **ministered unto him** of their means (Luke 8 : 3). But *there
were* **many other women,** *which came up with* Jesus *unto
Jerusalem* on His last passover journey. These, especially
the closer circle, were "forerunners of the noble army of
Holy Women, who were, in the ages to come, throughout
the length and breadth of Christendom, to minister at
many a death-bed out of love for Him who died "the
Death."—MACLEAR.

42–47. And when even was now come, because it was the Preparation,
that is, the day before the sabbath, there came Joseph of Arimathæa, a
councillor of honourable estate, who also himself was looking for the kingdom of God; and he boldly went in unto Pilate, and asked for the body of
Jesus. And Pilate marvelled if he were already dead: and calling unto
him the centurion, he asked him whether he had been any while dead.
And when he learned it of the centurion, he granted the corpse to Joseph.
And he bought a linen cloth, and taking him down, wound him in the linen
cloth, and laid him in a tomb which had been hewn out of a rock ; and he
rolled a stone against the door of the tomb. And Mary Magdalene and
Mary the *mother* of Joses beheld where he was laid.

Ver. 42. *When even* of Friday *was now come, because it
was the* **Preparation,** i. e. as Mark explains *the day before
the sabbath,*[1] which, always observed more strictly than
the festivals, was at this season an especially high-day
(John 19 : 31) that excluded all work to which burial was
reckoned ; therefore the burial of Jesus was now resolved
upon by, Ver. 43, **Joseph of Arimathæa,** the old city of
Rama in Benjamin (Judg. 4 : 5 ; 19 : 13 ; Isai. 10 : 29 ;

---

[1] Morison reminds of the German "Sonnabend."

Matt. 2 : 18),[1] possibly er-Ram, 5 miles north of Jerusalem. He was a **councillor** of the Sanhedrim, whose condemnation of Jesus he had not sanctioned (Luke 23 : 51), and *of* **honorable estate**, high social position, and wealthy (Matt. 27 : 57); **who also . . . the kingdom of God.** Joseph, a secret disciple (John 19 : 38), like Nicodemus, who assisted at the burial (John 19 : 39), was one of the quiet band of expectants in Israel like Simeon and Anna (Luke 2 : 25, 38). *He* **boldly went into Pilate**, regardless of men and willing to brave every danger, *and asked for the body of Jesus.* " As he exposed himself to the dislike and hatred of the whole nation and to great dangers, there can be no doubt that this singular courage arose from a secret movement of the Spirit."—CALVIN. Ver. 44. *And Pilate* **marvelled** *if* Jesus **were already dead**, for the crucified sometimes lingered three days, and scarcely ever died in less than 36 hours, wherefore the Jewish law, more merciful that the Roman, ordered the breaking of the legs (John 19 : 31). Ver. 45. Pilate called the *centurion* (ver. 39), was assured of Christ's death (John 19 : 33), and *granted the corpse* freely (cf. 2 Peter 1 : 3). Ver. 46. *And* Joseph *bought a* fine *linen cloth* (14 : 51), and *taking* the body *down* from the cross that still stood, **wound him in linen cloth**, which was cut up in strips (John 11 : 44; 19 : 40; 20 : 7), a small piece being reserved as a napkin for the head (John 20 : 7). This was accompanied by embalmment, which the Jews adopted after contact with Egypt (Gen. 50 : 2). Myrrh and aloes (John 19 : 39) were wrapped in with the cloths. And *he laid* Jesus in a **tomb hewn out of rock.** Such tombs, still found in the East, are caves, sometimes upright, some-

---

[1] This is the position of Robinson, Bleek, Meyer, Ewald, Keim, Keil, in "this most complicated and disputed problem of sacred topography." (Stanley.) Nebe, Ldg. II., p. 415.

times horizontal, the latter having steps for entrance. Within there are several chambers, one at times being lower than the other, on whose side-walls there are niches, about 7 feet long, into which the corpses are placed.[1] He *rolled* an immense (16:4) stone . . **the door**, the outer entrance, while, Ver. 47, Mary . . . **laid**. Jesus, to be made like to His brethren (Hebr. 2 : 17), went the way of earth (1 Kings 2 : 2), as He foretold (Matt. 12 : 40), and as faith now gladly confesses (1 Cor. 15 : 4). "As Christ did not die for Himself, but became flesh and dies for our sake, thus He lies in the ground for our sake, and His grave is our grave. But as He therefore has no grave, He does not remain in death and the grave, thus shall we through His resurrection be awakened at the last day and live with Him in eternity."—LUTHER.

[1] Robinson Res. I. 78 sq.; 2 : 175 sq.; 3 : 317. Thompson, II., p. 151 sq.

CHAPTER XVI.

1-8. And when the sabbath was past, Mary Magdalene, and Mary the *mother* of James, and Salome, bought spices, that they might come and anoint him. And very early on the first day of the week, they come to the tomb when the sun was risen. And they were saying among themselves, Who shall roll us away the stone from the door of the tomb? and looking up, they see that the stone is rolled back: for it was exceeding great. And entering into the tomb, they saw a young man sitting on the right side, arrayed in a white robe; and they were amazed. And he saith unto them, Be not amazed: ye seek Jesus, the Nazarene, which hath been crucified: he is risen; he is not here: behold, the place where they laid him! But go, tell his disciples and Peter, He goeth before you into Galilee: there shall ye see him, as he said unto you. And they went out, and fled from the tomb; for trembling and astonishment had come upon them: and they said nothing to any one; for they were afraid.

Ver. 1. **When . . . past**, Saturday evening that closed the Sabbath having come, **Mary . . . spices** to complete the embalmment so hastily performed on Friday evening. Their ministering love cannot rest. Ver. 2. **And very early**, before dawn (John 20: 1), **on . . . week**,[1] which was forever to become the Lord's day (Rev. 1: 10), they go out and *come to the tomb* (15: 46) as the sun is rising. "After the sad Sabbath brightly shines the day, which shall hold the primacy among the days; the first light glistens on it, and my Lord rises with triumph and says: This is the day which the Lord hath made, let us rejoice and be glad in it."—JEROME. Ver. 3. *And* the

---

[1] $\mu\iota\acute{\alpha}$ τῶν σαββάτων cannot be "an einem Sabbather" (Luther), because σαββάτων must here possess its derived meaning "week." See Stellhorn, p. 124; Thayer, p. 566.

women **were** ... **stone**[1] (15 : 46) ... **tomb** ? Now they remember the great hindrance, which in their eager love they had forgotten. Ver. 4. But **looking** ... **great**, and therefore they could see it so far off. God, who in His mercy had kept from them the thought of the stone and guard (Matt. 27 : 62), removed their care before it came (Isai. 65 : 24). Ver. 5. **Entering** ... **tomb** (15 : 46) ... **a young man**[2] ... **robe**. Angels, present at the birth of Jesus, dare not be wanting where heaven and earth are united in the Risen One (John 1 : 51). They appear as **young** men to represent the eternal youth of the heavenly life now given in Christ, and **sitting**, because this life is a rest for the people of God (Heb. 4 : 9), and **on the right side**, for God's right hand hath gotten the victory (Ps. 118 : 16). Their robes are **white**, transfigured by their heavenly glory (9 : 3), and symbols of victory and glory (Rev. 6 : 11; 7 : 9, 13). *And* the women *were amazed* at the emptiness of the tomb, and frightened by the brightness of the heavenly messengers like the shepherds at Bethlehem (Luke 2 : 9). But God, who has first humbled them by this mystery, "instantly mitigates their dread, that they may not sink under its oppressive influence; and not only so, but by the sweetness of His grace heals the wound which He had inflicted."—CALVIN. Ver. 6. For the angel speaking in short, quick sentences of deepest, joyous emotion, **saith Be** ... **amazed** (cf. Luke 2 : 10). There is no cause for fear, only joy is to be expected. **Ye seek** ... **the Nazarene**, as a human friend and human prophet, **which** ... **crucified**. His crucifixion leads you to seek Him among the dead, for

---

[1] The Rabbis called these stones Gulalim, which with the "rolling" indicates that they must have been round like millstones.

[2] Luke (24 : 4) mentions two angels, but Mark emphasizes only the prominent spokesman. Cf. note on 10 : 46.

you do not see the triumph of the cross. **He is risen.** Jesus, raised up by the glory of the Father (Matt. 16 : 21 ; 17 : 23 ; 26 : 32 ; John 2 : 22 ; Rom. 4 : 24), rises also in His own power (Matt. 17 : 9 ; 20 : 19 ; Mark 8 : 31 ; 9 : 9 ; 10 : 34 ; 16 : 9 ; John 10 : 18 ; Rom. 14 : 9), and bringing to light life and incorruption (2 Tim. 1 : 10), is the first fruits of them that slept (1 Cor. 15 : 20) and the proof and foundation of our justification (Rom. 4 : 25). "This is the great joyous article of our faith, which alone makes Christians."—LUTHER. **He . . . him!** The empty tomb is a visible proof of Christ's resurrection. "The place I will show you where He lay, but He is no more here." "If Christ is not here, a Christian must not be here."—LUTHER. Ver. 7. **But go, tell his disciples.** Become messengers, where men are silent, to the doubting eleven and specially to disconsolate *Peter* (14 : 72). **Jesus goeth . . you** (14 : 28). Although Jesus appeared at Jerusalem, He did not stay there to gather His scattered flock. This was done in quiet Galilee, where He had found more faith than in Jerusalem (John 21 : 1 ; 1 Cor. 15 : 6). Ver. 8. **And . . . them.** Christ's promise of resurrection had been forgotten, and now the announcement is so marvellous, that they waver between faith and unbelief. The unbelief that remains renders them so fearful. *And they* **said nothing.** Although later the women told the disciples (Matt. 28 : 8), for the present fear rendered them silent. " Untimely fear often hinders us in doing justice to our office."—OSIANDER, STARKE.

9–11. Now when he was risen early on the first day of the week, he appeared first to Mary Magdalene, from whom he had cast out seven devils. She went and told them that had been with him, as they mourned and wept. And they, when they heard that he was alive, and had been seen of her, disbelieved.

Ver. 9.[1] **Now . . . devils** (1 : 23 ; 5 : 9 ; EXC. II., p. 31).

[1] For the genuineness of v. 9–20, see Introduction, p. xix.

Mary Magdalene, who had come with the other women (ver. 1), ran back before entering the tomb to tell Peter and John that the tomb was empty. Then she returned with these two disciples, who left again, while Mary remained, and received the first manifestation of the risen Lord (John 20: 12). Jesus appears first to a believing woman. Ver. 10. **She . . . him**, the eleven and other disciples, *as they* **mourned and wept** (cf. Luke 24: 17) hopelessly for their crucified master, as He had told them (John 16: 20). Even, Ver. 11, **when . . . seen** of Mary, they **disbelieved**. "Their unbelief having deprived them of sound understanding, they not only refuse the light of truth, but reject it *as an idle fancy* (idle talk) as Luke tells us."—CALVIN.

12–13. And after these things he was manifested in another form unto two of them, as they walked, on their way into the country. And they went away and told it unto the rest: neither believed they them.

Ver. 12. *And after these things*, when Jesus had been seen of the women (Matt. 28 : 9) and Peter (1 Cor. 15: 5), *he* **was manifested** (ver. 14; John 21: 1, 14; Col. 3 : 4) *in* **another form**, for His body although the same (Luke 24: 39) was not subject to space and time (John 20: 19; Luke 24 : 31; Acts 1 : 3), which is a prophecy of our future (1 Cor. 15 :44; 1 John 3 : 2). He appeared **unto two**, Cleopas and an unknown disciple, *on their way to the country*, to Emmaus, distant about seven and a half miles (Luke 24: 13 sq.). Ver. 13. **They went away . . . they them.** It seemed impossible that Christ should manifest Himself at once to Peter and these two disciples within so short a time (Luke 24 : 33). How difficult is human unbelief to overcome. But the hesitation of the disciples is a proof that the resurrection of Jesus could not have been invented by them.

14-18. And afterward he was manifested unto the eleven themselves as they sat at meat; and he upbraided them with their unbelief and hardness of heart, because they believed not them which had seen him after he was risen. And he said unto them, Go ye into all the world, and preach the gospel to the whole creation. He that believeth and is baptized shall be saved; but he that disbelieveth shall be condemned. And these signs shall follow them that believe: in my name shall they cast out devils; they shall speak with new tongues; they shall take up serpents, and if they drink any deadly thing, it shall in no wise hurt them; they shall lay hands on the sick and they shall recover.

Ver. 14. *And afterward* on the same day **he . . . meat** (Luke 24:36; John 20:19 sq.); *and he upbraided their unbelief* (ver. 11, 13) *and hardness of heart* (6:52; 8:17), **because . . . risen.** They who are to be messengers of faith must have faith, and therefore judgment begins at the house of God (1 Peter 4:17). Christ reproves their unbelief that faith might follow; He upbraids their hardness of heart, that a fleshy heart full of love may come."—JEROME. Ver. 15. *And* shortly before His ascension He **said . . . world** (Matt. 28:19), for you are to do greater works than I (John 14:12), who was sent bodily only to Israel (Matt. 15:24). The whole world is to be your parish as apostles. "These are words of majesty, which can properly be called majesty, that He commands these poor beggars to go out and proclaim this new preaching not to one city or country, but to all the world, every principality and kingdom. This is such a strong, mighty command, that no order of this kind has ever gone out into the world, for every king's or emperor's decree does not extend further than his country and people; but this command extends to all kings, lords, country and people, great and small, young and old, learned, wise and saints."—LUTHER. **Preach . . . creation.** The first great work of the messengers is to bring the tidings of God's love thus to all men, that even creation will begin to rejoice in the freedom of the children of God with their hope (Rom. 8:18 sq.). But the gospel requires faith (1:15), therefore, Ver. 16, **He ... saved.** The faith, not like that of the devils (James 2:19), but firm trust in Christ, is the receptive organ for the blessings of baptism, which are washing away of sins (Acts 22:16; Eph. 5:26), regeneration and renewal by the Spirit, who is given in baptism (John 3:5; Tit. 3:5; Acts 2:38). In its administration it brings salvation not only as the foundation of our Christian life (Tit. 3:5), but as a constant present possession (1 Peter 3:21), and a future consummation (Mark 16:16). This power of baptism, due to the divine word (Eph. 5:26), is granted also to children (10:13 sq.).[1] It is only an ordinate means, and " of no profit without faith."—LUTHER. Therefore **he ... condemned.** Only unbelief, which will not receive the gospel and its initial ordinance (Matt. 28:19), condemns. It is not the omission but the contempt of the sacrament which brings judgment. " The whole world is divided into two parts, and separated by a great difference; the one to heaven, the other to hell; that there shall be no other judgment on the last day than according to this preaching, who believed or who did not believe."— LUTHER. Ver. 17. *And these* **signs** (6:2) *shall follow them that believe*, not only to strengthen their own faith, but to confirm their preaching to those that hear. *In* **my name** (9:37) *shall they cast out devils* (1:23). This power, exercised by the disciples during the lifetime of Jesus (3:15; Luke 10:17), was afterward used by Philip, the deacon (Acts 8:7), and Paul (Acts 16:18; 19:15), to

---

[1] The faith of children is wrought by the word of God in baptism. See note on 2:5, with which cf. Augustine, on Forg. & Bapt. I, XVII.; III, III.; on the soul and its origin, II, CXII.; Ag. the letters of Pelagius, I, CXXII. See also Krauth, Conserv. Reform., p. 576 sq.

show the power of Christ over Satan. *They shall speak* **with new tongues,** not only in various languages as at Pentecost (Acts 2:11), but also in the peculiar ecstatic words of the Spirit (Acts 10:46; 19:6; 1 Cor. 12:10; 14:2 sq.), to exhibit the new truth and uniting power of Christ. Ver. 18. *They shall* **take up serpents** without being harmed, as Paul did at Malta (Acts 28:5). **If . . . them,** as tradition relates of John, who was given hemlock, but not poisoned. All the dangers of nature can be overcome by the disciples, who **shall . . . recover.** This was effected e.g. by Peter (Acts 3:7) and Paul (Acts 28:8; cf. also 1 Cor. 12:29; James 5:14, 15). These gifts were not only for the early Church, but for all times whenever they are needed. "If I believe I can do it then it is in my power, for faith gives me so much, that nothing is impossible, if it be necessary. For Christ has not spoken that they always *must* go and do thus, only that they have power and *can* do it."—LUTHER.

19-20. So then the Lord Jesus, after he had spoken unto them, was received up into heaven, and sat down at the right hand of God. And they went forth, and preached everywhere, the Lord working with them, and confirming the word by the signs that followed. Amen.

Ver. 19. **The . . . spoken** to His disciples during the forty days and immediately before ascension such words as are recorded Matt. 28:16 sq.; Luke 24:44 sq.; John 21:1 sq.; Acts 1:7 sq., **was received up into heaven.** This reception into glory (1 Tim. 3:16) was also an act of Christ Himself (John 6:62; 20:17; Eph. 4:8 sq.), prefigured by the removal of Enoch (Gen. 5:24; Heb. 11:5) and the taking up of Elijah (2 Kings 2:11). It was the entrance into the Holy of Holies (Heb. 4:14; 7:26; 10:19) and the return to the Father (John 3:13; 6:62; 20:17), and therefore the completion of the resurrection.

But it is no local removal to heaven (Eph. 4 : 10). The God-man entered the heavenly omnipresent state (Matt. 28 : 20). "When He was on earth He was too distant from us, now He is too near."—LUTHER. For He **sat down . . . right hand of God** (12 : 36 ; 14 : 62). "Where God and God's right hand is, there is Christ, the Son of Man."—LUTHER. Having **taken captivity captive** (Eph. 4 : 8) He is now in glory and power as King, ever gaining victory (Ps. 110 : 1) until all things, even death, are subdued (Phil. 3 : 21 ; 1 Cor. 15 : 26). In such rule He is the ever-living high priest (Rom. 8 : 34 ; Heb. 4 : 14 ; 7 : 26 ; 1 John 2 : 1, 2) ; and the prophet, who speaks through His apostles. For, Ver. 20, *they went forth*, after tarrying a time at Jerusalem (Luke 24 : 49 ; Acts 1 : 4) as ordered, and **preached everywhere**. This was being fulfilled in the world as then known even in the days of Paul (Col. 1 : 23). Later tradition, though partly unreliable in details, seems correct when it relates how Thomas went to preach in Parthia, Andrew in Scythia, John in Asia, Peter in Pontus, Galatia, Bithynia, Cappadocia and Asia Minor, Paul into all countries from Jerusalem unto Illyria.[1] The *Lord* with His heavenly power (ver. 19) was **working with them** (Rom. 15 : 18 ; 2 Cor. 13 : 3) *confirming the word by the signs that followed* (ver. 17 sq.). **Amen.** This conclusion, though wanting in the best MSS., may be our confession of the truth of this divine word, as recorded by Mark. "Amen, Amen, yea, yea, it shall be so."—LUTHER.

---

[1] Origen as quoted by Eusebius, H. E. III. I. McGifford, p. 132. See also notes on 3 : 18.

APPENDIX.

APPENDIX.

WHEN DID CHRIST EAT THE LAST SUPPER?

AT first sight this question seems one of minor importance. It apparently involves only a chronological difficulty, which comes to the surface when the statements of the first three gospels are compared with the account of John. But in fact it is not merely a date which is involved; for upon the determination of the time depends the character of the Last Supper of Jesus with His disciples. As the chronological question is answered, this solemn Supper is either the passover or not. And it is not indifferent whether the Lord's Supper was instituted in connection with the passover-meal or at some other time: for the temporal conjunction of the passover with the Lord's Supper is important, because the former is the prophecy and type of the latter. The relation of both and the position which Jesus took is not insignificant, because by it the whole relation of the Old and New Testament, and the bearing of the old covenant, as that of promise, to the new covenant, as that of fulfilment, is indicated. And this indication is of no small value, for it is a very fundamental place which the passover held in the religion of Israel, and it is a very central position which the Lord's Supper occupies in our Christian faith, since it rests upon the fundamental fact and truth of the atoning death of Jesus Christ. It is true, that mere temporal connection or the want of it cannot destroy this relation. Nevertheless the time is the framework for the actual transfiguration of the old covenant into the new by Jesus, the great renewer. But this consideration dare not be used to influence the exegetical investigation, as the typical relation of the passover-lamb and the time of its sacrifice have been employed by some to fix the date of Christ's death, or at least to confirm it. The bearing of the time has only been shown to point out, that this question lies deeper than it appears. Its discussion, that has and must enter into minute details and particulars, is no straining of gnats.

Equally necessary does this matter seem in the light of the history of the Christian Church. A great controversy of the second century, reaching with its results into the third century and only determined finally in the fourth, turns upon the date of the celebration of the Lord's Supper. The exegetical question was not indeed the cause of the controversy, but in the discussions the apparently different chronological determinations of the synoptists or John were used, and John was interpreted by the synoptists or the synoptists by John. The history and development of the paschal controversy necessitate therefore an entering upon this point. The consideration and review of the discussions on the passover as relating to Easter will also cast much light upon the determination of this difficulty, and confirm by the testimony of the early Church the exegetical position attained independently. The understanding of the history of the paschal controversy will strengthen the proper view. But all this will be seen more fully in the sketch of the controversy, which will appear further on (see p. 342).

In addition, the date of the Lord's Supper is important

because this matter is so largely discussed by modern criticism, and used, though not always directly and with an expressed and pronounced purpose, to show a disagreement between the gospels. That which has been characterized in the Preface as the fault of modern exegesis will find a concrete proof here. Although to-day this subject is not seen in the dimensions which it assumed when the critical tendency of the Tübingen negativists first employed it, it is still treated by some of the most representative scholars and greatest exegetes in a manner destructive of the harmony and organic unity of the gospels. The spirit of this criticism appears in it; and sometimes scholars are affected by this tendency, who would be expected to be free from and uninfluenced by it. It is very necessary that all intelligent Christians should know at least in some particulars this modern destructive current in theological thought. At present it is most occupied with the Old Testament, but it is by no means idle in the department of the interpretation of the New Testament and in the question of the origin of the gospels and the early history and development of the Christian Church. The name of Harnack alone, who is such an authority and power not only in the theology of Germany, but is also largely influencing English and American theologians, will suffice to prove at once the existence and to point out the danger of the present trend of theological thought. Therefore it seems necessary and timely to discuss this question of the time of the Lord's Supper very fully. It is not merely for the value of this series of commentaries, then, that this subject, discussed at least to some degree in all commentaries, is treated at length, but especially for the suggestions which it is able to offer.

In the treatment of this matter, the case involved

will be stated and defined first. In the second place, the theories which accept a contradiction between the gospels will be discussed. After this various solutions that have been attempted, while permitting the statements of John and the synoptists to remain apparently contradictory, will be examined. Then the agreement advocated by some on the basis of John, and finally the agreement sought upon the foundation of the synoptists, will be considered. Under the last division, the objections apparently against the synoptists will be removed, and the confirmatory testimony of the paschal controversy, of the Church fathers and Luther, and of astronomical calculations will be brought out.

I.—STATEMENT AND DEFINITION ON THE QUESTION.

The reason of this discussion will appear on the statement of the case. If we possessed only the synoptical gospels the whole subject would be very plain, even though there are difficulties in their accounts. Matthew (26 : 17) relates as the time, when the two disciples, Peter and John, are bidden to prepare the "passover" as "the first day of the unleavened bread." Mark, who at the beginning of the fourteenth chapter says: "Now after two days was the feast of the passover and the unleavened bread," affirms in the twelfth verse that the time of the Supper was "the first day of unleavened bread, when they killed the passover." Luke emphasizes the idea of the peculiar day as that of the first when the passover-lamb had to be killed even more strongly, when he writes in chapter twenty-two, verse seven: "And the day of the unleavened bread came on which the passover must be sacrificed." In these statements the distinction of "passover" and "unleavened bread" by Mark does not point to two days of feasts which were originally distinct though not separate. The passover did originally begin on the fourteenth of Nisan, and the day of unleavened bread on the fifteenth, the holy day of convocation, but in Christ's day this distinction had long ceased. (See comment on chapter 14, verse 1, page 231; Smith's Bible Dictionary, American Edition, III., p. 2347, note.) Thus all the synoptists think of the fourteenth of Nisan, the first month of the Jewish ecclesiastical year beginning toward the end of March (Lev. 23 : 5; Numb. 28 : 16). All else related shows, as each evangelist says, that " they made ready the passover." For with this intention a guest-chamber was secured, as was customary with those who came from a distance (Matt. 26 : 18; Mark 14 : 13 sq.; Luke 22 : 8 sq.). In this chamber the Lord sat down with the twelve apostles (Matt. 26 : 20; Mark 14 : 17 sq.; Luke 22 : 14 sq.), being the head of this family, which had the proper number required for the celebration by Jewish law and custom. (See comment on chapter 14, verse 14, p. 236.) And Christ Himself said at the meal: " I have desired to eat *this passover* with you before I suffer " (Luke 22 : 15). In addition, the whole arrangement of the Supper, the dipping into the dish (Matt. 26 : 23; Mark 14 : 20), the passing of the first cup with the word about drinking of the fruit of the vine anew in the consummation of the kingdom of God (Luke 22 : 17), the taking of the "cup of blessing" (Luke 22 : 20; 1 Cor. 10 : 16; 11 : 25) with a repetition of the word about drinking of the fruit of the vine (Mark 14 : 25), and the conclusion by singing the Hallel, Psalm 115 to 118 (Matt. 26 : 30; Mark 14 : 26), seem inexplicable on any other supposition than that Jesus celebrated the passover. (See comments and notes on pages 237, 239, 241.) If then the passover was eaten by Christ with the twelve at the regular time on the fourteenth of Nisan, He was crucified on the fifteenth, the holy day of convocation. Then He laid in the tomb on the Sabbath-day, the sixteenth of Nisan, and arose on the seventeenth. But if we had only John, we would be led to conclude that Christ and His disciples ate the Last Supper on the thirteenth of Nisan, the day before the real and legal paschal meal. The Last Supper is apparently spoken of as having been held "before the feast of the passover" (John 13 : 1). And when during the Supper Jesus told Judas Iscariot : "That thou doest, do quickly," the eleven apostles supposed that it was "because Judas had the bag, that Jesus said unto him, Buy what things we have need of for the *feast;* or that he should give something to the poor" (John 13 : 27, 28, 29). In the early morning of the day, which followed the evening of the Last Supper and the night of the capture of Jesus, the members of the Sanhedrim will not enter the Prætorium, the palace of the gentile Roman governor Pilate, "that they might not be defiled, but eat the passover" (John 18 : 28). And when Christ is still before Pilate, just previous to His being led out to crucifixion, the time is stated to have been "the Preparation of the passover ; and about the sixth hour" (John 19 : 14). After the crucifixion the Jews are anxious, "because it was the Preparation, that the bodies should not remain on the cross upon the Sabbath (for the day of that sabbath was a high day)" (John 19 : 31). The chronology of John, on the supposition that he places the Last Supper on the thirteenth of Nisan, would then demand, that the crucifixion took place on the fourteenth, the day on which the passover-lamb was slain and eaten. Christ's body would then have been in the grave on the fifteenth, which was a high day or double sabbath, because the day of convocation occurred on the weekly sabbath. The resurrection must consequently have taken place on the sixteenth of Nisan.

The debate is therefore as to the day of the month, and it is not about the day of the week. Both the synoptists and John place the Last Supper on Thursday evening and the crucifixion on Friday. But Westcott (Introduction to the Study of the Gospels, page 341) thinks that the question of the day of the week is a point of inquiry. According to him, "long use and tradition seem to have decided this already, but it may be questioned whether there are not grounds for doubting the correctness of the common opinion." He, as later Seyffarth (see below, page 322), refers to Matt. 12 : 40, where the Lord tells the Jews seeking a sign, that He will give them "the sign of Jonah" in that "the Son of man shall be three days and *three nights* in the heart of the earth." From the separate enumeration of the nights, which cannot be "without any special force, or strictly speaking inaccurate," it is concluded that the day of crucifixion might have been another day than Friday, to whose acceptance the term "Preparation" interpreted in favor of Friday has led. The period from Friday to Sunday, even though the parts of a day be reckoned in full, would not be three days and *three nights*. Only if Thursday had been the day of the death of Christ would His prophecy have been truly fulfilled. In favor of Thursday the expression Matt. 27 : 62: "The next day that followed the day of Preparation," seems to argue strongly. This circumlocution is deemed inexplicable if applied to the Sabbath, but to be readily understood if the first day of "unleavened bread" (Matt. 26 : 17) is again referred to in this manner, because "no characteristic term remained for it." This first day could be "a great Sabbath" (John 19 : 31), without being a weekly Sabbath.

The whole Sabbatic period might extend from the fifteenth of Nisan to the *dawn* of the first day of the week. The greater interval between the death and resurrection of Jesus, than from Friday to Sunday, seems also to be confirmed by such expressions as "*after* three days" (Mark 8 : 31 ; 9 : 31 ; 10 : 34), "in three days" (ἐν Matt. 27 : 40 ; Mark 15 : 29 ; John 2 : 19 (?) ; διὰ Matt. 26 : 61 ; Mark 14 : 58), "the third day be raised up" (Matt. 16 : 21 ; 17 : 23 ; 20 : 19 ; Luke 9 : 22 ; 18 : 33 ; 24 : 7, 46), "it is now the third day" (Luke 24 : 21).

But plausible as this position appears, its only support is Matt. 12 : 40, which is interpreted regardless of the Jewish custom of calling any part of the whole period covering one night and one day "a night and a day." In the Jerusalem Talmud, cited by Lightfoot, a day and a night are an "onah," which is evidently the basis of the term of St. Paul, "night-day" (νυχθήμερον, 2 Cor. 11 : 25). In similar manner the "three days" are thus used popularly, and the parts stand for the whole. This is also apparent from the usage of this term in the Old Testament (Gen. 40 : 13, 20 ; 1 Sam. 30 : 12, 13 ; 2 Chron. 10 : 5, 12 ; Hosea 6 : 2). The argument derived from Matt. 27 : 62 rests upon the supposition that no circumlocution could have been used for the Sabbath, and it disregards the passover-season in reference to which the Sabbath was to be designated. But the whole theory receives its death-blow from the clear statement Mark 15 : 42: "it was the Preparation, the day before the sabbath." Here the day of crucifixion is unequivocally determined to be Friday, and "Preparation" is interpreted as "fore-sabbath," that is, Friday. Luke likewise says (chapter 23 : 54): "It was the day of preparation and the sabbath drew on," and in verse 56 he relates, that the woman, who had come to anoint Jesus, "rested the sabbath-day according to the commandment." Nor is John less distinct in this matter. In chapter 19, verse 31, the day of crucifixion is unmistakably designated as Friday, and only on this supposition is "high day" explicable. Westcott's explanation is altogether without warrant or proof. It must therefore remain settled, that the day of the Lord's Supper was Thursday evening. There can be no reasonable doubt as to the day of the week. The difficulty is only about the day of the month.

II.—The Theory of Contradiction.

This theory of contradiction is essentially a modern one. And the question of the time of the Last Supper, which has not been regarded as a real contradiction in former times, has, to speak with Stier, "assumed a threatening shape in modern criticism." The position of many in this matter has been well voiced by Pressensé, when he says: "Between the synoptists and the fourth gospel there exists concerning this subject a contradiction, which cannot be brought into agreement; and on the point, which of the two reports is objectively the more correct, uncertainty must remain" (Jésus-Christ, page 602). And strangely enough a scholar in other respects as conservative and evangelical as Steinmeyer has made a similar utterance in his history of the passion of the Lord (1882, page 29, footnote). The source of this position is to be found with Schleiermacher, who in his regeneration of modern theology has introduced much old rationalistic leaven, which in some form or other is still working in the most various minds. But the greatest impetus was given by Ferdinand Christian Baur, the genius and founder of the Tübingen school. This point of view must therefore be examined first.

The Tübingen school in its representatives Baur, Schwegler, Hilgenfeld, Strauss, Keim, Schenkel, Scholten, followed by Renan and Samuel Davidson, so far prefer the synoptists as to discredit John totally. In their argument from the early custom of the observance of the Lord's Supper in Asia, which rested upon the belief that Christ ate the Jewish passover with His disciples on the evening of the fourteenth of Nisan and died on the fifteenth, they claim that this observance is incompatible with the statement in John, which puts the death of Jesus on the fourteenth of Nisan, to cause it to coincide with the sacrifice of the paschal lamb in time and purport. The fourth gospel is therefore a late invention of the second half of the second century, and has a controversial tendency. It was introduced in favor of a new practice, and created sentiment against the old. One of its central thoughts, according to Keim, is the idea of the paschal lamb, as shown by John 1:29, and especially chapter six, verse fifty-one. This whole position is not disproved by a perversion of the actual practice, in claiming that it placed the death of Jesus and not the passover on the fourteenth of Nisan (Steitz, Weitzel, Wagenmann, Beyschlag), which will be seen to be untenable from the statement of Apolinarius, given below (page 344). But the better way is to disprove the existence of controversial tendency in the gospel of John. The idea of the paschal lamb rests upon Isaiah, chapter fifty-three, and is never stated as though a correction were to be made. It is likewise not as important and central in the fourth gospel as it is claimed. The typical relation of the passover-lamb had not to be asserted as a new idea. It existed and was commonly accepted in the second century upon the foundation of such biblical statements as are found in 1 Cor. 5:7; 11:24, 25; 1 Peter

1:19, and frequently in the Apocalypse. No one who reads John without prejudice can find in it any controversial trend. And the very passages involved in the paschal question are much too indefinite for such a purpose. Whenever John finds it necessary to differ from a current view no such supposition of a quiet correction can be accepted. This becomes evident from John 2:21 and 21:23, where John feels compelled to correct the impression of words of Christ that had been misunderstood and misapplied. He would, therefore, in all probability have clearly marked a correction, if one was intended to have been made in the statements of the time of the Last Supper of Jesus. It is nowhere apparent that the gospel of John intends to correct the synoptists, as little as they correct and improve upon John. And had John done so he would have been a very weak critic. His words are less clear and definite than those of the synoptists; and von Hofmann is correct when he asks: " How can it be explained that John departs from the synoptists without making this departure noticeable otherwise than in an intermediate manner? In this way he only makes us uncertain about that statement (i. e. of the synoptists), instead of giving a certain knowledge of the correct view in an unequivocal manner." But this whole theory of ideal construction has been thoroughly disproved. It is a mere phantasy of the brain ("ein Hirngespinst"—Beyschlag). At the present time it would be unnecessary to call attention to it, did it not appear sometimes where it was least expected in some modified form and in a mild shape. Thus von Orelli, positive and evangelical as he is, seems tainted by this old Tübingen idea, when he asserts: " That meal of the disciples in the night of suffering was an anticipated passover, since the fourteenth of Nisan came only upon

Friday, as is apparent from the gospel of John (19:14), which with *consciousness* (Bewusstsein) represents the death of Christ as that of the true paschal lamb" (Herzog-Plitt, Realencyklopädie, second edition, Vol. XI., page 268). Although John is not discredited, and the synoptists are read according to John, an opposite position to that of the school of Baur, yet the assertion of the manner of John's representation of Christ as the paschal lamb reasserts the core of the Tübingen error and imparts a characteristic to John which invalidates von Orelli's preference of John, and is subversive of it, if the proper deduction would be made. The emphasis given to the consciousness, with which John is supposed to have portrayed Christ as the paschal lamb, classes John among the writers of tendency (Tendenz-Verfasser), men who are a peculiar product of the nineteenth century. But by far more dangerous than von Orelli's single utterance is the whole position of Pfleiderer, who is a respectable survival of the Tübingen school, and who has of late in a number of publications exerted no small influence upon English and American theologians. He ascribes a " bold freedom " to John, and holds that John's peculiar " dogmatic idea caused a deviation." " The foundation of this deviation from the unanimous older tradition " is said to consist in this, " that the evangelist wished to put the Christian Lord's Supper out of all relation to the Jewish passover ; therefore the meal of departure was not to be a passover-meal, and therefore the institution of the Lord's Supper at this occasion had to be suppressed " (Urchristentum, page 725 sq.). It is a matter of surprise to find that Pfleiderer is so well acquainted with the wish and purpose of John, although there is no trace of such purpose in the gospel, and no indication that John from any tendency suppressed the institution of the Lord's

Supper. Pfleiderer has attributed to John the aim and bias of his own mind.

The majority of modern scholars, who have a predilection, even though but slightly, for the negative side, have changed from the Tübingen position, and accept John's account to the detriment of the first three gospels. They have returned to the view of Lücke, who followed Schleiermacher. Lücke, in the second edition of his commentary on John, asks the question "whether the synoptical gospels are just as certainly derived from immediate eye-witnesses as the gospel of John, and whether they have been kept genuine as they were handed down?" The answer is virtually negative. It is with some modifications the opinion of Neander, Siefert, Usteri, Bretschneider, deWette, Theile, Hauff, Steitz, J. Müller, and in a mild form of Farrar. But the three best known and latest advocates of this position are Meyer, Bernhard Weiss,[1] and Beyschlag. Before entering upon the consideration of their positions, two theologians must be mentioned, who are scarcely at ease in this company, but who have unfortunately chosen it on this point. Delitzsch (in Ed. Riehm's Handwörterbuch des Biblischen Altertums, second edition, 1893, Vol. II., page 1160) in the discussion of the passah favors John's apparent view altogether. And although a paschal character is ascribed to the Last Supper, it is not considered to be the paschal meal. All the Rabbinic quotations brought forward are against the synoptists; and no attempt or hint at reconciliation is made. The brevity of the article and the small space allowed will scarcely suffice to account for Delitzsch's complete silence on a

---

[1] In this point Johannes Weiss agrees with his father and interprets Luke in the interests of John. (See 8th German edition of Meyer's Commentary on Luke 22 : 7, page 615.)

possibility of agreement. This is to be lamented all the more as the lexicon of Riehm is for educated Bible-readers of every class. The influence of this last utterance of Delitzsch's on this subject is inconsistent with what was his personal position of faith. It is toward the negative tendency and implies the rejection of the synoptic account. In similar manner Prof. Otto Zöckler, in his article on Jesus Christ in Herzog-Plitt's Realencyklopädie, second edition, Vol. VI., page 669, states: "It will scarcely be possible to evade the admission of the existence of this difference between the first three evangelists and the fourth as actual, but at the same time not to prefer the account of John as the one inwardly and outwardly best accredited." Various apparent indications of the position of John in the synoptists are regarded as reminiscences, but no solution of the difficulty is really suggested or given. John is so preferred as to injure the synoptists, and Zöckler's testimony counts in the same direction as that of Delitzsch.

Meyer, in the discussion of John 18 : 28 (American edition, 1884, page 486 sq.), after he has mentioned the attempts at reconciling the statement of John with that of the first three gospels, and has rejected them with very brief and very insufficient arguments, asks on which side historical accuracy is to be found. The choice is for John "as the sole direct witness, whose gospel has been preserved unaltered." The date of the Lord's Supper in the synoptists is then opposed by arguments, which are considered further on (page 338). Thereupon the central point of the whole argumentation is presented, viz., how the synoptic account arose. Here Meyer is as bold a constructionist as the old Tübingen idealists. He says: "The question *how the correct relation of time in the synoptic* tradition *could be altered by a day*, withdraws itself from any solution that is demonstrable from history. Most naturally, however, the institution of the Lord's Supper suggests the point of connection, both by the references, which Jesus Himself in His discourses connected therewith gave to the Supper in its bearing on the passover meal, by the idea of which He was moved (Luke 22 : 15), as also by the view of the Supper as the antitypical passover meal, which view must necessarily have been developed from the apostolic apprehension of Christ as the Paschal Lamb (John 19 : 36; 1 Cor. 5 : 7), so far as He in the Supper had given Himself to be partaken of, Himself the perfected Passover Lamb, which He, simply by His death, was on the point of becoming. Thus the day of institution of the Supper became, in the antitypical mode of regarding it, an *ideal* fourteenth Nisan, and in the tradition, in virtue of the reflective operation of the idea upon it, gradually became an *actual one*, and consequently the preparation which was firmly established as the day of death became, instead of the preparation of the passover (fourteenth of Nisan), as John has again fixed it, the preparation of the Sabbath. This Sabbath, however, regarded, not as the first day of the feast, as in John, consequently not as the fifteenth of Nisan, but as the second day of the feast (sixteenth Nisan)."

This whole position attempts to read the mind of the early Christian Church in a manner for which there is no evidence. It begins with the assumption that the primitive Church supposed that the Lord's Supper ought to have been a passover-meal, because both are inwardly related and the latter is the type of the former. What was held to be proper became to be accepted as a fact, and was then clandestinely introduced into the first three gospels. How and when this occurred, and what was the cause which transformed an imagination into actual reality, Meyer has failed to account for. What invention was necessary to complete the synoptic account, what unnatural editing to make the story one, from the question of the disciples (Matt. 26 : 17) onward to every detail of the meal! It is the most preposterous assumption, and strikes at the very root of the veracity of the gospel. It makes the inconceivable actual, by an imaginary "reflective operation of the idea." This reflective power and operation is unexplained and inexplicable from the records of the history of the Church in the apostolic and sub-apostolic period. The supposition of Meyer leads to the conclusion, that the synoptic gospels, which by universal admission are the earlier ones, and must therefore have been already living in the Church and influencing every thought and activity when John's gospel became public, were so corrupted in such a matter of no small importance under the very eyes of the Church. The responsibility is in reality thrown back on the evangelists themselves. Could they, one of whom was present, and the others companions and direct scholars of the apostles, have been so mistaken? Have we reason to look upon them as unprincipled forgers? Such an error on their part invalidates not only the gospels, but it overthrows all historical credibility, which relies upon the testimony of eye-witnesses. All history cries out against such construction. Logic and common sense condemn it.

Weiss (Life of Christ, third edition, English translation, 1884, Vol. III., page 273 sq.) has essentially the same position as Meyer, although he has not dared to speak so authoritatively of what was in the mind of the primitive Church. His arguments are largely the impossibility of seeing a paschal meal reported in the synoptists, connected with the other apparent proofs generally urged from Jewish law and custom against it. In the "Life of Christ" there is almost an approach to reconciliation of the two accounts. The Supper which has been asserted to have been no passover-meal is given paschal character. But it does not appear wherein this paschal character, also held by Delitzsch (see above, page 299), consisted. Much is made of the impossibility of slaying all lambs in the temple on one evening, and an approximation is made to a temporary view of Ebrard, which he abandoned later.[1] He argues for two days as necessary for the celebration of the paschal supper. The whole tendency of Weiss's view is toward discrediting the account of the first three gospels. Weiss has, however, most strongly injured his theory, when he relates that the statement Mark 14 : 12 has brought about the common and prevalent mode of looking at John from the point of view of the synoptists. Over against this, the historical misstatement, that the earliest harmonists preferred John, is outweighed. The position, which Weiss otherwise accords to Mark, as an early source, must make a word found in Mark of much greater value because of its greater antiquity. Weiss is therefore altogether inconsistent in this

---

[1] Schaff in a footnote in the American edition of Lange's commentary on Matthew, page 456, has summed up Ebrard's consecutive positions in these words: "Ebrard held originally the other view, that Christ died on the fourteenth of Nisan, and was rather suddenly converted to the opposite side by Wieseler (Chronol. Synopse, Hamburg, 1843, pp. 333-390), but then he again returned to his first view in consequence of the clear, calm, and thorough investigation of Bleek (Beiträge zur Evangelienkritik, Berlin, 1846, pp. 107-146). Compare Ebrard: Das Evangelium Johannes, page 42 sqq., where he defends Wieseler's view, and his Wissenschaftliche Kritik der evangelischen Geschichte, 2d edition, 1850, page 506 sqq., where he returns to his first view with the honest confession: 'The plausible and acute arguments of Wieseler have since been so thoroughly refuted by Bleek that no false pride of consistency can prevent me from returning openly to my original opinion as expressed in the first edition of this work.'"

matter. His "Markusevangelium und seine synoptischen Parallelen" in its whole tendency and character is the opposite to the statements in the "Life of Christ." But Weiss's modifications are refreshing in comparison with the radicalism of Meyer.

Beyschlag, on the contrary, is very outspoken. He begins his treatment, in the "Life of Christ" (third edition, 1893, Vol. I., p. 390 sq.), with the characteristic words: "We pass by the many forced attempts to deny the tangible contradiction between the synoptic and Johanean account; to wrongly interpret the synoptists according to John or John according to the synoptists, or to distinguish two last meals of Jesus at each of which He said the same things about the betrayal of Judas and the denial of Peter, etc. All those, who do not, in order to maintain a preconceived notion of the authority of the Bible, cause it under circumstances to say the opposite of what it says, are agreed as to this, that the contradiction exists and that it is necessary to decide for one or the other account." After the Tübingen theory is disproved, Beyschlag mentions as three decisive arguments against the synoptists, the existing Sabbath-laws, the defilement that a trial would have brought upon the members of the Sanhedrim, the impossibility of leaving the passover-meal before morning. These arguments will be touched upon later (see page 339). They are also only incidental to Beyschlag's point of view, who has well described his own true motive, when he speaks of "the presupposition of the erroneousness" of the synoptical relation. The synoptists "were not clearly conscious of the confusion;" and the "original evangelist" (Urevangelist), who is Mark, is spoken of as coming "from rural Galilee." "The first evangelist" (Matthew) is claimed as belonging "to the Diaspora which was so careless in ritual matters." In short, "if one or the other had a doubt, whether such actions were legally allowed at Easter, he was undoubtedly completely quieted in his position as layman by the thought, that this profanation of the passover-night and of the holy day agreed well with the godlessness and the wicked spirit of the enemies of Jesus." All this is one fabric of imagination. Where is the proof that Mark was a Galilean? Everything points to his being a child of Jerusalem (see Introduction, page ix sq.). What evidence can be brought to show that Matthew was of the Diaspora? Equally gratuitous is the assumption that the synoptists were unacquainted with the most well-known laws and passover-customs of Jerusalem, although they must at all events have been there more than once. It cannot be proved that the Galilean and Hellenistic Jews were so ignorant. This ignorance would have been inexcusable even in Jewish laymen. It is clearly impossible among a people constantly so careful in all ceremonial laws and customs. The thought, that the wickedness of the Jews broke all laws, is to a certain extent true, and the accounts of John and the synoptists show this. But that this view, which silenced the conscience of the evangelists when noticing an error, determined the account is a baseless invention and imparts to the truthful Galileans, moved by the Spirit of truth, the seared conscience of modern critics, who, when they have adopted one principle, follow it to its bitter end against all contrary facts and all compunctions of conscience. Beyschlag has in his last imputation involuntarily written the self-confession of modern negative criticism.

All these attempts to find contradiction are not honest treatments, but prejudiced constructions. The authors are not as fair as Winer was, when he stated that " the differences between the gospels are to be recognized and an explanation must be abandoned." It can with all fairness be admitted that there are apparently quite some difficulties, and the individual may confess with Alford, "Of the solutions none satisfy me and I have none of my own;" and be led like Tholuck by a love of scientific truth to say "that the union of the two accounts is encumbered with very great difficulties." But the subjectivitism, which acts with such assurance and arbitrariness, cannot be sufficiently deprecated. Questions hard to solve may exist in minor points, which would not invalidate the historical truth of a fact. In other historical sources, which are contemporaneous, similar reports are found of occurrences that apparently contain a contradiction. But probably the reader not knowing an essential feature, which as being self-evident was omitted in the original report, sees opposition where the knowledge of the omitted detail would bring about harmony. To acknowledge such discrepancies and even contradictions, apparently altogether insoluble, in the Bible does not detract from its historical and canonical position. It only shows our inability for the time being to determine the exact facts, and it does not necessarily follow that the authors of the biblical books have committed errors. But in this question of the time of the paschal meal, involving the time of the death of Jesus, there could not have been uncertainty in the first Christian congregations. A change could only have been due to a designed purpose, which is nowhere evident. The whole early Church had no other opinion than that both accounts agreed. In the paschal controversy no party impugned the veracity of the account opposite to their views. Only the interpretation of the opponents was questioned, and their view was regarded as bringing the gospels into contradiction. Thus Apolinarius says against the observers of the fourteenth of Nisan: "They interpret Matthew as favoring their view, from which it appears that their view does not agree with the Law, and that the gospels seem, according to them, to be at variance." And in a later stage of the discussion Polycrates stated in favor of those who kept the fourteenth of Nisan: "All these observed the fourteenth day of the passover according to the gospel." It is only ignorance of the usage of the word "gospel," at that time, to suppose that "gospel" meant but one book, e. g. that of Matthew or John. Polycrates, who wrote after Theophilus of Antioch had died, and Irenæus had written his great work, and Clement of Alexandria was beginning to flourish, could not have invented a new use of the word unless there were evidence. His use of "gospel" must have agreed with that of his contemporaries, which applied "gospel" to the whole preaching and account according to all evangelists (see Zahn, Geschichte des N. T. Kanons, Vol. I., page 185, and note on chapter 1 : 1). Contradiction is no principle of the primitive Church, but only an invention of a criticism, which has grown up under anti-Christian philosophical and historical presuppositions.

III.—Solutions Suggested.

The attempt has been made by many to permit the words of the synoptists and John to remain in their apparently contradictory force, and to arrive at a reconciliation of both accounts by giving the preference and determining power to neither. Some of these efforts, which have not been few, and in the service of which much ingenuity and learning have been placed, will be noticed and discussed.

(1.) One method is to leave the synoptists intact and make the Last Supper the passover-meal, by placing the Supper related by John (13 : 1 sq.) at an earlier time. This seems to obviate the silence of John about the institution of the Communion. It has been advocated by Maldonatus on John 13 : 1, who in Matthew says of the Last Supper: "Jesus ate the passover in Jewish manner." Lightfoot has connected it with the feast at the house of Simon the leper at Bethany, which he wrongly puts two days before the passover (see chapter 14 : 3, page 232). The anointing of Jesus by Mary (Matt. 26 : 6; Mark 14 : 3), that took place at the meal in Simon's house, furnishes Lightfoot the opportunity for the remark: "While they (the disciples) are grumbling at the anointing of His head, He does not scruple to wash their feet." Bengel, who also maintains this position in its fundamental features, deviates from Lightfoot in supposing that the meal reported by John was eaten on the evening before the passover-meal (see on Matt. 26 : 17 and John 18 : 28). Kaiser in his "Chronologie und Harmonie der vier Evangelien," has also adopted this explanation. According to it the claim is made, that the description of the meal in John is not that of a paschal supper; and it is said to have taken place before the feast (John 13 : 1), for which Judas is ordered, as the other disciples suppose, to buy provisions (John 13 : 29). Only in John 14 : 31, when Christ says: "Arise, let us go hence," does He, it is maintained, depart for Jerusalem. Besides, the washing of the feet of the disciples by Jesus is thought to be incongruous with the paschal meal, although it is not made clear in what this incongruity consists. And Satan, whom John

(13 : 2) speaks of as coming to Judas, has according to Luke 22 : 3 entered into Judas before the feast. But the words of John do not regard the entering as a present act, but as a past occurrence; for Satan is spoken of as "*having* already put it into ($\check{\eta}\delta\eta\ \beta\epsilon\beta\lambda\eta\kappa\acute{o}\tau o\varsigma$) the heart of Judas" to betray Christ. And plausible as all the other arguments appear, they are disproved by a comparison of the synoptists and John. The setting of the meal in John 13 : 1 sq. is the same as that which the synoptists regard as the passover. The whole context argues for identity. Luke in chapter 22 : 24 sq. reports a contention of the disciples, which is explanatory of the washing of their feet by Jesus (John 13 : 1 sq.). And in connection with this supper all four evangelists tell of the announcement of the treachery of Judas by Jesus and the dipping of the sop in the dish (Matt. 26 : 21 sq.; Mark 14 : 18 sq.; Luke 22 : 21 sq.; John 13 : 21 sq.), of the foretelling of the denial of Peter (Matt. 26 : 31 sq.; Mark 14 : 27 sq.; Luke 22 : 31 sq.; John 13 : 36 sq.), and the going out of Jesus and the eleven apostles to the mount of Olives (Matt. 26 : 30; Mark 14 : 26; Luke 22 : 39; John 18 : 1 sq.). In addition, this solution does not at all touch the great difficulty connected with the "Preparation of the passover" (John 19 : 14).

(2.) Another supposition is, that Jesus celebrated two days. This double celebration is held to have been necessitated by various causes, or to have come about in various ways.

(*a.*) Serno, who ascribes the deviation from the regular passover observance to the Jews of the Diaspora, imagined that the difference was brought about by an error in the ocular observation of the moon. He supposed that in some regions the moon might be seen on the first appearance, and in others possibly obscured by clouds.

Thus the first day of the passover came to be doubled and the paschal meal could be eaten legally on either day. So it may have happened, that for the Galileans in Jerusalem that was the first day which for the inhabitants of Jerusalem was the day before the feast. The first error of this supposition is the identification of Jesus and His disciples as Galileans with the Jews of the Diaspora. The Galileans were never considered to belong to those Jews who lived outside of Palestine. And equally amiss is the notion that the determination of the passover was left to the mere ocular observation of any one and to the arbitrary will of the people. The authorities of the Sanhedrim at Jerusalem determined the first day of the month of Nisan, and according to their appointment of this day all computation was made. After the Sanhedrim had fixed the first day of the passover-month upon reliable testimony of the observation of the moon, it was announced by signals of fire all over the country. And when it occurred that the Samaritans at times deceived by similar signals of fire, it was enacted that special messengers should be sent to every district to make known the first of the important month of Nisan. (Rosch hoschana, IV., 1 sq.) Thus there could be no uncertainty on account of various computations of the new moon.

(*b.*) It has also been supposed that Jesus adopted the habit of the Sadducees, who are assumed to have eaten the passover one day before the other Jews that followed the pharisaic custom. This is virtually the position of Stier, although he does not name the Sadducees. One of the earliest advocates of this notion was Carpzov. And L. Capellus, Petronius, Iken and Kuinoel have so modified this explanation as to identify the observance of Jesus with the practice of the Jewish sect of the Karaites.

But the Karaites were much later than the time of Jesus. They are a sect of Judaism founded by Anan ben David about 761 after Christ. The only strength of the argument from the practice of the Karaites would lie in the proof, that they had perpetuated an older observance of the Sadducees. The doctrinal position of the Karaites was indeed related to Sadduceeism; and owing to their freer standpoint toward the Law, it was analogous to the opinion of the Sadducees. Anan ben David, the founder of the Karaites, also used Sadducean interpretations very largely. But these were obtained from Talmudic literature; and there is no certain proof that the Karaites arose directly from the Sadducees. In their rejection of many legalistic observances the Karaites were also moved by a totally different motive than the Sadducees. The latter occupied a critical and doubting position over against commandments of the Law and then traditional pharisaic enactments; but the former rejected the Rabbinism, which was pharisaically determined, because of their earnest zealousness for the Old Testament. They were different in spirit and attitude from the Sadducees (see Ryssel in Herzog-Plitt Realencyklopädie, second edition, Vol. 18, page 112 sq.). And even were it possible to demonstrate the connection of the Karaites with the Sadducees, it is altogether improbable that Jesus would except their position. He was no liberalist, and His attitude toward the Sadducees, as indicated by the gospels (Matt., 16 : 6, 11, 12; 22 : 23; Mark 12 : 18; Luke 20 : 27), was certainly not one of approval. If Christ had adopted the Sadducean practice, He would have employed it on previous passover celebrations. But such a departure from the prevalent observance would undoubtedly have been noticed and used against Jesus by the Pharisees.

(*c.*) It has again been assumed, that it was customary to keep two days, in order that those who had been prevented on one day might celebrate on the next. But for such cases in which, because of legal impurity or too great a distance from Jerusalem, the Jews could not keep passover, it was enjoined that it be observed on the fourteenth day of the following month (Numb. 9 : 9-12). This so-called "second or little passover" was never the day before or after the regular passover. On it also the full and regular passover-ritual was not observed. Leavened and unleavened bread might be kept in the house; the Hallel was not to be recited with the eating of the paschal lamb, of which a portion might be removed from the house; and the Chagigah, or thank-offering, was not allowed to be eaten with the lamb of passover import (Mischna, Pesachim, IX. 3; Maimonides, Hilchoth Korban Pesach, X. 15). All these enactments disprove that two days were conjoined. In addition, the character of the little passover is totally different from the meal described in the synoptists. And there is no proof that Jesus or His disciples were ceremonially unclean at that time; therefore no reason remains why Jesus should not eat the regular passover-meal.

(*d.*) Two days of the passover celebration are held to be necessary by others, because the multitude of lambs could not be slain on one day, between the hours of the evening appointed for this purpose. Josephus (Jewish Wars, VI. 9, 3) reports, that some years before the destruction of Jerusalem, upon the express order of the Roman governor Cestus, who was to report to Nero the number of Jews in Jerusalem at the passover-season, the number of passover-lambs was counted and found to be 256,500. Such a large number of lambs, it is claimed, could not have been sacrificed from the ninth to the eleventh hour (3–5 o'clock P. M.) by the priests. To accommodate them, Ebrard therefore conjectured, the poorer Galileans ate the passover a day sooner. But this opinion was soon abandoned by Ebrard (see page 303, footnote). It has, however, been taken up again by some later exegetes, notably Weiss. But this supposition is disproved by the express words of Mark (14 : 12), " the *first day* of unleavened bread when they killed the passover," and of Luke (22 : 7), " and the *day* of unleavened bread came, on which the passover *must* be sacrificed." Further, it rests on the conception that the priests had to kill every passover-lamb themselves. This was not so. After a threefold blast from the temple-trumpet, announcing the time of sacrifice, each Israelite slew his own lamb in the temple, as Philo (III. 146) relates. In two long rows stood the officiating priests, of whom on the passover-day the whole twenty-four courses were present, and as one priest caught up the blood from the dying lamb in a golden bowl, he handed it to his neighbor, who in return gave an empty bowl. The blood was passed up to the great altar, where it was thrown out in one jet at the base of the altar. With such arrangement and with all the priests present, all Israelites bringing a lamb could be accommodated, especially if we suppose that one row of priests passed up the full bowls and the other returned those that were empty. There is therefore no necessity for using the large number of lambs to be sacrificed, to prove that the evenings of two days were required. Nor is there the least historical evidence for this assumption, which is too much magnified by many.

(3.) A third plan proposes to solve the discrepancy by conjecturing that either Jesus or the Jews had changed the day of passover.

(*a*.) Jesus is supposed to have anticipated the passover for some cause or other.

(*α*.) One cause is held to have been His desire to be slain at the time of the sacrifice of the passover-lamb, and thus to bring the fulfilment into closest temporal connection with the type. This is the position of Clement of Alexandria, Origen, Tertullian, whose testimony will be considered in connection with the patristic view (see page 347). It has been reasserted by Erasmus, Calmet and others, although with stronger arguments than those of the Church Fathers. Nevertheless a dogmatic view is the centre of the whole proof. And dogmatic reasons ought not to decide this debate. Similar arguments might be brought to demonstrate the necessity of having the New Testament passover celebrated at the time of the Old Testament observance (see page 287). Christ also was too obedient to the Law to have inaugurated such a change (Matt. 5:17). He only opposed the contra-scriptural traditions of the Pharisees (see Mark 2:1 sq.; 7:1 sq.).

(*β*.) Another reason for Christ's anticipation is supposed to be, the postponement on the part of the Jews, who, to avoid two Sabbaths coming together, that of the passover on the fourteenth of Nisan and that of the week on the fifteenth, transferred the whole observance to the fifteenth. This is the opinion of Calvin, who on Matt. 26:17 says: " Now it is universally admitted, that, by an ancient custom, when the passover and other festivals happened on Friday, they were delayed till the following day, because the people would have reckoned it hard to abstain from work on two successive days. The Jews maintained that this law was laid down immediately after the return of the people from the Babylonish captivity, and that it was done by a revelation from heaven, that they may not be thought to have made any change, of their own accord, in the commandments of God. Now if it was the custom, at that time, to join two festivals in one (as the Jews themselves admit, and as their ancient writings prove), it is a highly probable conjecture that Christ, who celebrated the passover on the day before the Sabbath, observed the day prescribed by the Law; for we know how careful He was not to depart from a single iota of the Law. Having determined to be subject to the Law, that He might deliver us from its yoke, He did not forget this subjection at His latest hour; and therefore He would rather have chosen to omit an outward ceremony, than to transgress the ordinance which God had appointed, and thus lay Himself open to the slanders of wicked men. Even the Jews themselves unquestionably will not deny that, whenever the Sabbath immediately followed the passover, it was on one day, instead of both, that they abstained from work, and that this was enjoined by the Rabbis. Hence it follows that Christ, in departing from the ordinary custom, attempted nothing contrary to Law." The substance of this view was held by the Reformers, both Lutheran and Reformed, Luther, however, excepted (see page 351), and their scholars. It has such names in its support as Beza, Gerhard, Bucer, Calov and Deyling.[1] Acceptance was gained for it a long time largely through the influence of Scaliger and Causabon. There is a difference among all these, however, as to the day of the month, some holding that Christ ate His Last Supper on what was regarded the thirteenth of Nisan, but what was really the fourteenth. But there is no proof in history that such a practice existed at that time, when Jesus celebrated the passover. Nor is there any evidence that the Jews loved

[1] It was also advocated by Philippi.

work so much, that they objected to two consecutive holidays. In this they were no exception to the common human choice. Cocceius has shown, in a note to "Sanhedrim, 1, 2" of the Talmud, that the Rabbinic custom was later. This is now universally adopted. The further difficulty is, that it would have been impossible for Christ and His disciples to have obtained the sacrifice of the paschal lamb at a time not considered legal. Calvin's central argument about Christ's subservience to the Law of itself overthrows the whole theory of an anticipatory passover.

(γ.) Grotius has given another form to the suggestion of the passover of anticipation. He believed that Christ celebrated only a commemorative passover (πάσχα μνημονευτικόν), and not the actual sacrificial day (πάσχα θύσιμον). But such a distinction was of much later origin. It became necessary after the destruction of the temple, and to-day the Jewish passover is merely commemorative, because no sacrifice can be made in the temple at Jerusalem. But even the passover of commemoration cannot be proven to have been one of anticipation. It is celebrated on the actual day.

(δ.) Another expedient was proposed by Derenburg, who thought that in the year of Christ's death the first paschal day fell on a Sunday, therefore the lamb would not be slain on the previous day; nor could it conveniently have been sacrificed on Friday, the preparation for the Sabbath. It was therefore slain on Thursday to be eaten on Sunday, the fourteenth of Nisan; and Jesus, knowing that He would die before, anticipated the meal. But two points are detrimental to this theory: the long interval between the slaying and the eating of the lamb, which is contrary to all Jewish custom; and the express permission to slay the passover on Sunday given by the Mischa (Pesach. VI. 1). Nor is there any proof that the

Jews were eating the passover on the day of Christ's resurrection. The whole account in the four gospels leaves no such impression.

(ε.) The supposition that the Lord gave the directions for the passover meal on the thirteenth of Nisan, which were only to be carried out on the following evening, the fourteenth, is a makeshift contradicted on every side by the gospels.

(*b*.) It has been proposed in all earnestness by Eusebius of Cæsarea, whose view Bishop Wordsworth has repeated in modern times, that during the trial of Jesus the whole celebration of the passover was postponed on that year. But when Jesus was taken, of which there had been no certainty previously, nor could there have been, especially since the Jews in former attempts to take Him had failed, the passover celebration had already begun. All the steps necessary to the postponement of the passover would have been so difficult, that this is altogether out of the question.

The more plausible presentation of this argument is, that only the priests, when called to the trial of Jesus, had not eaten of the passover. But against this is the time of Christ's capture, and the statement of Mark (14:53): " And they led Jesus away to the high priest: and there *come together* with him all the chief priests and the elders and the scribes." The word " come together " ($\sigma \upsilon \nu \epsilon \rho \chi \omicron \nu \tau \alpha \iota$) shows that they were just assembling, and that they had not previously been gathered. Nor have we any proof that they had not begun to eat the passover in their homes, because they expected to be called to a meeting for the trial of Jesus. Therefore Archdeacon Watkins (Excursus F. on John in Ellicott's series of commentaries on the New Testament) is more correct, when he supposes that the priests and other Sanhedrists had been interrupted, and after they went back they ate, "turning the supper into a breakfast." But this and all postponement was clearly contrary to the acknowledged law (Lev. 23 : 5 ; Deut. 16 : 7), and the custom that "the pascha is not to be eaten but during the night, nor yet later than the middle of the night" (Schbach. V. 8). The hate of the Jews (Fairbairn) might have moved them to postpone the evening of the passover; but this transferral would not account for the whole difficulty, but would only solve John 18 : 28 ; and John 19 : 14, which is equally to be considered, is not at all cleared up.

(4.) A fourth general plan is to examine the exactness of time, either as to its legal determination on the fourteenth of Nisan, or as involved in the meaning of the phrase, "between the two evenings," or as to the interval between the death and resurrection of Jesus.

The advocates of this position are mostly of the last two centuries, although in the early history of the Church, even independent of the paschal controversy, there were differences on the score of the dates. Clement of Alexandria in his "Stromata" (Miscellanies) (Book I., Chapter XXI.) says : "And treating of His (Christ's) passion, with very great accuracy, some say that it took place in the sixteenth year of Tiberius, on the twenty-fifth of Phamenoth (March); and others the twenty-fifth of Pharmuthi (April), and others say that on the nineteenth of Pharmuthi the Saviour suffered."

(*a.*) The earliest representative of the attempt to unite the thirteenth and fourteenth of Nisan by calling attention to the fact, that the evening began the Jewish **day**, was Frisch (1758). His view was refuted by Gabler, but again maintained by Rauch (1832). His opinion, as summarized by Tholuck, is this : "The legal determination, by the fourteenth of Nisan, means not the *end* of the day, but its *beginning*, consequently the evening of the thirteenth. This is beyond dispute deducible from Josephus, Antiq. II. 14, 16, where we read that the Jews were obliged to select a lamb on the tenth of Nisan, and to keep it until the fourteenth and ἐνατάης τῆς τεσσαρεσκαιδεκάτης, 'at the begining of the fourteenth' to kill it. The day of the crucifixion would consequently fall on the fourteenth of Nisan. After it has been furthermore shown that in the strict sense the passover lasted only seven days, from the first day of the feast, the πρὸ ἑορτῆς τοῦ πάσχα, John 13:1, is interpreted, 'before the passover properly so-called'—which commenced, to wit, 24 hours later, on the fifteenth of Nisan. It is shown further, that on this view, John 19:14 and 31 allow of a very satisfactory explanation, since then John 19:14, the παρασκευὴ τοῦ πάσχα is the day before the passover proper, and in verse 31, that Sabbath is called μεγάλη, (high, great), because the *first* day of the festival fell upon it, which, just as much as the last, was regarded a grand day. In chapter 19:28, however, there remains no other resource than the supposition that τὸ πάσχα there is meant to designate not the paschal lamb, but the unleavened bread, τὰ ἄζυμα, which was eaten throughout the festival proper." The strength of this theory are some of the chronological statements in the Pentateuch. In Numb. 33:3, the day of the departure of the Israelites from Egypt is called "the morrow of the passover," which seems to be in favor of Rauch's supposition, as also the order in Exod. 12:22, that none shall go out "until the morning." But in the first passage, Numb. 33:3, it is said, that Israel went forth on the fifteenth of Nisan, and if the departure in agreement with Exod. 12:30 followed the same night, the passover must have been eaten on the fourteenth. This is the clear interpretation of the Jews, whose practice in the time of Christ, according to all testimony, was to celebrate the evening of the fourteenth of Nisan, and not the evening of the thirteenth. And the expression of Josephus cannot be used to denote the *daybreak* of the fourteenth, that is, its beginning on the evening of the thirteenth, because there is no comparison with another time of the day, but only the date is to be marked. Besides, "between the paschal meal, at which already unleavened bread was used, and the day of which was counted with the feast, between this and the first day of the festival proper, a day having no connection with the feast would be thrown in" (Tholuck).

(*b.*) The expression "between the two evenings" (Hebrew: bēn haärbāyīm), about the precise meaning of which there is dispute, has also been brought into requisition to explain this matter. It occurs in reference to the passover in Exod. 12: 6; Lev. 23: 5; Numb. 9: 3, 5; and has been employed in conjunction with the chronological data in Exod. 12: 18 and Lev. 23: 6 by Wratislaw, whom Alford quotes as stating: "that the time after 3 o'clock P. M. Thursday might be called by St. Mark 'the first day of unleavened bread, when they sacrificed the passover,' and by St. Luke 'the day of unleavened bread, when the sacrifice must be killed,' it being killed after the first and before the second evening on Friday, and thus loosely speaking within the day, which commenced at 3 o'clock, and strictly speaking within that which commenced at sunset Thursday. Similarly any time after three or sunset on Thursday might be 'Preparation.'" The disciples according to this explanation made preparation on Thursday for Friday. In like manner Ellicott regards the Lord's Last Supper as the paschal meal eaten twenty-four hours before the Jews, but "within what was popularly considered the limits of the festival." And Westcott holds that "the question of the disciples was asked immediately upon the sunset of the thirteenth. The Preparation is evidently contemplated as foreseen by the owner of the house, and need not have occupied much time. The evening of the Supper would thus be as St. John represents it, the evening at the beginning of the fourteenth. The same day after sunrise next morning is rightly described as a Preparation-day,—'the Preparation of the Passover,' though the Preparation, in the strictest sense of the term, was limited to the last three hours, from 'the ninth hour.'" Ingenuous as these explanations are, they fail because they always presuppose a passover sacrifice and meal of the disciples at another time than that kept by the other Jews. In addition, this term "between the two evenings" is applied to the evening sacrifice in Exod. 29 : 39, 41 ; Numb. 28 : 4, and in other connections (Exod. 16:12 ; 30 : 8), where it cannot be made to include the time from the evening beginning the day to the evening ending it. The interpretation of this expression is also disputed. It is taken to mean from the going down of the sun to its disappearance behind the horizon by the Samaritans, Karaites, Aben Ezra, Michaelis, Gesenius, Knobel, Keil and others. In support of this view Deuteronomy 16:6, "at the going down of the sun," is cited. But the Pharisees and Rabbis held that the first evening began, when the sun declined ($\delta\epsilon i\lambda\eta$ $\pi\rho\omega i a$), and that the second evening began with the setting of the sun ($\delta\epsilon i\lambda\eta$ $\delta\psi i a$). This opinion is supported by Josephus (Jewish Wars, VI. 9, 3), who says that the lambs were slain between the ninth and the eleventh hour, that is, from three to five o'clock ; and by the Mischna (Pesachim V. 1 sq.), which fixes the beginning at 2.30, and Maimonides, who says that the paschal lambs were slain after the evening sacrifice. Jarchi and Kimchi believe the two evenings to be immediately before and after sunset, from about five to seven o'clock (see Smith's Bible Dictionary, Vol. III., page 2342, note; McClintock and Strong's Encyclopedia, Vol. VII., page 735 ; Kitto's Encyclopedia, Vol. III., page 423, footnote). Whichever of these three interpretations be adopted, in one point they all agree, namely, in limiting the term " between the two evenings" to a few hours of the same evening. But those who argue from this expression generally make it extend to the following evening. Therefore there is no actual support for their supposition.

(*c.*) Among the advocates of a longer interval between the death and resurrection of Jesus to explain this difficulty are Schnekenburger, who contrary to all statements of the gospels holds that Jesus was crucified on Wednesday and lay four days in the grave ; and Seyffarth, who was well known to the older Lutherans of New York city. He virtually maintained the same view as that of Westcott described on page 293. According to him Christ died on Thursday, the fourteenth of Nisan, and was in the grave fully three days. The main argument is based upon astronomical calculations of the eclipse of the sun at the death of Jesus. He accepts as the years of the death of Jesus the year 33 or 786 of the founding of Rome, like Ebrard, Ewald and Renan. But most scholars contend for the year 30 (Wieseler, Winer, Tischendorff, Friedlieb, Greswell, Ellicott, Lange, Schaff, Caspari, Pressensé); and this is pretty generally accepted, although Ideler and Zumpt adopt the year 29, Keim 35 and Hitzig 36. The astronomical determination is of itself not sufficient, even though it were quite certain. It can only serve as a corroborative proof, but not as the establishing argument (see also, page 351).

Peculiar is the claim of Lutteroth, that the passover began on the tenth of Nisan, the day of the selection of the paschal lamb. On this day Jesus, as Lutteroth supposes, was crucified, and arose between the thirteenth and fourteenth after being in the grave fully three days and three nights. The first appearance of Jesus to His disciples was then on the morning of the fourteenth. To support this view rather forced exegesis is necessary. Mark 14: 12, "the first day of unleavened bread, when they killed the passover," may, says Lutteroth, be applied to the tenth of Nisan, because this day opened in general the passover-season. The relative "when" ($ὅτε$) is not to be referred to "day" but "unleavened bread," the whole festival in connection with which the lamb was sacrificed. Luke 22: 7, "And the day of unleavened bread came, on which the passover must be sacrificed," is said to contain no chronological statement as in the parallel passages, but to mean that the day appeared, when Jesus, the true paschal lamb, was to be sacrificed. Matt. 28 : 1 is interpreted to apply to the fourteenth of Nisan, the passover-day, which extends to a second sabbath, the fifteenth. But what proof is there that the fourteenth was a Sabbath-day? The statement of this strange exposition is at once its refutation. It is a far-fetched construction, but not an honest explanation. Most prominent in it appears what is characteristic of all the attempts at solution thus far mentioned. Violence is done to some direct word of the gospels, or some fact of history has been overlooked, and the custom of those times not properly considered. The interest of harmony has produced an unnatural agreement. All such efforts will not solve this difficulty, but only by reaction lead to the acceptance of the theory of contradiction. A more just mode of procedure is upon consideration of the statements of the two conflicting sources, John and the synoptists, to attempt to bring one in its totality and peculiarity into agreement with the other. This will be tried, first giving John the preference, and then the synoptists.

IV.—Agreement according to John.

This method, originally suggested by Apolinarius, has found its modern representatives in Movers, Maier, Weitzel, Isenberg, Kahnis, Caspari, Godet, Plummer and others. Its clearest and on the whole best statement is that found in Godet, whose arguments will be examined in their exegetical bearing. The historical and other proofs will be mentioned in the last division as objections to the agreement on the basis of the synoptists (see page 338).

The sense of the passages in John is first determined, beginning with 13 : 1 as the fundamental one. The words, "before the feast of the passover," are meant to refer to the evening before that on which the paschal meal was held, that is, the evening from the thirteenth to the fourteenth of Nisan. "Passover" is given the same import as in chapter 12 : 1, and applied to the meal, although it is admitted that the whole fourteenth of Nisan may be included. It is supported by a reference to Numb. 33 : 3, where the fifteenth of Nisan is called "the morrow after the passover." The supposition that "before the passover" may apply to the short time and the few moments before its inception is rejected; but no clear proofs are given for this procedure. In John 18 : 28 the eating of the passover is accepted as the eating of the meal in the narrow and specific sense in which this expression occurs in the synoptists. The Old Testament proofs for a wider meaning (see below, page 332) are not really weakened, nor is the usage of "eating" in its wider application disproved; nor "passover" in its narrow signification established as consistent with the general usage in John.

In consonance with these passages, thus interpreted, John 19 : 14, " the preparation of the passover," is viewed, as it is supposed that Greek readers might most readily understand it, namely, to mean the preparatory day for the first actual day of the passover, that is, the fifteenth of Nisan. It is claimed that "Preparation" cannot have its technical Jewish signification of Friday (see below, page 335), because it would otherwise stand alone and not be joined with " passover "; for it is self-evident that only the Friday of the passover-week is intended. But in verse thirty-one " Preparation " is employed in its special Jewish sense ; and the time of the death of Jesus is stated to be the fourteenth of Nisan. The fifteenth is called a "high day," because concurring with the weekly Sabbath. Verse forty-two of the same nineteenth chapter is explained in the same manner.

With this position the synoptists are to be brought into unison. And in endeavoring this, the direct passages are not approached first, but an incidental word is made the real basis, and is then strengthened by the interpretation of other expressions. Such a method is liable to create suspicion at once ; and it is at the very beginning an involuntary confession of weakness.

Matt. 26 : 18, " My time is at hand; I keep the passover at thy house with my disciples," is made the starting point. It is supposed to imply haste, and therefore to demand an anticipatory passover. But at such a view no one would arrive, who did not read the presupposed position of John into these words. Of themselves they do not say what is claimed. The earlier commentators, who favored this view, were wiser in interpreting " my time " as the time for the passover-meal. But the impossibility of such a usage of this expression, which in the gospels, especially John, always refers to Christ's death (John 7 : 6, 8), has led Godet and Reuss to abandon it. And with this abandonment the main support of this passage for the point of view of John is taken away.

Matt. 27 : 62, where the day on which the priests again came to Pilate to demand a guard for the tomb of Jesus, is called " the morrow, which is the day after the Preparation," is also claimed to be in favor of John. It is held that this expression would be very strange to designate the Sabbath ; for it would amount to calling it the day after Friday. And such a name for a day as important and marked as the Sabbath would be very unnatural and improper, because nearly always when two days are spoken of connectedly the less important and significant is determined by and named after the greater and higher day. This "morrow" therefore is peculiar only as the day of the death of Jesus ; in itself it is an ordinary week-day. But that there could have been no different term for the Sabbath is an assumption, the more without reason since the preceding Friday was no ordinary one. It is not necessary then to put the scene related Matt. 26 : 18 sq. on Friday, and to imply covertly that the fourteenth of Nisan is here meant by Matthew. The day following the " Preparation " was not omitted to be called Sabbath, because of the sabbatic character of Friday (Wieseler). But in the omission of " sabbath " and the special emphasis of Friday as the " Preparation," there lies a reproach of the Jews, since they used Friday not to prepare themselves for the stillness of the Sabbath, which for them was no true day of rest, but to bring Jesus to death. This Sabbath had been so violated by their wickedness, that it could no longer be called a sabbath (Lange, Keil, Nebe).

Mark 15 : 42, where "Preparation" is interpreted by Mark himself as "the day before the sabbath," is so weakened that "sabbath" in "fore-sabbath" (προσάββατον) is applied to any day of sabbatic character. But Mark writing to gentile readers at Rome explains "Preparation," which, as proved by Judith 8 : 6, can only have the meaning Friday. In addition, Luke in the same connection (23 : 54), says: "the sabbath drew on," that is, it began to be the evening of the Sabbath-day, which "dawns" with its glory. Only by a very forced and unnatural reading can Mark be construed to mean any day but Friday.

Matt. 26 : 17; Mark 14 : 12; Luke 22 : 7, in which the time is related when the disciples asked about preparing the passover, are certainly not indefinite. There is no possibility of applying them to the thirteenth of Nisan, the day called "the day before Preparation" (προετοιμασία) by Clement of Alexandria. Nor can any reasons, like that of the crowded condition of Jerusalem, be used to show the desirability of the disciples making their arrangements on the thirteenth of Nisan, as against the plain and clear statement of the first three gospels. Matthew's report of this day as the first day is confirmed by both Mark and Luke as the customary day for the sacrificing of the paschal lamb. There is an unmistakable identification. And Luke further confirms this, when he states that "the day of unleavened bread *came*, on which the passover must be sacrificed." The word "came" ($\tilde{\eta}\lambda\theta\varepsilon$) does not and cannot mean what Chrysostom, Puschke and Ewald desire. It is not equivalent to "be near" ($\dot{\varepsilon}\gamma\gamma\dot{\upsilon}\varsigma\ \tilde{\eta}\nu$). Joined by δε to what precedes, it denotes as aorist in this connection, that the day of the festival had come and begun. Whenever Luke uses the expression of the coming of a day ($\dot{\eta}\mu\dot{\varepsilon}\rho\alpha\ \dot{\varepsilon}\rho\chi\varepsilon\tau\alpha\iota$) it designates not the approach, but the actual beginning of the day (compare Luke

5 : 35 ; 23 : 29 ; Acts 2 : 20). The meaning of the chronological statements of the synoptists is evidently and undoubtedly that the day of the Last Supper was the fourteenth of Nisan ; and therefore any explanation according to the supposed position of John for the thirteenth will treat them unjustly. With so much against this supposition no force lies in citing customs, as that of drawing water on the evening of the thirteenth of Nisan, with which to bake the unleavened bread on the fourteenth. This custom is held to be indicated when the disciples are bidden to follow a man bearing a pitcher (see chapter 14 : 13 sq.). And thus the Last Supper is placed on the thirteenth of Nisan. But the order that the water to be gotten on the thirteenth could not be drawn until the first stars had appeared, makes it impossible that this custom was the opportunity of Christ's command. The time would have been too late for the two disciples to obtain the sacrifice of the paschal lamb and to make the other preparations after the stars had arisen. The result of this whole examination will be a *non-sequitur*. An agreement on the basis of the thirteenth of Nisan cannot be reached. Wherever it is pressed the inevitable consequence is to impute to some degree at least the correctness and veracity of the synoptists. And those who have begun with the purpose to reach harmony are led to pronounce contradiction. Godet unconsciously but well voices, what all advocates for the supposed view of John ought honestly to confess on their supposition, namely : " John wished (as often in his book) to correct this misunderstanding (of the day of the Last Supper) and to clear up the darkness of the synoptists (?), by which the misunderstanding could be furthered." The shadow here cast upon the synoptists is not that of our understanding, but that of their writing.

Their work is criticised. The darkness is not that of the depth of truth, which we behold as "in a mirror, darkly," but it is an obscurity in a plain date, which the evangelists could and ought easily have known. It helped a misunderstanding and therefore furthered error. And all this, the Spirit of truth, who led the writers of the gospels, is tacitly assumed to have suffered.

V.—Agreement according to the Synoptists.

In the examination of this last possibility of bringing John into accord with the synoptists, the passages Matt. 26:17, Mark 14:12, Luke 22:7, will be accepted, as they most naturally seem, to point to the fourteenth of Nisan. The attempt and failure to bring them into consonance with John confirms their peculiarity. It is also most widely recognized that by an unprejudiced exegesis they can only refer to the fourteenth of Nisan. A great majority of exegetes therefore favor this view. It is advocated by Lightfoot, Bochart, Bynæus, Reland, Schoettgen, Ohlshausen, Crusius, Hengstenberg, Tholuck, Guericke, Robinson, Ebrard, Bäumlein, Riggenbach, Norton, von Hofmann, Lichtenstein, Friedlieb, Langen, Lange, Andrews, Osterzee, Kirchner, Rotermund, Wichelhaus, Röpe, von Gumbach, Luthardt, Keil, L. Schulze, Nösgen, Nebe, T. Zahn, Plumptre, Morison, Schaff, Kendrick, Riddle, and others.

The question remains as to how the various statements of John will agree with the synoptists. This can only be determined upon careful examination of each passage in John pertaining to this matter.

(1.) John 13:1, beginning "Now before the feast of the passover," has been claimed to point to the thirteenth of Nisan. It must be first determined what is qualified by the phrase "before the feast." Some take it to refer to the action spoken of in verse four, and include the four verses in one sentence. But such an intricate structure would hardly accord with the style of John. And in the early divisions of the gospels a new sentence began at verse two. This is the acknowledged punctuation of the best textual critics. Godet desires to maintain the general application of the introductory words of John 13:1, and ascribes to them the character of a prologue. But of this there is no need. They can be connected with "knowing" ($εἰδώς$), and would then mean, "Jesus knowing before the festival that his hour had come," and refer back to such statements as are found in John 12:23; Matt. 17:9, 22 sq.; 20:17 sq. But this connection with "knowing" is very vague and indefinite, and, except by Nebe, has been generally given up. Even if it be retained it will thus have no bearing upon the passover question. The best interpretation, adopted by Tholuck, Luthardt, Meyer and others, is to have "before the feast" qualify "he loved them unto the end." The meaning then, with "loved" conceived of not "as an emotion, but as an act" (Gerhard), is, that before the passover, in view of His death, the love of Jesus was actively called forth toward His disciples, and manifested itself in actual proof unto His very end. Not only the washing of the feet of the disciples but every evidence of love, as related to the end of chapter seventeen, is included. Now if such an act of love is meant, "before the feast" cannot refer back a day or to any peculiar time, but it designates in general the time immediately before the feast. The nearer definition must be made by the connection, as "before" in itself is not definite. It is merely relative, and no inference ought to be drawn from it. John did not wish to mark a definite time as he had done in chapter 12:1.

The word "feast" (ἑορτῆς) is really festival and is equivalent to the Hebrew Chāg. It does not mean a single meal, but the whole celebration. Thus in Lev. 23 : 5, 6; Numb. 28 : 16, 17, the paschal supper is clearly distinguished from the Chāg, the whole festival. This really began on the fifteenth of Nisan. The evening before the fifteenth was the "Proëortion," the preparation for the whole passover "feast." It was the festival-eve (Vorfeier). With this the abrupt manner in which John begins the second verse and speaks of "supper" agrees. The statement "during supper" (δείπνου γενομένου) would be unclear, if it did not refer to the passover. Thus this first passage implies no contradiction with the synoptists. Even though the above explanation be not adopted, this much is evident, that it cannot of itself overthrow the synoptic position. In it there is no trace of any desire to correct.

(2.) In John 13 : 29, after Judas Iscariot has been told by Christ "That thou doest, do quickly," the disciples suppose that he is to buy something for the feast or to give some alms to the poor. But it is claimed that this thought of the disciples was impossible on the fourteenth of Nisan. What was there to buy if the passah had begun? But many things might have been required for the other days of the festival. And this as the whole celebration is indicated, as in verse one, by the word ἑορτήν. If these words of Jesus had been uttered on the thirteenth of Nisan, it is not explicable why haste was demanded, for a whole day was yet left. But on the evening of the fourteenth they are natural; and the eleven disciples may have thought that Judas was to purchase what was necessary for the thank-offering. Nor was it impossible to make purchases on the evening of the fourteenth of Nisan (see below, page 339).

(3.) The passage, which is the strongest and at first sight seems to be against the synoptists, is John 18 : 28, where it is related that the priests did not enter the Prætorium, that they might not be defiled, but that "they might eat the passover" (ἀλλ' ἵνα φάγωσι τό πάσχα). If "eat the passover" means only to eat the passover-lamb, then John places the crucifixion on the fourteenth and contradicts the synoptists. Now "eat the passover" has a limited sense in which it refers to the paschal meal. It is so used in 2 Chron. 30 : 18, especially in the Septuagint, from which many New Testament expressions arose. Besides, it is used five times in the synoptists (Matt. 26 : 17; Mark 14 : 12, 14; Luke 22 : 11, 15), and is always applied to the paschal meal. But in all these passages the context restricts this expression, which is not the case here in John. In addition, with so few parallels the meaning cannot be absolutely fixed, especially since only one Old Testament passage is cited. From the Old Testament where the root of the term lies its determination must begin. It is also unfair to settle John's usage from the synoptists, without searching whether there is any indication in John of a different application of either the word "eat" or "passover." To arrive at the answer to this question we must begin, however, with the whole New Testament use, particularly of the word "passover." This is not only used for "the paschal lamb" as in Mark 14 : 12; Luke 22 : 7; 1 Cor. 5 : 7, but also for "the passover-meal" in Matt. 26 : 18, 19; Luke 22 : 8, 13; Hebr. 11 : 28, and the five passages cited above ; and finally for *the whole festival*, comprising the seven days of unleavened bread (Luke 2 : 41, 43; 22 : 1; Matt. 26 : 2). This latter use is found frequently in John. Six times out of the nine in which "passover" is employed it has the broad meaning

(2 : 13, 23; 6 : 4; 11 : 55; 12 : 1; 13 : 1). If now "passover" be thus taken, "eat" is put in loose popular usage for *keeping* the passover (compare Numb. 9 : 2, 6, etc.). This expression occurs in reference to passover in 2 Chron. 30 : 22, which is literally "they did eat the festival seven days." "Festival" (hā mōēd) is explained by Bertheau and Keil as festive offerings (compare Exod. 23 : 15). The latter says that the term "keep the festival" in formed after "eat the passover." That eating was so understood is also evident from the Septuagint, which renders *vayōkēlū συνετέλεσαν* (fulfilled, kept). There is no strong proof that this translation is due to a different reading *vayakēllū*, as Godet supposes. *Vayōkēlū* is well attested. But this whole explanation does not seem to fit as well as it ought to the context in John. If the whole festival were meant the fear of defilement on the part of the priests would have been utterly senseless. A feast and a meal is evidently in the mind of the priests, which was to be held the same day. Therefore "passover" (πάσχα) must be taken not as applying to the passover, but in a broader sense. It is then by metonymy used for "paschal sacrifice," and designates the voluntary peace and thank-offerings, offered during the whole passover-season, and especially on the fifteenth of Nisan. This offering of the fifteenth was later called the Chagigah. The Old Testament knows of this wide use of "passover." A suggestion is offered by the passage quoted above, 2 Chron. 30 : 22. There *mōēd*, festival, stands for the offerings. And the previous verses fifteen, seventeen and eighteen, which contain *Pesāch* (passover) in its limited sense, prove nothing against the metonymy in verse twenty-two. But direct evidence is found in Deut. 16 : 2 : "And thou shalt sacrifice the *passover* unto the Lord thy God of the flock and herd." Here "passover"

(pĕsăch) is applied to sheep and oxen (zōn ŭbākār). Zon ŭbākār denote no additional sacrifices to the pesach, for they are in apposition with it. And the specific passover sacrifice cannot be meant, because it is a Cè, a yearling of the sheep and goats. Both Dillman and Keil, together with the Rabbis, refer this verse, therefore, to the Chagigah. And the Rabbis were certainly well acquainted with the law. "Passover" occurs also in the plural (pĕsāchim) in the same broad sense, and includes flocks, lambs, kids, small cattle, oxen, etc. (2 Chron. 35 : 7, 9). Similar to this usage of Pesach is that of Chäg in Psalm 118 : 27 : "Bind the feast (the festive offering) with cords, etc." (Compare in addition Exod. 23 : 18; Malachi 2 : 3.) It is then no uncommon usage by which Pesach in Hebrew stands for various offerings. And if it is claimed that the general meaning of sacrifice must of necessity include the special sense from which it is derived, the fact is overlooked that when words lose their special signification in a broader application, this cannot be used to designate the particular original meaning, if even though it might be included. But when by the figure of metonymy a part is denominated of the general sacrifices, the other parts, under which "passover" belongs, are necessarily excluded. The Talmud confirms the use of Pesach for the thank-offering. In it the question is asked: "What is Pesach?" to which the answer is returned, "The peace-offering of the passover, that is Chagigah" (Rosh Hashana, V. 1). Further confirmation is furnished by the fact, that the defilement, which the priests contracted when entering the palace of Pilate, belonged to those ceremonial impurities, which lasted only for a day. If the "πάσχα" were the passover-lamb, the defilement would have ceased by the evening when the passover was to be eaten. It could have been washed away by the so-called "ablutions of a day" (see Lev. 15:31 sq.; 17:15; 22:6, 7; Numb. 19:7 sq.; Maimonides on Pesach, VI. 1). Friedlieb is therefore correct, when, on the supposition that the Jews feared defilement as preventing them from eating the paschal lamb, he states, that it is "surprising that the Jews should have been afraid of rendering themselves unclean for the passover—since the passover could not be kept till *evening*, i. e. *on the next day*, and the uncleanness which they dreaded did not, by the law, last till the next day." But on the fifteenth, the Chagigah, which expressed joy, was eaten. It is true that it was sometimes slain on the fourteenth, and Maimonides says: "When they offer the passover in the first month, they offer it with peace-offerings on the fourteenth day, of the flock and herd, and this is called the Chagigah, or feast-offering of the fourteenth day. And of this it is said (Deut. 16:2) that 'thou shalt sacrifice the passover to the Lord thy God of the flock and herd.'" This, however, does not disprove the eating on the fifteenth; for, according to Lightfoot on John 18:28, the Chagigah was eaten on the fourteenth only when the paschal lamb was not sufficient, but the usual and regular time was the fifteenth (Pesach, IV. 4; X. 3). And to this eating the words under discussion can readily apply, and then there is no disagreement between John and the synoptists.

(4.) The next passage to be accounted for is John 19:14: "It was the Preparation of passover." The discussion here turns upon the word "Preparation" ($\pi\alpha\rho\alpha\sigma\kappa\epsilon\upsilon\acute{\eta}$). Does it refer to Friday in accordance with its usual Jewish meaning and designate Friday of passover-week? Or is it applied to the passover in itself, and does it mean the first day of the passover without reference to the Sabbath? von Hofmann attempts to avoid the whole difficulty by changing the accepted punctuation. He suggests the following: "And it was the Preparation. The hour of the passover was about the sixth." This would decide the question for Friday, but this punctuation is unwarranted, for "of the passover" would hardly be placed before "hour" were it to qualify the same. The answer of von Hofmann is in general in the right direction; it does not cause the conflict between the gospels, which the acceptance of "Preparation" as the first day of the passover brings about. In the New Testament *Paraskeue* (Preparation) is found five times in addition to this passage (Matt. 27 : 62 ; Mark 15 : 42 : Luke 23 : 54 ; John 19 : 31, 42). Mark defines it especially as fore-sabbath. Although it is not seen in the Old Testament, the general strict laws of Sabbath observance (Exod. 35 : 2, 3 ; 16 : 22–27) would lead to it; and so it occurs after the exile (Judith 8 : 6). In Greek the fore-sabbath was always called Preparation ; and in this sense Josephus uses it (Antiquities, XVI. 6, 2). This would therefore be a well-known term when John wrote. It has also passed into Syriac for Friday. In Rabbinic language it was *Arubeta*, and designated the eve of the Sabbath (ĕrĕb hā shābāt). This expression is not the same as passover-eve. There is no proof that at that time the "ĕrĕb hā pĕsăch" of the Talmudists existed (see page 342). It points to a time when the temple had been destroyed, and therefore the regular passover had ceased. In both Old and New Testament usage that evening belonged to the passover festival. And even if it be granted that it existed, it could only have embraced a few hours before sunset. But the *Paraskeue* includes the whole previous day. In the two other passage in John (19 : 31, 42) it is used in this sense, and means Friday. Against this view there is no grammatical difficulty, for the genitive τοῦ πάσχα can easily stand in a more "remote internal relation," and mean the Preparation, Friday, of passover-week. It would then be similar to saying " the Tuesday of Christmas-week." A further support is given to this mode of interpretation by the term " sabbath of passover" (σάββατον τοῦ πάσχα ; Ignatius Ep. to Philippians, 13); and by " sabbath of the feast " (σάββατον τῆσ ἑορτῆς ; Socrates, Hist. Eccl. V. 22). While there is every evidence for this use of *Paraskeue* for Friday, there is not a trace of proof that the festivals and peculiarly passover had any day of preparation, or that the day before the festival received this name.

(5.) John 19: 31, " for the day of that sabbath was a high day," is supposed to be applicable only to the first festival day of the passover, the fifteenth of Nisan, and not to the second, the sixteenth. But any day in the passover-week, whether the first or the second day, might be great. Even the last day in a festival not so important, that of Tabernacles, is called " the great day of the feast " (John 7 : 37), although it is not more sacred than the first (compare Lev. 23 : 33–36). But it was considered great as the " holy day of convocation ; " for the " calling of assemblies " (Isai. 1 : 13) is rendered by the Septuagint " great day." Therefore the day of convocation must have been held thus by the Seventy, who knew the Jewish mind, and who expressed what undoubtedly still obtained in Christ's day. Therefore the sixteenth day of Nisan would be great as the day of convocation. In addition, it was the day on which the first-fruits were presented with ceremonies in part above the Sabbath regulations. From it the fifty days until Pentecost (Lev. 23 ; 15 sq.) were reckoned. All this is more than sufficient to make it a great day, and there is no necessity of claiming another day.

All the passages thus far examined in John are in their interpretation not torn out of the connection of John's chronology. The supposition that they call for the same date as the synoptists agrees very well with the statement John 12 : 1, that Jesus came to Bethany six days before the passover. This time fits in perfectly with the whole structure of the synoptists, and the harmonists have found no difficulty on this point. Thus, as Ebrard maintains, the total chronology of the synoptists and John are not in conflict but agreement,

But against the fourteenth of Nisan, as the day of the Last Supper, and consequently the fifteenth, as the day of the crucifixion, a number of objections have been urged, which are held to arise from the accounts of the actions of Jesus and His disciples and the Jews reported in the gospels, when they are compared with the Jewish laws and customs of the passover. These objections centre particularly on the fifteenth of Nisan. This as the first day had high sabbatic character, and is therefore subject to the law of rest (Exod. 12 : 16 ; Numb. 28: 18). But on the acceptance of the synoptic chronology we find every kind of activity on that day. The various actions which are supposed to have been impossible are these :

(*a.*) In John 13 : 29 Judas is thought to have been sent out to buy something for the feast. It is claimed, that on the evening of the fourteenth this would have been impossible. But this and all subsequent objections rest fundamentally on the supposition, that the days of festivals which had sabbatic character, like the first and last passover-day, the day of Pentecost, the day of atonement, were above the weekly Sabbath in sacredness. This, however, was not the Jewish idea. The weekly Sabbath was prized above these days. For its transgression death was the penalty (Numb. 15: 32), but for the breaking of a festival only a beating was the punishment. The Sabbath-laws were enforced on strangers, but not the law of festivals. On them a much greater freedom of action was permitted. It is true that no servile work (Lev. 23 : 3 sq., 39 sq.) could be done, and the Talmudists later called them " good days." But according to Exod. 12: 16 the preparation of food was allowed. And under certain conditions, when a pledge was given, even the purchase of certain necessary articles was permitted (Maimonides, Hilchoth, Yom tob, IV. 19 sq.). Maimonides says: " All work needful about meat is lawful, as killing of beasts and baking of bread, and kneading of dough and the like. But such work as may be done on the evening of a feast-day, they do not on a feast-day, as they may not reap nor thrash, nor winnow, nor grind the corn, or the like. Bathing and anointing are contained under the general head of meat and drink and may be done on the feast-day." Now this and other quotations from Rabbis and the Talmud, although they are later than Christ's day, are not to be rejected ; for the reason, that there is no evidence that the stringency of the observation of festivals relaxed. The whole line of development after Christ was toward greater severity. Therefore there is a great probability that the exceptions and allowances made are older.

(*b*.) The Lord and His disciples, it is said, would have left the city contrary to the law (Exod. 12: 22) had they gone out to the mount of Olives on the same night on which they ate the passover. But it is questionable whether this was a permanent command, or whether it was not rather intended only for the first passover in Egypt, like the having on of the shoes and the holding of the staves in the hand. The later observation of the passover was changed from the first in a number of particulars. But even if this law had obtained, the departure on that night would have been no transgression, for at the passover-season the city of Jerusalem was reckoned as extending as far as Bethany. And on the passover-night the gates of the city were not closed.

(c.) The greatest hindrance is found by some in the action of the priests in sending armed men and in holding judgment on a day when it was forbidden. But bearing arms was permitted in danger. From the time of the Maccabees they were allowed at all times for self-defence. This might have been the excuse of those Jews who went out for the capture of Jesus. The arms on that occasion were, however, not borne by the servants of the priests, who had only staves, but by the Roman soldiers. As to the holding of judgment, the Mishna (Sanhedr. IV. 1) expressly forbids the examination of a capital offender on a night or day before a festival. But the Gemara has modified this. It assigns a special meeting-place for Sabbaths and feast-days. "On the sabbath and feast-days they assembled themselves within the *B*e*chil*, which is in the lower wall, which surrounded the greater, in the vicinity of the forecourt of the women." When a special offender was caught, and particularly one who had not obeyed the Sanhedrim, he was not punished at once, but his punishment was reserved for the feast at which he was taken to Jerusalem, that by his example all might be warned. Thus the Mischna (Sanhedr. X. 4) states: "An elder, who does not subject himself to the Sanhedrim, shall be taken from the place where he lives to Jerusalem, shall be kept there until one of the three feasts, and shall be killed at the time of the feast, for the reason stated Deut. 17: 13." Maimonides also reports this law and adds: "as it is said 'all the people shall hear and fear.'" And Rabbi Akiba tells of the same enactment. It is apparent how this law might easily be construed to cover the case of Jesus. But even though such commandments had not existed, the Sanhedrists would in their hate have condemned Jesus. They knew, hypocrites as they were (Matt. 23 : 1 sq.), how to evade the laws when desirable. They undoubtedly also believed by their acts to serve God. And previously a festival had not restrained them from attempting to seize Christ. On the last *great* day of the festival of Tabernacles they had been in session awaiting that Jesus would be brought before them (John 7 : 32, 37, 44, 45). When Jesus was teaching in the temple on the festival of dedication, they "took up stones to stone him" (John 10 : 22, 31). Their very decision to put Jesus to death reveals the fact, that the special season as such did not restrain them. They only said : "not on the feast, lest a tumult arise among the people" (Matt. 26 : 5 ; Mark 14 : 2). The fear of the people deterred them and nothing else. And on the day after crucifixion, which, by general admission was a Sabbath, and a "great day," the Sanhedrim applied to Pilate for a watch. And the priests themselves see that the sepulchre is sealed and the watch properly placed (Matt. 27 : 62 sq.). In view of all this, the objection that it ought not have been done fails utterly.

(*d*.) The entering into Jerusalem of Simon, who came from the country; the taking down of Jesus from the cross, and His embalmment and burial, are also urged as impossibilities on the fifteenth of Nisan. But Simon may have been within the passover-limit of the city and have been on the way to the temple. There is no certain proof that he came from work. Embalming and burying were permitted as appears from the words of Maimonides quoted above (page 339). And the burial of Christ could easily have been completed before the following great Sabbath-day.

(c.) Old Jewish tradition is also cited against the fifteenth of Nisan as the day of the death of Jesus. In the Gemara of Babylon, composed from old traditions about the year 550, it is related: "Tradition reports, that on the eve of passover (ĕrëb hā pĕsăch) Jesus was crucified (hanged), and that after a court-crier had publicly proclaimed for forty days; 'that he shall be stoned, the man who through his deception has led the people astray. Who has anything to say in his defence may come foreward and speak.' But nothing was found in his defence. Therefore he was hanged on the eve of passover" (compare Lightfoot, Hor. Hebr. et Talm., page 490). Admitting that this was an old tradition, the fictitious additions, which Jewish hate dictated, make it uncertain. It is a part of the many distortions of the Talmud about Jesus. And Joel, a Jewish writer, referred to by Edersheim (Life and Times of Jesus the Messiah, Vol. II., page 481), claims, that the original view expressed in Jewish writings was, that Jesus was crucified on the first paschal day, and that this was only at a later period modified to the "eve of the pascha" (Sanhedr. 43a, 67a).

With these objections removed we can approach to the testimony of Church history in favor of the fourteenth of Nisan, as it appears in the paschal controversy. This did not indeed arise from the apparent discrepancies between the gospels, nor was its main interest exegetical. The purpose was rather to attain uniformity of observance, while asserting the independence of Christianity in fixing its festivals. Schaff has well summed up the central issue, when he states (Church History, Vol. II., page 212): "The gist of the paschal controversy was, whether the Jewish paschal-day (be it a Friday or not), or the Christian Sunday, should control the idea and time of the entire festival. The Johanean practice of Asia represented here the spirit of adhesion to historical precedent, and had the advantage of an immovable Easter, without being Judaizing in anything but the observance of a fixed day of the month. The Roman custom represented the principle of freedom and discretionary change, and the independence of the Christian festival system. Dogmatically stated, the difference would be, that in the former case the chief stress was laid on the Lord's death ; in the latter, on His resurrection." But though this controversy, therefore, bears more indirectly on our question, its main stages must be shown in their historical connection, that it may appear that the inferences drawn are just. The history of this matter is not without its disputed points, and is in some respects difficult to determine with absolute certainty, but it seems, according to the most careful examination and the best and least prejudiced scholars, to have been as follows :

First Stage. Between the years 150 and 155 Polycarp, the bishop of Smyrna, visited Anicetus, the bishop of Rome. In their conference they found, among other differences between them, a disagreement as to the celebration of Easter. What occurred then has been preserved to us in a letter of Irenæus to the bishop Victor of Rome (Eusebius, Hist. Eccl. V., Chap. XXIV. 16). In it Irenæus says: "When the blessed Polycarp was at Rome in the time of Anicetus, and they disagreed a little about certain other things, they immediately made peace with one another, not caring to quarrel over this matter (observance of Easter). For neither could Anicetus persuade Polycarp not to observe what he had always *observed with John the disciple of our Lord, and the other apostles* with whom he had associated ; neither could Polycarp persuade Anicetus to observe it, as he said that he ought to follow the customs of the presbyters that had preceded him." Nevertheless both bishops communed together and Anicetus "*conceded the administration of the eucharist in the church to Polycarp*" and gave way in this celebration to his view (see McGifford's Eusebius, Nicene and Post-Nicene Fathers, second series, Vol. I., page 244, note 20). Thus they parted in concord, " maintaining the peace of the whole Church."

Second Stage. Some years afterward, about 170, a controversy broke out in Laodicea. About it Melito of Sardis wrote two books (Eusebius, Hist. Eccl. IV., Chap. XXVI. 2) in favor of the fourteenth day of Nisan as is evident from Polycrates citing him (Eusebius, Hist. Eccl. V., Chap. XXIV. 5). But they are lost, as also the work of Clement of Alexandria, with the exception of a fragment. The chief source is Apolinarius, bishop of Hierapolis, who wrote: "There are some now who, from ignorance, love to raise strife about these things, being guilty in this of a pardonable offence ; for ignorance does not so much deserve blame as need instruction. And they say that on the *fourteenth of Nisan* the Lord ate the paschal lamb with His disciples, but that He Himself suffered on the *great day of unleavened bread (fifteenth of Nisan)*; and they interpret Matthew as favoring their view, from which it appears that their view does not agree with the law, and that the gospels seem, according to them, to be at variance. The *fourteenth is the true passover of the Lord, the great sacrifice*, the Son of God, in the place of the lamb—who was lifted up upon the horns of the unicorn—and who was buried on the day of the passover." Apolinarius is here evidently an opponent to the practice called " Quartodecimanian : " (fourteenth-day). But is he, in protesting against what he considers an error of exegesis and chronology, the representative of the Asian Church? It will scarcely be possible to hold this, in view of the statement of Eusebius (Hist. Eccl. V. Chapt. XXIII. 1) that: "the parishes of *all Asia, as from an older tradition*, held that the fourteenth day of the moon, on which the Jews were commanded to sacrifice the lamb, should be observed as the feast of the Saviour's passover." Apolinarius was then the one who differed, and his introductory words must not deceive us. That he lived in Hierapolis and that the controversy was in Laodicea, is no difficulty, because Laodicea is so close to Hierapolis. And the position of Apolinarius does not prove his opinion to be the prevalent one. In the constant intercourse between the congregations at that time, it is not striking " that the representative of an Easter practice not current in Asia became bishop of a congregation there, gained some adherents for his view, and when, like Apolinarius, he possessed literary activity, took up the contention against the custom and view of those surrounding him, not without every prospect of success " (Zahn). There were in Rome also those that held the fourteenth day contrary to Roman custom, like Blastus. Therefore the "Quartodecimans" (observers of the fourteenth) could have been no Jewish party, as is likewise evident from the manner in which Apolinarius treats them. There is, too, no trace of various parties of Quartodecimans either in Irenæus, Eusebius or Hippolytus, although the latter (Hær. L. 1 sq.) speaks of various opinions held by them.

Third Stage. The most vehement controversy arose between 190 and 194. This distracted the whole Church, and caused many councils and letters (Eusebius, Hist. Eccl. V., Chap. XXIII. sq.), until finally in 325 the council of Nicæa adopted the Roman practice. This matter became so important, because the Roman bishop Victor demanded in an overbearing manner that the observance of the fourteenth of Nisan should cease. Against this Polycrates, bishop of Ephesus, remonstrated. His letter is very earnest and presents weighty arguments. It was, as reported in part by Eusebius (Hist. Eccl. V., Chap. XXIV. 1–7): "We observe *the exact day;* neither adding nor taking away. For in Asia also great lights have fallen asleep, which shall rise again on the day of the Lord's coming, when He shall come with glory from heaven, and shall seek out all the saints. Among these are *Philip, one of the twelve apostles,* who fell asleep in Hierapolis; and his two aged virgin daughters, and another daughter, who lived in the Holy Spirit and now rests at Ephesus; and, moreover, *John,* who was both a *witness* and a teacher, who reclined upon the bosom of the Lord, and being a priest, wore the sacerdotal plate.[1] He fell asleep at Ephesus. And *Polycarp* in Smyrna, who was a bishop and martyr; and Thraseas, bishop and martyr from Eumenia, who fell asleep in Smyrna. Why need I mention the bishop and martyr Sagaris, who fell asleep in Laodicea, or the blessed Papirius, or Melito, the eunuch who lived altogether in the Holy Spirit, and who lies in Sardis, awaiting the episcopate from heaven, when he shall rise from the dead? *All these* observed the *fourteenth day* of the passover *according to the gospel,* deviating in no respect, but following the rule of faith. And I also, Polycrates, the least of you all, do according to the *tradition* of my relatives, some of whom I have closely followed. For seven of my relatives were bishops; and I am the eighth. And my people *always* observed *the day when the people* (i. e. Jews) *put away the leaven* (four-

---

[1] This expression, according to Lightfoot, is either actual or figurative. It may point to John as of pontifical race; or it may be "the earliest passage in any extant Christian writing where the sacerdotal view of the Christian ministry is distinctly put forward."

teenth of Nisan). I, therefore, brethren, who have lived sixty-five years in the Lord, and *have met* with the brethren *throughout the world*, and *have gone through every Holy Scripture*, am not affrighted by terrifying words. For those greater than I have said, ' *We ought to obey God rather than man.*' " But Victor, not answering nor heeding these arguments, excommunicated the Asiatics. Then Irenæus, although agreeing with the Roman bishop, reproved him for his arrogance, called for peace, and reminded him that this had been kept by Anicetus, Pius, Telesphorus and Xystus.

Now from this whole controversy it is apparent:

(1.) That the oldest testimony, that of Polycarp, a direct disciple of the apostle John, is derived from the immediate observance not merely of the other disciples but of John himself. If then John observed the fourteenth of Nisan, how could he have meant the thirteenth in his gospel?

(2.) The Roman bishop Anicetus appeals only to the tradition of the Roman bishops. And may not the enumeration of Irenæus, when he writes to Victor, give an indication of the time of the origin of the tradition? The oldest bishop mentioned by Irenæus is Xystus. And though the tradition may have been older, was not the whole Asiatic tradition, as admitted by Eusebius, and as announced by Polycrates, for the fourteenth of Nisan? The tradition of Asia is also nearer the source and has much clearer and better proof of the chain of succession than the Roman practice.

The different opinions existing among the Church Fathers are easily explained. Why some of them, like Irenæus, Clement of Alexandria, Peter of Alexandria, Origen, Hippolytus, Epiphanius, differed, is to be seen already in the fragment of Apolinarius. At the close of his words, he argues for the fourteenth of Nisan, as the day of the death of Christ. In this argument the relation of Christ as the antitypical paschal lamb to the paschal lamb slain on the fourteenth of Nisan is clearly the determining point. The dogmatic factor outweighs the other considerations. The word πάσχα was commonly believed to be derived from πάσχω (suffer). This derivation is found first with Irenæus, who (Against Heresies, IV. 10) says: "Of the day of His passion, too, he (Moses) was not ignorant; but foretold Him, after a figurative manner, by the name given to the passover; and at that very festival, which had been proclaimed such a long time previously by Moses, did our Lord suffer, thus fulfilling the passover." Thus also Tertullian (Against the Jews, X.) writes: "The *passover of the Lord*, i. e. *the passion of Christ*." When in other places these same Fathers wrote of this matter, where the dogmatic idea is not directly present to their minds, they greatly favor the fifteenth of Nisan as the day of the death of Jesus. Irenæus says incidentally (Against Heresies, II. XXII. 3): "'He came to Bethany six days before the passover,' and going up from Bethany to Jerusalem, He there *ate the passover*, and suffered on the *day following*." A similar remark is made by Origen on Matt. 26 : 17. The "Constitutions of the Holy Apostles," late as they are, certainly express the idea arrived at most naturally and in the Eastern mind, when, having spoken of Friday still observed as a fast-day among the Christians, they state: "On *their very feast-day* they (i. e. the Jews) apprehended the Lord." The testimony of Justin Martyr, earlier than all these, is clear and unmistakable. Although in the "Dialogue with Trypho" (Chap. XL.) "the lamb which God enjoined to be sacrificed as the passover" is held to be "a type of Christ," this does not lead Justin to fix the date of the suffering and death of Jesus; but he clearly says in Chapter CXI.: "And it is *written*, that on the *day of the passover* you seized Him, and that also *during the passover* you crucified Him." There is no uncertainty here, for the time of seizure is clearly put on the night of the first passover-day, or the night before the fifteenth of Nisan. The statement that Christ was crucified "during the passover" (ἐν τῷ πάσχα), in which "pascha," in distinction from its restricted use in "the day of the passover," is used in its wider signification, proves that the fourteenth of Nisan could not have been meant. With the position of Justin Augustine agrees. He argues against the derivation of "Pascha" as a Greek word from "pascho, to suffer," and says "those acquainted with both languages affirm it to be a Hebrew word" (Letters LV. 1; Tractate LV. on John). Having given up this derivation, he does not permit the typical relation of the paschal lamb to Christ, which he asserts (On the Spirit and Letter, Chap. XVI.), to determine him. Without discussing this whole question, he simply accepts the Last Supper as being the paschal meal, as well in the "Harmony of the Gospels" (II. LXXX. 157 sq.), as in the "Tractates on John" (see Tract. LV. 1; CXX. 1). Perhaps the expression that at the time of the trial of Jesus "it was the commencement of the days of unleavened bread" (Tract. on John CXIV. 2) might indicate a difference, but it cannot overthrow the whole position of Augustine. He was evidently not wavering like Chrysostom, who in Homily LXXXI. on Matthew says: "By the first day of the feast of unleavened bread he (Matthew) means the day before that feast; but they (i. e. the Jews) are accustomed always to reckon the day from the evening, and he makes mention of this in which in the evening the passover must be killed; for on the fifth day of the week they came unto Him. And this one (of the evangelists) calls the day before the feast of unleavened bread, speaking of the time when they came to Him, and another saith on this wise, 'Then came the day of unleavened bread, when the passover must be killed;' by the word 'came' meaning this, it was nigh, it was at the doors, making mention plainly of that evening. For they began with the evening, wherefore also each adds, when the passover was killed." Obscure as these words in part are, they apparently place the Last Supper at the time of the paschal meal. And in Homily LXXXIV. of the same gospel Chrysostom seems to confirm this by stating of the priests: "For neither did they eat the passover, but watched for the other purpose. For John, when he had said, that 'it was early,' added, 'they entered not into the judgment hall, lest they should be defiled, but that they might eat the passover!'" But in Homily LXXXIII. 3 on John 18:28, he gives the choice of two interpretations, and as Meyer said, "wrote the programme for the whole of the later investigations," when it is stated: "Either he (John) calls the whole feast 'the Passover,' or means, that they were then keeping the passover, while He delivered it to His followers one day sooner, reserving His own Sacrifice for the Preparation-day, when also of old the passover was celebrated."

It is clear that the early patristic evidence is in favor of the fourteenth of Nisan, if it be properly considered. The deviation was not due to the most careful exegesis and the best tradition. The earliest and most trustworthy testimony concurs altogether with the conclusion arrived at from exegesis alone.

In conjunction with this testimony the argument sometimes used against the fourteenth of Nisan from the use of leavened bread in the Eucharist in the Eastern Church must be considered. Although this use is earlier by far than that of unleavened bread, yet its testimony is not older than the paschal controversy. It may simply have been used, as common bread was easier to obtain. The matter was not pressed in a legalistic spirit. Theophylact, the able theologian of the Eastern Church, although adhering to leavened bread, stated that it was not due to the original day of the Lord's Supper.

Luther, without discussing this subject, evidently held to the fourteenth of Nisan as the day of the Last Supper. In the "Auslegung über etliche Capitel des anderen Buches Mosi" (1524–1526), he states (Erlangen Edition 35, page 195): "Thus God has determined the festival that it should begin in the evening of the fourteenth day, that upon the fifteenth day of the first month might be the right Easter-day. That is this law; therefore it happened without doubt that the true, proper, beautiful and gracious lamb of Easter, our Lord Jesus Christ, on palm-day rode into Jerusalem, preached four days in the temple, then ate the paschal lamb with His dear disciples; soon after He was taken captive in the garden at the mount of Olives, mocked, spit upon, scourged, crowned with thorns, condemned to death, crucified and killed, and therefore properly sacrificed." Judging from the initial sentence of Luther, he supposed that Christ had died on the fifteenth, "the right Easter-day." And this interpretation is confirmed by the whole subsequent treatment of Luther.

In conclusion, the astronomical argument in favor of the fourteenth of Nisan may be alluded to. It depends upon the year of the death of Jesus. This is, according to most scholars to-day, assigned to the year 30. Now, Wurm and Oudermann, the astronomers, have shown, that in that year the Friday of the passover-week was the fifteenth and not the fourteenth of Nisan. Wieseler uses this date in his chronology. Caspari has sought to prove that Wurm's calculations show that Friday was the fourteenth. But Rotermund has answered Caspari. And although there are intricacies in the Jewish calendar, which are not sufficiently cleared up, this much is evident, that the trend of the best calculations is in favor of Friday being the fifteenth day of Nisan, and therefore the Last Supper on Thursday would have been the paschal meal. The majority of scholars, that have considered this proof, admit this. And those taking the opposite position either neglect the weight of this argument, or, like Godet, attempt to evade its force in confirmation of the exegetical position, which avoids contradiction and opposition of the gospels, and vindicates in this particular, what is possible in so many others, the verity of all the gospels, their agreement and organic unity.

The American Church History Series.

BY SUBSCRIPTION, IN TWELVE VOLUMES, AT $3.00 PER VOLUME, OR $30.00 FOR THE SET.

Vol.	I.	The Religious Forces of the United States.	H. K. CARROLL, LL.D., Editor of The Independent, Supt. Church Statistics, U. S. Census, etc.
Vol.	II.	Baptists, ...	REV. A. H. NEWMAN, D.D., LL.D., Professor of Church History, McMaster University of Toronto, Ont.
Vol.	III.	Congregationalists, .	REV. WILLISTON WALKER, Ph.D., Professor of Modern Church History, Theological Seminary, Hartford, Conn.
Vol.	IV.	Lutherans, . . .	REV. H. E. JACOBS, D.D., LL.D., Professor of Systematic Theology in the Ev. Lutheran Seminary, Phila., Pa.
Vol.	V.	Methodists, . . .	REV. J. M. BUCKLEY, D.D., LL.D., Editor of the New York Christian Advocate.
Vol.	VI.	Presbyterians, . . .	REV. ROBERT ELLIS THOMPSON, D.D., Philadelphia, Pa.
Vol.	VII.	Protestant Episcopal, .	REV. C. C. TIFFANY, D.D., New York.
Vol. VIII.-		Reformed Church, Dutch,	REV. E. T. CORWIN, D.D., Rector Hertzog Hall, New Brunswick, N.J.
		Reformed Church, German,	REV. J. H. DUBBS, D.D., Professor of History, Franklyn and Marshall College, Lancaster, Pa.
		Moravian, ...	REV. J. T. HAMILTON, D.D., Professor of Church History, Theological Seminary, Bethlehem, Pa.
Vol.	IX.	Roman Catholics, . .	REV. T. O'GORMAN, D.D., Professor of Church History, Catholic University, Washington, D. C.
Vol. X.-		Unitarians, . . .	REV. J. H. ALLEN, D.D., Late Lecturer on Ecclesiastical History, Harvard University, Cambridge, Mass.
		Universalists, . . .	REV. RICHARD EDDY, D.D., Providence, R. I.
Vol. XI.-		M. E. Church, So.,	REV. GROSS ALEXANDER, D.D., Professor Greek and N. T. Exegesis, Nashville, Tenn.
		Presbyterians, So., . .	REV. THOMAS C. JOHNSON, D.D., Professor Ecclesiastical History and Polity, Hampden-Sidney, Va.
		United Presbyterians, .	REV. JAMES B. SCOULLER, D.D., Newville, Pa.
		Cumb. Presbyterians, .	REV. R. V. FOSTER, D.D., Professor Biblical Exegesis, Cumberland University, Lebanon, Tenn.
		Disciples, ...	REV. R. B. TYLER, D.D., New York.
		Friends, ... -	Prof. A. C. THOMAS, M.A., Haverford College, Haverford, Pa. R. H. THOMAS, M.D., Baltimore, Md.
Vol. XII.-		United Brethren, .	REV. D. BERGER, D.D., Dayton, Ohio.
		Ev. Association, .	REV. S. P. SPRENG, Editor Evangelical Messenger, Cleveland, Ohio.
		Bibliography, . .	REV. SAMUEL MACAULEY JACKSON, New York.

www.ingramcontent.com/pod-product-compliance
Lightning Source LLC
Chambersburg PA
CBHW030349230426
43664CB00007BB/587